WHITE HOT HATE

Also by Dick Lehr

NONFICTION

Dead Reckoning: The Story of How Johnny Mitchell and His Fighter Pilots Took on Admiral Yamamoto and Avenged Pearl Harbor

The Birth of a Movement: How Birth of a Nation *Ignited the Battle for Civil Rights*

Whitey: The Life of America's Most Notorious Mob Boss (with Gerard O'Neill)

The Fence: A Police Cover-up Along Boston's Racial Divide

Judgment Ridge: The True Story Behind the Dartmouth Murders (with Mitchell Zuckoff)

Black Mass: Whitey Bulger, the FBI, and a Devil's Deal (with Gerard O'Neill)

The Underboss: The Rise and Fall of a Mafia Family (with Gerard O'Neill)

FICTION

Trell: Nothing but the Truth

WHITE HOT HATE

A True Story of Domestic Terrorism in America's Heartland

DICK LEHR

MARINER BOOKS
An Imprint of HarperCollins*Publishers*
Boston New York

 For information, address HarperCollins Publishers,
195 Broadway, New York, NY 10007.

marinerbooks.com

Library of Congress Cataloging-in-Publication Data has been applied for.
ISBN 9780358359906 (hardback)
ISBN 9780358359968 (ebook)

Book design by Chloe Foster
Map by Robert Cronan, Lucidity Information Design, LLC

Printed in the United States of America
1 2021
4500837915

For my family: Karin, Nick, Christian,
Chloe, Holly, and Dana

And for infinite hope

Barasho horteed ha i nicin.
Get to know me before you reject me.

— SOMALI PROVERB

CONTENTS

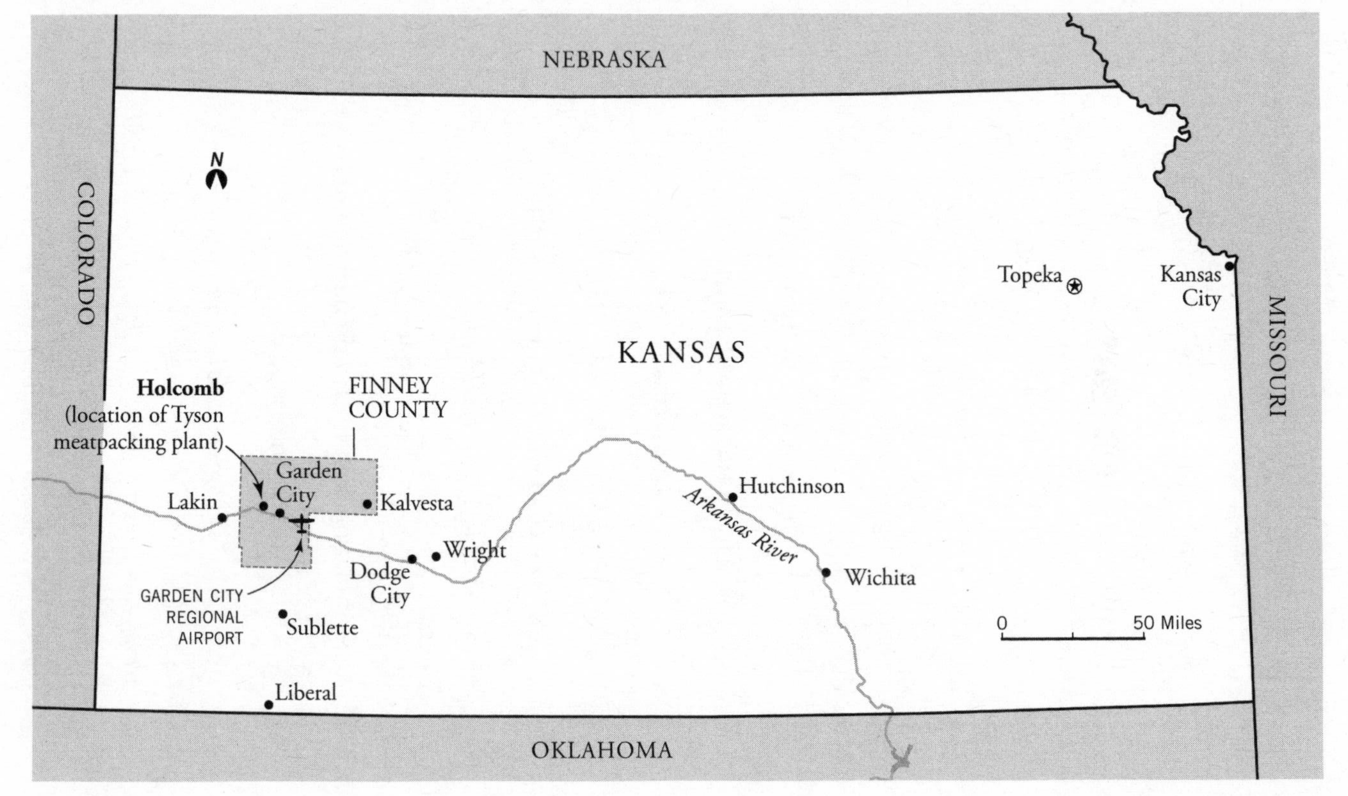
NEBRASKA
COLORADO
MISSOURI
OKLAHOMA
KANSAS
N
Topeka
Kansas City
Holcomb
(location of Tyson meatpacking plant)
FINNEY COUNTY
Garden City
Lakin
Kalvesta
Wright
Dodge City
Hutchinson
Arkansas River
Wichita
GARDEN CITY REGIONAL AIRPORT
Sublette
Liberal
0
50 Miles

AUTHOR'S NOTE

White Hot Hate is a work of nonfiction about real people, real events, and a real place. No one's name has been changed. The book is based on personal interviews and on thousands of pages of sworn testimony and documents from a federal district court trial, a federal appeals court review, and investigatory records from the Federal Bureau of Investigation and the US Department of Justice. The latter includes at least a hundred hours of secretly recorded (audio and, at times, video) conversations involving the FBI informant Dan Day, the FBI undercover agent "Brian," and the three Crusaders. Either by letter or other means I requested interviews with the three incarcerated defendants, Patrick Stein, Curtis Allen, and Gavin Wright. They did not respond. I therefore relied on their recorded statements, information in their sentencing memorandums, and other records submitted to the courts by their respective attorneys. The scenes and dialogue are based on either the extensive audio and video recordings or the recollection of at least one participant. The language on those tapes frequently includes profanities and racist slurs. For grammar and clarity, I occasionally altered the verb tense in a quotation or made other minor edits. Key interviews include those with Dan Day, Brandon Day, Alyssa Day, Cherlyn Day, Adan Keynan, Ifrah Ahmed, Halima Farah, Mursal Naleye, Benjamin Anderson, former assistant US attorney Anthony Mattivi, FBI agent Amy Kuhn, and retired FBI agent Robin Smith. During several trips to Kansas, I visited Wichita, Garden City, Dodge City, Liberal, Kalvesta, Sublette, Holcomb, and other locations where events in the book took place. The various sources that I relied on are summarized in chapter notes at the back of the book.

PROLOGUE: A CALL TO ARMS

SHORTLY AFTER 2 A.M. on June 12, 2016, a young man named Omar Seddique Mateen parked a rented van in a lot adjacent to the popular Pulse nightclub in Orlando, Florida. Mateen, twenty-nine years old, was armed with a SIG-Sauer MCX semiautomatic rifle and a Glock 17 9mm semiautomatic pistol—both purchased legally. The SIG-Sauer MCX is a lightweight rifle with a sixteen-inch cold hammer-forged barrel that is marketed as a sporting rifle, even though bullets explode from it in a staccato rapid-fire sequence.

Dressed in tan cargo pants and a plaid shirt, Mateen strode into the nightclub's front lobby. It was last call, but several hundred patrons still packed the gay bar for a Latin-themed night of dancing, which was finally winding down in the wee hours of Sunday. Within seconds, the gun-toting Mateen shot the first person he encountered. Without hesitation he continued onto the main dance floor, firing in every direction. Pandemonium erupted as terrified patrons tried desperately to escape. Some ran out through exit doors to the parking lot; others crawled into bathrooms to hide in stalls. The gunman killed or wounded anyone in his path. When, thirty minutes later, an Orlando police negotiator reached the shooter by phone and asked for his name, Mateen replied, "You're speaking to the person who pledged allegiance to the Islamic

State." Seconds later, the gunman continued: "My homeboy Tamerlan Tsarnaev did his thing on the Boston Marathon, so now it's my turn."

In less than five minutes, the terrorist fired roughly two hundred rounds. He killed forty-nine people, injured another fifty-three. Following a three-hour standoff, during which police safely extracted dozens of patrons from various parts of the club, Mateen, who once had worked as a security guard, was killed in a shootout with a SWAT team. Police entering the club found bodies strewn on the dance floor and piled on the stage, a slaughter unlike anything they had ever seen. It was the deadliest attack on US soil since September 11, 2001.

Reaction that Sunday morning was swift, as public officials across the country denounced the violence and proclaimed that mass shootings would not intimidate Americans. Condolences for the victims' families flooded the airwaves and the Internet, although one presidential candidate somehow found a way to turn the carnage at the club into a moment of self-praise. Donald J. Trump, at the time the likely Republican presidential nominee despite sky-high unfavorable ratings, said he'd been sounding the alarm about President Barack Obama and also Hillary Clinton, a Democrat who would soon oppose Trump in his run for president. Both Democrats were weak on terrorism, openly inviting trouble, said Trump. "Appreciate the congrats for being right on radical Islamic terrorism," he tweeted at noon. "I don't want congrats, I want toughness & vigilance." Claiming that Muslims were pouring into America and "trying to take over our children," Trump repeated his campaign promise to ban them from entering the United States if he was elected president.

FORTY-EIGHT HOURS after the mass shooting, and nearly sixteen hundred miles from Orlando, Dan Day heard his cell phone ring at daybreak in his ranch house in Garden City, a tiny city in rural southwest Kansas. Dan was slow to answer. He was unwell—in a stupor of sorts, half-awake, half-asleep, and feeling awful. He'd overdone it the previous day, helping his son with his landscaping business, working in the hundred-plus-degree heat, and failing to eat enough and, more important, keep his stocky, forty-eight-year-old frame hydrated. A native of Garden City and a lifelong Kansan who had worked just about every kind of job growing up, whether on a farm or at the giant meatpacking plant on the outskirts of town, he should have known better. Now he was paying the price—dizziness, clamminess, a splitting headache. He'd barely slept.

Calling him was Patrick Stein. He was the XO, or executive officer, of the southwestern division of the Kansas Security Force militia, and so when Dan answered, knowing he had to, Patrick filled his ears with the same fast, angry talk Dan had come to expect. Dan referred to these over-the-top tirades as "going Stein"—words firing rapidly like bullets from Patrick's mouth. Patrick instantly picked up where they'd left off the previous night, when he and the others in their private circle had held a conference call using Zello, the push-to-talk application that worked much like a walkie-talkie, to express high-voltage outrage at ISIS and the slaughter in Orlando. Patrick, then and now, was shouting that he'd had it. He was done, "*fuckin' done,*" he said, with waiting for someone else to step up and do something decisive about Muslim terrorists hiding in plain sight everywhere across the great United States.

"*Shit's got to fucking stop,*" Stein raged to Dan about Mateen's massacre, screaming for a final solution. He told Dan he'd already set a meeting for later that same day, and Dan sensed from Patrick's tone that his friend was at long last ready to blow like a volcano. For months Patrick had talked about taking action, but in the wake of Orlando it seemed some kind of switch inside him had flipped. The time had finally come, as Patrick kept saying, to stop the Muslims "*somewhere, sometime, somehow, someway.*" Sure, Trump yakked about preventing Muslims from entering the country at the borders. Patrick had no argument with that, but he and the others were thinking they needed to go further—toward outright expulsion or, even better, "*extermination.*" They'd take their first step that afternoon, at an organizational meeting. Toss around ideas —and whatever the eventual plan, Patrick promised that it would be "*something a lot more crazy than this fucker*" in Orlando.

Dan listened intently, waiting for Patrick to finish. He knew he had little choice, no matter how groggy he felt or how much he didn't want to budge from his home in the Garden. Patrick Stein, forty-seven, was his XO in the KSF militia, and for that reason, among others, Dan knew he had to heed the call to arms.

THAT SAME morning, at about 9 a.m., a Somali businessman in Garden City named Adan Keynan parked his white minivan in front of 912 West Mary Street, got out, and unlocked the entrance to the African Shop. Adan, thirty-one, a trim-looking man of medium height, often wore a rounded cap called a taqiyah and dressed in either an ankle-length, robelike garment called a khamis or a tan suit—suits were favored by Somali businessmen like him. He was accompanied by his wife, Sara, who typically wore a full-length, loose-fitting dress and covered her head with a scarf that, when worn by a married woman, is called a shash.

Adan was following what was pretty much his daily routine: opening up at about 9 a.m. after attending morning prayer at the mosque down the street in the apartment complex where he lived, and then overseeing, along with Sara, the comings and goings of shoppers throughout the day. One side of the store's small front room was devoted to foodstuffs; there, on hand-built wood shelves, Adan stocked Kenyan tea and sacks of rice, beans, spices, and other food items imported from East Africa. The other side of the front room featured decorative East African household accessories such as curtains, pillows, and rugs, as well as shoes and clothing—the scarves, caps, wraps, and garments that Somalis customarily wore. To replenish the shelves, Adan periodically made road trips to Minneapolis–St. Paul, where more than fifty thousand Somalis lived, the largest Somali diaspora in the United States. He drove the roughly eight hundred miles, which took about twelve hours, loaded his van with goods from the larger markets in the Twin Cities area, and then made the return trip to Garden City.

Soon after his arrival here, in the summer of 2007, Adan had identified a need for a business where refugees could find familiar foods and other goods. His shop was a short walk from the apartment complex at 312 West Mary Street, which was occupied mainly by Somalis, including Adan and Sara, as well as a second complex across the street, which was filled mostly with Burmese refugees but also more Somalis. With its spacious back room, Adan's store had become a hub where Somali elders and others gathered to socialize, especially on weekends when they weren't working.

Its success notwithstanding, Adan felt apprehensive as he opened his shop that Tuesday morning. The mass shooting in Florida over the weekend, a tragedy felt everywhere and covered nonstop by media around the world, was on his mind. That the shooter had pledged allegiance to ISIS, or the Islamic State of Iraq and Syria, had unleashed a torrent of hostile commentary against all Muslims, no matter their country of origin. ISIS had originated years earlier in Iraq, but the dialed-up anti-Muslim speechifying in the United States didn't make a distinction between its place of origin, which was in the Middle East, and the African nations. In fact, ISIS barely had a footing in Adan's African homeland—a few hundred fighters at best—and ranked a distant second to the dominant Islamist terrorist organization in Somalia, al-Shabab.

But a second, and more personal, source of unease was closer at hand—a formal letter from the city, which was sitting atop his desk inside the store. It was a one-pager from the Garden City Neighborhood and Development Services Department, dated June 1, and it began: "This letter is to inform you that your business is in violation of the Zoning

Regulations of the City of Garden City." Adan, who barely understood English, was baffled by the zoning and land-use terminology, which, truth be told, would confuse most citizens who were fluent in English. The letter, for example, said his business was located in a part of town "zoned I-2, Medium Industrial District." More pointedly, it said, "The I-2 district does not allow a retail business such as your business as a permitted use." Although the abundance of official wording was mostly beyond Adan's grasp, the missive's bottom line was crystal clear: "You have thirty (30) days from the date of this letter to discontinue retail use at this location."

The ultimatum was a gut punch. The hard work Adan had put into the store to make a go of it, and the vital role the business now played in the lives of his Muslim neighbors—suddenly that all seemed to be in jeopardy. Thirty days, and the clock was ticking. As he worried about what to do next, he couldn't help but wonder if the letter, relying on the trappings of zoning and land-use restrictions, was a sneaky way of saying *Get out: we don't want your kind in Garden.*

WHILE DAN DAY managed to heed the command to meet Patrick for a ride to the meeting, it didn't mean he felt any better. In fact, as the day wore into evening, Dan's condition worsened. He felt dizzier, maybe even feverish. His throat was as dry as a Kansas riverbed at midsummer. As he rode with Patrick to the God-forsaken middle of nowhere—somewhere west of Wichita—Patrick, complaining they were late, wouldn't even stop at a convenience store so Dan could get some water. The AC in the truck wasn't working either. To make up time, Patrick tried shortcuts on a bunch of dirt roads, which threw Dan's stomach into further tumult.

Dan was a tottering mess once he, Patrick, and a couple of others in the KSF militia began their hastily called session shortly before dusk. But despite how muddled he was, Dan did register the absence of two men who in recent weeks had emerged alongside him and Patrick as the most hardcore in their commitment. Curtis Allen, forty-seven, their KSF commander, was en route, having had business to attend to near Kansas City. Patrick had been in touch with Curtis by phone, and Curtis said he would show up eventually. Gavin Wright, forty-nine, however, would not be able to make it; he had a previously scheduled meeting with some Chamber of Commerce types in connection with the mobile and modular home company he co-owned with his brother. Patrick had talked to him too, though, and planned to update Gavin after the meeting. "He's fucking game on!" Patrick assured Dan. Patrick saw Gavin and Curtis as key assets. Both men were steeped in guns and other weaponry, and they possessed impressive collections. Curtis was former military, after all, having served in the National Guard in Iraq.

The meeting was all Patrick's. The "Orlando deal" was a tipping point, Patrick said, and the moment was now upon them to finally do something about the Muslims in their midst. "Garden City is a main fuckin' hub that they're bringing them into," he said.

Patrick continued: "I wanna start cleaning house."

That meeting on June 14, 2016, marked the formal start of a criminal conspiracy—although at the time Dan Day was in no condition to recognize its legal significance. He was struggling to keep up with the others, to add a comment here and there. But it was a failed proposition. He gasped for air at one point, prompting someone to comment, "You look hot or something. You doin' all right?"

Dan tried sipping water, but it didn't help. He began to waver; the voices around him were going in and out, the way sound does on a radio when someone plays with the volume. He stumbled forward. "I'm seeing stars," he announced, not to anyone in particular but more to himself, as he realized he was beginning to lose consciousness; and as he did, as he continued to stagger and fall in the empty field in rural Kansas, a cold panic took hold. Dan wondered what would happen if they searched his jeans after he passed out. Yes, they would find his pocket carry—gun talk for the compact Ruger SR9c pistol tucked snugly into its soft leather holster. That was not what worried him. He carried; they all carried. It was the other thing—his overwhelming concern. What if they found the recording device?

I

THE ACCIDENTAL INFORMANT

Eleven months earlier, on July 17, 2015, Dan Day had watched approvingly as his son, Brandon, worked up a sweat jogging the perimeter of Harold Long Park under a hot midmorning sun. Formal preseason training for the varsity wrestling team wouldn't start until the fall, but Brandon, a rising sophomore, was determined to arrive in shape. Wrestling had a long, glorious history in Garden City, with a steady string of state champions whose photographs—each posing crouched, in uniform—were showcased in the school gym. Dan had wrestled some himself while in school in the 1980s, although without much success. He mainly served as training partner for his best pal, Terry Johnson, a true talent who was second in the state in the 135-weight class and later served as his best man when he and Cherlyn got married. Brandon had wrestled in middle school but had given it up to try junior ROTC his freshman year. He'd realized he missed the sport, though, and was now aiming to make the team and compete in the 145-weight class.

Dan liked his son's work ethic, the notion that Brandon wanted to work out over the summer rather than wait for preseason training, when most kids began getting in condition. He was also likely a bit envious, for there was a time when Dan was as lean and supple as his son. Not anymore; he'd filled out, a polite way of saying he'd gotten heavy.

No way he could be jogging alongside Brandon. In shorts, T-shirt, and sneakers, Dan walked around the park while Brandon jogged—and kept lapping him.

Most mornings this was their routine. Dan had time—the free time that came from being out of work. He'd lost his job as a probation officer the year before, on the losing side of a bitter workplace dispute. Intensive supervision officer had been his job title, and the work at the county's corrections facility consisted of monitoring convicts who were on probation. Dan would meet with clients and their families, administer urine tests if drug charges were involved, and sometimes accompany police on unannounced checks at homes or local bars, all part of making sure the felons assigned to him were living up to the terms of their court-ordered probation.

Dan had liked the job. He'd worked already for more than a decade in criminal justice—in the broadest sense—having previously been a guard and then a shift supervisor at the local juvenile prison, which was called a detention center. He'd dealt with some hardcore youthful lawbreakers, especially starting around 2009, when West Coast–based gangs made their presence known even in a place as remote as Garden City. Quelling jailhouse fights and fielding personal insults and menacing threats were all part of it. But Dan always felt that his personality—low-key, even-keeled—was well suited to the work, along with his knack for sizing people up. This proved especially handy when he started the new job as probation officer in 2012 and was regularly called on to assess a client's credibility—whether the client was telling him the truth or trying to pull a fast one as to their employment, schooling, or use of drugs or alcohol. "I could see through their bullshit," Dan said.

The pay in the new job was pretty good too—about $42,000 annually, plus overtime. It allowed him to rent a home on the east side of Garden City, with the intention of buying it. And the health plan provided the coverage needed for Cherlyn, who had diabetes and suffered bouts of depression. Moreover, the hours were better than what he'd had at the juvenile prison. Now he could give Brandon and his daughter, Alyssa, rides to school and dependably attend their sports games or whatever activity they might be involved in.

For eighteen months things were great. Then trouble erupted. Dan butted heads with the department's top manager. It was an oil-water type of thing—the two just didn't mix. Dan began receiving warnings that he wasn't moving his caseload fast enough. He resisted the pressure to process people as if they were on an assembly line. This wasn't like the meatpacking plant, where you butchered cuts of beef, dangling on hooks or carried on conveyor belts, as they went quickly past you. His clients were human beings, and many were looking to restart life after a falling-out with the law.

Dan proved no match for the managerial moves made against him, however. His boss called in a state investigator to question him after a bunch of holiday gift cards went missing, as if Dan had had a hand in their disappearance. But the investigator suggested lousy clerical practices were more likely the problem than any skulduggery. Despite this, in early 2014, his boss placed him on a thirty-day "retraining" regimen, an administrative review to reevaluate his future employment. The feedback on Dan's work had swung like a pendulum, from "superior" in his first year to "not making the grade" in the second. Dan fought back as best he could but realized that the daily nitpicking about his performance meant he didn't have a chance. In anticipation of the official word that he was a goner, he packed some personal items into a box on his desk, including a decorative scene of Mary and the baby Jesus in the manger, which he'd displayed at Christmastime.

Then the thirtieth and final day of the review came. Dan was at home when a deputy sheriff he'd known for years arrived with the formal letter of termination. The sheriff said something about Dan probably expecting the bad news, and Dan replied, "Yeah, I seen it coming." The sheriff asked Dan to hand over his badge and keys, and then he mentioned the box.

"The what?" Dan said.

The sheriff acted sheepish, given that the two had known each other for some time, and then went on to explain that the boss who was out to get Dan was worried the box on his desk might contain explosives and had alerted the bomb squad.

"Gimme a break," Dan replied, in total disbelief.

The sheriff asked for assurance that he wasn't going to get blown up if he inspected the box—some of the other deputies were saying they should send in the bomb squad's disposal robot.

"No, no, no," Dan said, "you won't get blown up."

Dan was livid—a bomb threat? The phony gift-card investigation was one thing, but this was the dirtiest of dirty tricks. Pathetic—but humiliating as well. Dan and the sheriff shook their heads at the craziness of it all, and a few minutes later the deputy drove off. He promised to get Dan his box with the baby Jesus in it.

WHEN BRANDON first began training, they measured the park's loop: 0.36 of a mile, which meant that for a three-mile workout Brandon would run nine laps. Then, while Brandon jogged, Dan walked, staying as best he could in the shade of trees that city leaders had been smart to plant throughout town in the middle of the previous century—walnut, Chinese and American elm, and locust. During the 1950s irrigation systems had been improved, which helped farming in western Kansas become more reliable than it had been since the dust bowl days of the 1930s. Garden City's population topped ten thousand, and the state of Kansas became known as "the Wheat State," with farms working the thousands upon thousands of acres of land so flat and unobstructed, you could look across the horizon to where the sky touched the ground. But even with major advances in pumping water out of the vast underground Ogallala Aquifer, farming remained the feast-or-famine venture it had always been. The driest year ever in Garden City was recorded smack in the middle of a decade-long growth spurt—only 5.68 inches in 1956. But fears of a possible prolonged drought ended the next year, when 21 inches of rain fell.

There was simply no immunity from the Heartland's ups and downs, which for many caused a lifetime of stress and poverty. The cycle was certainly part of Dan Day's family history. His father, Lee Day, had first arrived in Garden City as a boy in the 1930s—his family traveling from Missouri in a covered wagon because his parents could not afford a car. The family grew wheat and corn. Everyone pitched in, including Lee, along with his fifteen siblings. The family struggled—money was sometimes as scarce as rain—and when Lee returned after serving in World War II as an army sergeant in the Pacific, he continued farming. To add to the household coffers, Lee also fought. When he was a teenager, he'd earned a reputation as a barroom brawler, a sport of sorts in those days, with plenty to be made from the wagering on the fights. Lee was quick with his fists, able to take on bigger men despite his modest size. And in the army, he'd fought for his unit in organized bouts. Returning home, he jumped into the ring whenever a traveling circus came through that staged fights featuring cash prizes.

Dan's father was just doing what came naturally in southwest Kansas, where farming was too fickle to rely on solely: he was tapping another skill for extra income. But when he hit his midthirties, he quit the fight game and settled down. In 1961 he married a woman named Iris Willson from an Oklahoma farm family. The need for more money never abated, however. So Lee always worked two jobs, alternating between his small farm outside town and his work as a mechanic. Iris, a widow whose first husband had drowned during a family outing, had six kids of her own, and when Danny Ray Day was born on April 3, 1968, he became the youngest of the blended family's nine children.

Over the years Lee Day's heart proved weak, yet he still found a way to work. He bought a small spot of land in Garden City in the early 1970s, when Dan was a toddler, and built a tiny three-bedroom ranch, into which the sprawling family somehow fit. The family attended church on Sundays, while at home Dan's father frequently spoke about God and the importance of Christian values, alluding vaguely to how he'd "calmed down" since his youth.

And he instilled in Dan a love for guns and hunting. The memory of the first shot he ever took stayed clear in Dan's mind. His dad was headed out for target shooting one day and brought him along. They drove across the dry riverbed of the Arkansas River to a remote spot that had been turned into a makeshift dump for car wrecks and broken-down appliances. Lee Day, a marksman, took aim at a beat-up truck and fired his .22 rifle, *pop-pop-pop,* shot after shot, until he'd spelled out his son's name with bullet holes: DANNY. The youngster beamed. Then Lee told Dan it was his turn. Lee helped his son hold the rifle so that Dan could aim and pull the trigger. The gun's power shook the boy. Following that first shot, another clear memory became embedded: his father talking to him, in all seriousness, about the importance of gun safety, imparting three lessons that decades later Dan would drill into his own son, reciting them as if his father were talking:

- *Always treat a gun as if it is loaded.*
- *Don't point a gun at anything you don't plan to kill.*
- *Red is dead,* meaning that if a gun's red indicator is visible, its safety is *off.*

Before an ailing Lee Day died at the age of forty-eight, he gave each son a gun from his collection. Dan received a 20-gauge shotgun—a prized possession but one little Dan could barely hold, even though it was smaller and lighter than a 12-gauge. Now that his father was suddenly gone, one of Dan's older half-brothers, also a terrific shot, became a surrogate and regularly took him hunting. Arranging permission from a farmer, the boys drove off-road into an empty pasture to hunt for rabbits, pheasants, even coyotes. Dan rode in the truck's bed, ready to shoot at whatever popped up. Back then, a coyote pelt netted twenty-five dollars. The money was always welcome at home, as was a rabbit or pheasant for that night's dinner table.

For all of his family's hardships, Dan considered his childhood generally happy, built solidly around family life and Christian faith. Even after his father died unexpectedly in 1973, during heart surgery—when Dan was just five years old—the family forged ahead, determined to make ends meet. On the Great Plains, coping with unexpected setbacks—no matter what form they took—seemed like a fate one generation passed on to the next.

NOW DAN, his wife, Cherlyn, and their two kids were in the midst of coping with the unexpected. Ousted from his job as a probation officer, Dan had tried ever since to elude poverty's grip and ride out their "famine." Things initially got worse, though. He'd managed for a while to keep up rental payments, but early in 2015 he couldn't do so. They lost the house they'd dreamed of buying. They spent several weeks in February and March bouncing around, staying in motels when friends pitched in to help pay for a room, or even, one time, in their car. Cherlyn's diabetes worsened, and she required several hospitalizations. Because the family had no health benefits, the medical bills piled up.

But more recently, circumstances had begun to stabilize. In June, Dan moved his family into his boyhood home, once he got relatives who'd been occupying the house to vacate. He was not happy that the house had not been kept up the way his father would have expected; its exterior siding was now torn and shabby, but at least he and Cherlyn and the kids had a rent-free roof over their heads. Cherlyn then became eligible for medical disability payments, which helped with her health care, and Dan succeeded in piecing together income by working side jobs—landscaping or other outside work—along with monitoring the Internet daily for retail deals. He'd scour Facebook, eBay, and other sites, looking for opportunities. It might be tires, an antique sewing machine, guns or ammunition—any possibility for profit. "I'd offer them, like, half of what they wanted and negotiate with them." Or if he saw that the Walmart a few blocks from their house was having a sale on ammunition, he'd rush to the store to purchase the maximum allotment per person before it sold out. He'd make money reselling the items online at higher prices. "It was enough to pay the bills and buy food."

Throughout Dan faced the family crisis head-on, with an equanimity that seemed rooted in his steady personality and his upbringing in a part of the country where the unexpected was to be expected. When the power was shut off in late spring, for example, Dan calmly went down to the power company's office and squared things away so that the lights were back by nightfall. And he constantly juggled what funds they did have to stay atop payment plans for utilities, car insurance, and anything the kids needed for school or sports. Dan may no longer have been a Sunday churchgoer, but he possessed a kind of spiritual stoicism that helped him look hardship in the eye and stay the course. He prayed regularly, believing God always had a reason, and put his head down, leaned in, and did what he could to provide for Cherlyn, Brandon, and Alyssa. His mantra? *It is what it is.*

Plus, there was a silver lining: he got to be with his wife and kids more. Family was everything to him, and he fully appreciated the fact that he and his wife were close with their two teenagers—which wasn't the case in a lot of families. For Dan, this was the norm—he'd grown up the youngest and, with a slew of older siblings, had never had to worry about getting picked on. In fact, after his dad died, his mother married a roofer named John King, and John already had five sons. Fourteen kids in all, and three more bedrooms were put in the basement of the three-bedroom home his father had built. Someone was always around —either in school or in town—to look out for him, and Dan carried on that same ethos in his own much smaller family: all for one, one for all.

Dan and Cherlyn gave new meaning to the proverbial Sunday drive. Their town had only a single movie theater and they had to be ever mindful of finances even during good times, so their idea of family entertainment was to pile everyone into the car and head out. Brandon and Alyssa may have never yet seen an ocean, but starting at an early age they got full exposure to the Great Plains. Dan drove into the country, down old highways and dirt roads, or along the Arkansas River, its riverbed either barely a trickle or bone dry. The kids grew to embrace the simple, uncluttered beauty and muted colors of the prairie—the sea of green sprouts in early spring, waves of suntanned wheat at harvesttime, and the endless brown stubble that followed.

They'd pass locations Dan had roamed as a kid, which might prompt a boyhood story, like the one that had even made headlines. That was the summer of Dan's junior year, in 1985, when heavier-than-usual spring rains had swelled the Arkansas River and filled a large sandpit in the middle of nowhere, south of town and about a mile west of US 83. Over the hot Memorial Day weekend several hundred people had turned out to swim and paddle around in the pop-up "pond." Dan and his pal Terry Johnson were riding downstream on rubber tire tubes when they spotted three kids in distress where the river fed the sandpit. Terry knew how to swim, but Dan did not. Because his mother's first husband had drowned as her whole family watched helplessly, Dan's half siblings became frightened to death of the water. Dan splashed around as a boy, doing a dog paddle, but that was it.

Terry was therefore the one who dove in to help. For Dan, the next minutes seemed to happen in slow motion. Terry reached the little kids, but they were panicked and climbed all over their rescuer. Terry was the one now yelling for help, and Dan, tossing caution aside, joined the scrum, paddling as best he could and then clawing the boys off Terry. Together they managed to get the kids safely to land, where dozens of onlookers had gathered. It all ended well, and two days later Dan and Terry's pluck was front-page news in the *Garden City Telegram;* a headline mentioned that "One Rescuer Couldn't Even Swim." As Dan retold the story over the years, when describing the confluence of factors—the tubing, strong current, and timing, and how a near tragedy had been averted—Dan saw it all as preordained, saying, "God put us right there, right then."

To keep the road show going, when Dan ran out of memories, he'd switch to spinning made-up stories, adventure tales set in the vast prairie. Or he'd turn the radio dial to the local country station playing its top-forty countdown. He might even force his vocals on the family—to their collective cringing—when a favorite, such as Johnny Cash's "A Boy Named Sue," came on the radio. The boy in the song didn't have a dad while growing up and had learned to tough it out. Dan found encouragement in the lyrics, given that his dad died when he was little. The relaxed ride-arounds added up to what parenting gurus call "quality time." Surely, Dan didn't like being without a steady income, but he did treasure his family time. He'd do anything for his wife and kids. "It's how I was raised," he once said.

Being out of work also meant that in addition to accompanying Brandon on workouts, Dan had more time to share in his favorite pastime—hunting and target shooting. He and Brandon had a couple of favorite places, including Dan's sister's place in Holcomb, just seven miles west of Garden City. That was where one of the state's most notorious murders had taken place, a decade before Dan was born. On November 15, 1959, two ex-convicts, thinking the farmer Herb Clutter possessed a safe full of cash, broke into his house and shot Clutter to death, along with his wife and two children. The town became a national sensation when the writer Truman Capote wrote about the killings in a bestseller titled *In Cold Blood.* The farmhouse itself became a macabre tourist attraction for a period in the 1990s, when the family that owned it charged five dollars for a tour. Arriving at Dan's sister's spread, father and son spent hours firing at stationary bull's-eye targets or clay pigeons. From a young age Brandon had shown a facility as a natural shot, just as Lee Day had been.

Like his father, Dan had acquired a variety of guns over the years, including a .357 magnum revolver, a 12-gauge pump-action shotgun, and an AR-15 semiautomatic rifle. And he carried a weapon wherever he went—to him it was an accessory as basic as a belt. Without a gun he felt "naked," the gun owner's term for being weaponless. Kansas was an open-carry state, which meant a person with a permit could display a firearm openly. Dan rarely did that, feeling open-carry was too showy. He preferred to tuck his Ruger SR9c 9mm semiautomatic handgun in a pocket holster or the small of his back.

That Ruger was on him as he walked around Harold Long Park on the Friday morning in July 2015. With the sun climbing higher into the sky, Brandon approached and slowed his jog. Dan asked, "You ready, Punk?" The coarse-sounding nickname was actually a term of endearment, short for "Punkin'," which Cherlyn had made up when Brandon was little. The boy was now ten days shy of sixteen—growing up fast, it seemed. Taller than his father too, which was obvious as the two stood next to each other, both sweating profusely and feeling thirsty. Brandon said he was done, which meant the next stop in their daily routine was the air-conditioned library a few blocks away, to get a drink, cool off, and look up sports scores and other news.

DAN WOULD LOG ON to one of the desktop computers lining a wall in the Finney County Public Library. He actually spent a fair amount of time every day on the Internet, using either the library's computers or his iPad. He needed an online presence to conduct his buy-sell business, but he also took time to consume the news. He liked to keep up with what was going on, both locally and beyond. His news sources ran the gamut—CNN, MSNBC, FOX, and, on occasion, Breitbart or Alex Jones, whose radio show he considered a "fake-like Internet talk show." Dan shook his head in disbelief at some of the stuff Jones pushed, like his rant that the federal government was building tunnels to connect Walmart stores in Texas, where President Obama planned to hide troops for a surprise raid on the Lone Star State. Walmart had felt the need to respond, releasing a statement from its corporate headquarters in Arkansas to deny the conspiracy theory. It was almost comical, Dan thought, and Jon Stewart had spoofed the whole nonsense in a bit on *The Daily Show.*

Dan, a fanatical fan of football's Kansas City Chiefs and, less so, baseball's Kansas City Royals, kept up on sports scores. He'd also begun paying some attention to the presidential race, ramping up for the primaries. To him, the cluster of Republican candidates seemed a mess. He didn't know what to make of the New York hotel magnate Donald J. Trump, who in June had officially jumped in. Dan had watched Trump's TV show, *The Apprentice,* and read a couple of his self-promotional books. He saw Trump as a liar who was so full of himself that he made up stories about his alleged feats, and so Dan didn't really cotton to him. But he did like the way Trump stood up for America and, most important, strongly backed gun rights. Meanwhile, Dan had no use for Hillary Clinton, largely because she favored gun reform. The issue of gun rights was pivotal to him—a litmus test. That was a big reason why he'd never cared much for Obama. It wasn't about race, he'd tell people, complaining that everyone seemed to think it was racial bias when you said you didn't support the first Black president. Dan liked to point out that Obama's mother, Ann Dunham, was born in Wichita, and *her* parents were native Kansans, making Obama a native son of sorts. Dan just didn't like a slew of Obama's policies on the economy, health care, and abortion rights, and felt generally that his administration meddled too much in state and local affairs. "I didn't hate the government," he said, "but there was things I didn't like in the way it was run."

While skimming campaign news about an election that was more than a year away, something else captured Dan's attention: the twentieth anniversary of the Oklahoma City bombing, which had killed 168 people, including 19 kids under the age of six. The bombing was the deadliest act of domestic terrorism in American history, and Dan had not forgotten the fear and shock caused by the explosions on April 19, 1995. At the time, he and Cherlyn were living less than three hours north of Oklahoma City in the tiny city of Bartlesville. They had first met in Garden City through church—the Trinity Wesleyan Church—where Dan's father, Lee, used to go and where Cherlyn's uncle was the pastor. One weekend, Cherlyn attended a barbecue that Dan's mother was hosting for folks from church, and she and Dan hit it off. Marrying in November 1993, the couple moved to Bartlesville. Cherlyn already knew the town well; her parents, siblings, and cousins had all gone to the small Christian college there—Oklahoma Wesleyan University. Soon after the move, Dan landed a part-time job as a security guard at the college, and he planned to take a course in business management to add to the credits he'd earned while briefly enrolled at Garden City Community College. Few in his family had graduated from high school, never mind taking college courses. And Bartlesville, an out-of-the-way community in eastern Oklahoma known mainly as the longtime headquarters for the oil giant Phillips Petroleum, became the only place outside Garden City where Dan ever lived.

The couple had been residing in Bartlesville for about a year when, on a bright April morning, Timothy McVeigh, an army veteran of the Gulf War, parked a rented Ryder truck packed with explosives in front of a federal office building in downtown Oklahoma City. Dan and his wife watched the nonstop news coverage of the blast, destruction, and death, listening intently to early speculation about possible reasons for the bombing and whether investigators had any leads. The speculation included potential next targets—namely Bartlesville, because the headquarters of Phillips Petroleum were located there. The threat felt so near, and terrifying. "Like a 9/11 for us," Dan would say later, in reference to the terrorist attacks of September 11, 2001, which left 2,996 dead and many thousands more injured.

In April 2015, as the twentieth anniversary of the Oklahoma City bombing garnered more media coverage than anniversaries in prior years, Dan read one story after another. Bill Clinton was the keynote speaker at the memorial service, addressing a crowd of more than a thousand gathered at the spot where the nine-story building McVeigh destroyed had once stood. The former president praised the Oklahomans for showing courage in rebuilding their lives. "You chose farsighted love over blind hatred," he said, his voice breaking. Joining Clinton was the FBI director, James B. Comey. "For twenty years, you have sought the good coming out of the darkness," Comey added. Neither mentioned McVeigh, who was convicted in 1997 and executed in 2001. He had said, after being captured near Bartlesville, that he was hoping to inspire an uprising against the federal government, which he saw as tyrannical. For Dan, the memorial service churned up a range of discomforting emotions—the fear he and Cherlyn had felt at the time, the sadness at so many deaths, and the utter disbelief that Timothy McVeigh, in his twisted mind, somehow saw his anti-government point of view as justifying a deadly act of terrorism.

McVeigh's violent radicalism—two decades past, by 2015—came at a time when government counterterrorism resources were targeting far-right groups and extremists like him. With good reason: three years before McVeigh, there had been the siege at Ruby Ridge—an eleven-day standoff in a remote corner of Idaho between federal agents and the white-separatist Randy Weaver. The ensuing firefight left a US marshal and Weaver's wife and son dead. Ruby Ridge became a rallying cry for the militia movement and its anti-government ideology. Then, a year after McVeigh's bombing, there was the pipe-bomb explosion at the Summer Olympics in Atlanta on July 27, 1996, set off by a white American terrorist named Eric Rudolph, which killed one woman and severely injured more than a hundred others. Because of those cases and a handful of others, federal efforts—by the FBI, the US marshals, and the ATF (the Bureau of Alcohol, Tobacco, and Firearms)—were focused on combating domestic extremism.

But then came a monumental event, changing everything—the international terrorist attacks of September 11, 2001. From that moment on, and with the creation of the Department of Homeland Security, just about every possible law-enforcement resource at both the federal and state levels was directed at international terrorism—namely, the Muslim extremist group al-Qaeda, started by Osama bin Laden and responsible for the 9/11 attacks, and eventually the militant Islamic State of Iraq and Syria, or ISIS. Over the next decade, hundreds of criminal cases, relying on new anti-terrorism laws that explicitly designated al-Qaeda and ISIS as terrorist organizations, were brought against suspected international extremists. In July 2015—the month when Dan and his son had begun their daily workouts—the director of the FBI appeared before a Senate committee to emphasize that radical Islamist terrorism remained "among the highest priorities for the FBI and the Intelligence Community." There could be no letup, James Comey warned, saying that ISIS, now outpacing al-Qaeda in attracting extremists in the West, had "proven relentless in its violent campaign."

It was hard to overlook news about ISIS-inspired cases, especially when one was local. On April 10, 2015, a Topeka man was arrested by the FBI as he made ready to detonate a thousand-pound car bomb at the Fort Riley military base in Manhattan, Kansas. The FBI had been tracking John T. Booker Jr., age twenty, for months as he rounded up explosive materials to attack the base and kill as many soldiers as possible. His arrest was covered nationally in the press: "Kansas Man John Booker Indicted in ISIS-inspired Bomb Plot," reported NBC news. Meanwhile, the *Huffington Post*'s story was headlined "John T. Booker Jr., Kansas Man, Arrested in Plot to Suicide Bomb Fort Riley for ISIS." The case fell smack in the FBI's counterterrorism wheelhouse—dealing with a radicalized Muslim extremist. James Comey even referred to young Booker in his July speech to the Senate, saying the homegrown Islamist terrorist, who'd made online videos denouncing America and supporting ISIS, had "systemically carried out steps to attack a US military institution."

But over the same time period, there had also been a resurgence in far-right domestic extremism. In 2014, Kansans saw firsthand this brand of violence—and with a sadly different outcome than Booker's attempt. Frazier Glenn Miller, seventy-three, claiming he was an "activist for white rights," gunned down three people at a Jewish Community Center in Overland Park, a city across the state from Garden City, in eastern Kansas. Though Miller, a former Ku Klux Klan leader, afterward said he was looking to kill Jews with his pump-action shotgun, none of the dead were in fact Jewish. Miller's upcoming trial for murder was scheduled to start later in the summer, in Olathe, Kansas. In another case, an avowed racist named Robert Doggart was arrested in Tennessee before he could carry out his lethal plot. Doggart had stockpiled weapons and was about to head north to upstate New York to burn down a mosque in the Muslim community at Islamberg. The sixty-three-year-old Tennessean believed the community at the foothills of the Catskill Mountains, consisting of about forty families, was a training ground for Islamist terrorists bent on attacking New York City.

Doggart was stopped in time, whereas Miller was not—yet terrorist plots involving far-right extremists were not getting the same level of official attention from counterterrorism agencies as were those involving American and foreign-born jihadists. Part of the reason was that white supremacists like Miller and Doggart tended not to be viewed as actual terrorists in the eyes of the law. Unlike Booker, an ISIS devotee who was indicted under federal anti-terrorism laws, the others were accused of civil rights violations, hate crimes, conspiracy, or, in Miller's case, murder. Another reason was that federal officials weren't saying much publicly about the uptick in far-right violence. Comey did not make mention of either Miller or Doggart—or anyone involved in domestic terrorism—in his address to the Senate in early July. Instead, the idea of terrorism had come to be equated narrowly with radical Islamist groups like ISIS as the main threat to the country's security; it did not encompass far-right groups as well—a double standard that, at least indirectly, fueled anti-Muslim sentiment. This modern strain of Western xenophobia had much in common with the "yellow peril" and the "red scare" of a century prior. Asians during World War II and then Communists during the Cold War were demonized as an immediate existential threat to America's survival. Now, in the twenty-first century, many political leaders and presidential candidates jumped on board to help calcify the new viewpoint. The Republican Donald Trump was especially outspoken; his call for a ban on Muslim immigrants became central to his campaign. He attacked US refugee policies as porous, enabling terrorists to easily sneak into the country. "We have no idea who these people are," he said, referring to Muslims as he spoke on the campaign trail. "This could be one of the great Trojan horses."

NO MATTER what extremists like Miller and Doggart were called, Dan gleaned information about them during his regular checks of online news sites. But it was on Facebook and YouTube, where content was largely unchecked and unedited, that he could most clearly detect a change in the country's political climate. "News" such as the story about the Walmart tunnels, which he considered utter nonsense, took on a life of its own, featuring extensive and passionate testimonials "proving" that President Obama was ordering the tunnels built. John T. Booker of Topeka had relied on Facebook to broadcast his intentions to "wage jihad." The year before his arrest he'd posted that "getting ready to be killed in jihad is a HUGE adrenalin rush." It's how the FBI got on his tail; a citizen who'd seen Booker's Facebook post had alerted the bureau. Just as noticeable, if not more so, was the wave of white-supremacist postings, reflecting the heightened nativism and anxiety of many white nationalists during Barack Obama's presidency.

New Facebook accounts and conservative groups sprouted all the time, either to condemn Obama, and then Hillary Clinton and her run to succeed Obama, or to push an angry, heated anti-Muslim message. Though Dan and every other Facebook user did not suspect it at the time, in a few years US law enforcement would uncover the fact that a number of the accounts and groups had been created by Russians as part of a covert operation to foment divisiveness in the country's 2016 presidential election. There was, for example, Being Patriotic, a phony grassroots group that created anti-Clinton, pro–gun rights advertisements —two themes dovetailing with Dan's own views. Or, in the months to come, there was Stop A.I., or Stop All Invaders, which circulated virulent anti-Muslim advertisements. In one, a photograph of women wearing face coverings was accompanied with text saying the coverings were putting Americans at risk: "We must not sacrifice national security to satisfy the demands of minorities. All face covering should be banned in every state across America!" And there was Secured Borders, another anti-immigrant Facebook group with a following that eventually topped 130,000.

Dan created his first Facebook account in 2009, after he found that everyone else in his extended family, spread out over southwestern Kansas, seemed to be on Facebook. He took the moniker D-Day, and by 2015, he was using the account as one way to conduct his online business to earn some money and support the family. He frequented a gun site, for example, looking for opportunities to buy a gun cheap and then resell it at a markup, as he did with the ammunition he bought at Walmart. Mostly, though, he used Facebook to broadcast his dual passion for the Kansas City Chiefs and his family. "Can't believe this girl Alyssa Day turned 14 today!!!" he wrote on his page on January 3. "She is beautiful and wise beyond her years!!! I have been blessed to have a daughter like this!!! Happy Birthday!" Or he'd occasionally share an unexpected slice of life: "Wow, Mountain Lion spotted in Garden City, KS!!! Yep, seen it with my own 4 eyes! ☺."

Facebook was also how he'd reconnected with one particular former co-worker. Dan had first met Terrence Taylor in the late 1990s, when both worked as guards at the juvenile detention center. They fell out of touch once Dan left the youth prison in 2012 to take the job as probation officer. Now they'd reunited as Facebook friends, and Dan couldn't help but notice Terrence's over-the-top patriotism and denunciations of ISIS and immigration. Terrence posted photos of flag-waving, muscle-bound white men dressed in camo and armed with AK-47s. Then he posted a close-up of a big, shiny machine gun with the caption "ISIS bring your best men with their sharpest knives, we the people are waiting." And he posted a photo of President Obama holding a microphone, with the caption "Excuse me. I'm not done lying yet." Dan remembered Terrence as something of a big talker, a guy with a full mustache who was overeager to please and to fit in. Because the militia movement was now gaining popularity, he wasn't surprised to see that Terrence had jumped onto the bandwagon and joined the Three Percenters of Southwest Kansas, a far-right anti-government group that Terrence was constantly promoting on his Facebook page. In June, Terrence shared a black-and-white photo of a heavily armed militia member with the words "Three Percent: Liberty or Death." Dan followed Terrence's page, curious about the militia, and he suddenly noticed that militia recruiters were all over in cyberspace—voicing love of country and gun rights as well as anger at ISIS and the federal government. He didn't disagree.

It was why Terrence Taylor came to mind right away that Friday morning when Dan spotted a peculiar-looking poster tacked to a bulletin board in the lobby of the Finney County Public Library. The poster, hanging in the middle of the Community Bulletin Board, consisted of a Palestinian flag—three horizontal stripes in black, white, and green, overlaid by a red triangle. In big lettering, the poster said, STOP ISRAEL and LET PALESTINE BECOME A FREE STATE, with a telephone number printed at the bottom.

The poster was an anomaly, so strikingly different from the typical fare—notices about upcoming tag sales, community meetings, and other town events. Dan was irked. The anti-Israel message went against his Christian beliefs. He was no biblical scholar; his son, Brandon, was the one in the family who could quote passages. But he had always been strongly pro-Israel concerning that nation's endless conflict with Palestinians over control of the Gaza Strip. "I believe that Israel had the right to have their own country, that God had given them their country," he'd say. He even wondered if the poster might have something to do with Hamas, the Islamic fundamentalist group that was also fighting Israel's occupation of the strip. His position reflected views common to the Midwest, espoused on Bott Radio Network's string of conservative Christian radio stations, including 107.9 FM in Garden City, which broadcast the weekly "Friends of Israel Today" segment.

Dan stared at the poster, thinking, *Really? In Garden City?* He didn't imagine for a second that folks from Garden City would ever get involved in something like *that,* meaning any action that was pro-Palestinian and anti-Israel. The poster's message continued to irritate him as he and Brandon walked into the library to get a cool drink. He was thinking, *How weird,* a Palestinian flag on what was basically a pro-Hamas poster appearing in the lobby of the public library. He viewed the poster as an endorsement of terrorism. Dan was offended, and so on his way out he studied it again, as if to confirm it was real. Then he ripped it down. His reasoning? "If they have a right to put it up, I have a right to take it down."

And Terrence Taylor came to mind. Terrence would be keen to know about this.

When dan day was born, in 1968, his hometown was establishing itself as the apex of what would become known as Kansas's meatpacking Golden Triangle. In farming, the emergence of center-pivot irrigation —long-armed sprinklers attached to wheels—had been transformative, turning thousands upon thousands of acres of marginal land into viable growing fields. From a plane in the sky, the southern Great Plains offered a new visual geometry: a quiltlike pattern of seemingly endless circles and squares. In addition to larger corn yields, inexpensive cattle feed—grain sorghum, commonly called milo—was being harvested in record amounts. That, in turn, helped spur explosive growth in large-scale feedlots, where cattle were fattened for slaughter. Meanwhile, the meatpacking industry was reshaping its business model, choosing to abandon urban areas for rural locations closer to feedlots and to labor that was both cheaper and generally non-union. In 1980, Iowa Beef Processors opened the world's largest meatpacking plant in Holcomb, just west of Garden City. Within three years another meat company, Monfort, reopened and expanded an idle plant on Garden City's east side. Soon enough, the two plants were operating two shifts daily, six days a week, and employing about four thousand workers.

Southwest Kansas had become the epicenter of feedlots and meatpacking, as both the farming and the cattle industries were consolidated, swallowing up smaller family operations. With meatpacking plants opening in nearby Dodge City and Liberal, Kansas—about an hour's drive to the east and south of Garden City, respectively—the three points gave rise to the Golden Triangle tagline. By century's end, the plants employed about ten thousand workers, who were butchering and packaging more than twenty thousand head of cattle daily. The roads surrounding Garden City became filled with huge, rumbling tractor-trailer haulers, transporting loads of cattle from the feedlots to the slaughterhouses. Depending on the time of day and the direction of the breeze, the odor of manure could linger in the air throughout Garden City's neighborhoods. The stink was pervasive enough that visitors readily took olfactory notice—it was hard not to—but locals like Dan only chuckled; they were long used to it, tended not to even notice. City leaders, when asked, put a positive spin on the odor, calling it the smell of money.

Typical of working-class families in the greater Garden City area, most of Dan's siblings had worked in a meatpacking plant at one time or another. Dan's turn came in early 1986, during his senior year in high school, a period of uncertainty for him as a question loomed: what was he going to do after graduation? Joining the marines was something he'd thought about, having grown up with stories about his dad and his uncle Ray Day, from whom he got his middle name. Both had served in the army during World War II, his dad in the Pacific and Uncle Ray in Europe, where he'd taken part in the D-Day invasion at Normandy, in June 1944. He was later killed in action, in 1945. Uncle Ray, a private in a field artillery unit, was buried in Belgium at the Henri-Chapelle American Cemetery, along with nearly eight thousand other American war dead. Dan was drawn to the idea of serving his country, although his childhood asthma, even if no longer much of a bother, likely would pose an obstacle. What about college? Most of his stepbrothers and half brothers were high school dropouts. Some had had run-ins with the law, even spent a night or two in jail, usually the result of fighting. If Dan headed for college, he'd basically be breaking new ground. Work? He'd always worked part-time while in high school, mostly at a gas station, where he pumped gas, changed tires, or replaced brakes. He wasn't keen on being a grease monkey for life.

The future wasn't something he'd thought too much about. His junior year he mainly was interested in hanging out with his wrestling pal Terry Johnson and another lifelong friend, John Franco, born two days apart from him in the same Garden City hospital. John's grandparents had emigrated from Mexico years ago. Dan would help Terry with his wrestling training, but mostly the threesome filled their days with hunting, off-road four-wheelin', and looking for the next party to crash. But by the second semester of his senior year, in January 1986, Dan's consistently solid grades meant he'd already earned enough credits to graduate. The official ceremony was still months away in June, and Dan found himself done with school, free and clear. He decided to take his turn at the meatpacking plant, where workers were always needed and the $6.50 hourly wage was just fine for a high schooler.

Dan took his friend John Franco with him down to the employment office at the Monfort beef packaging plant on the east side of Garden City, the one that had reopened three years before. The plant consisted of a grouping of white buildings and steel bins situated on about 330 acres. Dan, seventeen years old, lied about his age in order to qualify for the minimum hiring age, which was eighteen. He could tell they just wanted workers and didn't care about the letter of the law. John Franco was put to work on the dock, loading boxes of packaged meat onto trucks, physically demanding but one of the safer jobs in the scheme of things, while Dan was assigned to one of the hardest: boning chucks.

Dan was outfitted in a steel-mesh apron and a pair of steel-mesh gloves. In one hand he held a hook and in the other, a razor-sharp straight knife. When a heavy piece of meat approached on the conveyor, his job was to hook it onto a cutting tray and quickly hack the slab into three pieces. The meat then continued down the line, where it was trimmed of fat and cut into even smaller pieces. Dan's slabs had to be cut in a certain way, and supervisors yelled at workers for not doing it right or for being too slow. The first week or so, the meat looked to Dan like a giant blob—one blob after another coming at him all shift long, barreling down the conveyor nonstop for eight hours. He tried his best to slice it as he'd been instructed, but he kept messing up. New workers were given six weeks to get the hang of it. Dan took the deadline as a challenge; he endured the yelling from his managers as he put to memory exactly where to butcher the meat, and soon it no longer looked like a hulking mass when it approached. He spotted his targets as he hooked a slab and made three clean, quick cuts with the knife.

His forearms, tired and sore at first, got stronger, and he didn't mind working hard. Even so, although he'd made the grade at the meatpacking plant, he didn't see a future in boning chucks—the grueling shifts, the same dull red meat on the conveyor, a stagnant wage, and workplace dangers. Dan still counted ten fingers on his hands, but that wasn't the case for plenty of co-workers. The hard life at the slaughterhouse seemed to scare him straight—and his stint became an impetus to continue with school. The marines wouldn't have him due to his asthma, and so, come the fall of 1986, he enrolled at Garden City Community College. For money, he drove a UPS truck part-time. He wasn't sure what to study; he declared a business major—something everyone else at school seemed to be choosing. When he added classes in the trades—automotive, mechanics, and welding—he liked them so much, he began thinking maybe he'd become a shop teacher. But the next year, UPS encouraged him to come on full-time, an offer Dan decided he could not refuse—not at $19 an hour, and with only a high school diploma. He stopped school and drove a UPS truck for five years. He earned $45,000 annually, with lots of overtime, and then one day he attended a cookout at his mom's house, where he met the love of his life, his future wife, Cherlyn.

Life was good, an upswing in the cycle of feast and famine.

WHEN DAN worked at the meatpacking plant, he noted that he was one of the few "white boys" on the line and that hardly anybody spoke English. Jobs at slaughterhouses did not appeal to most folks in the Heartland, given the dangers of butchering, generally poor working conditions, and comparatively low non-union wages. By the time Dan was boning chucks, as the meat industry took off, immigrants were the go-to labor pool. Mexican immigrants had always had a presence in Garden City, albeit a minority one. In 1980, for example, they made up 16 percent of the population. (Hispanic families with longtime ties to the town were sometimes called "Texicans.") Then a surge in new Hispanic workers, filling jobs on the kill floors and processing lines, fueled a dramatic demographic makeover. By 1990, they made up 25 percent of the population, a figure that continued to climb, reaching 44 percent in 2000. Joining them in the slaughterhouses were refugees from Southeast Asia who had fled the Vietnam War and then the fall of Saigon in 1975. They'd been steered to the area by recruiters for the meatpackers, and Catholic groups helped settle them in town. Signage around Garden City—in restaurants, school buildings, and the plants' lunchrooms, and even notices that posted tornado warnings—began featuring three languages: English, Spanish, and Vietnamese. Noticeable too were new markets, bakeries, and restaurants catering to the burgeoning immigrant populations. There was the Phở Hòa 1 Vietnamese Restaurant, for example, which opened in 1987, and the El Remedio Market. Both were located on busy Fulton Street, near the railroad tracks. School enrollments spiked too—part of the city's overall population growth—and the school district partnered with the community college to create learning centers that would provide the new arrivals with language instruction and other educational support.

The influx of immigrants did not stop there. By the mid-1990s, Somali refugees had arrived in small numbers, working first at the plant in Liberal and then mainly in Garden City. Local newspapers periodically ran stories that in journalism are called "explainers"—articles full of information about the "strangers from a strange land." One lengthy chart gave a description of the Islamic religion—the veneration of the prophet Muhammad, born in Mecca in about 570—and adherence to the Quran, which requires five daily prayers and prohibits behaviors such as drinking alcohol and having sex outside of marriage, which are considered unclean. The chart provided Somalia's population (8,050,000 in 1993), its language (Somali), and details about the traditional African Islamic robes and scarves the Somalis wore. It explained the reason for the diaspora, the violent civil war in a homeland located on the Horn of Africa, along the Indian Ocean. Longtime Garden City residents were particularly curious about the way Muslim women were wrapped in brightly colored full-length dresses, with headcovers hiding their hair. The newspaper article sought to provide context, explaining that while the attire might make the women appear "tribal to Americans," it wasn't as if they had spent "their days in Somalia hauling water jugs atop their heads." To the contrary, the women came from all walks of life. One refugee was a former bank accountant, another had been a teacher, but no matter their prior occupations, they had fled Somalia's civil strife to find a new life in the Golden Triangle.

In 2008, the number of Somalis in Garden City rose dramatically when Tyson Foods closed a meatpacking plant in the town of Emporia, located about a hundred miles southwest of Kansas City. The company offered bonuses to nearly four hundred Somalis to relocate to Garden City and work at the plant in nearby Holcomb, which it had purchased from Iowa Beef. Smaller numbers of Burmese and Ethiopian immigrants also began appearing in the city, drawn by the promise of instant work. To further attract new immigrants and to make Garden City a Muslim destination, the company made additional accommodations: it allowed Somalis two prayer breaks per eight-hour shift in specially designated prayer rooms at the slaughterhouse. Prayer rugs were provided, as were compasses, so that Muslims could pray in the direction of Mecca. And foot-washing stations were installed in some bathrooms. In relatively short order Muslims began filling some of the lower-cost apartment complexes. The largest concentration was at the single-story Garden Spot Apartments on West Mary Street. Tenants, with the landlord's okay, had even converted one apartment into a mosque.

It wasn't as if the immigrants' arrival in Kansas had been friction-free, though. Tyson had closed the Emporia plant in part because tension had erupted when Somalis began working there in 2006. Many in Emporia had been welcoming, but a hardcore group was not. "The town is going downhill," one angry resident wrote anonymously on the local paper's blog. "The Somalis are rude, inconsiderate, and ungrateful. They drive terrible . . . No one wants them here." In Garden City, Hispanic residents periodically complained about a race-based double standard, saying police were more likely to crack down on drunkenness or worse at the handful of bars they frequented rather than at the mostly white country club. Or Hispanic students were punished more severely than whites for the same infraction of school rules—and sometimes even disciplined for speaking Spanish. Change brought challenges, to be sure—in housing, health care, education, and race relations—but city leaders saw those complications as preferable to the economic malaise, or even ruin, that other communities in the High Plains (the western part of the Great Plains) were experiencing. Overall, amid rapid demographic change at the end of one century and continuing into the next, the old and new coexisted fairly well. It was more like "to each his own," as longtime residents recognized that the newcomers were hardworking and largely kept to themselves.

In fact, Garden City's new diversity drew the attention of anthropologists and journalists. This was not a place that resembled in any way a coastal megalopolis, such as Los Angeles or New York City. It was one of most rural and remote spots in America—"an unlikely multicultural mecca," as anthropologists came to refer to it. Experts studied the explosive growth of the meatpacking industry and the immigrant population and examined what one anthropologist called Garden City's "quiet accommodation" of its foreign newcomers, in spite of language and cultural barriers. The experts produced articles for the *Journal of*

Rural Studies and gave presentations with titles like "Harvest of Change: Meatpacking, Immigration, and Garden City, Kansas."

In 2010, a reporter from the *Wichita Eagle* named David Klepper came to town to work on a long feature about the melting pot that was Garden City. Headlined "Garden City: America's Future?" the article included extensive comments from both longtime residents and Somalis. "I feel like I belong here," one Somali man told the reporter. "Muslim—not Muslim—it doesn't matter." In a democratic country, he continued, "we are all the same."

Census data bore out the shifting demographics. Garden City had once been overwhelmingly white—82 percent as recently as 1980—but starting with the 2000 census, the percentage of white residents was shown to have fallen below 50 percent. The city was being transformed into the first community in the state where Hispanic, Vietnamese, and Somali residents, along with those of other ethnic backgrounds, made up a majority. Such a startling ethnic makeover might prompt homegrown lifers like Dan Day to wonder, as Dorothy once did in Oz, whether they were even in Kansas anymore.

On Saturday, July 8, the very next day after Dan and Brandon's respite in the air-conditioned library, Dan and his son walked across Terrence Taylor's small front lawn toward the single-story house, with its light brick facade. WELCOME THREE PERCENTERS! screamed a handmade sign planted in the ground. *Just like Terrence,* thought Dan; the showiness was a reminder of the man's loud personality. Near the sign an American flag flapped red, white, and blue in the breeze, and beneath it hung a second flag, resembling the US flag except that in place of fifty stars was the militia's symbol: the large Roman numeral III encircled by stars. Terrence was at least consistent—big talker, big mustache, big sign. Nothing discreet about Dan's former co-worker from the juvie prison.

The poster of the Palestinian flag, which Dan had ripped down in the library Friday morning, had become an excuse to connect with Terrence later that same day. Dan had guessed right. Terrence was not only interested in the poster; he got all worked up. He eagerly wanted to make a duplicate, using the library's copying machine. Dan said that wasn't necessary; he had no reason to keep the poster. Terrence could simply have it, save himself ten cents. Terrence then kicked into good ol' boy mode, mentioning that he was having some friends over for a cookout the next afternoon—Dan and Brandon should come. The former co-workers kidded each other a bit, with Dan saying he might show if he knew Terrence was grilling steaks. Terrence, laughing, promised to do just that. The encounter on Friday was their first in who knew how long, and Dan couldn't help but notice the words on the big new tattoo taking up most of Terrence's forearm: MOLON LABE. The words were Greek, roughly meaning "come and take them," a menacing phrase that was becoming all the rage with militia members and gun owners.

Dan had been noncommittal, but on Saturday, curiosity got the best of him. Even though he was following Terrence Taylor on Facebook and saw that Terrence had joined the Three Percenters, neither he nor Brandon knew much about the militias beyond the fact that, generally speaking, they were pro–gun rights and anti–federal government—positions Dan held to some degree, especially the former. Besides, as Saturday morning wore on, he and Brandon joked that a free meal was a free meal. They decided to go, and late that afternoon they made their way across the lawn to the backyard patio where Terrence met them heartily. Picnic tables and folding chairs had been set up, the grill was fired up—but no steaks, just the basics: hamburgers and hot dogs. The afternoon was scorching hot. The Taylors had put up a canopy for shade, even set up fans from the house, but neither provided much relief. Brandon overheard Terrence's daughters grumbling that they were doing all the work setting up. Terrence was busy showing off his new tattoo.

Dan looked around, counted at least a dozen guests, with more arriving. Many were dressed in fatigues. Most were carrying, which wasn't a surprise. What riled Dan was that, seeing the sign out front and hearing the talk underway on the patio, he realized this was not a simple family and friends cookout. It was a recruitment meeting. He wished Terrence had been up front about that. Dan might be curious about the Three Percenters, but he had no interest in joining them or any other unit. He wasn't about to turn around and walk out, though, and decided to grin and bear it. He and Brandon each got a plate of food and sat down together. They started small talk with a couple seated at their table, while nearby a cluster of men were talking up the militia, guns, tattoos, and the country's sorry state of affairs.

One fellow in particular seemed to control the conversation, loudly introducing himself as a proud new member of the Three Percenters—and also the proud new owner of a Glock semiautomatic handgun. Dan glued his eyes on the guy as he drew the new handgun and began waving it around. Usually low-key to a fault, and hardly the type of person to make waves or draw attention to himself, Dan was already irritated at the true purpose of the cookout. He couldn't stand down as the gun-slinging Three Percenter showed off so close to him and his son. He was an absolutist when it came to gun safety. A Glock did not come with a manual safety, so Dan stood up and abruptly snatched the handgun away from its startled owner.

"Don't point that fuckin' gun at me," he said.

"It ain't loaded," the gun owner snarled.

Dan ignored him. He pushed the button to eject the gun's magazine. The Glock was made to hold twenty rounds—nineteen bullets in the magazine and the twentieth in the chamber, ready to fire. Dan instantly saw the magazine did indeed contain bullets. He didn't count how many, and anyway it did not matter—the Glock was loaded. He held it up to display his findings to its owner. The guy was dumbfounded, his swagger suddenly gone, and he went quiet.

The small ruckus notwithstanding, Dan and his son blended in, ate their free meal. There was plenty of talk about the Three Percenters, a national militia founded in 2008, shortly after Barack Obama's election as the country's first Black president. It was part of a wave of new far-right paramilitary groups promising resistance to gun control and the intrusion of Obama's federal government into their lives. The group took its name from the myth that during the Revolutionary War, only 3 percent of Americans had actually taken up arms to repel mighty Great Britain and achieve independence. It wasn't true; historians put participation at 15 percent and likely even higher, noting that for any country at war, having 6 percent of its population in service was a sizable proportion. But 3 percent sounded good, and around the country local militia units were formed, some affiliated with the national organization, some not.

Dan and Brandon listened in as guests talked about the weapons training they hoped to do and their plans for stockpiling food and material — talking the talk of "preppers" getting ready for a natural disaster or an invasion. They complained about big government, dropping phrases like "founding fathers" and "martial law" in a pseudo-intellectual way. Eventually Terrence came over to introduce Dan to Jason Crick, who was the founder and head of the local group, the Three Percenters of Southwest Kansas.

Crick, who was from nearby Dodge City, told Dan that he'd created the militia only a few months earlier, in April 2015, and that they were just getting underway. He said he'd been recruiting members through a Facebook page and at gatherings like Terrence's cookout. A key motivating factor, Crick said, was that "Obama was still president." He and the like-minded people he'd been assembling all agreed that the future looked ominous and that *something was coming:* "I don't know if it's like an uprising or I guess you could say like a government takeover, basically, of everything." Patriotic folks needed to be ready to defend themselves against the federal government and also new waves of immigrants — Muslim terrorists among them — that Obama was allowing into the country.

Crick then got ready to deliver the recruiting message to the entire group. As people finished their food, Terrence introduced Crick as head of the newly formed Three Percenters of Southwest Kansas. Crick pulled out the poster of the Palestinian flag that Dan had found in the library and began his talk. Waving it around, Crick cited the Israeli-Palestinian conflict, praising Israel and denouncing the pro-Palestinian movement. Then he veered into a tirade about ISIS terrorists and against Somalis, saying the local Somalis were supporting ISIS in opposing Israel. In their own backyard, Crick was saying, terrorist cells were likely proliferating. Dan perked up, startled of course to see the poster. But more than that, he was flabbergasted to hear Crick making a giant leap, connecting the pro-Palestine poster to local Somalis and ISIS terrorism. And he thought, *What the heck?*

LESS THAN a half mile and a minute's drive away from Terrence's house stood the Garden Spot Apartments, a complex consisting of thirty rental units in eight single-story brick buildings, laid out in a U-shape, with an entrance and exit onto West Mary Street. Across the street, at 305 West Mary, sat another sprawling single-story complex. Both were filled to capacity with Somali and Burmese refugees. "They are people and need a place to live just like anyone else," the owner of the two complexes had once said.

Despite their proximity, Terrence's cookout and the refugee-occupied apartments might as well have been worlds apart, given the great divide in language, culture, and understanding. The Somalis mainly kept to themselves, living quietly. Nearly all of them were employed at the Tyson meatpacking plant, and while Terrence grilled burgers on his backyard patio, the Somali tenants worked the plant's two Saturday shifts, butchering and packaging beef.

In all likelihood, Terrence Taylor, Jason Crick, Dan Day, and other attendees at the Three Percenters of Southwest Kansas recruiting cookout did not know a single Somali by name. Some, especially the ones living in Garden City, like Terrence and Dan, would be aware of one prominent Somali refugee, the local entrepreneur Adan Keynan—if not by sight, then by occupation. Adan's business, the African Shop, was situated a bit farther down from the apartment complex on West Mary Street and just around the corner from a shopping center featuring a new Walmart. Few residents of Garden City might know a Muslim refugee, but they could not miss Adan's business on the busy thoroughfare.

Adan Keynan's long journey to America mirrored that of many Somalis. In the early 1990s, when he was just a boy, the Somali government had collapsed, and thousands of Somalis were dying in fighting between rival clan warlords. His family had fled their war-weary homeland. In 1992, the United Nations dispatched a peacekeeping force to Somalia to restore order, but the situation worsened. Gun battles the next year between US special forces and local militia fighters during the two-day Battle of Mogadishu resulted in the deaths of nineteen US soldiers and hundreds of Somalis. The fierce, close combat included the downing of two US Army Black Hawk helicopters by rocket-propelled grenades, or RPGs, which became the basis for a bestselling book, *Black Hawk Down.* The UN forces had pulled out by early 1995, having failed to achieve peace.

Adan, though born in Mogadishu, recalled little of the capital city. His family had escaped to nearby Ethiopia. "When your country collapses, you go wherever you can in Africa," he said. They became part of a Somali diaspora that would continue into the next century, with more than a million Somalis eventually living in exile in countries around the world. In Ethiopia, the Somali refugee population exceeded 200,000. Adan said, "The camps, it's very hard to live." Like every family, his was seeking asylum. Taking first steps to enter a US program that allowed foreigners fearing persecution or death in their home country to resettle in America, his parents registered with immigration officials and were interviewed. Then they waited. Adan and his eight siblings grew up in a camp and had little or no formal education; their family's main focus was day-to-day survival.

Nearly fifteen years passed before Adan finally got his chance. He was twenty-two that spring of 2007, and by this time a new Islamist terrorist group had asserted itself in Somalia—al-Shabab, which in Somali means "The Youth." The militant group had strong ties to al-Qaeda and a shared fundamentalist view of jihad, or holy war, against purported enemies of Islam, while adhering to a strict interpretation of the Quran. Its guerrilla attacks included suicide bombings and assassinations, and over the years, al-Shabab gained control over parts of central and southern Somalia. By 2008, the group's Islamist-nationalist fighters had grown from a few hundred into the thousands, and that year the US State Department designated al-Shabab a foreign terrorist organization.

In March 2007, Adan arrived in New York City and then traveled immediately to Columbus, Ohio, where some relatives and family friends had already settled. His final destination was Missouri—just a spot on a map of the United States to him but a place where friends had said he could find work. In June, he left Ohio and headed west, albeit on a circuitous route, because the two men giving him a ride were not bound for Missouri but were heading farther west, to Garden City, Kansas. To Adan, everything about the United States was a mystery, and when he arrived at Garden City on June 24, he thought that it was a village in the middle of nowhere compared to an urban center like Columbus, Ohio. He intended to stay only until another friend from Missouri could come for him. Then his plans took a turn. An immediate departure became impossible because of High Plains weather—fast-changing conditions that occur when cold, dry air from the Rocky Mountains collides in the Kansas sky with warm, humid air from the south. Within a few days of his arrival, a downburst thunderstorm swept through Garden City, tossing cars, toppling tractor trailers, and smashing windows. Parts of the apartment building where Adan was staying collapsed. "It was like, what is going on? Why is the house breaking?" Adan relocated to another apartment already overcrowded with Somalis, where, he drily observed, it felt like he was back in a refugee camp.

Then there was an unexpected job offer. He barely knew the Somalis he was temporarily staying with, but they told him that the Tyson meatpacking plant in nearby Holcomb was hiring. Adan was encouraged to go see for himself, and so he went to the plant the next day. To his surprise he was offered work on the spot. His first day on the job was July 7, the Tuesday after the fierce thunderstorm had ripped through town. During orientation he and other new hires were shown videos on how to slaughter cattle, remove their skin, and then butcher and package the various cuts. He'd never seen anything like it—the efficiency of massive industrial slaughter, and for the next week he had dreams about the slaughterhouse. He was put to work on the line, or "the chain," as workers called it, hanging cattle carcasses by their legs on hooks, which then carried them forward for butchering. Within a few months he hurt his shoulder, in part due to the wear and tear that the heavy, demanding, repetitive work put on his slight build. He was treated for the injury, did some physical therapy, and was reassigned to knife work, cutting and trimming the meat.

What began as a stopover had become home. He became part of Garden City's growing Somali population. He met a Somali woman named Sara, eighteen years older, and in 2009 they married and moved into a one-bedroom unit at the Garden Spot Apartments. But like Dan Day before him, Adan did not see a future in meatpacking. He wanted off the grueling line, and as he settled into life in a small city with an unusually diverse population, an idea began to take hold. It started when he and some friends decided to go out to dinner one night. The restaurant they chose was buffet-style, and Adan found himself standing in the line, not knowing what he could eat. The Quran forbade consumption of pork, and Adan wondered if the food offerings contained any. The outing highlighted for him the difficulty his people had in finding acceptable foodstuffs. Even when he and Sara cooked at home, using ingredients purchased at Walmart, he worried that some might contain pork products.

He'd grown frustrated that Muslims in Garden City, now numbering well in the hundreds, didn't have access to food that was their own. He saw markets catering to Mexicans and Vietnamese, and he wanted Africans to have one too. So in March 2009, just two years after his arrival, he opened a store that he called the African Shop. It was a short walk from the apartment complex, across an empty lot and right next to a Dollar General. To stock it, he bought a used white van and drove to Minneapolis–St. Paul, home to the largest Somali diaspora in the United States. He and Sara loaded the van with imported teas, spices, and all kinds of food and clothing from the markets there and made the return trip home.

He learned on the job how to run a business, establishing connections in Minnesota to create a reliable stream of commerce, and the African Shop proved a success. He'd become a full-time merchant, and as demand for African goods continued to increase, he outgrew his original store. In late 2013, he moved to a much larger space a few blocks away, at 911 West Mary Street. He set up a retail area in front and converted a spacious area in back into a community center, with a pool table, a small kitchen where tea and native dishes could be prepared, and a large-screen TV. In addition to soccer matches and other sports programs, the Somalis' favorite shows included *Law and Order: Special Victims Unit.*

AS OF the summer of 2015, Adan Keynan, then thirty, had lived and worked in Garden City for eight years. Yet he'd never mastered English. He was able to follow a bit of basic English, but speaking the language was another matter. He generally leaned on others when the need for translation arose. Two younger Somalis in particular were emerging in the community to help him and any Somali cross the language barrier —Mursal Naleye and Ifrah Ahmed. Both were in their twenties, outgoing, and multilingual. Adan had come to America from a refugee camp in Ethiopia, while Mursal and Ifrah arrived from camps in Egypt and Uganda, respectively. But no matter the route, they shared the sense of dislocation and disruption symptomatic of coming from a homeland in constant turmoil.

Mursal had grown up in a small town outside Mogadishu, where his father had once had a thriving medical practice until the endless fighting changed everything. He immigrated to the United States in 2010 and had lived in Garden City since early 2013. It took time for him to find his footing, but having an easy smile and language skills, he began to successfully navigate between the growing Somali population and the broader community. He first worked at the Tyson plant as a butcher but was soon certified as a translator and transferred to departments where language skills were at a premium, namely, inspection and training. He was unable to move into the fully occupied Garden Spot Apartments on West Mary Street, where Adan and many Somalis lived, so he rented at Labrador Apartments on the east side, which was also popular with refugees. By 2015, Mursal had a good job and a girlfriend, played soccer with friends, and socialized at Adan's shop.

Ifrah Ahmed also arrived in Garden City in 2013, several months after Mursal. She was a newborn when her family fled to a refugee camp in Nairobi, Kenya, where her mother, a teacher, found work teaching English. Ifrah learned English, Swahili, and some Arabic. When she was a teenager, Ifrah moved to Uganda and the Nakivale refugee camp. It was at Nakivale in 2012 that she received word that her bid to immigrate to America had been approved. In her early twenties Ifrah was sent by Catholic Charities to Kansas City. The next year, she decided to move to Garden City, where a distant cousin was living.

Ifrah's adjustment to her new surroundings did not come easy. Like Mursal before her, she was accustomed to living in and around a big city —in her case, Nairobi. She liked the bustle of urban life, its culture, and the sense there was always something new to try. The Great Plains felt barren. But she was fortunate to find work. Right away, Tyson hired her as a translator. Ifrah devised a plan to save money, buy a car, and move to metropolitan Minneapolis–St. Paul. Then her plan changed. In Garden City, she got to know other Muslim refugees from Somalia and elsewhere in Africa, and she started making new friends. One day shortly after moving into town, she walked into the African Shop. It was late in 2013, just when Adan Keynan was preparing to relocate the store farther down West Mary Street. Ifrah had been curious to meet its proprietors and to see what they had for sale. Introducing herself, she learned that Sara, Adan's wife, had grown up in Kenya and also knew Swahili, the language Ifrah had spoken in the Nairobi refugee camp. Ifrah was beside herself. She couldn't remember the last time she'd been with someone who spoke Swahili. The two women spent the entire afternoon together. In her free time, Ifrah began going to the shop to visit with Sara and Adan and to help out if they needed it. Even better, a year later, in March 2015, Sara's daughter Halima arrived from Pakistan, where she had been studying at the university. Ifrah Ahmed and Halima Farah were the same age, with similar interests in music and culture, and both spoke Swahili. They became fast friends. In just over a year, Ifrah had found an extended "family." She dismissed any thought of departing Garden City for a bigger place with tall buildings and busy streets. As she explained it, "For the first time in the United States I felt like I belonged somewhere, and so I stuck around."

EVEN THOUGH Mursal and Ifrah were now available, Adan didn't need their services as interpreters all that frequently. In large part his daily life in Garden City—like that of most Somalis—was self-contained. The Garden Spot Apartments and other residential complexes where they lived were located on the northwest edge of town, right next to the highway. From there those employed at the Tyson plant in Holcomb had a quick, direct commute. For their worship, two mosques were right at hand, one at the Garden Spot Apartments and another across the street, in the 305 West Mary Street apartments. In their free time, Somalis played soccer together on city fields, mingled outside their apartments, or socialized in the community room at the back of Adan's store. They purchased food at Adan's and walked to the Dollar General and a nearby Walmart for anything else they needed. There was little reason to deviate from a daily life centered on Tyson, the mosque, the apartments, and their own people and, with that, little opportunity to interact with anyone speaking English.

Longtime residents generally accepted this separation; it's basically how things had always been during past influxes of immigrants and the city's increasing diversity. Mexicans had kept to themselves at first, as had the Vietnamese, and now the Somalis and other Africans. Some, however, wanted more of a connection. City officials and Catholic charities initiated programs aimed at providing housing, education, and other support services. Late in 2015, a progressive-minded veteran of the police department, Michael D. Utz, was named chief, and one of his first initiatives was to invite Muslim elders to meet with him on a regular basis. Getting this going proved a challenge, and the language barrier wasn't the only difficulty. Because the refugees had feared or experienced violence at the hands of the authorities in the homelands they'd fled, they did not trust the police. Looking around for help, Utz heard about the young Somali Mursal Nayele. He reached out to Mursal and asked if he would act as liaison. Mursal agreed, and the meetings got traction. Moreover, Utz hired a Somali to join the department's patrol division of about thirty officers.

In 2015, two members of the region's health-care community also became convinced that getting to know the Somali people was in everyone's best interest. One was a family doctor named John Birky, a Kansas native who had done volunteer medical work in Africa. The other was Benjamin Anderson, who had recently been named CEO of the twenty-five-bed Kearny County Hospital in Lakin, about twenty miles west of Garden City. Benjamin's wife was a Kansas native. Both men were in their midthirties, faith-driven and committed to social justice. They decided that to get to know the Somalis personally and culturally—and to lessen the group's isolation—was one way to achieve their goal of bringing health care to the burgeoning refugee community. In a bid to break the ice, they began stopping by Adan's store to buy tea, dates, or honey. Neither knew much about Somalia beyond periodic news reports on al-Shabab's latest acts of terrorism—and so they did harbor some suspicions. Benjamin worried that some refugees might actually be a step or two removed from al-Shabab, while Dr. Birky, who considered himself open-minded, felt some apprehension about the Somali strangers when he shopped. Both men got stares from the store's owner whenever they went in. Transactions were completed in an instant, with an exchange of money for goods and barely a spoken word. *No warmth there,* Benjamin thought.

Yet the two pressed on. "Jesus said that the first command is love God, and the second command is love your neighbor," Dr. Birky later told a reporter. And, he noted, the neighbor whom Jesus had cited in his teachings was someone "of a different culture."

Then, over the summer of 2015, Benjamin had a new idea. He was spearheading a fundraiser to benefit hospitals caring primarily for children, which were known as Children's Miracle Network Hospitals at Via Christi Health. His hospital and the city of Garden City were co-sponsoring a concert by Time for Three, called Tf3 for short. The string trio had wide appeal; they performed a range of pop music, from Katy Perry to Kanye West, and had played at venues such as the Indy 500 car race and during halftime at NFL games. Earlier in the year, more than twelve thousand young people had attended three sold-out shows in Wichita. Benjamin had high expectations for the event, to be held on the first Saturday night in October. He wondered what might happen if they invited some Somalis—let the music make a connection that the awkward purchases at Adan's shop had not. Benjamin talked the idea over with Dr. Birky, and he liked it a lot. Benjamin mentioned the concert to a Somali who'd been to the hospital and spoke English. He asked him to see if he could round up a group to attend.

WHILE BENJAMIN and Dr. Birky mulled over ways to get to know Somalis, Jason Crick and the Three Percenters at Terrence Taylor's cookout fumed that Muslims were soiling Garden City, turning it into a breeding ground for ISIS terrorists. As he displayed the poster of the Palestinian flag, Crick continued to harp about ISIS, claiming that a "recruiting sheet" for the terrorist group had accompanied the poster on the bulletin board. But Crick had no idea what he was talking about. Hamas was the terrorist group based in Palestine, not ISIS. ISIS was based in Iraq and Syria. Both groups might hate Israel, but they also hated each other. It mystified Dan that discussion of the poster with a Palestinian flag had morphed into the sounding of an alarm about ISIS.

Even so, the militia leader's comments triggered heated speculation that local Somalis were either ISIS militants or raising funds for the group. Some even claimed that several Somalis had been seen hovering around the poster. Dan tried to take it all in. Yes, he'd noticed a couple of Somalis at the library when he and Brandon had gone inside to cool down—but they were there as patrons. What a stretch to now claim that the Somalis were responsible for a recruitment poster for an international terrorist organization. When Crick was finished, militia members turned to him, asking questions about what was now being accepted as an important discovery. Others suggested they should put Somalis under surveillance, while a few huddled around the poster to snap pictures of it with their smartphones.

Dan was fed up, feeling that Terrence must have twisted their exchange about the poster into something it wasn't. Some fast-moving, off-the-wall fiction was developing, and it felt as false as the underground tunnels connecting Walmarts, which he'd read about. He headed home, incredulous. The cookout's strange turn didn't end there, however. Later that Saturday night, and throughout the next day, Dan and Brandon watched on Facebook as a photograph of the poster and the "news" of ISIS recruitment in Garden City went viral. Just as crazy, militia members were saying a Somali had stood guard at the poster in the library's lobby. That was the story spreading on Facebook, and it was gaining momentum, as one follower after another vouched for "it"—something that had not happened but nonetheless was taking on a life of its own.

Only in the digital age, Dan thought.

Then two days later, on Tuesday morning, Dan's cell phone rang. It was Terrence Taylor. He asked if Dan would come over to his house; he wanted to talk.

Dan was in no mood, not after the cookout scene. "What the hell for?" he said.

Terrence wouldn't say exactly. Just that Dan needed to come—now.

NOT LONG AFTER THE call, Dan and his son pulled up in front of Terrence's house. Dan instructed Brandon to wait for him—and to call 911 if he heard anything peculiar, like loud noises. Then Dan got out. He had no idea why Terrence wanted him to come over. Maybe Terrence was looking to introduce him to top people in the statewide militia, thinking Dan was interested? Which he wasn't. Maybe Terrence wanted to discuss the fiery online discussion that the poster with the Palestinian flag had provoked? He just didn't know. Dan walked across the lawn, and Terrence met him at the front door.

Brandon stayed behind, seated in the passenger seat of the family's four-wheel-drive Chevy Blazer. The street was quiet compared to the previous Saturday. Gone were the cars and trucks belonging to militia members who'd attended the cookout. The handmade WELCOME THREE PERCENTERS sign was gone too, although the militia's flag still hung beneath an American flag on the front-yard pole. The teenager fidgeted, looking for any sign of movement coming from inside the house. Nothing. Then, after a half hour or so, the front door finally opened. Out walked his father. The door closed behind him. Brandon could tell there was more than one person in the entryway, but he could not get a good look.

His father walked toward the Blazer, strode around the front, opened the door, and climbed into the driver's seat. Brandon could see that something was off—there was a blankness to his father's expression. But before Brandon could say anything, Dan muttered, "FBI."

"What?"

"*FBI.*"

Brandon asked his father what he meant.

"Two FBI agents," Dan said. Two agents had been waiting for him in Terrence's living room. To talk about what transpired at the cookout—especially the poster. Dan sat still, then shook his head as if to wake himself, looking at once confused and annoyed.

He was confused about the wholly unexpected meeting with federal agents and annoyed at Terrence for having blindsided him twice now, first at a cookout that was actually a militia meeting and second with the FBI ambush. If ever the old saying fit a situation, this was it: With friends like Terrence, who needed enemies?

THE NEXT day, Dan heard from one of the agents, who suggested that they meet again — this time at the FBI office in Garden City, and without Terrence Taylor. Dan agreed; at Terrence's he'd felt like the proverbial deer caught in headlights, even though the agents, after introducing themselves, had assured him he was not in trouble. They'd explained they were just trying to gather information about a recruiting poster at the library, following a tip regarding online rhetoric about the poster and a possible ISIS cell in Garden City. They were looking to separate fact from fiction, they said. They'd managed to track some of the online dialogue to Terrence and learned about the militia-sponsored cookout he had hosted at his home on Saturday. With Terrence's cooperation, they'd traced the poster back to Dan. They just had a few questions for him about that poster, about ISIS recruiting, and about Somalis standing guard in the library's lobby.

Dan had listened half in shock but still thought he'd be able to debunk the bizarre ISIS angle. He couldn't get comfortable, though, and had mostly mumbled his way through the conversation. So when a second meeting was suggested, he welcomed the chance to have a more coherent conversation and to make clear what had actually happened.

The FBI field office was located on Campus Drive but easy to miss. Like an unmarked police vehicle, it had no identifying signage and no listing in the building's directory. The front glass was reflective, as in a one-way mirror, and its entrance was kept locked. It was hidden in plain sight in a nondescript brick office strip called Palo Verde Place, alongside a dentist's office, a chiropractor's office, and the branch office of the First National Bank of Hutchinson. In back was a row of trees shading an alley with parking spaces out of view from the street.

Dan hadn't even known there was an FBI office in Garden City. He pressed the buzzer on Wednesday morning, July 22, and was let in. There was no clerical staff to meet him, just the resident agents, Amy Kuhn and Robin Smith. The two had separate offices, but after greeting Dan they took him down a short hall and into a windowless conference room. Their manner was friendly and polite, just as it had been at Terrence's house. They thanked him for coming in and reiterated that in no way did they think he'd done anything wrong. They just wanted to talk some more. Robin Smith was the senior agent of the two; prior to joining the bureau he'd served in the Army National Guard. Amy Kuhn had a law degree and had worked as a prosecutor before deciding she wanted to be out in the field, solving crimes rather than trying them in court. Both came across as personable in a Midwestern way, and Dan learned that they were native Kansans. Kuhn had grown up in southwest Kansas, not far from Garden City. For the private meeting they were dressed casually in blue jeans, and each carried a Glock pistol in a belt holster.

The conversation covered the same ground as the one at Terrence's the previous day, but it was less stressful. Dan more calmly described finding the poster with the Palestinian flag in the library's front lobby, how it had irked him, given that he was pro-Israel. He'd torn it down on his way out, deciding that if someone felt they had the right to post it, he had the right to remove it. He told about handing off the poster to Terrence and then, the next day, attending the recruitment event for Jason Crick's militia; he'd gone to it thinking it was an afternoon cookout and nothing more. Then he addressed one of the agents' primary concerns: the ensuing Facebook chatter about terrorist activity. Contrary to the story that had later circulated online, Dan emphatically said he'd never seen Somali refugees protecting any ISIS-related materials during his library visit with Brandon. That would have alarmed him to no end; he saw no indication whatsoever of ISIS activity.

"Meaning Crick and others were jumping to conclusions?"

"Hell, yeah," Dan replied.

"Okay, that's solved!" Robin Smith declared.

The joke relieved any lingering discomfort, and the FBI agents used the moment to pivot to a matter of equal concern to them: Jason Crick's Three Percenters of Southwest Kansas. They asked Dan a series of questions about the gathering. What did members discuss? Were they armed? Did they have plans? Dan recapped the members' agitation once Crick had waved the poster and falsely asserted that Somali refugees were aiding and abetting ISIS. "Everybody's angry that they were there guarding—standing guard over the flyers, and they just couldn't believe it, and they were getting angry." He quoted members saying that "Somalians were either part of, like, terrorist groups or supported—raised money to support terrorists, ISIS." The Three Percenters seemed pretty "trigger happy," he added, the way they handled their weapons, disparaged Somalis, and advocated shadowing them.

"They were very eager, when they were talking, very eager to find Somalians, a terrorist group maybe," he said. "They thought that there were terrorist training grounds nearby."

The agents listened, paused, and then asked Dan whether he was planning to join Crick's militia.

"No," he said. He'd been curious but had no plans to do that.

Then Amy Kuhn carefully asked Dan a question. If he changed his mind, and if he were to join, would he consider staying in touch with them?

Dan asked the agent what she meant by that.

Kuhn continued: *If* he were to join and *if* he were to learn about either suspected terrorist activity or militia plots against the Somalis, would he let them know?

Lots of *ifs*. But Dan understood. The agents wanted him to infiltrate Crick's militia, serve as their eyes and ears, and report back to them about anything he felt might be criminal. Dan was fast to admit that there was plenty about the federal government he did not like, especially during the Obama presidency, but one thing he wasn't was a government hater across the board. He believed strongly in law enforcement, especially an agency like the FBI, and that made the agents' offer intriguing, even though there was no talk of money or other benefits. The idea played into his own background in criminal justice and interest in public safety. And there was more. While never in his wildest dreams would he have imagined the recent chain of events, he was not one to question life's ups and downs, its booms and busts. It was his default position to accept what may come—he had faith in a greater plan, one covering the present circumstances as it would any other. And so Dan Day resolved that the offer was "something I needed to do, something I was supposed to do."

So his answer was yes. He would do it. He would follow Crick's militia for the FBI.

IN THAT moment a partnership began, however casually and informally. Over the remaining weeks of the summer the agents and Dan continued to meet, feel each other out. Dan stepped up his online "research," combing through Facebook pages for the Three Percenters and members like Terrence Taylor, learning what he could about the group. On July 28 he sent agents Kuhn and Smith screenshots he'd taken of some of the members' Facebook pages featuring anti-Muslim rants. He then contacted Jason Crick and said he wanted in, and right off, without fanfare—without further interviewing or vetting—Crick accepted him as a new member of the Three Percenters of Southwest Kansas.

On his own Facebook page, Dan's postings took a noticeable turn. Previously an outpost for sports cheerleading and family high-fives, Dan began showcasing his new militia commitment. In late August, he reposted a photograph of predatory vultures, captioned "ISIS has surrounded us, Here's the Plan . . . Kill them, Every last one of them." He replaced his profile picture with a Three Percenters emblem and the words "Together We Stand." On September 8, he added a picture of a growling wolf with the headline "We Are the Three-Percent And We Are Coming For You . . ." Dan Day suddenly appeared all in.

In a hotel conference room that same day, September 8, when Dan Day was making it clear on Facebook he'd joined Crick's militia group, the FBI agents Amy Kuhn and Robin Smith appeared as guest speakers at the Garden City Noon Lions' monthly luncheon. The two mingled easily with the local civic group. Smith even wore a suit for the occasion instead of the blue jeans and collared shirt he preferred. During their talk, they described in general terms their work as the resident FBI agents for the Garden City area, how they were responsible for the western third of the state, and how they reported to a special agent in charge, or SAC, stationed in Kansas City. They described the types of cases they handled—political corruption, money laundering, Internet security, and so on.

But they made no mention of their counterterrorism work, specifically the fact that FBI agents in the West and the Midwest were quietly paying more attention to the militia movement nationwide—and the rising threat of domestic terrorism in the deadly style of Timothy McVeigh. And they certainly made no mention of Dan Day and his efforts on their behalf. In fact, privately, and after weeks of informal contacts, the agents had begun the process of formalizing Dan's new role. It needed to be put in writing in official bureau documents. The case agents would be Kuhn and Smith; Kuhn would become Dan's "handler." They would come up with a number and code name to use in classified FBI reports. And they'd need to sit down with Dan to review policy and procedures. Then if Dan was willing, he would have to sign the document on the dotted line. And if he did all that, Dan would be officially a confidential human source, or CHS, for the Federal Bureau of Investigation.

2

MINUTEMAN

THE FBI, AS AMERICA'S top law-enforcement agency, has always depended heavily on informants to bring to justice all manner of criminal organizations—be they the Ku Klux Klan, the Mafia, or an international drug cartel. But along the way the efforts had sometimes gone appallingly awry, with agents undertaking illegal bugging operations or committing rampant civil rights violations—Martin Luther King Jr. had been one well-known target of gross FBI malpractice during the civil rights era. In another, the worst known informant scandal in FBI history, the legendary Boston crime boss James J. "Whitey" Bulger was protected by a band of corrupt agents in the FBI's Organized Crime Squad in Boston in return for tips about the Mafia. In practice, Bulger had a license to kill, with free rein to conduct a criminal enterprise, knowing the FBI had his back.

By definition, the recruitment and monitoring of informants have always proved problematic; illegal conduct on the part of the informant or, less likely, the agent remains an ever-present risk. For agents, the challenge increases exponentially when the people enlisted to provide inside information on criminal activity come with substantial baggage of their own. It could be a prior criminal record, a history of drug or alcohol abuse, or a pending criminal case, with the informant angling to lessen the charges or the eventual punishment by means of sub rosa work for the government. One or more of these possibilities further complicate the already tricky task of constantly assessing an informant's reliability and trustworthiness: was the individual trying to con the bureau? Even if a tight leash is maintained and an FBI investigation eventually succeeds in bringing criminal charges against the targets, the informant's baggage persists as cause for concern in a case's final phase—the trial. Defense attorneys typically pounce on it, arguing that the government's evidence is either tainted or concocted by an informant trying to please his master and improve his own dire situation. In instances when the informant has been paid by the government for her undercover work—a not uncommon scenario—that additional fact further buttresses claims that the informant's testimony was bought and paid for, and therefore unreliable. From start to finish, the credibility of informants with unclean hands is a vexing matter for agents tasked with managing them.

In this regard, FBI agent Amy Kuhn liked what she found in Dan Day. In the broadest sense, Dan's prior work as a guard at a juvenile detention facility and later as a probation officer made him a fellow member of the criminal justice world. Even though his last job had ended badly, Dan was forthcoming about his firing. He'd come across as honest; she and her partner were mostly used to lies. "Everybody lies to us—that's the norm," Smith once said. The agents then conducted further checks, contacting a trusted counterpart in the Kansas Bureau of Investigation, or KBI, who basically verified Dan's accounts. The instance of the missing holiday gift cards and the "bomb scare" on Dan's last day of work came across as nasty office politics and the result of personal vendettas.

Even so, Anthony Mattivi, the Topeka-based assistant US attorney who oversaw national security investigations, remained skeptical. To him, Dan Day at first glance had plenty of baggage: he'd been fired from his job, his employment history included other controversies, and now he seemed to be bouncing around. Dan might not have the level of personal baggage seen in drug or Mafia cases, with informants who often had criminal records, but Mattivi nonetheless imagined he'd have a hard time selling Dan to a jury, especially after defense attorneys had at him during cross-examination. In his line of work, Mattivi preferred having an undercover agent—a true professional—infiltrate a potential terrorist group. He worried that a civilian would come across as "a wannabe cop," someone of shaky reliability.

Kuhn pushed back, however. She liked the fact that Dan was homegrown, a local more likely to fit in with Crick's militia. An "imported" informant posturing as a rural Kansan might use mannerisms and speak in a way that would come across as forced. Put bluntly, posturing as a redneck among rednecks would not be a stretch for someone with Dan's working-class background. Moreover, even though the agents had learned that Dan was out of work and spent a fair amount of his time scrambling to provide for his family, he had not once brought up the subject of getting paid for infiltrating the militia. The FBI agents had no intention of paying, certainly at the start of the relationship, and the fact that Dan never mentioned money worked in his favor as they assessed his suitability. The internal document prepared late in September 2015 to formalize the arrangement—paperwork that Dan would sign—stipulated that there was "no promise of financial compensation." It also included a section where the handler—in this instance, Amy Kuhn—had to characterize the informant's motivation for agreeing to work secretly on the bureau's behalf. Often the motive was money or a reduction in a criminal charge or pending sentence. But not this time. Instead, as the summer ended and Dan had begun providing information and screenshots from the militia's private Facebook sites, Kuhn noted in her assessment that he was doing so for the greater good. "His biggest concern was that there might be somebody wanting to do something bad in his area," she said. "He wanted to make sure that members in his community were safe." In the official internal FBI form, she kept her description of Dan's motivation short and simple: "Patriotism."

DAN DAY'S tenure officially began in early October 2015, and as an informant, he was given a five-digit identifying number for internal FBI record-keeping: 73282.

Amy Kuhn then came up with his code name: Minuteman.

But it wasn't as if the newly enlisted FBI informant Dan Day was on a par with an FBI agent, state trooper, or local police officer working undercover. Extensive training was required for an investigator to adopt a phony identity as a mafioso, cocaine trafficker, or international arms dealer. For someone like Dan—a civilian confidential human source—there was no formal instruction.

The agents did review some do's and don'ts with him, a quick course you might call Informant 101, in the run-up to his official start. The most critical ground rule boiled down to the distinction between a sting and an entrapment. The former was legally permissible, allowing Dan to participate in militia business, react to others' comments, and gather intelligence. It meant that once someone introduced a plan, Dan could play along with the cabal insofar as giving feedback and even, at a later date, reminding the others of an idea or proposal they'd previously discussed. Entrapment, however, was not okay. Dan could not initiate an illegal action or coerce militia members into taking such an action against Muslim refugees if the militia would not have otherwise undertaken it. The bottom line: Dan was never to plant ideas; plans had to start with someone else. But once such an idea was put in play, he could brainstorm with the rest of them.

Legally, the stakes were huge. The notion that the accused had been entrapped by an infiltrator working secretly for the government was a standard defense strategy in subsequent criminal prosecution. It was a defense raised in several federal counterterrorism cases brought in the years following 9/11, cases that had relied on the FBI steering an undercover agent to get close to a suspect. Indeed, in the local case of John T. Booker Jr.—arrested earlier in 2015 near Fort Riley in Manhattan, Kansas, as he prepared to detonate what he thought was a car bomb—critics argued the ISIS-inspired Booker had been entrapped by a government agent who orchestrated Booker's deadly terrorist plan.

But Dan wasn't too concerned about joining Crick's militia with so little formal coaching. Perhaps naive, he was confident in his ability to get by on his wits and the low-key personality that gave him time to read people and tease out the subtext of a particular interaction. Besides, over a lifetime filled with stretches of hardship, and surrounded by a large and toughened cast of siblings and extended family, he'd learned not to be intimated by any person or situation. If someone got into his face, he'd hold his ground—a simple rule for survival he liked to summarize this way: "I don't care if they're bigger than me or whatever. Even if they could kick my butt, you know, I ain't going to be intimidated." It was part of the overall outlook, come what may.

The FBI agents had also talked about the "persona" Dan would need to cultivate as a member of Crick's Three Percenters, but he didn't see much of a problem in that. Militia members liked guns; so did he, as big a fan of Second Amendment gun rights as any hardcore member of the National Rifle Association. He wouldn't have to pretend there. Militia members also had strong anti-government attitudes; on Facebook he'd observed militia members and white nationalists of all kinds as they ranted nonstop about how the federal government was totally corrupt and overrun by the Muslim Brotherhood. Though Dan did not feel utter hostility and hatred toward the government, he had plenty of complaints about it that he could share. Slightly more difficult would be the vile and virulent xenophobia he would have to express. When Dan was growing up, one of his best friends, John Franco, was Mexican

American, and he'd never had a beef with the Vietnamese refugees or, more recently, the Somalis. Bigotry wouldn't come naturally, but he still figured he could act as if he hated Muslims as much as others did. For him, the worrisome part was watching what he said in order to stick to the cardinal rule against entrapment—reacting to actions but not initiating them, just being a fly on the wall that took everything in.

Dan didn't feel out of his league and believed he could get along to go along. That's why he was matter-of-fact when he presented his work in progress with the FBI to his wife, son, and daughter as the summer ended and a new school year began. "No big deal," he said, by way of explanation; he was just doing the right thing. "Part of God's calling," he continued, and he even tried making light of any potential danger, calling the assignment an "adventure." During family briefings he also talked about the need to keep confidential what he was doing for the FBI, and that included keeping his work separate from the family. "It's what the FBI wants," he said. But even as he spoke, Dan knew that this would be easier said than done. There were few secrets in a family as close as his—living in close quarters too, in the tiny ranch house his father had built.

Dan's wife, Cherlyn, had needed some reassurance, whereas Alyssa, starting her freshman year at Garden City High School, thought that her dad's new work sounded like an episode from her favorite TV show, *Criminal Minds,* a long-running series about FBI profilers investigating murders. She watched it all the time on Netflix. Then in real life, she and her brother experienced a moment that seemed like a plot twist a television writer might concoct. Alyssa had decided to join the high school debate team alongside Brandon, then a sophomore and a returning debater. The two went to an organizational meeting where that fall's topic was presented, as chosen by the National Speech and Debate Association: *Resolved: The United States federal government should substantially curtail its use of domestic surveillance.* The siblings exchanged knowing looks. The strange coincidence became their private joke in the weeks that followed, as they worked with teammates researching evidence to support an argument for or against the use of all manner of surveillance practices, technological or human, including informants. The two whispered about how they could tap their father as Exhibit A in support of whatever side of the topic they were tasked to argue. That was a joke. At the start their father's covert work, keeping tabs on a local militia for the FBI, seemed more abstract than real—and *kinda cool.*

THROUGHOUT THE AUTUMN, DAN continued insinuating himself into Jason Crick's Three Percenters militia, joining the private Facebook chat-room conversations and attending meetings. His online moniker became "Dangerous Dan"—"D-Day" for short. Crick had certainly taken a liking to him. He appreciated Dan's steady nature; other members were half-cocked half the time, like a bunch of overheated pickup trucks without mufflers making a ton of noise signifying nothing. Dan came across as more thoughtful and methodical. By November, Crick had appointed Dan to serve as his vetting officer. This meant that a wannabe Three Percenter who'd reached out to Crick through the group's Facebook page had to be evaluated by Dan, who would then make a recommendation to Crick as to whether the person was the right fit for the militia.

Following up on the "evidence" seized in July at the library regarding local Somali support for ISIS, Crick and his supporters felt it was their duty to put Somalis under surveillance. Crick decided to focus on stores where Somalis shopped—the one in Dodge City, where Crick was from, and the African Shop on West Mary Street in Garden City, owned by Adan Keynan. On the designated night, eight to ten armed members split up into teams of two, each equipped with a radio. Living in Dodge, Crick found it easier to watch the store there, and so they conducted three stakeouts in Dodge to one in Garden City.

The militia's additional "probable cause" for shadowing Muslim refugees came from observations that Somalis often gathered after hours at the Dodge City store. The Three Percenters theorized that the refugees had to be up to something nefarious. Fueling this notion was the regular appearance of a cargo van, around midnight. Militia members watched as Somalis unloaded or loaded boxes and canvas bags. No one could detect their contents for certain, but the group suspected that the packages contained contraband—illegal drugs, ammunition, guns. One member insisted he'd recognized a rifle bag, while another wondered if the

Somalis might be engaged in human trafficking. The Three Percenters believed that the Somalis were either raising funds for ISIS or directly involved in a terrorist cell. The militia would love to tail the van to its destination—maybe an ISIS training ground?

Dan joined Crick on the outings, and at the start of one nocturnal stakeout, the two decided on impulse to enter the Dodge City store and look around. The proprietor was friendly enough, offering each a bottle of juice, which they drank. While standing there, Dan and Crick noticed that the store's shelves were sparsely stocked, and through a partition they could see a back room and a group of men playing cards. Several wore expensive-looking suits; Dan later said he guessed they were custom-made outfits costing in the thousands. Then, beneath a coat hanging on a coatrack, Dan thought he noticed the butt of a rifle leaning against the rack.

The militia leader Crick interpreted the goings-on as further proof of the refugees' skulduggery, later telling members the store wasn't really a store—just check out the empty shelves. It was instead a front for illegal gambling and drug trafficking—just look at the cardplaying and the $3,000 custom-tailored suits. Plus, the hidden rifle. According to Crick, the Somalis were up to no good, and the militia needed to ramp up its scrutiny. But Dan didn't think they'd really seen anything untoward. Even the rifle butt—about which he was uncertain—wasn't cause for alarm. This was Kansas, after all, an open-carry state. In fact, he and Jason Crick were armed with handguns when they'd walked into the store.

Dan kept his actual thoughts to himself, however. Instead, he eagerly endorsed Crick's take on the situation. And soon after, when Crick instructed Dan to check out a rural location rumored to be an ISIS training ground, Dan dutifully replied that he would. Dan brought Brandon along when he headed out in his Chevy Blazer—perhaps not a textbook parental decision, taking a fifteen-year-old along on militia business. But Dan was in adventure mode and hadn't detected any real danger. Besides, Brandon knew how to take care of himself, and the two always did spend a lot of time together. When they scouted along the riverbed of the Arkansas River east of Garden City, all they found was a group of paintballers having fun.

STARTING OUT, Dan's double life had little impact at home. Daily challenges hadn't been altered: he scrambled online to earn enough to make ends meet, drove his kids around to meet their various school and sports obligations, and cared for Cherlyn and her health needs. The main difference was that every week or so, he'd go off to a meeting called by Jason Crick or to vet a possible new recruit. In fact, a bigger distraction—and a pleasant one—was enjoying the Kansas City Royals' bid to break a thirty-year World Series drought. The series against the New York Mets began in late October, and Kansans everywhere were holding their breath, hoping that the 2015 fall classic would not end as a heartbreaking repeat of the previous year, when the Royals had lost the best-of-seven series to the San Francisco Giants in the final game.

Dan and Brandon had jumped on the Royals bandwagon, joining the crowd at the Time Out Restaurant, a sprawling sports bar in Garden City, to catch the action. For the series clincher, they drove to the home of one of Dan's nephews, who was the proud owner of a giant-screen TV. Everyone cheered and then celebrated with folks statewide when the Royals won the game, 7–2, on that Sunday, November 1, and with that, the World Series crown. The next day, under bright, sunny skies, more than 800,000 fans turned out for the victory parade in Kansas City.

Dan's unhurried start as an informant presented a chance to work out a few kinks with the FBI agents. Right off, there was the matter of Dan's gun. Robin Smith insisted that Dan not carry a weapon while working as a civilian informant. FBI policy, he said: no *ifs*, *ands* or *buts*. This guideline made sense in many instances, such as when an informant recruited by the FBI was a convicted felon; for that person to carry a weapon would constitute a crime. Dan, however, saw the matter differently and was equally insistent. He'd shot guns his entire life and had legally carried a handgun for almost three decades. He wasn't about to go "naked" because of some FBI policy. It was a standoff, with neither party willing to budge, and FBI agent Amy Kuhn had to intervene as mediator of sorts. In this situation, if Dan was not carrying when most everyone in Crick's militia was armed, it might seem odd and draw unwanted attention. Dan had no priors, so for him to carry was perfectly legal, and besides, he didn't come across as some jacked-up, trigger-happy dude—he was more like a poster boy for gun safety. In other words, his moniker notwithstanding, "Dangerous Dan" was altogether different from the usual informants the FBI tapped. Besides, it wasn't as if he'd have any FBI backup while at militia meetings, which were often held out in the boonies, and Robin Smith ultimately conceded that point: Dan needed to have some way to protect himself if the need ever arose. It was settled: he could carry.

Dan took a liking to the pair of agents, saw how they complemented each other. Robin Smith, in his early fifties, a six-foot-plus veteran of the National Guard, eschewed suits and preferred blue jeans, an open-collared shirt, and cowboy boots. Of the two, he got worked up more easily—not hotheaded but excitable—and sometimes his partner had to tamp down the emotion. Maybe it was the lawyer in her, but Amy Kuhn was quieter, more methodical; her shoulder-length brown hair was always neatly cut. Beneath the professional veneer Dan saw a "real cowgirl," a gun-toting, cowboy-boot-wearing native of southwest Kansas.

Through what would become regular in-person meetings, Dan kept the agents informed about Crick's up-and-coming militia group. That he was Crick's vetting officer gave him a bird's-eye view of new members. His job was to examine a recruit's beliefs—about the Constitution and gun rights, for example. They came from all around, from all kinds of backgrounds. He met with a firefighter, then a welder, and a mechanic. Everyone liked guns, but there were dissimilarities. Some were "preppers," or persons mainly preoccupied with stockpiling food, guns, and ammo to defend themselves against a natural disaster or, as wild as it seemed, against an invasion of foreign terrorists or troops ordered by President Obama to take over the nation. Others, Dan found, acted all gung-ho, as if they were hoping to join a motorcycle gang, with a clear Wild West desire to ride out and find someone to shoot at.

Dan would meet the recruit either online or in person, then send Crick a short summary about the person through Facebook, mentioning any "red flags." He figured that by early December he'd vetted between thirty and forty people for the fledging Three Percenters. What Jason Crick did with the assessments was his own business. The vetting didn't seem to matter too much; Crick seemed ready to allow anyone in who wanted to join. Crick acted more interested in the numbers game than anything else — meaning he wanted to brag to other militia groups around Kansas about how big his had gotten. By December, the list of members had grown to at least a hundred names, even though Dan hadn't met the majority of them, and no more than a dozen turned out for meetings.

To Dan, Crick wasn't all that impressive. Crick was lousy — or lazy, Dan couldn't tell which — at organizing, whether it was a Somali store stakeout or a field training, and it wasn't hard to pick up on militia members' growing frustration with him. They expected Crick, their putative leader, to schedule exercises where members would assemble in a remote area and spend hours on tactical operations and shooting practice. But these exercises were too few and far between, as were their private group sessions using Zello, the application that functioned much like a walkie-talkie; they dwindled as the fall months wore on. One time, Dan went to Crick's house in Dodge City and found him playing a shooter video game — hyper-focused on virtual combat against a teenage player who was somewhere else, in his own home. The forty-nine-year-old Crick barely paused long enough to talk; he played video games for hours on end, it turned out. Dan didn't say anything but wanted to ask, *Was that how you got your training and experience—via video games?* Others grumbled about Crick's wife, how she was always by his side at militia business, ready to tangle with anyone who challenged her husband's authority. Dan got along with her okay, but others complained she acted more in charge than Crick did. Some called her "the voice of Jason." Sniping only got worse when Crick appointed his brother-in-law as second in command of the Three Percenters. Few recalled ever seeing the guy at a meeting.

Dan briefed the agents about all of this, but most important, he reported that over the course of the fall, Crick had grown ever more heated about the perceived Muslim threat and, by ordering the stakeouts, was aiming to advance the group's crucial agenda: "hating Somalis." The covert intelligence became enough of a concern that on December 7, 2015, the two agents opened a formal investigatory file on the militia leader. In a confidential FBI report, Kuhn wrote that beginning on and after October 15, the CHS code-named Minuteman had witnessed Crick and his militia associates use "derogatory language and hateful speech to express their desire to harm Muslims, deface their property, impede their business and/or impede or prevent their practice of the Muslim faith."

Even so, whether the agents liked it or not, there was nothing illegal yet about Crick's actions: forming a militia, staging gun drills, or even championing bigotry, which was constitutionally protected free speech and assembly under the First Amendment. But the stakeouts and the shadowing of refugees leaving the store were tilting toward illegal harassment and possibly a hate crime. Crick's group had a "high risk potential," the agents wrote, of "becoming extremist." That was the concern —possible domestic terrorism, particularly given the national context, the documented spike in militia groups, especially in the Midwest and the South, and a corresponding groundswell of violent white-supremacist rhetoric. People like Crick had become increasingly emboldened in their hostility to Barack Obama's presidency—and were hardly alone in their anti-Muslim bombast. The same day the agents opened the Crick file—December 7—the Republican presidential hopeful Donald Trump told supporters in South Carolina that if elected he would order a "total and complete shutdown," allowing no Muslims to enter the United States. The campaign promise came fresh on the heels of his outrageously false assertion that Muslims had celebrated the 9/11 terrorist attacks. "I watched when the World Trade Center came tumbling down," he claimed at a Trump for President rally in Alabama, "and I watched in Jersey City, NJ, where thousands and thousands of people were cheering as that building was coming down. Thousands of people were cheering."

On a Saturday afternoon two days into the new year, and about thirteen hundred miles northwest of Garden City, the self-anointed patriot Ammon Bundy took control of the main building at the Malheur National Wildlife Refuge in Oregon. That night, Bundy, along with a dozen or so armed followers, recorded a video for release on his Facebook page the next day, Sunday, announcing publicly the surprise takeover by his group, which he was calling Citizens for Constitutional Freedom.

By 2016, the bearded cattle rancher was widely known in militia circles. In early 2014, he and his father, Cliven, had stared down the federal government when their long-running quarrel over use of federal land near their ranch in Bunkerville, Nevada, came to a head. In all, the family had racked up $1 million in unpaid grazing fees owed to the US Bureau of Land Management. When federal officials, with a court order, began rounding up and confiscating the family's herd, the Bundys and a contingent of anti-government supporters stood their ground. Eventually, what became known as the Bunkerville standoff ended peacefully. The Bundys were allowed to keep their livestock, and their staggering debt remained unpaid. The family declared victory. In YouTube videos and on Facebook, Ammon Bundy had become a social media star in the sprawling Patriot Movement.

Now he'd traveled to Oregon, arriving on Saturday to take up a new cause. He'd come to show support for a local cattle rancher and his son who'd been prosecuted federally on arson charges. Bundy and a growing number of protesters saw the case as a cover for federal officials' true motive—seizing the ranchers' land. The two were facing five-year prison terms, and Bundy appeared in time on January 2 to attend a midday rally in the town of Burns, Oregon. Despite the icy weather, nearly three hundred demonstrators turned out, including members of the Idaho Three Percenters, who had been publicly championing the ranchers' cause for weeks in a bid to drum up support.

Bundy decided afterward that the rally wasn't enough; further direct action was called for. Before nightfall, he and his followers—some of them had been at his side during the 2014 clash—drove the thirty miles south of Burns to the Malheur refuge. In the video that he released the next day, Bundy was seen accompanied by a group of men in beards or goatees, some with wraparound sunglasses, carrying AR-15-style rifles and other assault weapons. Bundy asserted that the federally run refuge belonged to "we the people" and that he and those standing with him were "out here because the people have been abused long enough." He announced they would not end their occupation until the ranchers were freed. "We're planning on staying here for several years," he said, and he called on like-minded people to unite with them. "We need you to bring your arms."

Joining the takeover of the wildlife refuge was Robert LaVoy Finicum, a rancher in his early fifties from Arizona who, inspired by Bundy, had recently stopped paying his grazing fees. Finicum quickly emerged as a major spokesman at news conferences and on YouTube dispatches, where his cowboy hat, earmuffs, and army jacket became a familiar sight. "The federal government has no authority to own and control one-third of America's landmass," he told reporters upon his arrival, echoing Bundy's words about people's sovereign rights.

Within days the FBI set up a command center in nearby Burns, a federal presence that soon totaled a couple of hundred agents, along with dozens of state and local police. National news coverage tracked Bundy, Finicum, and their followers on a daily basis.

EIGHT MILES outside of Dodge City, Kansas, one farmer in particular was among the thousands, even millions, who followed the occupation, mainly on YouTube and Facebook rather than mainstream news. His name was Patrick Stein, and he was from the tiny town of Wright, Kansas, population about 160 and barely a blip along US Route 50, the seemingly endless road running the length of America's waistline, from Sacramento, California, to Ocean City, Maryland. Wright had a post office and a senior center on a main street that extended only a few blocks. Its single church, school, and cemetery were near the town's edge, and hard by the highway stood a towering grain co-op. To the east a few miles along Route 50 was the neighboring town of Spearville, "Home of Windmills," with its sleek turbines filling thousands of acres as visual proof of that town's newest industry—wind power. Just a decade old, the expanse of white towers, their massive fiberglass blades rotating slowly in the wind, dominated what had for centuries been an unbroken horizon across the Great Plains. Each one soared 265 feet tall, nearly the length of a football field.

Patrick had worked the family farm in plain view of that striking topographical alteration, just as he'd witnessed other changes in the Kansas he'd known growing up. About five foot nine, he had the physique typical of a farmer—stocky, with thick, muscular forearms made strong from a lifetime of physical labor. He kept his hair cut short—and unkempt. Until the recent appearance of hints of gray, it was dark-colored. He wore blue jeans, work shirts, and well-worn work boots. He liked baseball caps. Though he came from an intact family, there'd been plenty of hard times. For one, he was born in 1969 to an alcoholic mother. She eventually beat her addiction and even put the experience to good use, becoming a substance abuse counselor for Catholic Charities. But that came much later, and as a boy Patrick was the child assigned the chore of keeping a beer in his mother's hand. No one was surprised when he had his first drink when he was ten.

For Patrick, there was always the farm work with his brothers and their aging father, harvesting wheat, corn, and milo. But as he came of age, Patrick bounced around a fair amount, a dusty tumbleweed rolling across the rutted plains. He did manage to finish high school and briefly worked at the meatpacking plant in Dodge City. He then took off for a bit, employed as a truck driver traveling the region. He tried his hand at selling used cars, was an emergency medical technician, or EMT, and a volunteer firefighter. He tried marriage too but couldn't match the longevity of his parents' relationship. His two marriages went bust; his parents meanwhile celebrated a fiftieth anniversary. Patrick did become a father to two sons but was neglectful. Or, as one of his lawyers once said, he was "too busy chasing windmills to spend time with his family." It was a generous characterization. For unlike Don Quixote's chivalric quest against windmills imagined as giants, Patrick's tilting into the proverbial windmill was dark and self-destructive. He was fourteen when he was put into an inpatient drug and alcohol program for the first time —with more stints in detox to follow. He was known to guzzle a twelve-pack of beer in one sitting, and there were periods when he'd opt for a half bottle or more of Everclear grain alcohol, which he'd drink straight. He tried methamphetamine, became addicted, and for a time set up a lab to illegally make the drug for himself and to sell. Over the years, he'd been arrested ten times, mostly for minor infractions of the law, but he did serve jail time once in connection with a drug deal gone bad. In early 2014, he completed his most recent inpatient detox program, but soon after he suffered a relapse and began drinking excessively and using meth again.

Patrick Stein, now in his late forties, lived alone in a trailer that his parents owned. For several years running, he'd worked long, hard days in the family fields, stewing all the while about changes he despised in the world around him—and he didn't mean the giant wind turbines in nearby Spearville. He meant America as a whole; he believed that the country was going to hell in a bucket. He did feel fortunate about one thing, however. He'd discovered a new focus for his disaffection, fresh ways to channel what he regarded as his patriotic zeal. He'd become a fanatical consumer of right-wing news and ideology. On his smartphone or his iPad, he followed three conspiracy theorists and conservative talk-show hosts in particular: Michael Savage, once barred from entering Britain for his fiery anti-Islam rhetoric; Alex Jones, once called the most paranoid man in America for his belief that the 9/11 attacks, the Boston Marathon bombing, and even Timothy McVeigh's Oklahoma City bombing were either staged or orchestrated by the federal government; and on Fox News, Sean Hannity, who'd recently emerged as Donald Trump's biggest cheerleader, parroting Trump's nativist rants — Patrick couldn't get enough of Hannity. Patrick now marched to Trump's anti-Muslim drumbeat, fueled by the belief that Islamist militants were pouring into the country. During nightly forays online, Patrick often continued beyond his three favorite "news" sources into a cyberspace abyss to view grainy videos displaying ISIS terrorists burning captives alive or drowning them in cages. He printed out a poster declaring NEVER EVER TRUST A DIRTY FUCKING MUSLIM and hung it in his trailer.

He no longer felt alone; his disaffection, his hate — they felt normal. Then, as a next step, he sought out the company of the like-minded. While online during the fall of 2015, he came across a statewide militia that was forming a local unit — and so he joined. It was called the Kansas Security Force, First Division, which geographically covered the western third of the state. The commanding officer, or CO, was a Kansan named Curtis Allen. Curtis was busy throughout the fall, posting warnings on Facebook about the increasing number of Muslim refugees moving into the greater Garden City area. In mid-November, he urged people to take action, stating that "we as Kansas have to take the next step here!! If anyone hears they are bringing these refugees into our state we have to spread the word immediately!! We can meet buses at state lines and shut them down or take more drastic matters to stop this invasion!"

Curtis was an ex-marine who, after an honorable discharge, had enlisted in the US Army National Guard and was deployed to Iraq in 2003 as part of Operation Iraqi Freedom. Though his camp north of Baghdad was subject to regular enemy mortar fire, Curtis did not see much combat. In all, he was in the military for nearly two decades, but after he returned home, his service ended on a sour note—after going AWOL from training drills in 2007, he was officially "separated" the next year. Curtis had trouble holding a job afterward. He fought depression and was officially diagnosed with post-traumatic stress disorder in 2010. He drank heavily and had been arrested several times on domestic assault charges. He also collected firearms—an activity that was illegal, due to a domestic battery conviction—and he nursed a deepening animus toward both the federal government and Muslim refugees. Most recently he'd moved to Liberal, Kansas, a small town about seventy miles south of Garden City, on the border with Oklahoma. He lived in a trailer with his on-again, off-again girlfriend, Lula Harris, and inside the front door they hung an American flag. For the first time in a long stretch, Curtis held a steady job; he was a traveling salesman for a national company, marketing and installing alarm systems for homes and businesses.

Patrick and Curtis had hit it off as Curtis got his KSF unit up and running—so much so that Curtis appointed Patrick as his executive officer, or XO. Through Curtis, Patrick met another new KSF member whose mobile and modular home business, G&G Home Center, was located in Liberal. His name was Gavin Wright. Gavin had grown up in Garden City, where his father had founded a successful mobile home company in the early 1970s. In high school, Gavin was a few years ahead of another local boy named Dan Day, although the two didn't know each other at the time. For most of his adult life, Gavin had worked as an electrician in another part of Kansas, but following his father's sudden death in 2013, he teamed up with his older brother Garrett to run the family business. They named it G&G, standing for Garrett and Gavin, and during the summer of 2014, Gavin moved to the Liberal area to open up a second, satellite office to sell their mobile homes and trailers. Curtis had dropped by one day, looking to drum up new business. He asked Gavin about a contract for installing security systems into the homes G&G was selling, and they got to talking. Gavin hadn't known anyone when he'd moved to the area and was glad to have a new friend.

By the end of 2015, Patrick, Curtis, and Gavin had become close cohorts. Given his strong personality and initiative, Patrick was often mistaken for the one in charge, rather than Curtis. For one thing, as executive officer, Patrick brainstormed ways to proactively expand their group, and he wondered what might happen if they poached from other militias. With that idea in mind, he contacted a nearby militia he'd run across on Facebook—the Three Percenters of Southwest Kansas. It turned out that its leader, Jason Crick, lived in Dodge City, a few minutes' drive from Patrick's home in Wright, Kansas. They communicated via a private chat room, and after Patrick gave Crick a rundown about his beliefs and concerns, Crick surprised him by saying it all sounded good and he wouldn't need further vetting. Crick welcomed Patrick aboard and promised to be in touch about upcoming meetings and field trainings. It was a quick, easy transaction, and each man believed he would benefit from it. Crick, a leader who first and foremost liked numbers, had added yet another warm body to his roster of Three Percenters, while Patrick now had access to a ready-mixed pool of militia members to recruit for KSF.

THAT WAS the beauty of the Internet—so much got done without a face-to-face, even when, as with Patrick and Crick, the parties lived literally minutes apart. The Web erased distance—which had proved crucial for enabling Patrick, Curtis, and Gavin to forge their connection, given the fact that Patrick lived more than an hour's drive from Liberal. Using their smartphones and iPads, the three were just clicks away, able to link up secretly online in a network of paranoia and doomsday ideology. It was a bonding that came not from spending extensive amounts of time together in person but through hours and hours on social media —be it Facebook, texts, or calls on the group application Zello, which everyone liked for its added security feature: when someone joined the call, the user name was displayed. No one could sneak in anonymously. Like others in the movement, the threesome embraced the Internet as a source of authentic, credible information, as if it were a public library. They seemed oblivious to the false claims and bogus websites that proliferated online. They routinely shared posts and "news" from right-wing media and militia sites that at once united them with like-minded "patriots" and corroborated their belief that everyone should be "prepping" for when the SHTF (Shit Hits the Fan). This event could be a natural disaster, a Muslim terrorist attack, or even an attempt by the federal government to eliminate sovereign rights—any event during which personal liberty could become a matter of life and death. People needed to be armed and ready, with stockpiles of food and other goods. Likewise Patrick, Curtis, and Gavin had begun storing munitions. For his KSF militia, Curtis obtained green T-shirts printed with the statement WHEN TYRANNY BECOMES LAW, RESISTANCE BECOMES DUTY. Threats seemed evident all around, and apparently were mounting—from gun-control activists, illegal immigrants, Islamist terrorists masquerading as refugees, and an out-of-control federal government that was unconstitutionally crushing property rights and other personal freedoms at the behest of a second-term president Patrick Stein liked to refer to as "the nigger in the White House."

It was no wonder, then, that in early 2016, Curtis and Gavin joined Patrick Stein and the legions of supporters closely following the anti-government crusader Ammon Bundy's occupation of the Malheur National Wildlife Refuge in Oregon. The Facebook page for the Bundy Ranch regularly streamed updates and posted videos from Oregon, many of them featuring co-leader LaVoy Finicum delivering a dose of anti-government polemic to the press assembled there. In one, Finicum reiterated the statement that the occupation was "intended to be peaceful," while at another briefing he made clear that his resistance was unyielding. "I'm not going to end up in prison," he said. "I would rather die than be caged." Patrick Stein grew particularly restless, and as days passed, he began thinking more and more about heeding Bundy's call and heading north to Oregon to take a stand alongside the occupiers.

Then things changed. Late in the day on Tuesday, January 26, LaVoy Finicum was shot and killed in a confrontation with authorities. Finicum, whose fifty-fifth birthday was to be the next day, was driving one of two vehicles stopped on a rural road at a roadblock set up by Oregon state troopers. Riding with Finicum in his white truck were three others, including a young Kansan—the eighteen-year-old singer Victoria Sharp, whose Christian music group, the Sharp Family Singers, had traveled to Malheur from their home south of Topeka to offer support to the occupiers at the wildlife refuge and entertain them with gospel songs. In the second vehicle was the leader, Ammon Bundy. Bundy and the two men with him were arrested on the spot, but a few minutes later, Finicum gunned his truck and sped off. He raced down the road and then veered into the snow at a second roadblock. Exiting with his arms raised, he was shot dead seconds later, when he lowered his right hand; police believed he was going for a handgun kept in the left side of his jacket. The standoff soon fizzled. Its leaders were taken into custody; Ammon Bundy's father, Cliven, was arrested at an airport after declaring he was en route to Oregon to join the cause; and the remaining handful of armed occupiers gave up in early February, following talks with FBI officials.

Instantly, LaVoy Finicum was lionized; the Bundys posted a tribute to him on their Facebook page the morning after his death: "LaVoy has left us, but his sacrifice will never be far from the lips of those who love liberty. You cannot defeat us. Our blood is seed." Supporters saw Finicum as the innocent victim of a government ambush, his death symbolic of the federal abuses that formed the core of their protests. Patrick Stein was of course in full agreement, but during the aftermath of LaVoy's death, he was seething because there'd been no vengeance, and he questioned whether, after all was said and done, the occupiers even had the stomach to put up the fight necessary to take back the country. "LaVoy was murdered, you know, in broad daylight, fucking point-blank," he complained to his KSF cohort. "How many, how many patriots were out there at that time?" he asked rhetorically, as he began a rant on the way he thought things should have gone down. "How many, how many fucking bullets were sent the other direction?" he continued. "Big ol' fucking goose egg. Yep, zero. That's got me concerned a little bit. I mean, if you asked me, there should have been a goddamn onslaught like they've never fucking seen before, but they got, didn't even get the click of a fucking misfire, you know? The ol' hammer fucking dropping and nothing going anywhere? Shit, we didn't even get that. So I don't know there; I don't know."

Dan day also closely monitored the occupation of the Malheur National Wildlife Refuge during the month of January. Not only because the takeover was a big news story. There was that, certainly. But mainly because he too was making ready to head north to Oregon to join Ammon Bundy, LaVoy Finicum, and their followers. If he went, he'd present himself as a militia member from southwest Kansas, a Three Percenter, although his reason for making the pilgrimage would be different from that of the others at the refuge. Soon after the takeover, his FBI handlers Amy Kuhn and Robin Smith had asked if he'd be willing to join the occupation and provide inside intelligence to the FBI force on duty there. He said that he would, seeing the request as an extension of what he'd already signed on for as an informant, or confidential human source. The agents were pleased, and Dan, while continuing as Jason Crick's vetting officer, was on standby for service in Malheur.

Then LaVoy Finicum was killed, and the occupation ended soon after. Dan's anticipated infiltration of Bundy's group became moot. In fact, it later emerged that the FBI had managed to insert a number of informants over the course of the month—nine in all, with their time at the refuge ranging from a few hours to twenty-three days. During the climactic stop at the roadblock that resulted in Finicum's death, the driver of Bundy's Jeep was actually an FBI informant who'd helped coordinate the encounter with the police. The informant had been the FBI's most valued inside source; he'd inserted himself into Ammon Bundy's inner circle nearly from the start, posing as a member of Three Percenter militia from Arizona.

For dan, 2015 had ended quietly enough. He'd proved he could juggle his online buy-sell work, his kids' sports and debate competitions—one of their tournaments that fall had taken them to Topeka—with his new role in Jason Crick's militia. Then, for the holidays, the family had done the usual: they spent Christmas with Cherlyn's parents in Salina, Kansas, a four-hour drive from Garden City. Given their financial struggles, Dan wasn't able to give the kids more than a gift or two. For him, though, that was not without precedent. Growing up in a large family in relative poverty, he was used to just one or two presents—and as a boy, he learned to cherish mightily whatever was given. Dan knew his kids would appreciate whatever gifts came their way. Family was what mattered most.

December also marked the first time the FBI had paid him; early in the month, at their office the agents gave him a check for $300. Dan had been surprised. He'd never asked for money and hadn't expected any. In four months he'd certainly incurred expenses—gas money, for one thing. This would cover costs, he figured. Every penny helped.

However low-key the year had ended, 2016 began with an altogether different vibe. Jason Crick had shown himself to be a weak leader, seemingly more interested in losing himself for hours playing shooter video games than in running a quasi-military outfit. He'd gone underground in December; few could reach him, leaving Dan and some other members, staying in touch on social media and increasingly annoyed, to conclude Crick had decided to shut down for Christmas without telling anyone. Even though the FBI had opened a file on Crick, Dan realized that Crick was probably less of a concern than some of the characters drawn to his Three Percenters. One guy, for example, talked about how he was building up an arsenal by converting semiautomatic pistols and rifles into automatic weapons—the latter was illegal.

Then there was the guy Dan had known previously through an online gun website. The guy had had a handgun Dan was interested in purchasing for a quick resale, but the deal fizzled when they couldn't come to terms on a price. Now in January he surfaced as a new member of Crick's Three Percenters militia—one of the acolytes Crick had okayed on his own, which Crick would do even though the putative protocol was for Dan, as vetting officer, to first meet the candidate.

The guy was happy to reconnect with Dan and, knowing that Dan was gung-ho about munitions, was eager to share a secret about an amazing find—Claymore mines. Dan was taken aback: Claymore mines? These combat explosives were unlike conventional land mines, which were set off by a trip wire and exploded every which way. A Claymore was capable of being aimed at a specific "kill zone" and detonated by remote control. It discharged hundreds of steel balls toward the target, with a range of up to a hundred yards. It was often described as the equivalent of a sawed-off shotgun.

Dan asked to know more, and the guy claimed to have run across the explosives while mowing a farm field. He was nervous, though—scared even, and not just because possessing Claymore mines was illegal. They were so incredibly dangerous, way beyond his limited expertise with handguns and rifles. He wasn't looking for any money, just wanted to be rid of them. He thought Dan might have a use for them, seeing as he was in the buy-and-sell munitions game. Or maybe Dan wanted to take possession on behalf of the militia.

Immediately Dan notified his FBI handlers, and over the course of the next few days he got his first whiff of an FBI field operation. The last thing the FBI wanted was to see Crick or any member of a militia get ahold of explosives—if that's indeed what was on offer. Instead, they wanted to steer the matériel safely into federal hands. To do that, Dan concocted a story: he said he had cousins in Oklahoma who'd be interested in the Claymores, implying that his relatives were part a black-market organization trafficking in guns and drugs. Together with his FBI handlers, Dan then arranged a handoff. He drove to the guy's house outside Garden City. Meanwhile, agents surrounded the place, unseen. When Dan arrived, he called the guy on his cell to say that he was sitting out front in his Chevy Blazer. The guy came out and climbed into the SUV. They made small talk as the guy deposited a package on the front seat. Dan then read him the riot act, how he had to keep his mouth shut and not tell anyone about the package's destination—not Jason Crick or anyone—because the outfit in Oklahoma meant business. He warned him, "You got to understand, you don't fuck with these guys that I'm taking these to." The guy seemed sufficiently put on notice and hustled back into his house.

Dan drove away and turned onto another street, and suddenly agents pulled up to take the package from him. As it turned out, the package didn't contain explosives but rather military fuses used to detonate a mine—anticlimactic, in a way. Even so, Dan had felt an adrenaline rush and was all pumped up, feeling this FBI op was the real deal. Everything about the exchange had gone down so quickly and smoothly. As he'd sat in his Blazer, talking to the guy, he knew that agents were in hiding all around, although he could not detect a single one. Then, as soon as he'd left, they'd seemingly come out of nowhere. In the end, Dan had held the possible explosives for all of what, five minutes? He was impressed.

Having never been schooled in undercover work the way agents or other police are, often at the FBI training academy in Quantico, Virginia, Dan got important on-the-job training from the Claymore mine episode. His credible-sounding bluff about cousins who belonged to a criminal enterprise, his private worry that he might actually handle a dangerous explosive dumped in his lap by a reckless militia member, his staying cool while at the center of an FBI recovery operation—it was all good practice.

By this point Dan felt comfortably embedded as a Three Percenter, able to switch on his persona as a white nationalist and project a calm swagger as the group's vetting officer. Through Facebook, he'd networked his way deeper into militia culture across the state of Kansas. He was Dangerous Dan from Garden City, hooking up online with other militia leaders as the FBI's eyes and ears. And he felt good about being able to anticipate next moves, so that when Crick finally resurfaced from his holiday sabbatical and called for a training exercise in Cimarron in February, Dan made a point of meeting with Crick beforehand. He wanted to inform Crick about the so-called Claymore handoff, just in case the new member, despite Dan's warning, didn't keep his mouth shut. Better to have Crick hear it from him rather than someone else, which would have Crick suspecting him of dealing behind his back.

They met on Saturday morning, February 13, at a convenience store on Highway 50 in Cimarron. Dan jumped into the cab of Crick's truck to fill him in. He explained everything about the mines, which were *not* as advertised—fuses of some kind, it turned out—and his confession came off as he intended. No big deal. Crick had been curious, asked a few questions, but that was it. Besides, Crick was in a rush to meet a local sheriff to get keys to unlock the gate to the shooting range. The remote public range was about four miles south of Cimarron, along the Arkansas River. Crick wanted Dan to head down to the gate and greet the others while Crick retrieved the keys. He told Dan that ten, maybe twelve guys were expected to turn out for the exercise.

And then, as Dan started to exit the truck, Crick called out.

Almost forgot, he said.

What?

There'll be a new guy, Crick said.

Oh yeah?

Dan kept a poker face but was semi-annoyed, thinking Crick had once again gone and added yet another warm body without going through the militia's vetting process.

The guy lives outside Dodge City, Crick continued. It was as if he had read Dan's mind and was justifying the deviation from protocol. Crick said that he'd reached out to him directly. They'd met for coffee. He'll be good, Crick promised.

And his name?

It's Stein, Crick said.

Patrick Stein.

DAN ARRIVED at the gate along the unpaved road before anyone else. Through the fence he saw that the firing range was as basic as they came. Some ranges had wooden shooting platforms. Not this one—a pile of dirt adjacent to the river. Some had targets already on hand. Not this one, and Dan hoped Crick remembered to bring some.

He'd been there only a few minutes when a red Chevy 4×4 truck, equipped with a light bar on its roof, pulled in next to his Blazer. The dirt-stained truck kicked up dust.

"You Patrick?" Dan said to the man jumping out from the cab.

"Yep," Patrick replied.

The two men shook hands and made small talk. Patrick mentioned that he came from farming in Wright, just outside of Dodge. But Dan didn't need telling. He could see from looking at Patrick that he was a farmer—the grittiness about him, the stockiness, the strong upper body. They talked a bit about the Three Percenters. Dan mentioned that he was the vetting officer, and they chuckled at the fact this was their first time meeting, the vetting officer and the newest member. Patrick joked that he'd been a Three Percenter since January, when Crick met with him and let him in. This seemed to be Patrick's opening; he began badmouthing Jason Crick nonstop. It surprised Dan a little—a new member so freely criticizing the militia leader. But Patrick seemed unconcerned. And he had a list of grievances—that Crick seemed lazy and disorganized, that he'd been waiting for more than a month for Crick to get something going. It seemed like amateur hour to Patrick.

Dan nodded along. Okay, what else was new?

The others began arriving, and then Crick, who unlocked the gate. For the next couple of hours, the ten or so Three Percenters worked on shooting and tactical drills. From Dan's perspective, the performance was unimpressive, even nerve-racking. One drill called for the men to split up into pairs and, armed with rifles and handguns, move as a team from station to station while firing at targets. One of the teams included a member who had never shot before, and Dan thought he was viewing a circus act as the guy tugged and struggled to pull a handgun from its holster, only to have the gun pop up out of his hand and into the air like a hot potato. The gun did somersaults before the guy caught it, and then, awkwardly, began firing—to Dan's horror, he nearly shot his partner. That's when Dan intervened, basically called a time-out to get the group back to the basics of gun safety. He reviewed best practices in the handling of handguns as well as the AR-15 semiautomatic rifle. He grabbed a handgun and ticked off the same safety commands his father had once drilled into him: never point a gun at somebody; always assume it's loaded. He held the gun and removed its magazine. He barked, "It's unloaded now, right?"

Some nodded yes.

Then Dan took aim at a target, pulled the trigger, and fired the gun: *BAM.* Dan looked hard at the group. "Wrong," he said.

Several of the men were surprised, taken aback that a bullet was still in the gun's chamber. Dan continued his tutorial, saying some guns were now manufactured so they wouldn't fire once the magazine was removed. But that wasn't the case with most guns, especially older ones. Even without a magazine, a bullet remained in the chamber. He repeated the message: never point a gun at someone, and always assume a gun is loaded.

The demonstration got the men's attention, and they resumed their exercises with a bit more discipline. Dan saw that some members were clearly inexperienced while others knew how to handle weapons. Patrick Stein was among the latter; Dan noted he was a good shot. When they were finished, and before leaving, everyone hung around for a while, and that was when Patrick began to stand out, and not simply for his shooting prowess. He had initially come across to Dan as pretty low-key, talking about his farming, about last year's harvest and his expectations for the upcoming season. But once the conversation turned to current events, his personality seemed to change abruptly.

The occupation at the Malheur National Wildlife Refuge had ended just a few days earlier, and members had plenty to say, especially about the killing of LaVoy Finicum. Patrick's comments grew more heated than anyone else's, though, as he expressed his belief that the failure to retaliate immediately against those responsible for Finicum's death was reprehensible. Then, when the discussion turned to militia matters, such as munitions, someone brought up explosives and how it might be a good idea to have access to them for when the Shit Hits the Fan. Patrick piped up again and, as if to show his worth as a new member, said he knew someone in Hays, Kansas, who might have some.

Dan's radar was activated; he wondered whether another situation was about to arise in which he'd be chasing illegal explosives for the FBI. He joined this conversation to probe Patrick's claims. He talked up the idea, saying explosives would be a good idea, and he made mention of the ruse he'd used in the previous incident—that if it didn't pan out for the militia, he had contacts in Oklahoma who'd be interested. Dan wasn't able to figure out if Patrick was all talk or what; he talked a good game, though.

Then when Jason Crick brought up Somalis—suspicions about an ISIS cell and the fact that a mosque in Dodge was often filled with Muslim worshippers—Patrick became even more vocal. He made clear in no uncertain terms he had no use for Somalis, and his face turned red as he spoke. He told the group he'd even taken it upon himself to stake out the Somali store in Dodge City but was frustrated at not spotting any shady goings-on when he knew they must be up to something. He'd monitored the store at various times during the day, even used binoculars, but saw nothing.

Crick admonished him; his timing was off. "You need to go at midnight," he said. "That's when everything's happening."

Patrick seethed. "Fucking motherfuckers."

The meeting broke up, the men scattering in all directions. Dan's route once he reached Garden City was circuitous. Before heading home, he had to swing by the FBI office on Campus Drive. It's what he did now as part of the routine—meet the agents to debrief following a militia outing. He'd park his Chevy Blazer at a nearby bank and walk down the narrow drive behind Palo Verde Place, where the bureau office was located. The idea was to minimize the chance of being detected.

He'd head to the third door in from the mall's right rear side, the only one painted gray, which Dan never understood: why the FBI's back door was gray when the rear doors to the bank and dental practice were reddish. He'd knock. The FBI had an overhead camera aimed at the back entrance—the only wall-mounted camera at the complex. The agents would check to see that it was him. They'd let him in, then take him to the windowless conference room.

Today, as usual, the agents were expecting him and the latest news. Which was Patrick Stein. Patrick was the headline: the new face Dan planned to bring up first thing.

PRACTICALLY OVERNIGHT, IT SEEMED Dan had acquired a new best buddy in the militia. He and Patrick Stein exchanged contact information before breaking up that day in Cimarron, and Patrick began calling and texting regularly. He wanted to talk about anything militia-related, and Patrick, Dan realized, could talk a mean streak. Dan got to thinking Patrick was high half the time, on meth or something like it. On one call, Patrick got all excited, eager to tell Dan about an opportunity to finally help out in the aftermath of the Malheur debacle, if only in a small way. He'd signed on to work security for the Sharp Family Singers when they left Oregon and returned home to Auburn, Kansas, just south of Topeka. Others in the Patriot Movement were fearful that federal agents would hound, or even terrorize, the family for having joined the occupation to serenade Bundy, Finicum, and their followers with gospel and patriotic songs. There was particular concern for Victoria Sharp, the eighteen-year-old who'd been riding in the back seat of LaVoy Finicum's truck during Finicum's deadly encounter with the FBI and the Oregon state troopers. The teen hadn't been charged and, following her release, she'd been vocal about the fatal shooting of LaVoy Finicum. In interviews on CNN, on the radio, and with newspaper reporters, she called the rancher's death a police killing in cold blood. Even though a video released by the FBI showed Finicum reaching toward an inside jacket pocket, where a loaded handgun was found, Victoria insisted on national television, "He was just walking with his hands up." She sang at Finicum's funeral, called him an "amazing patriot," and vilified the federal government at every opportunity. "People lost their lives for our freedom," she said, blaming the FBI. Some began calling her the "new face of the Patriot Movement" and the "patriot princess."

Patrick Stein had stepped up and responded to the call for volunteers. It was the least he could do, he thought, since he'd never made it to Oregon before everything collapsed. He told Dan he'd be gone a few days and that he was heading east with a few friends to work the security detail. Guys from another militia group, he said. Dan wouldn't know them — and then Patrick pivoted to a pet peeve — Jason Crick, leader of the Three Percenters. Patrick resumed badmouthing Crick, a harangue that was now a theme in his talks with Dan — that Crick was not up to the task, that his group was just child's play. Patrick said Dan should see these other guys doing security with him — they were the real deal, part of a new group just getting off the ground.

When their conversation was done, Dan alerted his FBI handlers about the security detail, and the agents notified their counterparts in Kansas City. The bureau did in fact stake out the Sharps, and Dan later picked out Stein in surveillance photographs taken by agents. The security detail ended after a few days, as did the FBI surveillance, without incident. For Dan, the other takeaway from Patrick's call — and others like it, when he griped about Crick — was that Patrick clearly favored this second militia group, which he called the Kansas Security Force. His advocacy was hardly subtle, and Dan decided that, as Minuteman for the FBI, he should learn more about KSF and what it was all about.

Jason Crick surprised Dan and some other Three Percenters when he announced during a private militia Zello call on Thursday night, February 25, that he wanted to put the Somalis in Garden City under surveillance in two days, on a Saturday night. It was a bit surprising because they'd just come off a field training and they weren't accustomed to Crick organizing another exercise on short notice. But Crick said he'd gotten a tip — uncorroborated — that several buses filled with refugees were headed to Garden City, and the last thing the place needed was a new surge in Muslim resettlement. One of the militia's core tenets was that refugees were bringing about the country's ruin; it was therefore their patriotic duty to keep tabs on the unwanted interlopers.

In response, ten or so members said they'd be able to make it; the group included Dan and Patrick. The men would split up into pairs, with each pair assigned to stake out one of the several locations where Somali people gathered. They'd communicate using handheld ham radios, in the hope of developing their version of probable cause: that Somalis were engaged in trafficking either illegal guns or drugs or were actually planning acts of terrorism. Crick wanted everyone to bear arms, but that went without saying—it was a standing militia order.

In any case, Dan never went anywhere without a pocket carry. He had recently begun to favor a Ruger SR9c, a compact, nine-millimeter semiautomatic pistol, instead of his Glock pistol, though he liked it a lot. The Glock was hugely popular with law enforcement and gun enthusiasts, but the Ruger had a couple of features that made pocket carrying a little less risky. For one thing, the Ruger had a manual safety lock, whereas the Glock had no safety feature at all. Compared to carrying the Ruger, carrying a Glock in his pants pocket seemed to Dan like an accident waiting to happen. The Ruger also came with a bullet indicator, and the Glock did not. When Dan left the house, he always wanted to have a bullet loaded in the chamber, ready to fire; if he ever needed to use the weapon, he did not want to lose a half second or more to loading a bullet. That half second might cost him his life. With a Ruger, he could at any time confirm that the chamber was loaded by running a finger along the top of the slide to feel for the protruding indicator, which confirmed that a bullet was in place.

Then Dan got a call from Patrick the next day. Patrick had an idea. There was a gun show in Garden City on Saturday he wanted to check out, and Patrick was thinking they could meet up after. They could drive around so that Dan could point out, in daylight, the different Somali locations they'd monitor at night. Dan agreed. He notified his FBI handlers that his Saturday militia operation had evolved and now had two parts—one with just Patrick and one with the group after dark. Dan and the agents arranged to debrief at the end of the night, as was their usual practice.

Dan and Patrick agreed to meet at the Dollar General. That Saturday afternoon when Dan turned off West Mary Street into the store's concrete parking lot, he spotted Patrick's red Chevy pickup. Dan left his Blazer and climbed into Patrick's passenger seat. The skies were cloudy and the temperature was in the seventies—unseasonably warm for late February, when a fifty-degree day was the norm. Patrick's windows were powered down. The two greeted each other and sat still for a minute as Dan explained the game plan. He noticed that Patrick had a black Glock pistol wedged between the driver's seat and the front console. Resting on the cab's back seat was a bulletproof vest and an assault rifle. Patrick seemed ramped up, which got Dan wondering again if Patrick was high on something.

The truck happened to face east, in the direction of a flat, empty lot, beyond which were the Garden Spot Apartments, the low-slung complex at 312 West Mary Street housing many Somalis. A well-worn footpath ran diagonally across the scrubby lot, created as a shortcut for anyone walking from the apartments to the Dollar General and then back. Dan noticed two Somali women completing the short trek across the field. They wore traditional headscarves and colorful robes, which would undulate in the occasional gust of wind. The two slowly made their way in front of Patrick's truck. Dan could hear the women's voices. They spoke Somali. He couldn't understand them, but they were smiling and seemed happy.

Patrick said, "Here come a couple of fucking raghead bitches." He wasn't quiet about it, either.

The women looked their way, which only seemed to stoke a fire.

"Yeah, you!" Patrick yelled out the window, swearing at them, angry and unfiltered words gushing from his mouth. His face turned a hot red, and his torso turned and twisted in the truck's seat, like he was a caged tiger wanting to break free. The abrupt explosion stunned Dan. He could tell that the women did not understand Patrick's words, but they clearly grasped that the tone was threatening. Dan could see the fright in their eyes.

Patrick turned to Dan. "I ought to fucking knock 'em off, kill 'em right there." He had dropped his right hand onto the Glock wedged next to the console. He screamed at the women some more, his head sticking out of the truck as he wrapped his fingers around the pistol's grip. "Kill the motherfucking bitches!" Patrick shouted. He said he could just open fire on the two Muslims, splatter their brains all around, and really make a statement.

Dan had to do something. He yelled, "C'mon, man, chill out!" He continued: "Someone's gonna call the cops. Chill out!" Patrick kept at it, though, his head jutting from the truck as he swore at the Somali women and then jerking back toward Dan as he proclaimed that, goddamnit, he was going to shoot them, right there, right now.

Dan felt panic. He lowered his right hand onto his Ruger in a way that Patrick, lurching around in his seat, could not see. Each man now gripped a semiautomatic pistol. Dan knew a bullet was loaded in his Ruger's chamber, all set to go. And in that instant, which seemed to unfold in slow motion and take several minutes rather than seconds, Dan concluded that if Patrick continued on his deadly course, if Patrick lifted his Glock from the console and took aim at the two women who were now frozen in place, puzzled and scared, then he would pull the Ruger from his pocket and shoot Patrick. He was not going to let Patrick kill a couple of innocent Muslim women, and he was prepared to stop him.

He also, during that swirl of seconds, continued yelling at Patrick to cut it out, countering Patrick's hate-filled tirade with his own reason-filled rant: "Be fuckin' smart, man! Someone's gonna call the cops if you don't stop! Chill out!"

It was a standoff of words and of weapons.

And then, just as suddenly as he'd erupted, Patrick grew calmer. He released the grip on his weapon, although the river of hate did not completely let up; he repeated the smear "Fucking raghead bitches," albeit in diminished volume. It was easy to see that he ached to heap violence upon the Somalis, as he did each and every time he saw any of them.

Patrick glared coldly at the women as they disappeared into the Dollar General. Dan let out a deep breath.

THE TOUR of Somali venues didn't take long—all were within walking distance of the Dollar General and, coincidentally, were only about a mile from the FBI's Garden City office farther down Mary Street in an easterly direction, at the intersection of Campus Drive. Dan directed Patrick to one Somali store, on a side street a block or so off of West Mary Street, called the Somalia Wany Mall, which seemed shuttered more often than not, without regular hours. It was located behind the main Somali market located right on busy West Mary Street—the African Shop, owned by Adan Keynan, a hub for Muslim shopping and socializing.

"I was ready to kill those raghead fucking bitches," Patrick muttered at one point, as he steered his truck along West Mary Street, following Dan's directions. It was as if he wanted to make sure Dan understood that he hadn't been fooling around. Dan just nodded.

Patrick already knew a bit about the lay of the land, informing Dan that he wanted to be sure to cruise through the Garden Spot Apartments. He said Jason Crick had mentioned the complex was deserving of special attention, not only because it housed several hundred Somalis but because the tenants had apparently turned one apartment into a mosque.

The complex consisted of several buildings accessed by a one-way U-shaped driveway. Dan indicated to Patrick that he would need to enter at one end, proceed around the U, and exit at the other end. The loop bordered buildings with apartments. Cars and minivans were parked in front of each unit. The mosque was apparently in one of the buildings that sat in the inner part of the U. The whole setup resembled a large roadside motel.

Patrick entered the driveway. Somalis seemed to be everywhere, either hanging out in small groups outside on sunlit patches of grass or strolling in clusters down West Mary Street toward the market. The display did not surprise Dan. The unusually warm February day was like a summons from Mother Nature for everyone to get outdoors. Plus, Saturday was a day off for most refugees from their jobs at the Tyson meatpacking plant. But Patrick, glancing all around as he steered the truck, couldn't believe how many of them there were. He'd had no idea. "God, look at 'em all," he said. "Living right here."

Dan had remained tense since the outburst at the Dollar General, nervous that Patrick might erupt again, and he stayed alert, ready to urge calm. Fortunately, Patrick was preoccupied, taking everything in, and his anger never went beyond the smoldering stage. "Fucking cockroaches," he repeated with disgust, in reference to the numerous Somalis they passed while edging along the driveway. Unsolicited, he provided Dan with a primer on his view of the problem. "Muslims are like cockroaches," he explained earnestly. "You can't kill just one of them; you have to kill all of them." Patrick acted as if he held some kind of advanced degree in Islamophobia: "Unless you exterminate 'em all, they'll just keep coming back." He seemed proud of the analogy—equating Muslims with vermin—and to enjoy the hard sounds in the epithet he repeated like a mantra: "Fucking cockroaches."

Dan, however, had never heard this appalling analogy before. In fact, he'd never heard anyone talk the way Patrick did—and he'd heard plenty of awful stuff. Heck, the gatherings of the Three Percenters bubbled with bigotry. But this—Patrick's rage—was not something he'd ever encountered. Dan didn't know what to say in response; he sat in the cab and listened, his concern unabated that Patrick, at any moment, here in the middle of the Somali apartment complex, might draw one of his weapons. Dan was rattled, scared even. It wasn't as if he'd never before seen people threaten violence. In fact, when he was a probation officer, some clients had called him a motherfucker and promised to kill him. He'd regarded them as idle threats and brushed them off. But Patrick? Nothing seemed idle about his threats, either during the brief, tense moment at the Dollar General or as they drove around Garden City.

Moreover, Dan was unnerved by the fact that at the Dollar General, he'd suddenly found himself ready to shoot Patrick Stein. He had just been in a situation where he was poised to use a gun against another person. Never in a lifetime of guns had that happened. He was no killer, yet suddenly, for an instant, he'd been ready to kill. Even though it would have been done to prevent the killing of innocent people, Dan could not shake off the harrowing feeling the experience had left him with.

When the two completed the tour of the apartment complex, the ride-around was over. They headed back to the Dollar General so that Dan could get his Blazer. Dan was eager to go, but as he was exiting the truck, Patrick told him to hold on, he had one more thing to say. Dan paused, and Patrick said he wanted to share a confidence: he actually belonged to that other militia he'd mentioned previously, in passing—the Kansas Security Force. Moreover, the only reason he'd joined the Three Percenters was to recruit members for the KSF. In effect, he'd infiltrated Crick's group to poach its people. He then made his pitch: Dan was better than Crick's group, and the KSF could definitely use someone like him. The KSF, he said, was hardcore, serious about "exterminating the cockroaches."

The disclosure didn't come as a huge surprise, not after the way Patrick, in the short time Dan had known him, had disparaged Crick while plugging the KSF militia for providing the Sharp Family Singers with a security detail. Patrick then continued selling the KSF, explaining how the local unit was a startup with a commanding officer, Curtis Allen, who had been in military service, while another member was from Garden City originally, a great guy named Gavin Wright. Dan recognized the Wright family name: Gavin was ahead of him in high school, although Dan never knew him. True patriots, both of them, Patrick said.

Patrick also said that no one in Crick's group had any idea about Patrick's covert role, and he wanted it to stay that way. As he spoke, Patrick lifted his Glock pistol and placed it atop the center console. Dan looked at the gun resting there. It was pointed forward, not at him, but he still took the move as a warning. Patrick stressed again that he didn't want anyone to find out.

It was time for Dan to go. Patrick thanked him for meeting up. Dan nodded, sure thing. They'd reconvene later and do it all over again with the militia. Patrick drove off. Dan sat alone in his Blazer. He needed a few minutes to gather his thoughts. He dreaded the idea of going back out at night with Patrick and the Three Percenters. He wanted to make sure too that Patrick wasn't following him home. No way did he want Stein to know where he lived.

Along around this same time, Benjamin Anderson, CEO at the county hospital in nearby Lakin, got an unexpected call at home. It was shortly after 10 p.m., which was late for him. His wife and four kids were asleep already; in fact, he was heading to bed when his cell phone rang. He wondered who could be calling so late, and when he answered, the woman on the other end said, "Hello, Benjamin? Benjamin? It's Halima Farah."

Despite the hour, Benjamin perked up, hearing that the caller was the stepdaughter of the African Shop's proprietor, Adan Keynan. Benjamin had only recently begun to feel that he and Dr. John Birky were making any real headway with the Somalis, which wasn't the case after the initial attempt in early fall, when they'd invited Somalis to the Time for Three concert, the fundraiser his hospital had co-sponsored with the city of Garden City. Halima was among a handful of Somalis who did attend, but they didn't arrive until well after the music had started. When they left early, before Tf3 had finished and before either Benjamin or Dr. Birky had had a chance to talk with them, Benjamin felt the overture had been a big flop. Nothing seemed to come of it. Benjamin continued to go to the shop every couple of weeks to purchase honey, dates, and tea—he had enough tea at home now to last a lifetime, it seemed—but he was still met with the same coolness, as if he were an undercover city inspector looking for code violations. Dr. Birky tried again later in the fall; he and his wife, Lisa, invited Halima and Ifrah Ahmed, the young refugee who worked as a translator at Tyson, over to their house to carve pumpkins with their kids at Halloween. The two Somali women—friends, multilingual, and relative newcomers—seemed more outgoing than most, up for trying new things, curious about American culture and pastimes. Halima, Ifrah, and the Birkys enjoyed themselves with the carvings, seeming to get to know one another a bit better. Still, contact was infrequent, progress slow; it felt like watching an ice cube melt.

Then in February, nearly six months after the Tf3 concert, Benjamin got his first call out of the blue from Halima. She phoned him at home, and at first teased him, saying he hadn't been to the store in a while. Then she pivoted and explained the reason for the call was to introduce a newly arrived Somali, a pre-med student who had just started a six-month internship at St. Catherine Hospital in Garden City. The student, named Mohammed Abdi, got on the phone, and Benjamin had what he considered a breakthrough conversation. Abdi was from Kansas City, where he'd lived since immigrating to the United States at the age of twelve. He was glad to be interning in Garden City because of its sizable Somali population but was disappointed to discover that "his people," meaning Somalis and East Africans, lived apart and largely in isolation. Abdi was thinking that before his internship ended, he'd like to organize some kind of cross-cultural event. Halima had said Benjamin might be someone to talk to about that. Would he help?

Benjamin was floored, replied that of course he would help, and the two promised to begin brainstorming a plan.

On the heels of that surprising call, Benjamin now found himself taking a second unexpected call from Halima, this one well after hours, no less.

"My uncle wants to meet you," Halima announced.

"Really?

"Yes."

"Where?"

"At his home."

"When?"

"Right now."

Benjamin didn't say anything right away. He couldn't help but think the invitation was strange. Halima's tone of voice was matter-of-fact, however, as if casually inviting someone to dinner at this late hour was not out of the ordinary.

"Okay," he answered. "Okay."

He changed out of his pajamas and into jeans and a lightweight hoodie. He considered waking his wife but decided not to; she'd likely think going out at that hour was crazy, and then she'd stay up worrying until he returned home. He did want company, though. He called Dr.

John Birky, and not surprisingly, the doctor was game, ever eager to work on closing the divide between the Somali and hometown communities.

It was already after 11 p.m. when Benjamin and Dr. Birky pulled into an open space at the Garden Spot Apartments. Following Halima's instructions, they located the second apartment in from the U-shaped driveway's entrance, the unit with a white minivan out front. Adan Keynan and Halima were waiting and took the two men inside the dimly lit apartment. When the door closed behind them, Benjamin wondered whether he and Dr. Birky were being foolish to enter a Muslim refugee's home. He felt hesitant, but then in the same instant felt embarrassed. He knew that this reluctance—worry, even—stemmed from unfamiliarity.

The apartment was tiny and dark. Drapes covered the front window, and thick rugs were spread over the wall-to-wall carpet. It was basically one large room, with two small bedrooms. The living area was separated from the compact kitchen on the right by a dining table. Sara was in the kitchen, and she turned to greet them. The room was filled with the smell of African spices, reminding Benjamin of Adan's store.

Adan had them sit at the table. Halima served as translator, and Benjamin and Dr. Birky were treated to dinner. Benjamin had eaten hours earlier but nonetheless consumed everything Sara put on the table—sambusas, the triangle-shaped pastries filled with ground beef; the onions and spices, rice, goat meat, bananas, and more. The gathering was awkward at first, with little talk, as everyone slowly warmed to the situation. Adan showed the visitors how to eat with their hands, as was the Somali practice, and they gave it a try.

Then, as the dinner neared its end, conversation flowed in earnest. Adan thanked the guests for coming and, through Halima's translation, began asking a series of questions he said he and his Somali peers pondered endlessly: What if he wanted to start a restaurant in the back of his shop—how would he go about it? How could a Somali refugee get a driver's license if the test was only in English and Spanish? For Somalis wanting to learn English, how could they do that while working double shifts at the meatpacking plant?

Benjamin and Dr. Birky fielded the questions as best they could, as the back-and-forth between the visitors and their hosts became more relaxed. It was past midnight when they finished the meal and ran out of questions—at least for the time being. Then it was Benjamin's turn. He wanted to ask Adan a question that had come to mind over the course of the evening: how often had Adan hosted white people like him and Dr. Birky in his home? Adan answered that they were the first ones to ever visit his apartment in the decade he'd lived in Garden City. And then, when it was time for the guests to leave, Adan put his hand on Benjamin's shoulder and said he and Dr. Birky were no longer strangers in his home and, having shared dinner, were now his brothers.

Benjamin had gone into the apartment wondering about his safety and left feeling the opposite—as safe as could be. On the ride back to Lakin, he and Dr. Birky knew the impromptu gathering had marked a turning point in their effort to open up channels with the refugee community.

WHEN DAN arrived home from the Dollar General late in the afternoon of February 27, he was still shaken from the ride-around with Patrick Stein. His family could tell something was not right, and so Dan shared a short, alarming summary of Patrick's outburst. He felt it was imperative to reach his FBI handlers right away, so he called agent Amy Kuhn. This was a departure from the plan to debrief later, at the end of the long day and night, but Dan needed to talk now, to alert the agents to Patrick and to steady himself. He ended up having a couple of brief calls with Amy, conversations broken up in part because it was the weekend. The agents had planned for a nighttime debriefing, not a daytime one. They were off duty, enjoying the good weather with family. Over the course of these quick calls, Dan's narrative came across as choppy and out of sequence, as he ricocheted between describing some of Patrick's actions, information about the KSF, and his own tangle of emotions. He told Amy at one point that Patrick had called the Muslim women "raghead bitches" and made clear his view that Patrick was dangerous and unpredictable, a breed of militia member unlike any he'd come across so far. For the first time too, Dan voiced apprehension, telling his FBI handler that he wasn't keen about participating in anything else that day, meaning the nighttime operation with Crick's people.

The FBI agent had a different take: Patrick's conduct meant that Dan's involvement was vital, especially with Patrick's disclosure about the KSF, a militia group that had not been on their radar. Between their calls she conferred with her partner, and though she was unable to break free from her obligations, Robin Smith quickly rearranged his evening plans. He'd patrol Garden City, out of sight and in an unmarked car, keeping an eye on the militia's field operation—in other words, keeping under surveillance the militia members' surveillance of the Somalis. Amy Kuhn did not tell Dan about the backup and instead gave him a pep talk, that he was onto something, that he needed to be part of the night's operation. He was to stay as close as he could to Patrick, to gather additional intelligence and be the voice of reason in case Patrick heated up again.

Having calmed down some, Dan was persuaded. He told Amy he'd go. His earlier sense that undercover work would be an adventure, something *cool,* felt long outdated now, even naive. During all the weeks with Jason Crick, he'd felt some semblance of control, so that if Crick ever did veer from racist rhetoric into plotting an actual hate crime or another illegal maneuver, he felt he'd be able defuse the situation and minimize the harm. Dan would say, "I can control Crick," an expression of his confidence in his ability to reason with Crick, talk him out of something if need be. But he thought Patrick Stein was "real radical," and after only two encounters he was already afraid Patrick was crazy enough to simply start killing Muslims.

Ten militia members, most outfitted in camo clothing, met after nightfall in the parking lot of a convenience store in Garden City. Jason Crick ran through a series of checks to make sure everyone was armed and their handheld ham radios were in working order. When Crick began assigning the men to pairs and matched Dan with some guy he barely knew, Dan did what he had to do. He'd have preferred teaming up with anyone other than Patrick Stein but nonetheless spoke up, bucking Crick's authority and telling the militia leader he wanted to ride with Patrick, who piped up to second the motion. Patrick informed Crick that he and Dan had hung out earlier in the day and that Dan had showed him around. Their pairing made sense, and Crick accepted the switch.

Crick directed a couple of teams to stake out the two Somali stores, especially the African Shop. When a team spotted a Somali leaving a store, they were to notify everyone by radio, and another car would then tail the Somali to his destination. If they were lucky, the Somali would lead them to something ISIS-related—possibly a camp or a supply depot.

Dan and Patrick took Patrick's truck. They drove around, retracing their steps from the afternoon. They approached the second Somali store, the Somalia Wany Mall, from the rear, roaring across a dirt lot. The store was dark, and closed. Then they responded to a call about a Somali leaving the main store, the African Shop, and they tailed the car as it turned off West Mary Street and into a neighborhood less than a mile away. They watched a young Somali couple exit the car and enter a small ranch house. Patrick took note of the street number, recording the fact that these Somalis were living outside their group's usual confines, and Dan observed that the house was a few doors down from Terrence

Taylor's. Dan knew their fellow Three Percenter would not be pleased to learn that a Somali was living on his street.

The two were next assigned to the Garden Spot Apartments at 312 West Mary Street. They parked on a side street facing the buildings. Dan was already thinking the mission was an exercise in the absurd. He'd even asked Crick what the plan was if they saw Somalis doing something irregular or perhaps illegal. Call the cops? He knew no one in the militia had any intention of contacting the authorities for any reason. They avoided the police like the plague. So what was the plan? Crick never gave Dan a direct answer.

Patrick cut the engine and turned off the lights. They sat in the dark, the truck shielded partially by a stop sign and a tree limb. Dan felt drained by the earlier events of the day and didn't really want to talk. Patrick, meanwhile, though not nearly as combustible as before, had plenty to say. He spoke about the weaponry and other equipment he had on hand, including the tactical bulletproof vest and the AR-15 semiautomatic rifle with a night-vision scope. He pulled out a pair of night-vision binoculars too, for Dan to try. Dan did, and he was amazed at the clarity and immediacy of what he could see as he panned across the street, looking at the cars and apartments. Through it all, Dan was realizing how much Patrick liked to hear himself talk, and as they sat there killing time, something about the moment reminded Patrick of the Oklahoma City bombing. Patrick brought up Timothy McVeigh, a name that for Dan always triggered an eerie memory of that horrific, deadly bombing, which took place when he and Cherlyn were newly married and living in Oklahoma, near where McVeigh was captured. Patrick rambled on about explosives, naming the materials McVeigh had used—such as ammonium nitrate and fuel—and as his eyes locked onto the apartments the Somalis called home, he made the observation that a fertilizer bomb could knock out a whole building. Dan added little to the conversation.

The crackle of the radio brought Patrick's musings to a halt. The African Shop was closing up, a voice reported on the radio. The lights inside were switching off, a couple was stepping outside, and the man had stopped to lock the front door. The voice grew excited, saying the two were each carrying a bag—a big bag—and they were loading them into a white minivan. With that, other voices jumped in. One, possibly Crick's, commanded another team to follow the van. Patrick got on to remind everyone of his and Dan's location, right across from the apartment complex and less than a half mile from the African Shop.

Leaning forward, Dan could see the white van, carrying a man and a woman, driving down West Mary Street from the direction of the African Shop. The van slowed as it approached and turned right off of West Mary into the apartment complex. Patrick was barking into the radio, "We got 'em, we got 'em, they're coming to us."

The van pulled into the first space on the right. Patrick continued as play-by-play announcer: the van had parked, and now two Somalis were getting out. Each removed a bag and headed to the first apartment. Dan could tell the man had a slight build and was dressed like a businessman, in what looked like a brown suit. The woman—*Must be his wife,* Dan thought—wore a traditional robe, her face covered with a scarf.

Other voices interrupted, asking Patrick and Dan if they could make out what was inside the bags. Cash? Drugs? "Must be," the others insisted, but Dan and Patrick couldn't tell. Instead, they watched as the couple entered the apartment. The lights inside went on. Then a few minutes later they were turned off—and all was quiet across the street.

"Whaddya got, whaddya got?" the others implored. "What are they doing now?"

Finally Patrick answered. "Nothin'," he said.

The night had fizzled; the moment was anticlimactic. Overall, it had been an unremarkable outing. After several hours of surveillance, all the militia had to show for the effort was their tracking of a few Somalis going into and out of the African Shop. Crick spun it positively as having been good practice. And there was still the mystery of the Muslim shop owner's bags: what exactly was hiding in them? Something to keep in mind for future surveillance.

For his part, Dan just wanted to get out of there. Patrick had a few choice words before departing, though. "Remember what we talked about," he told Dan. "The KSF offer stands: come with us."

Dan nodded, said he'd think about it.

3

CRUSADERS 2.0

On a weekday night later that spring, Dan went into the bedroom he shared with Cherlyn, closed the door, and got ready for the call. He placed his cell phone on the bed. Next to it he put the voice recorder the FBI had given him. The setup was hardly high-tech—a basic audio recorder positioned to capture voices emanating from his cell phone's speaker. But it was what his FBI handlers, Amy Kuhn and Robin Smith, had provided, and it was what he'd been using for regular group chats with the new militia he'd joined. Dan then activated the FBI's recorder, identified the date, and said, "This is Minuteman. I'm recording a Zello conversation that took place at 9:30 p.m. with, uh, Patrick Stein, Gavin Wright, and Curtis Allen, and others of KSF." And he waited.

By this time, Jason Crick's Three Percenters militia was history as far as Dan's undercover efforts were concerned. His FBI handlers had instructed him in March to turn his attention to Patrick Stein and the fledging Kansas Security Force. The KSF—and Stein in particular—was new to the FBI, and Dan was the only informant positioned to infiltrate it. He was hardly eager to do so after Patrick's trigger-happy tirade in late February. But soon after the long, stressful day spent stalking Somalis, he'd notified Patrick that he would bolt Crick's group and accept the offer to join KSF.

Patrick was psyched, and a few days later Dan received a text message from Curtis Allen, the commander of the KSF's First Division: "Hey, how you doin'? Give me a call." Their brief chat went well, and then on March 13 Dan accepted a Facebook friend request from Curtis. Once Dan had done that, he was given access to a private Facebook page for KSF members only. To throw off any potential snooping by law enforcement, KSF leaders called their page "The Art of Changing Diapers." Within days, Dan became friends on Facebook with several other KSF members, most notably Gavin Wright, and he began closely following their posts and communications, most of which were rants either against the federal government or against Muslim immigrants. In one posting that month, Curtis issued a warning: "The time is coming soon to make a choice and we the people either need to make a stand and make a loud statement or this nation will soon be lost." He titled a later posting "I Promise, This Country Will Become a Muslim Country."

Dan passed along key names to his FBI handlers—and, like Patrick, neither Curtis Allen nor Gavin Wright had been on the FBI's radar when it came to suspected militia extremists. Dan got to meet Curtis in person when he went camping with KSF members in late March at Cheney Lake, a state park and reservoir about thirty miles west of Wichita. Curtis, nearly six feet tall, fit, and sporting a buzz cut, made a strong first impression. He arrived outfitted in full camo, with guns, his trailer, and a pup tent, looking "ready for war right then," as one member noted. The gathering reunited Patrick, Curtis, and another militia member, Brody Benson. Brody was a short, stocky farmer with a big cowboy mustache whose farm was just outside Hutchinson and due north of the lakeside campsite. The three had worked together on the security detail for the Sharp Family Singers, following the family's return the prior month from the occupation of the Malheur National Wildlife Refuge. For the Cheney Lake event, Brody brought along a giant homemade smoker set on a two-wheel trailer. In honor of the late LaVoy

Finicum, he'd painted Finicum's cattle brand on its side—a design with the letters L and V in red.

The overnight was billed as a KSF family affair so that members who'd been in contact only on social media could meet in person and introduce their families. Dan came alone, of course. He was not about to expose his family in the FBI undercover operation. Curtis came alone too, although he'd been talking to his then ex-girlfriend Lula Harris about getting back together. In 2015 she'd left for El Dorado, Kansas, to help her son with his kids as he went through a divorce. While there, she was diagnosed with tonsil cancer, and in early 2016 had begun chemotherapy and radiation treatments. Curtis was urging her to return to Liberal to be with him while she recovered, and she'd said that she would. For everyone who came, the camping was a good time, featuring hard drinking, Brody's brisket, and plenty of talk about saving America. Curtis handed out new KSF patches.

The bonding continued as late winter turned to spring, even as some members, including Patrick, had to devote themselves to planting corn on their farms. Gavin Wright hadn't made it to the Cheney Lake event, and Dan got to meet him at a KSF meeting held at a café in the tiny town of Sublette, which was south of Garden City and en route to Liberal, where Curtis lived and where Gavin's business was located. Gavin was on the husky side, with streaks of gray in his bushy hair and goatee, and a few years older than Dan. The two traded stories about Garden City. Gavin, it turned out, had never graduated—indeed, his high school years had proved difficult for him. His parents divorced when he was a freshman, a breakup that for Gavin came totally out of the blue, since he and his older brother Garrett had rarely seen their parents argue. Gavin did a fair amount of rebelling, which occasionally erupted in conflict with his father. One time he got an ear pierced without telling anyone and afterward showed up drunk at his father's place. His dad flipped out, yelling, "What are you, a fucking girl now!" Calling Gavin a sissy, his father reached out and ripped the earring from his ear. Blood splattered all over. Gavin would recount the story as a lesson learned. "Needless to say," he'd tell people, "I didn't do shit to my body after that." No tattoos for him, and no jewelry of any kind.

Gavin trained as an electrician and for more than a decade had lived in Manhattan, Kansas, where he ran his own electrical business. He got married, then divorced, and took custody of the couple's two sons. He liked to brag to Patrick, Curtis, and Dan that "back in the day" he'd cooked and sold crystal meth—and had been way smarter than any local cop and never got caught. Indeed, for all of his rowdiness and drug dealing, Gavin had never once been arrested, which wasn't a claim Patrick or Curtis could make. Besides a clean record, another point of pride was his gun collection. It was an interest he had shared with his father, and the family's hand-me-down collection included guns of all kinds—shotguns, rifles, and plenty of antique muskets.

Gavin had been back in the area for only a little more than a year to oversee the Liberal satellite office of G&G Home Center, the company he and his older brother created to carry on their late father's mobile and modular home business. He wasn't living in Liberal itself; he had instead found a place just across the border in Oklahoma, a small house where he was staying with one of his teenage sons. Gavin didn't really know anyone at first, and then he met Curtis, and through Curtis, he'd met Patrick, and now Dan Day.

Given the locations of their hometowns and their schedules, in-person KSF meetings like the one in Sublette were irregular. Far more frequent contact was through Zello, and in the roll call for the members-only KSF group, Curtis was known as "Ichiban," a Japanese word for "Number 1," which was fitting, since he was the KSF commander. Gavin was "Sparky," and Dan was "D-Day." Patrick never tired of extolling his code name, "Orkinman," which was based on his self-anointed role as the exterminator of human pests, namely Muslims.

During nighttime calls, which could include ten or so members, the talk ran a gamut of topics. They might discuss efforts to beef up the numbers in their KSF division. Curtis had proposed setting up a booth at upcoming fairs, and he'd also had KSF business cards made up to leave around while traveling to sales appointments for the alarm systems he sold on commission. They might talk about scheduling trainings —either medical training or field exercises—or about "prepping," the stockpiling of food and weapons for when the SHTF. They might talk about gun rights or current events. There was the ISIS-inspired terrorism case of John T. Booker Jr., for example, who had been arrested in 2015 in Manhattan, Kansas—where Gavin used to live—for trying to set off a bomb outside the US Army's Fort Riley. In February, Booker had pleaded guilty in federal court in Topeka to one count of attempted use of a weapon of mass destruction and one count of attempted destruction of government property by fire or explosive. To Patrick, Curtis, and the others, a terrorism case like Booker's was proof that Muslim militants were closing in.

They vented profusely about Muslims, illegal immigration, and even the notion that in the event that she won the presidency, Hillary Clinton was going to declare martial law and enlist NATO forces to ensure her takeover. They therefore viewed the 2016 race for the White House as critical to America's future, and the one candidate who seemed to channel their concerns about jobs and the country's security was Donald Trump. During an interview with CNN's Anderson Cooper on March 9, Trump ramped up his anti-Muslim rhetoric, asserting flat out that "Islam hates us." In his call for a Muslim ban, the distinction between the religion itself and radical Islamist terrorism meant little. "We can't allow people coming into this country who have this hatred for the

United States," he said. When pressed the next day on national television during the Republican debate if he actually thought that 1.6 billion Muslims worldwide hated America, Trump didn't budge. "There's tremendous hatred, and I will stick with exactly what I said."

The militia members were inspired by the candidate's Islamophobic cheerleading, and Zello meetings and Facebook postings became an echo chamber for their strident bigotry concerning Somalis and other Muslims living in Garden City. Beyond that consensus, however, debate often erupted over the spring months about what to do with their hate. Patrick Stein, for one, become a persistent advocate for action—from Orkinman, no less could be expected. More than once he wisecracked about simply picking off Somalis. Grab a .22 rifle equipped with a silencer, he said, ride into town, kick down the doors at the Garden Spot Apartments, and silently slay Somalis, one by one. It was as if he saw himself in a starring role: a gun-slinging Christian on a crusade against a Muslim takeover.

Dan referred to Patrick's outbursts as "going Stein"; other KSF members, even some who could be considered Muslim haters, saw Patrick's dark dreams as off the charts. Preparing defensively for a race war might be acceptable; going on the attack was not. When Patrick recognized a gulf between those he viewed as all talk and no action and those favoring the eradication of Muslims, he set up a new Zello channel exclusively for the latter. Curtis was all in, as was Gavin, and so was Dan. In creating this KSF subgroup, Patrick again showed a knack for code names. He called the new Zello channel Crusaders 2.0.

DAN PARTICIPATED in (and recorded) the Zello sessions, using his two-gadget setup as he assumed the persona of a like-minded hater of Islam. It didn't take long to notice how Patrick stood out as the most vocal; in fact, anyone listening might assume, based on the way Patrick took charge during group calls, that he, not Curtis, was the commander of the KSF. Curtis proved a quiet participant—too quiet, given that he was the actual commander. Eventually Dan figured out why. Curtis believed the federal government had the capability to monitor them. He thought the National Security Agency's data center in Bluffdale, Utah, was omniscient, capturing every word they—and everybody else, for that matter—said. "That motherfucker is two million square feet of computer," Curtis warned them. "Every single phone call. Every credit card transaction. Every X." Patrick might revel in the wonders of social media and its ability to unite him, Curtis, Gavin, Dan, and others—all living at least an hour's drive apart—on an almost daily basis. He might have faith in the password-protected, encrypted Zello channel. But not Curtis; he was suspicious. In fact, the pair's differing views became a source of low-grade tension. Curtis rebuked Patrick at times, advising him to "tone down his verbiage." Other times Curtis signed on to a Zello call, said little, and got off before the meeting had even ended. In his opinion, Zello talk should always remain vague, or be spoken in code, with anything specific saved for in-person meetings. "They've probably got every fucking word we say on that NSA motherfucker," he said.

The other significant development over the course of early spring was that Dan spent more and more one-on-one time with Patrick—mostly by phone but also in person. He was emerging as Patrick's sounding board about potential recruits and trainings, and even his occasional complaints that Curtis was uptight and slow-moving. "You know, at least I'm, uh, not like our commander," Patrick commented during one call in early May.

Dan chuckled. "Yeah."

"Sit on your fuckin' nuts," Patrick chided. "But do nothin'."

Patrick, the live wire, ran ideas by Dan, often about ways to raise money to buy guns, grenades, explosives—whatever might be needed down the road. He shared that for years he had operated a homemade meth lab and done pretty well. He proposed drug trafficking as a possible revenue stream for KSF, claiming to have a connection for obtaining high-quality meth. Dan saw in such moments an opportunity to enhance his militia bona fides—and he revived the ruse he'd first tested early in the year to secure the handoff of the alleged Claymore mines. He told Patrick he had his own connections too—"friends of his cousins down South," he said, people in Oklahoma who could get them guns and explosives. Dan had built this off partial truth; he did have cousins who'd tangled with the law, but with Patrick he whipped up that kernel of reality to build an impression of big-time illegality, and he was purposely vague about details in order to create mystery and suggest that his contacts were "badass people" in a criminal enterprise not to be trifled with. Patrick ate it up and liked it even more because of Dan's unwillingness to reveal too much, taking this as a sign of Dan's trustworthiness. Dan's standing with Patrick solidified, and by the start of spring Patrick, as XO, had appointed him to serve as both the group's vetting officer, a role he'd filled with Jason Crick's militia, and its intelligence officer. The latter meant Dan was charged with doing research on any matter or current event that arose during Zello meetings. In the few minutes prior to calls, Dan took to scanning online news sites, mainly CNN, to see what was going on in the world. The others were impressed by how knowledgeable he always seemed.

As Dan's infiltration of the group deepened, he found himself spending more and more time on militia matters, whether on group calls or vetting new recruits that Patrick, continuing to poach from Crick's group, steered his way. Dan met regularly with his FBI handlers for debriefings, but it wasn't as if they had much to offer by way of support beyond pep talks and reminders that, given the laws against entrapment, he could react to the group's ideas but must not introduce any specific plans. And he worried about saying the wrong thing.

Then there was his personal safety. He worried about that too. He might attend meetings carrying a Ruger SR9c, as was his custom, but there would be no FBI backup in the event that an unexpected variant of SHTF went down—like, what if his cover got blown? Dan was on his own in just about every way, untrained and inexperienced, making it up as he went along, as he did with the canard about his "cousins down South," which Patrick had liked so much.

Dan's ties to the XO seemed to put extra wear and tear on him. Patrick wouldn't think twice about calling Dan at any time of the day or night. He even phoned Dan while riding his combine in the fields, and the two would end up hollering to each other to be heard over the noise of the farm machinery. Patrick was so intense, so determined to eradicate Muslims, and so unpredictable. One weekend, for example, Dan arranged for Patrick to meet a couple he'd already vetted who were from the nearby town of Lakin. They'd been part of Crick's militia but were open to switching to the Kansas Security Force the way Dan had. They all met at the IHOP in Garden City, and that meeting went smoothly. Dan and Patrick then went to McDonald's to meet another potential recruit. That went okay too. Dan was ready to head home, but Patrick wasn't done. He suddenly asked Dan to show him around town, as Dan had in February. Patrick wanted to inspect again the locations where Somalis lived or gathered, places the militia would likely target.

Like before, Patrick drove, and for Dan, it was déjà vu. This time, Patrick was looking to use Google Earth on his cell phone to pinpoint Somali stores and clusters of apartments. As they did the drive-around, they'd pull over at a location so that Patrick could work his phone. But Patrick had a terrible time dropping a pin on a particular spot. He fumbled around, trying to make the function work to his satisfaction. Dan sat patiently in the passenger seat, watching as Patrick's temperature rose. They were parked outside Somali-occupied apartments near Garden City Community College when Patrick began venting his frustration by alternately swearing at the phone and hissing at Somalis who were out and about on that mild, comfortable day. The truck's windows were open, and as Patrick cussed at the Somalis, Dan grew tense. He looked out the window to distract himself, hoping Patrick would not "go Stein." He spotted a Somali woman walking with a little girl, maybe two years old and probably the woman's daughter. They were dressed alike in traditional outfits, and Dan fixated on the little girl and her colorful garment. *She is so cute,* he thought, and his mind went to picturing his own daughter, Alyssa, who was fifteen but as a toddler had always loved to play dress-up.

Patrick had looked over to see what Dan was watching so intently, a sight that sent Patrick's mind to an entirely different place. "There's another little baby cockroach motherfucker," he said. "We should take her out too." Patrick then made a gun with his finger, aimed it at the Somalis, and simulated pulling the trigger.

"Kill the little fucking cockroach."

Patrick may have assumed that Dan, whom he believed to be a fellow Muslim hater, was having the same thought, but in fact the words not only shattered Dan's reverie but also made him angry. Patrick was talking, without any semblance of remorse, about killing a little girl. Because of her race and religion, Patrick had concluded the girl apparently deserved to die. *No way,* Dan thought. *What if this were my daughter?*

Dan was shaken to the core. But he had to be careful not to put his cover at risk. "You need to keep it down or the fucking cops are gonna be here," he commanded.

Dan had never talked to Patrick like that—in a tone loaded with anger, even contempt. But the actual words he spoke fell within the boundaries of his undercover persona, meaning he'd managed a misdirect that had shielded his true feelings.

He could not contain himself, however, once he got home. Practically in tears, he paced the living room as he told Cherlyn, Brandon, and Alyssa. Dan looked at his daughter, who'd always been his "baby girl," and recounted how Patrick had pointed a finger-gun at the Somali girl. His family had never seen him so upset. Dan later also told this to his FBI handlers, and he got emotional with them too. There seemed to be no bottom to Patrick's hate.

The FBI opened a formal investigation of Patrick Stein on April 21, 2016. "Sufficient predication exists which identifies Patrick Stein as being a leader of an organized group of individuals who advocate and threaten force or violence to achieve both political and social goals," Amy Kuhn and Robin Smith wrote in the report. Four days later, Patrick was added to FBI's Terrorism Watch List, a central database for monitoring suspected terrorists.

Over the course of the year, the state of Kansas was demonstrating growing hostility toward immigrants, a trend following Donald Trump's lead. Governor Sam Brownback, a Republican, issued an executive order in April that barred state agencies from any further collaboration with the federal office that assisted Muslim and Syrian refugees resettling in the United States. The governor said that under President Obama, the Office of Refugee Resettlement had failed to vet refugees thoroughly, raising the specter of Muslim terrorists sneaking into the country. "If I have to choose between the safety and security of Kansans and the relocation of refugees, I will take action to protect Kansans," the governor said.

Practically speaking, Brownback's order amounted to political grandstanding, with little tangible impact on refugee resettlements. The federal office didn't require state assistance; it worked directly with humanitarian groups, such as Catholic Charities or the International Rescue Committee (IRC). And most Kansans, including those in the Kansas Security Force, were not fooled by Brownback's putative stand against the flow of Muslims. "He goddamn sure knows they're here and they're comin' in," Patrick groused.

Government ineptitude and a belief that Muslims were already arriving en masse to the Garden City area were fuel to Patrick's conviction that the militia had to get smarter about the unfolding crisis, and to advance the cause he came up with a brilliant idea involving his intelligence officer. He told Dan to volunteer at the local office of the IRC. Dan's infiltration would be a twofer for the group. He'd be in a position to identify IRC workers and volunteers they might decide to harass, or worse, at some point. More important, he'd be able to obtain the arrival times and addresses of new refugees, intel the militia could use to pinpoint locations for possible action, such as an ambush.

Following the XO's orders, Dan called the IRC office in Garden City, picked up an application, and submitted it. But he slow-walked the entire process, making it seem as if he were jumping through the bureaucratic hoops to become a volunteer but in fact doing next to nothing. When he eventually got a call from the IRC office to report for an orientation, he did not go, and whenever Patrick or Gavin or Curtis nagged him for an update on his application, his stock response became "Hey, I'm trying, man." In fact Dan had no intention of working as an IRC volunteer, which would expose him to the kind of insider information the others would demand that he share—such as names of workers to add to their potential hit list or accurate data about refugee arrivals and resettlements to factor into the group's plenary sessions. Dan could not tell them what he did not know.

FOR DAN, being the intelligence officer was proving tricky. On the one hand, the role enhanced his persona as a militia member committed to opposing Somali refugees. The group relied on him to do research, give updates on current events, and, most important, provide information about Garden City, his hometown. This was his value-added—but he could not contribute much to the intensifying discussions about potential anti-Muslim actions. He might know plenty about guns, but meth labs and drugs? Homemade explosives? Virtually nothing. It wasn't as if the others were experts, yet each brought a modicum of experience that gave him a head start—Curtis's military background, Patrick's drug dealing, and Gavin's craft as an electrician.

But the role that helped solidify Dan's standing also frequently placed him in a fix—as was the case with the IRC assignment. He worried that if he completed a particular task thoroughly and efficiently, it might put someone at risk or advance the cabal in a material way. For example, meetings that late spring and into summer focused on how to solve "the Muslim problem." There were wide-ranging discussions about methods of attack and possible targets, and all sorts of people were mentioned for inclusion on their hit list—city officials, police, social workers, churchgoers, and any do-gooder playing a role in bringing in and sustaining the refugees. Perhaps most vociferously they talked about eliminating local landlords—they were seen as guilty by association for harboring ISIS sympathizers. Types of punishment were debated. "I want to put a bullet in his fucking head so bad, dude," Patrick said about a particular landlord. Gavin Wright suggested at another point that rather than take out that landlord, they should go after the man's daughter and kill her. "Make it look like Muslims did it," Gavin riffed sinisterly. The landlord's suffering would be big time, he added, living "with that guilt the rest of his fucking life. He brought them motherfuckers in and put 'em in his house and they killed his daughter."

Dan was expected to contribute to the discussions, help answer the others' questions: Which rental complexes housed Muslim refugees? Who owned them? How many did each landlord own, exactly? But Dan didn't want to do or say anything that might put a landlord or a member of the landlord's family in imminent danger, and so he began to practice an intel sleight of hand that gave the appearance of providing support. During the buzz of reaction to Gavin's murderous inspiration concerning a landlord's daughter, Dan offered to find out where she lived. He did this in order to seem helpful. But what he actually planned to do was report back with a fake address after notifying his FBI handlers. To him, this would help keep the woman safe and allow the FBI to keep tabs.

This ad hoc strategy was about containment, allowing Dan to do his best to fit in, *saying* things and *reacting* enthusiastically to the others' ideas, however outrageous they might be, without furthering their cause substantively. He and his FBI handlers had become concerned that one of the group might go rogue and commit an impulsive act of violence.

To monitor the militia's movements closely, Dan had to maintain his status as a valued cohort.

IT WAS a high-wire act for an informant, with Dan constantly trying to maintain his credibility as a militia member while limiting the group's knowledge of those who supported the Somalis. Come early June, Dan was about to find himself in yet another pickle. In the *Garden City Telegram,* an item appeared that piqued everyone's interest. The brief notice described a community event on June 4 that would showcase Somali culture — henna painting, African music, "a welcoming speech at 5 p.m.; an African dance ceremony presentation at 6 p.m.; and an open public dance at 6:30 p.m." The gathering, said the newspaper, had been organized by a "group of volunteers from various backgrounds and cultures who have come together to develop organized sustainable strategies to meet the needs of the African community." All who were interested in meeting and learning more about their Somali neighbors were welcome.

Dan said he was free that day and could check it out — knowing he probably wouldn't even show up and then lie and tell the others that he had. But Patrick was eager to go, although his motivation to meet Somalis was hardly what the event organizers had in mind. Patrick wanted to size up the scene, see who showed up, identify backers of the Somalis. There had been talk around town about the opening of an African community center in the near future, and Patrick saw that as a whole new target to consider. The upcoming summer social seemed a potential jackpot of intel about Somalis and their local supporters, who, by helping them, had betrayed America.

Patrick proposed that he meet up with Dan so they could attend together. Dan pushed back. He wanted to avoid two things: Patrick identifying individual Somalis and local citizens firsthand, and then, given his volatility, Patrick getting into it with attendees and jumping ugly. Dan argued that he should go by himself. Easier to blend in that way. Plus, it was more convenient for him to drop by, since he lived in Garden City; Patrick would have to drive in. Finally, he was the intel officer, and this assignment was central to his duties. He insisted that he could take care of it by himself. The others, trusting him, said fine, go for it.

IN THE DAYS leading up to the social on June 4, which was to be held in a gymnasium at the Horace Good Middle School, event organizers busied themselves with final arrangements. This group included Ifrah Ahmed and Halima Farah, whose friendship since Halima's arrival the prior year had grown to the point that they felt like sisters, and also Benjamin Anderson, the hospital CEO, and Dr. John Birky. Benjamin and Dr. Birky had raised about $1,500 for groceries, while Ifrah and Halima and Halima's mother, Sara, had overseen food preparation, doing much of the cooking in the kitchen of the spacious back room of Adan Keynan's African Shop. Benjamin bought a bunch of T-shirts from Adan's shop to give away, featuring the colors of the flag of Somalia —a light-blue shirt with a white star and the message I LOVE SOMALIA. He and Dr. Birky spread the word through their medical network, inviting friends and doctors from the Garden City area and as far away as Wichita. Then, just days before the social, they hit on the idea to dress in Muslim attire as a gesture of cultural unity. They hurried to the African Store, where Adan helped them pick out African outfits. Dr. Birky chose a traditional ankle-length khamis, while Benjamin selected a skirtlike macawis and a white shawl to drape over one shoulder and across his chest. This getup also allowed him to put on and show off one of the special I LOVE SOMALIA T-shirts.

When Saturday came and people began arriving, Benjamin saw that some Somali men were dressed in suits. He worried they'd made a terrible mistake, that he'd insensitively appropriated an element of Somali culture with the clothing he wore. The awkward moment turned into an icebreaker, though, as the men from different worlds took stock of one another and a kind of mutual appreciation settled in, a realization that the event was a celebration of Somali culture. When others arrived in all manner of dress, Western and Islamic, it became clear that what people wore didn't matter. Everyone could join in as they saw fit. Adan arrived in an all-white suit. Ifrah and Halima looked stunning in brightly colored robes and the veils called hijabs—Ifrah's was a bold blue and Halima's a softer peach color. Both wore bright-red lip gloss, a finishing touch that conservative Muslim women would have eschewed but one they considered fit for a celebratory occasion.

The background music was African, and food platters were displayed on tables—Somali rice mixed with dry spices, garlic, tomatoes, and red peppers, triangle-shaped sambusas packed with either ground beef or lentils, the unleavened flat bread known as chapati, and a host of other dishes, including noodles with a thick Somali-style sauce of beef and vegetables, seasoned with turmeric. The start of the event seemed a bit formal, as certain Somali elders were introduced, followed by some of the organizers, including Dr. Birky and Benjamin, who were asked to say a few words. Everyone was thanking everybody else for coming together on a Saturday afternoon. It impressed everyone when Benjamin's brother, Daniel Anderson, a member of the air force's official chorus, the Singing Sergeants, sang the national anthem. A classically trained opera singer, Daniel had performed with the Air Force Band and sung "America the Beautiful" at Arlington National Cemetery on Memorial Day in 2013, with President Obama in attendance. Now the tenor's delivery of "The Star-Spangled Banner" boomed across the spacious Garden City middle school gymnasium.

Once the formalities were out of the way, the socializing began in earnest. Benjamin stood at the two sets of doors leading into the gym, greeting the arrivals—friends, doctors, a smattering of city officials and police officers. He happened to spot a husky man at the door who was dressed in jeans and a plain shirt. The man seemed hesitant, and the two briefly made eye contact. The man then turned away and began looking around the gym in a way that conveyed uncertainty, as if he wasn't sure he wanted to go in. Benjamin took notice because the visitor, by his apparent tentativeness, stood out from the others streaming freely through the doors, and Benjamin thought, *This is good, this is the very kind of person the event was intended to reach, someone who was uncertain about his Somali neighbors but was curious enough to come to learn more.*

THE MAN was Dan Day. He'd been staring at Benjamin as he welcomed people because of the way he was dressed—in a skirt, with some ropey thing draped across his chest. Dan was wondering what that was about—was he a Muslim? Then, when he realized that Benjamin had noticed he was giving him the once-over, Dan turned and headed into the gym, where clusters of people were already chatting.

Dan had brought along his son, Brandon. He'd assessed the situation as no-risk and thought Brandon could serve as a kind of prop in a father-son tandem—an easy sell as normal for a social. The attire worn by the man at the doors had Dan thinking about one of Brandon's teachers, who'd converted to Islam. He was a history teacher, ex-military, and Brandon liked him a lot. When the teacher became a Muslim, Brandon said he'd grown a long, full beard, which wasn't so unusual anymore; long beards were now a popular redneck thing too. Dan scanned the room, noticed that a few other white guys were also wearing ankle-length—what were they—dresses? He had no idea what the clothing was called. Maybe all of them were Muslims, like Brandon's teacher. Who knew?

Dan caught some of the introductory remarks, although he had a hard time understanding the Somalis who spoke in broken English. Things went more smoothly when a young woman with a blue head-covering and bright-red lipstick was called upon to translate. Dan could follow her. He saw a whole bunch of Garden City police officers working the room, and a spokesman said something about how the police in Garden City supported every resident, including newcomers like the Somalis. Dan figured the Somalis were probably scared of police because of where they came from, so the Garden City officers were reassuring them, inviting the Somalis to trust them.

Had Dan been true to his assignment as the KSF's intel officer, he would have proactively inserted himself into the occasion, walked around, and introduced himself, maybe starting with that white guy in the skirt. Take down names of sympathizers to add to the group's list of the unwanted. Instead, he stood on the sidelines, talking with Brandon about the decorations, the music, the attendees. The number of people who had showed up did surprise him—if he'd had to guess, he'd say at least a hundred.

He just wanted to be able to say he'd attended. He had no intention of sticking around for long. And so when the buffet was opened and people began to get in line, he nudged Brandon. He had no interest in trying the ethnic food. He'd seen enough.

TWO HOURS later, as the gathering wound down, it was photo time. Benjamin and Dr. Birky, their wives, and other guests posed for picture after picture with Ifrah, Halima, Adan, and Sara, along with other refugees. Pictures included twosomes, foursomes, and large groups; many people were decked out in colorful Muslim dress and wearing the I LOVE SOMALIA T-shirt. Folks had dined together—broken bread together, as Benjamin liked to say—danced, sang, and laughed. The event had turned into a party, and a successful one.

Over the three years he had lived in the area, Benjamin Anderson had seen that the police chief, Michael Utz, and the city manager, Matt Allen, were progressive-minded leaders who valued the city's historic diversity. They held meetings with Somali elders to express goodwill and a spirit of cooperation. The chief had even enlisted Mursal Naleye to assist him in coordinating his department's meetings, and the extroverted Mursal had done wonders rounding everyone up. He was at the social too, enjoying every bit of it.

But making a connection with the African community, given the cultural, religious, and language differences, hadn't been easy. Somalis continued to largely live in isolation, and while some city leaders spoke of unity, others' actions suggested otherwise. Just days before the social Benjamin had learned from Adan Keynan, one of the best-known members of the Somali community, about a shocking notice he had received from the zoning office. In a letter written on June 1, Adan was told that the African Shop violated Garden City zoning regulations—as a retail business in a zone where such business was not permitted. Adan had been given thirty days to stop doing business at his West Mary Street shop.

Adan had turned to Benjamin, nearly in a panic about what to do. To his credit, the shop owner had managed to enjoy himself at the Saturday social despite the city's order hanging over his head; he looked striking in his white suit. And right away Benjamin knew that he and Dr. Birky, and perhaps others, would be stepping up to help. The Somali community could not afford to lose the African Shop. But for now, in the dinner's afterglow, Benjamin was relishing the moment—as were Adan and the rest. He left the middle school gymnasium on cloud nine, feeling that the efforts of the past ten months were really beginning to pay dividends.

LATER, WHEN militia members brought up the social during a Zello call, they asked Dan for a rundown. How many people showed up? Were police there? Or city commissioners, or anybody else from the local government?

Dan was ready. He downplayed everything, saying, yeah, a tiny bunch of people turned out, including a few police officers and some people from Garden City looking to make Somalis feel at home. "The mayor, the PD that came to show support, you know." Dan claimed that he didn't recognize many folks, a dodge so he wouldn't have to identify persons by name. He stated that the whole thing had been pretty boring and pointless; he didn't stick around. When the Somalis started dancing to "their jungle music," he'd split.

This summary triggered a run of hate-mongering—a reaction Dan found unsurprising. It confirmed his hunch that it had been right to keep other members away from the social. The idea that there were white Kansans who supported immigration in general and Somalis in particular drove them batty, as had the fact that white landlords rented apartments to Muslims.

Curtis jokingly proposed a macabre way to punish these traitors. "Need to get some signs made up," he said. "Hundreds of 'em. Kinda like the redneck deal, 'Here's Your Sign.'"

This was a reference to the comic Bill Engvall's blue-collar routine in which he states that people he thinks are stupid should be required to wear a sign around the neck to warn the world: I'M STUPID. In one of these skits, the comedian would describe driving an eighteen-wheeler and, having misjudged the height of an overpass, getting stuck beneath the bridge. A cop responding to the accident asks him, "So, is your truck stuck?" Engvall would take a long pause, then continue: "I looked at him, looked back at the rig, and then back to him, and I said, 'No, I'm delivering a bridge.'" Shouting over the audience's laughter, Engvall would deliver the punch line: "Here's your sign."

Curtis proposed that the militia make a variation of the I'M STUPID signs to hang around the necks of Muslim sympathizers in Garden City. Their version would have a longer message: I SUPPORT ILLEGAL IMMI-

GRATION. I GO AGAINST THE CONSTITUTION ON A DAILY BASIS. I DO NOT HAVE ANY CARE FOR MY FELLOW CITIZENS IN THE STATE OR THE TOWN THAT I REPRESENT.

And then Curtis delivered a punch line fit for the militia: "We blow the top of their heads off," he said, and "just put that around their neck."

Dan listened to Curtis's joke, thinking about the white guy at the gym dressed in the skirt. He could picture him as one of Curtis's targets for beheading. Meanwhile, Gavin and Patrick howled in amusement —especially Patrick.

"I like that idea," Patrick said.

THE WEEKEND AFTER THE successful social in Garden City, America awoke to news that in the wee hours of Sunday morning, June 12, a heavily armed gunman pledging allegiance to ISIS had opened fire in the Pulse nightclub in Orlando, Florida. He succeeded in killing forty-nine people and injuring fifty-three others before he was slain in a shootout with a SWAT team.

Reaction that day to the deadliest terrorist attack on US soil since 9/11 cut across all segments of society, from politics to pop culture to the growing militia movement. "It's horrific, unthinkable," Bernie Sanders, the Vermont senator running for president, told NBC's *Meet the Press.* The singer Katy Perry lamented to nearly a million followers on Twitter: "I just can't believe this is the world we live in today."

Neither could Patrick Stein, although his outrage came from a wholly different place than the singer's. The Zello call Patrick ran that night for the Kansas Security Force had an urgent intensity to it.

"XO checking in," Patrick said at the start of the call.

"Sparky checking in number two," Gavin said.

"D-Day number three," Dan said.

Members continued to join as Patrick, after a few niceties, basically declared the Pulse nightclub massacre an act of war. "How long is this shit been going on now, in this country?" he asked angrily. They could not sit back any longer and wait for the do-nothing federal government. "There's got to be a fucking line drawn somewhere," he said, "and when that line is crossed, there has to be some kind of action taken. I mean, am I wrong in that thought process?"

"Not in my eyes, XO," Gavin said.

Patrick said they should start thinking about a plan.

What kind of plan?

Dan asked, "Say there was an ISIS attack in Garden City, you know. Someone went into Walmart and mowed down a hundred people, you know. What would we do? Is that what you mean by getting a plan, XO?"

Patrick wasn't sure, exactly. He just knew they needed a new strategy. His skin was crawling, and he ached to do something, "I'm ready to just start fucking taking them out," he fumed, reviving his cowboy crusader fantasy. "Kick in doors, and I mean just start fucking cleaning house."

Patrick was not alone in visualizing payback. The Internet and social media were afire with calls for vengeance made by right-wing extremists, and on Monday, Donald Trump used the slaughter to fan the flame and score political points.

"It's too bad some of the people killed over the weekend didn't have guns attached to their hips," the presidential hopeful said in a series of interviews. If these patrons had had weapons, he fantasized, and then "this son of a bitch comes out and starts shooting, and one of the people happened to have it, and goes *boom boom.* You know what? That would have been a beautiful, beautiful sight, folks."

DAN SPENT most of Monday working outdoors with Brandon on his son's lawn-care business. The day was sunny, dry, and hot, with temperatures in the high nineties, and he should have known better. He didn't take enough breaks, forgot to drink enough water, and didn't take into account that he was not in shape—far from it. When he arrived back home Monday evening, he was dehydrated and whipped. He practically passed out, dizzy and nauseated, when he went to bed. He figured he'd sleep, rest, and recover.

But then Patrick called first thing Tuesday morning, came on like a fast-moving storm across the Great Plains, to announce he was organizing a meeting for later in the day. Patrick said he didn't want to be just another "keyboard warrior" complaining about ISIS and the Orlando shooting, and he told Dan he'd arranged to use another member's spread in Hutchinson, just west of Wichita. Patrick said Dan would probably remember Brody Benson from the March campout at Cheney Lake; Brody had also worked the security detail with Patrick and Curtis for the Sharp Family Singers, following the Sharps' return from the occupation in Oregon. Brody's place "south of Hutch," Patrick said, was rural and remote—an ideal location since from now on they needed to plan for more in-person contact and watch what they said on the phone or during their Zello meetings. Patrick knew this would make Curtis happy, since the commander suspected the government was somehow listening to everything.

Their first step, Patrick said during this high-octane wake-up call, was to get some meetings going. Count heads, he said. "You're either with me or you're not."

Dan took it all in, thinking the last thing he felt like doing was driving three hours to a militia meeting. He didn't want to get out of bed. But when he got off the call, he phoned his FBI handler Amy Kuhn and alerted her to the unexpected development. She listened intently to his report, including the part about how awful Dan felt. But the agent seemed to sense, from the way Dan described Patrick's summons, that they'd come to a turning point in the case. She told Dan that they needed to meet right away at the FBI office.

Proof of the FBI's escalating concern awaited him. Agents Kuhn and Smith of course wanted Dan to go to the militia meeting, but they also wanted something more. They asked him to carry a concealed recording device. Up until now, he'd gathered information by recording the Zello meetings using the crude phone setup in his bedroom. He'd basically been in the safety of his own home, capturing the talk from a distance. This would be different; he'd be smack in the midst of the militia members while secretly recording their conversations.

Dan balked—for a whole bunch of reasons. For one thing, he felt terribly unwell. The three sat in the windowless FBI conference room. Dan, after a long pause, reluctantly said he just didn't think he'd be able to make it through the day. It was unsettling to think that he wouldn't be at the top of his game the first time he'd be recording in person. What if they caught him? He'd be in the middle of nowhere, without any backup. Sure, he carried, but he'd be easily outnumbered. He even had the passing thought that maybe the group had figured out he was working for the FBI, and the long drive to a distant location was in fact a setup to confront him. He had no evidence pointing to that possibility, but feeling so physically depleted left him vulnerable to paranoia. He told the agents he wanted to call Patrick back, tell him he was sick and would have to take a raincheck.

The FBI agents pressed him. They weren't overly aggressive, but they made clear how much they needed him to go. They emphasized the potential importance of the meeting—the starting point of some sort of plan, or so it would seem, based on the way Patrick had described the purpose of the hastily arranged gathering. And the agents reassured Dan about the recording device. It wasn't like in the movies, where a microphone taped to the upper body had wires running to a device secured in the small of the back. Surveillance technology had come a long way. Dan would carry a tiny recording device the agents could turn on when he left, and it would then run on its own until his return. He wouldn't have to fuss at all with it. The device had enough power to record for hours on end.

Dan felt the weight of the moment. He didn't like the idea of letting down the FBI, and so he reversed himself; he decided to do it. While the agents improvised an operational plan, he drove home to get ready. He explained the turn of events to Cherlyn and said he'd be with the militia until deep into the night. Then, as he was about to hurry back to the FBI office, he realized his wallet was missing. He searched the Chevy

Blazer but couldn't find it. He must have dropped it somewhere. He couldn't go without his wallet, without any money, his driver's license. He called the agents, fretting that they might think, *Oh, brother, what's up with this yahoo, reversing himself again, saying he can't go, saying he's lost his wallet, which is probably not even true and just an excuse.* Dan hated thinking they wouldn't believe him and would conclude, at this pivotal time, that he was unreliable. In a panicky voice he told them he had a new problem—the wallet. He guessed it might have fallen out of his pocket in the lot behind the FBI office. Robin Smith hustled outdoors, checked around, and got back on the phone to say Dan's hunch had been correct. Smith found the wallet sitting in the grass strip separating the FBI office from the adjacent bank.

Dan was relieved. One crisis averted—but hardly the last. He returned to the FBI office to hear about the impromptu plan the agents had devised. Kuhn was to follow Dan to the north side of Dodge City, where Patrick had said he'd be waiting for him—at the McDonald's next to the Village Square Mall. Smith was to drive separately to Dodge and, out of sight, keep an eye on things. Dan and Kuhn left hurriedly in a two-vehicle procession, heading east on Highway 50 for the hour-long drive.

But Dan didn't get very far—at about a mile past the Garden City Regional Airport his Chevy Blazer started acting up. He slowed down as the engine overheated and then stalled. He rolled to a stop and tried starting the engine. Nothing at all. The SUV had broken down and died.

Kuhn pulled in behind him in her unmarked FBI vehicle; what now? Dan thought the problem might be the water pump, but they had no time for diagnosis or attempts at a quick fix. Kuhn called Smith, and while the two agents were adjusting the operation on the fly, a Kansas Highway Patrol cruiser pulled into the breakdown lane next to Dan's

Blazer. Still woozy, Dan felt his mind spinning as he tried to think of what to tell the trooper. But Kuhn took charge, conferring with the trooper and assuring him the situation was under control—that she'd call for a tow and would give her friend a lift home. Then she and Dan got into her car and she began the drive to Dodge City.

Meanwhile, Smith raced ahead to the McDonald's, to scout out where Dan was supposed to go. He called to report he'd spotted Patrick and then described an entrance to the mall's vast parking lot opposite to the McDonald's. Kuhn could enter there from Highway 50 to drop Dan off without being seen. Dan could then cut through the mall on foot and come out right across from the McDonald's where Patrick was waiting in his truck.

With Kuhn at the wheel, Dan rested up as best he could, relishing the car's air conditioning. They continued east on Highway 50, across the prairie and past ranches and wheat fields. He knew by the overpowering stench of manure when they reached Ingalls, at about the halfway mark. In its sprawling feed yard, cattle by the thousands were fed and fattened up in crowded, fenced-in pens for eventual transport to the meatpacking plants. The car slowed as Amy and Dan passed through Cimarron, another of the region's historic Wild West towns, and when he saw they'd reached the Boot Hill Casino and Resort on the left, and then the Dodge City High School, he knew they were getting close to the McDonald's.

Kuhn turned in to the lot where Smith had instructed them to park. She readied the recording device. Tiny and nondescript, it basically looked like a phone charger. Dan was to carry it in his pants pocket for this meeting. If he were to continue recording in the future, the device could be concealed elsewhere on him, with a different look to disguise it. Kuhn spoke into the recorder, her voice flat and firm: "This is SA Amy Kuhn. It is June 14, 2016. It's approximately six o'clock p.m., and I am turning on a recording device to give to Minuteman to go to a meeting with Patrick Stein." She handed Dan the device, and he exited into the day's lingering heat—in the high eighties, with sunset still several hours away.

DAN CLIMBED into the cab of Patrick's truck, which was idling outside McDonald's. "Oh, sheez," he panted. "Talk about a bad fucking day."

Patrick said, "Well, I guess so."

Dan was late. Patrick was not happy.

"Sorry about that, man," Dan said. "Oh, shit," he said, as he realized how late they'd be. "Gonna make it in time?"

"Meeting ain't starting without me."

Dan noticed right away, as they pulled onto Highway 50, that the air conditioning in Patrick's truck was broken. He opened the window and leaned against the door to catch a blast of fresh air.

"Wind feels good," he said.

Dan asked where near Hutchinson they were headed—to Brody's house?

"No," Patrick said. "We're meeting out in the middle of a fucking pasture."

Patrick was still acting annoyed. Dan tried explaining his lateness, hoping that would help—the lost wallet, the Blazer breaking down. He was living proof of Murphy's Law—when something can go wrong, it will. "I just hope I didn't blow my fucking motor up," he said. At least he'd been able to call a friend for a lift to Dodge in time to salvage the day.

Patrick, seeming dismissive, changed the subject. He asked Dan if he'd seen the story on Fox News out of Texas, the shooting at a Walmart? Dan had not—he'd been too busy working outdoors, falling ill, and then scrambling to meet up. News reports initially said two people had been taken hostage by a Walmart worker identified as a Somali or, as

Patrick said, "another goddamn cockroach." Later reporting said the incident was actually a workplace dispute and that the gunman, who'd been killed by police, was in fact not Muslim. Patrick didn't buy it and considered the later version a cover-up for Islamist terrorism, which for once had had a happy ending. "SWAT team fucking capped his ass," he said.

DAN ASKED about Gavin and Curtis—were they coming? Gavin wasn't, Patrick explained. He had a business meeting he couldn't reschedule on such short notice. Even so, Gavin was good, ready to go, and Patrick had no concerns about him. Curtis? Patrick said he'd reached Curtis at daybreak just as he had Dan. He said he'd told Curtis how he'd come to a decision that morning, as if he'd been struck by lightning. "And I said I'm putting together a meeting for tonight, and it's probably going to be over in the Hutch area."

Patrick said Curtis was on board too. But Curtis was in Topeka on business, and so the plan was for him to meet them at Brody Benson's on his way back. Patrick said he'd tried to reach Curtis several times over the course of the day, but his calls kept going to voicemail. "I forwarded him, you know, directions, on how to get where we're going to be."

After a little while Patrick tried again to reach Curtis, and when he was done dialing he turned to Dan with a surprised look on his face. "His phone is finally fucking ringing," he said. But seconds later Patrick put the phone down. "Fucking voicemail."

Dan asked, "You try texting him?"

Patrick said he hadn't. Dan said he would. Patrick said, "Ask him what the fuck is going on. Tell him XO wants to know where the fuck you're at." Patrick was growing impatient. He wanted to be sure the KSF militia commander would be in attendance. "His goddamn Zello is never on busy like it has been today. He always returns phone calls."

Dan sent a text that included a red flag, saying, "911, call," and within minutes Curtis was back in touch.

"Where are you at, Commander?" Patrick asked. "Been tryin' to get ahold of ya and couldn't so I was getting a little bit concerned." Patrick reiterated the agenda: "Got a meeting over here at eight o'clock west of Hutch, out here by Brody's.

"Gonna start putting a plan together."

Curtis said he was on his way but was still up near Topeka, more than two hours away. Patrick repeated directions. "West of Hutch about fifteen miles and then back south." Curtis said he would get there as soon as he could.

"All right man, be safe," Patrick said.

He turned to Dan. "He starts getting close, he's going to call."

Dan nodded, then coughed, as if gasping for air.

"Tired," he mumbled. "It's fuckin' hot."

Dan found himself worrying about his broken-down Chevy Blazer; it was his family's lone vehicle. If it was totaled, he had no idea what they'd do for transportation. But almost immediately, he chastised himself for thinking about the SUV. He had far more serious considerations—the fact that he was not feeling any better as the day wore on made him wonder if he was suffering from heatstroke. And Patrick was so fired up, racing across the plains for the initial plenary session Dan was supposed to record secretly.

He felt uneasy, which was maybe why he felt the need to offer Patrick reassurance, especially since he'd screwed up the start of the trip and had kept Patrick waiting. Unprompted, Dan haltingly began discussing his conversion to the view that Muslims posed a clear and present danger to the country. "It took me a long fuckin' time to come around to that way of thinking." He said that for as long as he could remember, he'd bought into the notion that America was a nation of immigrants, a safe haven for refugees fleeing other countries. As for Muslims, he'd never been around them and had just assumed "not all Muslims, you know, are radical." But what a mistake to have thought that way. "You start reading the Quran, the whole fucking Quran," he said, "and everything it says is fucking anti-Christian, anti-, anti-everything we fucking believe in."

The affirmation hung in the air. Maybe Dan hadn't needed to say this, but it eased his anxiety. He didn't want Patrick doubting him—Crusaders 2.0 all the way.

"Yeah, that's right," Patrick said after listening to him.

Minutes later, as Dan began to drift off, Patrick took a call. Dan couldn't tell who it was; he was able to pick up only Patrick's side of the conversation. But based on Patrick's reaction, it had to be someone he knew pretty well.

"What's up, brother!" he'd shouted over the sound of the wind blasting into the cab.

There was some talk about farming and then Patrick got to the point —the Muslim problem. "I'm just at a point, dude, I don't give a fuck anymore," he declared. The uproar on Facebook over the shootings in Orlando had made him realize that now was the "time to capture that fucking steam that's building.

"Shit's got to fucking stop," Patrick said.

He described how he'd had an epiphany that very dawn. "This morning, I don't even know why—goddamn switch flipped, and I went into organization mode."

He was en route now, he told his friend, to a meeting he'd set up, the "very first number-one initial meet, ya know." It would involve a "select few" for a "brainstorming meeting, just to get everybody, everybody's thoughts and, uh, ideas and don'ts and do's and, you know."

His words amounted to another one of his Islamophobic sermons.

"I'm tired of sitting on my ass being patient and seeing this shit go down and happen all over the goddamn country, and absolutely nothing gets done about it. Nothing. Zero. Nada. Zilch."

And if it meant sacrificing himself for the greater good, he'd come to terms with that. "I'm done waiting, and that's how I gotta go out, so be it. I really don't give a fuck anymore. At least it'll be going out doing something for this goddamn country that ain't nobody else fucking doing."

Patrick was jacked. "Orkinman," he promised, "is coming to life!"

The call lasted for fifteen minutes or more. Dan stirred awake as Patrick was wrapping up, saying, "All right, be careful, brother." Dan may have faded in and out and missed much of Patrick's diatribe, but the recording device in his pocket had not. It captured everything Patrick had said.

"I think I fell asleep for a little bit," Dan said.

Patrick didn't respond.

Dan asked, "Hey, do you mind, uh, could you drive by a convenience store? Stop and get—I can run in real quick and get a pop or something?"

"We ain't gonna be goin' by any more convenience stores."

"No? Gosh dang it."

Patrick said, "Unless there is some after we turn south."

"I left a full fucking thing in my car," Dan moaned. "Ugh, man."

For long stretches, neither said a word. They continued east on Highway 50 across the Great Plains under a high blue sky, past miles upon miles of fields. Occasionally a small town appeared, or a farmhouse off in the distance surrounded by a cluster of tall trees that broke up the prairie's flatness, having been planted decades ago to provide a farm family with shade against the blinding, relentless sun. Dan sat still, staring out the truck's window and noticing that a number of wheat fields had been harvested. As they passed more fields, he saw combines working their way across the land.

Patrick saw them too. "These motherfuckers are cutting the hell over here."

"Have you got started at all on yours?" Dan asked.

Patrick said no. "Bunch of wheat back home still got a shitload of green in it yet."

"Really?"

"They're always about two weeks earlier than we are," Patrick said.

Dan wondered if the workers they saw were custom harvesters—itinerant cutters, also known as "Wheaties," who followed the wheat trail north and worked for hire harvesting the ripened grain, a practice dating back a century. "My stepdad was a custom harvester," Dan said. "They would go all the way up to fuckin' Montana."

"Yeah," Patrick said. He'd done that too, in addition to minding his family's fields.

Dan experienced more wooziness. "Damn," he said in frustration.

He was determined to hold it together but continued to feel utterly exhausted. He tried a bit of humor to convey to Patrick that he might be struggling but would be okay.

"I don't need a pop," he said. "I need a fucking beer."

Nearing dusk, and before reaching Hutchinson, they turned south off Highway 50. Minutes later they were cruising down the main street of Partridge, Kansas—with a population shy of 250 residents. "Looks like a nice little town," Dan said.

"Old little town," Patrick said. "Kinda off the beaten path."

There was a post office, a library, and an elementary school, and then they spotted their turn. They'd driven past the town in an instant, heading farther south. Dan said, "Man, this is out in the boonies." Patrick followed Brody's instructions for another few miles.

"You say he is waiting on a hill?" Dan said.

They saw Brody just as Dan spoke, as well as another KSF member who was also just arriving, a woman named Shelby. Patrick pointed to a house and told Dan that it belonged to Brody's parents. The family owned about two thousand acres, which Brody had talked up as perfect, given its remoteness and hilly terrain, for constructing a bunker, or "bug-out" spot, to retreat to in the event of a natural disaster or civil war. Like most militia members, Brody was a prepper who was eagerly planning for the day of reckoning.

Dan and Patrick also noticed a shooting shack under construction a bit off in the distance. "He's got a goddamn trap," Patrick said, pointing to the poured concrete base and adjacent shooting range.

But Dan already knew about the project from photographs Brody had posted online the week before. "He put it on Facebook," he told Patrick.

Brody strode over to greet them, and for a few minutes they stood around talking about others who'd been invited but were unlikely to make it. Patrick brought up Gavin Wright's schedule conflict, adding that he planned to brief Gavin the next day. Brody joked about a militia member named Derek who got so drunk during a Sunday outing on a nearby river that he still couldn't see straight. "We had moonshine and all kinds of shit," Brody said.

Dan nodded knowingly—another Facebook moment. "I seen the video," he said.

What about the commander?

"Curtis is, he will be here but he's gonna be late," Patrick explained.

Patrick then gave a nod to the shooting shack, expressing an itch to use it. "Goddamnit," he told Brody, "you're going to make me get my fucking gun out, ain't you."

IT WAS at sunset that the foursome strode across a pasture to the shed. Inside were a few stools they went to sit on. They made more small talk. Dan had a hard time getting comfortable. He asked Brody, "You wouldn't happen to have a bottle of water or anything, would you?"

Brody did have some. "You need a sip?"

"Oh, you mind?"

"Go for it."

Dan was thankful. He mentioned he'd had a jug of water that he'd left behind in his car after it broke down.

"No shit," Brody said.

"Just outside of Garden, by the airport," Dan said, and then he lied: "Luckily, uh, a friend of mine was going to Dodge, so I had them drop me off and, uh, to catch a ride with Patrick. Otherwise I'd be sitting on the side of the highway still."

They were basically killing time, not wanting to get started in earnest until Curtis joined them. Brody mentioned his divorce, heatedly describing a bitter child-custody battle. They talked militia politics—about the different groups, personalities, and training exercises. They even talked about wildlife—cougar sightings in Kearny County. Dan mostly listened, only occasionally adding a comment. Brody noticed he seemed ill at ease.

"You look hot or something," Brody said. "You doin' all right?"

Dan said, "Aww man, yeah, well, fuckin' I lost my wallet."

Brody laughed.

"Then my fuckin' car broke down. I've just been, like, it's been a long day."

Patrick called Curtis for an update, and he learned Curtis was now in Salinas, still about ninety minutes away. They might as well get going, Patrick said once he got off the phone, and start putting some ideas out on the table. They revisited the Pulse nightclub shooting, with everyone seething. Brody reminded Patrick, "When you called me today, you was all hot and bothered."

"Still am hot and bothered," Patrick said.

The foursome had pivoted from shooting the breeze to brainstorming about shooting Muslims. Patrick reiterated his overarching goal to "clean house," as well as his fantasy to start "kicking fuckin' doors in with a goddamn Mark 2 and a silencer."

Shelby was skeptical. "You're gonna get, just *maybe,* as many as that dude last weekend," she said, referring to Omar Mateen's death toll at the Pulse. Patrick had to think bigger, she seemed to be suggesting. And she voiced skepticism that a core group of militia members would be able to stem the flow of Somali refugees. "I don't see a small number being able to stop that," she said.

Brody begged to differ, arguing that going small could still yield huge dividends. "Take a look at ISIS," he said. "How their small little organizations tip the bounds of the whole world. That's what we need to be looking at." It was guerrilla warfare, Brody said a bit later. "Like the Vietcong, you hit and run," he said. "We create as much terror on them as they're doing on us, that's how you get it done."

Patrick was the first to concede he didn't have answers yet—except that because of the reconnaissance he and Dan had conducted on the Somalis, he knew without a doubt they should focus on Garden City. "You know they got these apartment complexes over there with Muslims in every fuckin' apartment—that's all it is, fuckin' goddamn cockroaches." What if they were to employ rocket-propelled grenades? "I'll run some RPGs right through, I'll blow every goddamn building up, right there—boom."

Shelby, once again, was unconvinced. "We gotta be realistic," she told Patrick, "because I can't get any of those, and you can't either."

Dan chuckled, but Patrick seemed to feel slighted. "Well, there's ways," he said.

The talk went around and around. Dynamite was brought up, as was the idea of a diversionary tactic to draw police to another part of Garden City while the militia launched its plot against Somalis—whatever the eventual shape of that plan. "I wanted this meeting to toss around ideas," Patrick said, adding, "This ain't something that's gonna kick off right now." It'll take a month or two, he said. "Maybe three. I don't know. We'll see."

DAN PUSHED himself to stay involved, to overcome his sorry state and show the others he wasn't a deadbeat. He supported the idea of a diversionary tactic, for one thing, and interjected at different times references to his work as intelligence officer. He mentioned how he'd attended the Somali social "to see what it was about," and he reminded them of his bid to infiltrate the Garden City office of the International Rescue Committee so that he could track the arrival and relocation of Muslim refugees. "They gotta do a background check on me," he said by way of providing an update, adding that the fact he formerly worked as a probation officer meant "I should be able to get in."

Dan even revisited the subject of his awakening to the nation's dangers, which he'd mentioned earlier to Patrick. "I'm pretty mellow," he told them. "I mean, I was tellin' him on the way up here. Fuck, a year ago, I haven't had this train of thought. I mean, you know, but I fuckin' been waking up."

Patrick interrupted. "I've been waking a lot of people up."

Dan finished his thought: he truly believed, he said, "it's time to do something."

But in that moment—and after about an hour into the meeting—Dan took a sudden turn for the worse. The others had just begun discussing possible ways to spread their anti-Muslim messages on social media when he cringed in pain.

Shelby noticed. "What is it?"

"Cramp," Dan said. The pain worsened.

Patrick and Brody, unaware of Dan's distress, kept talking.

"Oh, my gosh," Dan said. He put everything into trying to stabilize himself and wasn't sure anymore what the others were saying. "Oh my goodness," he said, as the shed seemed to wobble. Or was it him? He was going downhill fast.

Shelby gave him some water. "I got more," she said.

Dan had turned pale and sweaty. "Huh, oh," he moaned. "Oh, gosh."

"You need salt?" Shelby asked.

Dan's breathing became heavier and more strained.

"You gonna pass out?" she asked.

Brody finally took notice. "You all right, dude?"

"I just dehydrated." Dan couldn't even make a complete sentence.

Brody said they should walk over to his truck, turn on the air conditioning.

Dan liked that idea. But after taking a few steps from the shed and feeling more light-headed with each step, he stumbled, fell against a fence, and then dropped to the ground.

"You all right?" Brody said, hovering over Dan.

Dan looked up. Everything spun. He was afraid—that he would lose consciousness, that they would rifle through his pockets. Finding his pistol would be okay, but the recording device? What if they emptied his pockets and came across the tiny thing that looked like a phone but wasn't? What if they began interrogating him? The fear he'd felt previously—that they'd already discovered he was working for the FBI—returned. Would they torture him? Kill him? Bury him? Had he been poisoned? Ordinarily, when he felt in any way endangered, he'd start working up an exit strategy in his head, some plan he could implement if needed, something that made sense to him. But in this instance nothing made sense. He was having wild and crazy thoughts. What could he do? He was so weak, unable to think straight. He was a helpless mess—and this was, no less, his first time bugging the group.

"I'm seeing stars" was all he could say, and he wasn't talking about the ones dotting the night sky. The others helped him back up to his feet.

"There, c'mon," Brody said.

Dan never made it to the truck. He moaned, "Uhhhh," staggered, and collapsed a second time. He lay on the ground, going in and out of consciousness. He heard Brody making a call. Brody's voice sounded distant, even though he stood next to him. Brody was calling his parents' house, and Dan could hear Brody asking for someone. Next he could detect another presence; it was Brody's sister-in-law, who'd hurried down from the house. She was a nurse. Through the haze, Dan could sense that the nurse was assessing his condition.

And when she told Brody to call for an ambulance, he felt relief—as if he'd been rescued.

4

"THE COCKROACHES GOTTA GO"

Before an ambulance carrying Dan left the rural outpost, Brody Benson asked if he wanted him or Patrick to ride along to the hospital. That was the last thing Dan needed—their company would only create trouble in terms of his ability, in his condition, to maintain his cover. Even half-delirious, he managed to reject the offer, muttering something about getting his parents to come for him. Dan wasn't sure what made him think of the couple; his mother and stepfather were long dead. But maybe on some level, in some weird way, his two FBI handlers, Amy Kuhn and Robin Smith, were "parents."

Dan improved rapidly once the EMTs got him going with IV fluids. But what a close call; in fact, the entire day had been one close call after another, as if he'd spent the past eighteen hours teetering on the edge of a cliff. During the ambulance ride to the Hutchinson Regional Medical Center, about twenty miles away from Brody's place, one EMT asked what he and the others had been up to in the country after dark, and Dan answered they were checking out the new shooting range. Dan then felt for his pants pocket and was surprised to find both his handgun and the recording device still there. He expected the EMTs would have searched him. Then he had a new worry—that at the hospital, some attendant, security person, or nurse would find them. But when the ambulance arrived, he was taken into the ER and immediately wheeled into a cubicle where nurses began coming and going, taking his blood pressure and vital signs.

No one disturbed his clothing—a relief. Miraculously, he began feeling perky. The first chance he had, he called Amy Kuhn on his cell. The agent was shocked at the news of his hospitalization: was he okay? Robin Smith jumped onto the call. Dan learned that he'd been under loose surveillance, meaning that agents from the Wichita office had been dispatched to within a fifteen-mile radius of Brody's place. Hearing that, Dan wondered how their presence was supposed to help. He told the agents he felt terrible about losing consciousness. The distraction caused by his illness, the continuous struggle to stay lucid, and then the fact that he'd passed out meant that he had only a fuzzy recollection of the long day spent with Patrick.

Kuhn told him not to worry and then cut to the chase: "Do you still have everything?"

It took Dan a second to follow. Then he understood—she meant the recording device. He needed to choose his words carefully, not only because there was a nurse in the cubicle but also because the recording device in his pocket was probably still running.

"Yep, I got everything," he said.

"Everything everything?" Kuhn repeated the word.

"Yep," Dan said. "*Every*thing."

Smith then announced that he and Kuhn were on their way.

It was well after midnight by the time Dan, still in the hospital, called home. Alyssa, the only one awake, answered. He gave his daughter a bare-bones description of his calamitous day. He reassured her that he was fine but wasn't exactly sure when he'd be getting home; he was waiting for the FBI. The agents arrived in what seemed to Dan like record time, and to the hospital staff they presented themselves as part of Dan's extended family. Smith stood in Dan's cubicle, asking him and the nurse about his condition. Kuhn was at his bedside, leaning in close. Dan slipped her the recording device. The agent left briefly, in order to turn the device off in secret.

The nurse mentioned a possible CAT scan, but Dan refused it. He hadn't been injured in the fall. He'd just needed hydration, and now that he was feeling rejuvenated, he wanted to leave. The nurse was not pleased, but there was little she could do to stop him. First thing the agents did was to stop at a convenience store, where they bought Dan a large bottle of Gatorade. The night air felt refreshing—so cool in contrast to the high heat of daytime.

Dan then realized how the agents had managed to arrive at the Hutchinson hospital so quickly. Robin Smith had raced across Highway 50 at speeds exceeding a hundred miles per hour, as if part of a Hollywood-style Steve McQueen car chase. Kuhn sat in back, taking down notes on everything that Dan could remember from the day.

The first hint of dawn appeared in the sky as the agents dropped him off. Cherlyn was awake and greeted him, full of worry but relieved to see him. He shuffled into their bedroom, fell into bed, and slept past noon. He'd made it home safely but was troubled that the day might have been a bust, ruined by his faltering, then failing condition. What a crazy way to start recording Patrick and the others.

The picture changed practically overnight, though. The recording was immediately transcribed by the FBI. Kuhn and Smith listened to it as well, and they told Dan everything had worked—the sound was scratchy at times, for sure, especially during the long ride when wind blasted into the truck's cab. But it was all there, starting with Patrick Stein, the moving force who, in his own words, was kicking into "organization mode" and moving past his bucketloads of hateful, angry bombast toward waging a violent attack against Muslims in Garden City. Patrick was determined to count heads, see who would jump on board with him. It was all there.

Dan had done it. He just needed to stay the course. Maintain his cover. Get more.

IN CONTRAST to Patrick, Curtis wasn't so sure they needed more Crusaders. Ever cautious, Curtis believed that for security purposes, the fewer people the better. Besides, he was convinced a core group could accomplish plenty, especially if using explosives. Patrick was vehement, though. "The only fuckin' way this country's ever going to get turned around is, it will be a bloodbath," he said in a nighttime Zello call at the end of June. Patrick thought that with additional warriors, "I think we can get it done, but ain't going to be nothing nice about it." Curtis let him have his way. Most of July was spent feeling out possible collaborators—the first phase, of sorts, in their scheme.

The group convened two key meetings. Noticeably missing from any further activities were Brody Benson and Shelby. In the days after his medical emergency, Dan had heard from each of them; they'd wanted to check on him, make sure he was okay. But that was it. Despite the gung-ho posturing at the June 14 session, both soon dropped from sight. Patrick wouldn't talk about them, and Dan didn't want to set Patrick off by pressing the issue. The FBI briefly monitored Shelby but quickly realized she'd distanced herself and was no longer involved. For his part, Brody was already harboring doubts by the end of that first night. Curtis had arrived at the shooting range after Dan was carted off to the hospital. Shelby had gone home by then too, and it was while Patrick and Curtis were talking that Brody got a clearer sense that they weren't simply blowing off steam. The start of their secret meeting had been like playing a shooter video game, with everyone fired up in righteous recreation, sharing in a virtual seek-and-destroy of a mutual enemy. They were gamers in the throes of the action. But the more Patrick and Curtis talked, the more Brody realized their intent was real. Brody might hate

Somalis, but murder? Within days, he submitted his formal resignation to the Kansas Security Force.

The first of these two meetings, held on July 9, was a marathon, hosted by a KSF member named Trish at her rural spread twenty-five miles west of Garden City. It followed a Zello call the night before, during which Patrick said it was time, in effect, to separate the wheat from the chaff. Gavin unfortunately had a sales meeting that particular Saturday at G&G Home Center in Liberal. Trish's husband had to work too. But Curtis was on board to assist Patrick in gauging who might rise to the occasion, be it Trish or a few others slated to attend.

Dan showed up around 9 a.m. He was no longer driving the familiar Chevy SUV. The Blazer's engine was beyond repair, which meant that Dan had been housebound for the latter half of June, unable to meet with Patrick, or anyone for that matter, in person. The timing couldn't have been worse. The investigation had taken a critical turn, and Dan needed to be in the thick of things. But he had no savings, and little income to speak of, to pay for a new car. So, when he arrived in a used Chevy Impala, which had cost $6,000, he did so courtesy of the FBI.

While waiting for Patrick, Trish showed Curtis, Dan, and another militiaman named Nathan around her property. She was proud of its potential as a shelter against the storm—or whatever SHTF. "Commander, just so you know, water well over there," she said.

Curtis asked, "Do you have a plan for a generator to run it?"

Indeed she did—her father-in-law had one. "Shit hits the fan," she added, her in-laws would be coming to stay with her. Trish talked up the fact that her land was covered in medicinal plants—tumbleweed, which the Navajo had used to treat smallpox and the flu; horseweed, to treat diarrhea and hemorrhoids; sunflowers, to treat spider bites, snakebites, and sores and, boiled into a tea, to treat fever. Preppers—that's what they were—just like any bona fide militia members preparing for the worst. She ticked off dozens of homegrown foods, much of which could be stored—corn, pumpkins, watermelon, cantaloupe, zucchini, pole beans, peppers. "Carrots, okra, strawberries, tomatoes," she said. "I'm so excited."

"What about dog food?" Dan asked.

"Huh?" Trish said.

Dan had spied her dog, Sampson. "You stocking up on dog food?"

She realized he was razzing her. "Rabbits," she deadpanned.

Trish took them into an outbuilding that had been fixed up and furnished for an extended stay—if ever necessary. Her husband had bought a couch featuring cup holders in each armrest. "That is cool," said Dan, admiring the place. "I could bug out here." Everyone in the group was carrying, prompting a lively discussion about armaments, about guns they'd just purchased or had their eyes on. Dan described his new Ruger SR9c, which he said he'd acquired to replace his Glock as a pocket carry because of its safety. As he withdrew the semiautomatic pistol, he inadvertently hit it against the concealed recording device—making a sound that later proved jarring to the FBI transcriber.

Curtis, meanwhile, talked about the ammo business he was trying to get off the ground. "Trying to get financing on it," he said. "Trying to find five people that would put up five grand. Double your money the first year."

It was militia-minded small talk to pass the time until Patrick got there.

LIKE CURTIS, Patrick showed up in his Kansas Security Force T-shirt—Dan had forgotten to wear his. They went inside Trish's house to get down to business. "Do you guys have a whiteboard or something we could draw on?" Curtis asked. Trish did not. Curtis announced that he wanted everyone to start using the code words he'd devised for their communications, but Patrick said he hadn't had time to make copies to hand out.

Other men came and went over the course of the day while Dan, Curtis, and Patrick were constants. In the afternoon, the threesome queried one newcomer, a machinist named David, to see if he had easy access to the shop at work. Patrick said the reason for asking was that his father had once worked in a machine shop and, on his own time, was able to make things for free. "He built so much shit that we used on the farm," Patrick said, "and they didn't care." Patrick wasn't interested in having David make them farm tools, but what about silencers? Could David surreptitiously do that?

David hesitated. "You get into silencers, you are crossing a line," he noted. But for the militia and its greater good, he said, "I feel comfortable doing that." It turned out David was also tech-savvy; he delivered a lecture on how cell phones were hardly private or secure. "How many cell phones are in this room right now?" he asked. Everyone had one, and David insisted that "most of them are drawing, no matter whether they're on or not." It left them vulnerable to surveillance, he said. Curtis, in particular, perked up, and a new policy was adopted in response: cell phones had to be left in cars prior to any future gatherings. For his part, Dan had no beef with the rule; the FBI recording device was not in any way connected to his phone.

Yet another newcomer to Trish's table, a friend of Curtis's named Daniel, at one point pushed the group to think deeper about their options, challenging the notion that going after local Somali refugees in Garden City would be the most effective approach. He likened the Muslim threat to a bush, and said, "If you're just killin' Muslims, you're just taking off leaves here and there." He continued: "I don't see takin' off leaves as trying to fix the problem." He suggested that they could go further and attack their mosques—which he likened to branches on the bush. But he didn't think that would solve the problem either.

Daniel suggested the best course of action was to go after the "root" of the problem: "Where these people comin' from? Who's backin' 'em? Who's bringin' 'em in? That's where we oughtta be goin' after 'em."

The series of questions hung in the air until Patrick broke the silence. "Fuckin' nigger in the White House," he said with finality. "There's your root." President Barack Obama, his cabinet, and Congress were the heart of the problem, Patrick said, with Obama personally responsible for opening the floodgates to Muslim refugees.

"Well," Daniel said, "take that root out."

"I'd be there in two fuckin' seconds if I had the equipment to do it," Patrick said.

It was yet another dark fantasy to add to Patrick's list.

PATRICK, LOCKED in organization mode, alternated between probing recruits for their potential assets, ranting about the severity of the Muslim crisis, and openly lauding himself. He asked David, "You hear 'em being called cockroaches?" Not waiting for an answer, Patrick bragged, "I kind of started that because in my mind that's exactly what the hell they are, and you can't just kill one. You gotta go kill every fuckin' one of 'em, if you want to get rid of them. That's a cockroach."

Patrick was eager to take credit, and Dan took his cue. He flattered his XO as making history for inventing the slur. "Muslims, cockroaches — it's gonna be famous," Dan said.

Trish chimed in, stoking Patrick's ego. "I'm going to go ahead and add that to Wikipedia!" If they checked Wikipedia, however, they'd have learned that the Hutu majority in Rwanda had dehumanized the Tutsi minority by calling them cockroaches to justify the killing, or extermination, of 800,000 people in the 1994 genocide. The one-liner, however fitting as a catchphrase expressing Patrick's hate, was hardly his invention.

The highlight of the day, though, was the argument between Patrick and Trish that flared late morning, a climactic debate of sorts during which they pressed competing views of a militia member's duty and responsibilities regarding the perceived Muslim infiltration.

"Where does Miss Trish stand on all this?" Patrick said to start things off.

Trish acted puzzled. "What?"

"The cockroach situation," he said. "There's only one way to take care of that problem."

"Well," Trish said, "I'm not gonna just go up and start shootin' at 'em."

With that, the lines were drawn.

Trish made it clear that if ever there was an Islamist terrorist attack, "I will be there." But her mindset was defensive, all the way. "We're a militia," she asserted. "We are here to back up and protect our state." She could tell Patrick was upset. "I know that's probably not what you wanted to hear." She wasn't against spying on Muslims, but if militia members gathered intel about an imminent attack, they should alert the police, work with them.

"I can promise you right now we won't be workin' with the police," Patrick said.

Dan tried to help out. He emphasized the urgency of the Muslim threat, the necessity of a first strike—and their need to know exactly what Trish meant. "What do you feel about if we struck first?" he asked her.

"I won't be the one," she said flat out.

Dan probed further. "Okay, what if some of the rest of the group strike first?"

"Just don't tell me what you're doin'," she said.

But Dan, in his role as the group's intelligence and vetting officer, wasn't satisfied. Given what she was saying, might she pose a security threat to the group? "I mean, are you calling the law enforcement on us?" he said.

Trish laughed. "Hell, yeah, I'm gonna call 'em."

Dan and the others didn't think she was funny.

Realizing that, Trish said no, she wouldn't tell police. She reminded them that she had kids, and that on top of her view that militias were only for defensive purposes, she wasn't going to do anything that put her family at risk.

Patrick grew frustrated. He said, "If your kids are your number-one concern, you know what? Those motherfuckers will kill your kids just as fast as they kill you." Not only that, but he'd watched a slew of videos on YouTube showing Islamist terrorists training their young boys to be mini-terrorists. "I've seen four- and five-year-olds practicing literally on fuckin' teddy bears how to fuckin' behead somebody."

"I'm not saying they're good people," Trish said. "If they start comin' at me or any of this group, my friends, my family, I'm right there. But, I'm more a defensive person."

"Somebody's gotta strike first," Dan said a few minutes later.

The back-and-forth continued for more than forty minutes, as the three Crusaders put on a full-court press, trying to win Trish over. "Has there not been enough fuckin' American people die at the hands of these motherfuckers?" Patrick asked incredulously.

Curtis implored her to get real, saying she sounded like so many others in the movement—patriots all, but with their heads in the sand. "If we wait for them to do something, like you're sayin,' it's gonna be too late." He turned to history, citing the run-up to World War II. Americans' reluctance to confront Islamist radicals, he argued, reminded him of Jews who were in denial as Hitler consolidated power. "This is just like 1935 Germany," he told Trish. "Everybody's like the Jews sittin' in their store. You know, just waitin'. They're not gonna do nothing;

they're not gonna do nothing." Then the brownshirts came, he said. "They kicked the doors in and took 'em all to the fuckin' camp."

Patrick, not to be outdone when it came to invoking history, went even further back in time. "It's the way the Christians fucked up how many thousands of years ago," he said. "It's called the Crusades. The Muslims almost wiped out the Christians." The reason he chose to name their militia offshoot the Crusaders was to take up the baton, not let history repeat itself. "The Christians were playin' Christian, you know —turn the other cheek. Be the mister nice guy. Let's try to love 'em into fuckin', you know, not killing." Not possible, Patrick said. "Motherfuckers don't believe that way. They're taught from the time they're this old, if you're a Christian or a nonbeliever, my job is to kill you, period."

Patrick, Curtis, and Dan kept arguing the point: before it was too late, a first strike was necessary. "We do something in Garden City, then the next week it's something in Dodge, then Wichita," Curtis said. "Once we start, I think the public's gonna wake up."

Trish didn't budge. She liked them all, she said, but rejected the call to action. Daniel, it turned out, felt the same way.

Patrick was worn down. "Conversation done," he said finally. Except it wasn't. He and Trish tussled a bit more, and at one point, as Patrick began to see that Trish and Daniel were not coming on board, said, "I'm just sayin' there better not be a fuckin' word said nowhere, no how, by nobody." He then threw them a lifeline: as he, Curtis, Gavin, and Dan started drawing up plans, they'd be kept out of the loop. "It's literally for your own good," Patrick said. "You don't have to try to lie to the fuckin' cops or the feds or whoever, if for some reason you get questioned. You really don't fuckin' know!"

Trish, turning comedic again, mimicked a police interrogation: *"Who is Patrick Stein?"*

"Exactly," Patrick said. And also acting like a cop, he demanded: *"Who?"*

Trish had a punch line ready. "Oh, that's that douche bag."

Everybody laughed. The tension broke. "Right, yeah," Patrick said. He offered another putdown that could be used to feign ignorance with the police: "That's the dumb motherfucker from over around Dodge, isn't it?"

Trish, picking up on Patrick's drift, got off one more wisecrack: "I didn't even know he was smart enough to do all this stuff."

The debate was over; they'd just have to agree to disagree.

"I'm not gonna argue with ya on the Muslims anymore," Patrick said.

Trish replied, "No reason beatin' on a dead horse."

Then someone noticed the time—already almost one o'clock. Trish offered to drive into town and buy hamburger patties to throw on the grill, but they decided to pile into a couple of cars and get take-out chicken at a nearby U Pump It service station. The lunch break went quickly, and the core group resumed the meeting for several more hours, by which time Daniel had left. But for all their effort over many hours, and despite plenty of rah-rah anti-Muslim feeling, the head count at day's end was unchanged. Still just the core four: Patrick, Curtis, Gavin, and Dan. It was late afternoon when Dan returned to Garden City. "It's still July ninth," spoke FBI agent Robin Smith into the recorder after Dan got back to the office, "and I've just recovered the recording device at 5:14 p.m., terminating the recording."

THE CRUSADERS AGREED TO meet again nine days later, on July 18, at the Kearny County Fair in Lakin. Elsewhere in the country the big news was Donald Trump's announcement at the Republican National Convention in Cleveland that Mike Pence, the arch-conservative Indiana governor, would be his vice-presidential running mate. But in the Garden City area the fair was the big deal, a five-day happening featuring a livestock show with swine, sheep, and calves, a kiddie tractor pull, a fish fry, a country music band, and the Fifty-Second Annual Turtle Race. The race was one of the most popular events, sponsored by a local 4-H club, with more than fifty kids paying a half-dollar to enter a pet turtle. Multiple heats, each with ten turtles, were scheduled. One group of ten was placed in the center of a roped-off circle ten feet in diameter and, with onlookers cheering wildly, the competition began. The first turtle to pass beyond the roped-off area would move up to the next round.

Curtis had set up a booth at the fairgrounds for the Kansas Security Force militia. His on-again girlfriend, Lula, had finally agreed in June to move back in with him, and although still worn out by her cancer treatment, she'd helped him get his recruiting materials together. His mood was upbeat. So far he and Lula were getting along fine, and they'd done a home-improvement project together—painting the midsized rocks positioned along the edge of the trailer's tiny lot in three colors: red, white, and blue. And then they planted a Trump sign out front.

Curtis had spent the afternoon at the fair handing out KSF cards and talking up the militia's patriotic work. The plan was to conduct a second, private meeting at night with a couple more supporters they knew, to see if they might join. Trish lived the closest to the fairgrounds, and she had agreed to let Patrick, Curtis, Dan, and Gavin use her house for the sake of convenience, even though she wanted no part of their scheme. She and her husband stayed behind to mind the KSF booth.

Besides, their pre-teen daughter had a turtle entered in the race—in fact, the girl's turtle eventually finished first overall.

It was close to 8 p.m. and getting dark when the foursome arrived by a dirt road at Trish's house. "Hey!" Dan yelled to Gavin as they were all climbing out of their vehicles. "Your light's out on the passenger side. Fuckers around here will pull you over for that."

Dan was just trying to be helpful, but if Gavin appreciated the heads-up, he didn't let on. "What are you, my mother?" he said.

Dan rolled with the dig, just as he did a few minutes later when Patrick razzed him for passing out at the meeting on June 14. "You hydrated all right?" Patrick asked as they walked toward the house. The day's heat was unrelenting even at nightfall, with temperatures stuck in the low nineties.

"Yep, I'm good to go," Dan said.

"We don't have anybody on call," Patrick joked, referring to EMTs.

The others laughed as Patrick recalled, "He wasn't even walking last time."

Dan said, "Man, I don't remember the last twenty minutes, what you guys said, before I went out." He continued to recall that bizarre night. "I knew something was wrong. I didn't know what the hell it was."

Curtis interrupted. "All right, all right, we got it."

EXCEPT FOR a cat and Sampson the dog, the house was empty, and dark, when they let themselves in. Curtis looked around for the light switches while Dan and Gavin made sure the pets didn't sneak outside. They settled in at the table and started a discussion that would last several hours, as they worked through a range of issues. Curtis reminded everyone that their strategy going forward was to be "preemptive, and not just sitting on our asses." He mentioned a timetable: "We are less than—maybe at the max sixty days—probably less than fifty or forty days, when something major happens." The plot's details still needed to be hammered out, however, so they spent some of the time brainstorming scenarios. No one disputed their main target—Somalis. That was a given. But should they go wider? Patrick had drawn up a target list. Topping it were the landlords renting to Muslims, whom they'd previously talked about attacking. Then came city and county officials who, Patrick said, "are directly involved with bringing these motherfuckers in here." He said, "They're a fucking target too, in my mind. They're part of it."

Businesses large and small were on his list. The meatpacking plants, for example. "Tyson, National, and Cargill," Patrick said. Just yesterday at breakfast, he continued, he was complaining to his parents that the slaughterhouses were filled with refugee workers when it dawned on him they should be targeted. "I was like, what goddamn company in their right fucking mind would hire all these motherfucking employees that don't even speak your fucking language." Small businesses, such as the African Shop, were on the list too. Patrick again condemned city leaders for permitting Muslim businesses when they should be saying, "Fuck you, no, you're not opening up a goddamn store like that in this city." These myriad targets clearly were just a wish list, but they helped the Crusaders define their goals.

IDENTIFYING EACH person's talents, really spelling them out in deliberate fashion to realize their collective strengths, was yet another item on the agenda. The idea was Patrick's. "We might as well jump right into this," he said. "Give me your skill sets."

Gavin spoke first. "Anything electrical."

"Good, yeah," Patrick said.

"I can make power out of nothing, a weed eater and a motor," Gavin said. "I can make a generator out of it. I mean, not to brag, but I know everything about everything when it comes to electricity.

"I'm not a bad shot," he added, and then a little later thought of something else. "I'm a pretty good welder too. I don't know if that matters."

Next up was Dan. "Talk to me," Patrick said to him.

Dan said, "I have a different set of skills." He was good at planning: "Help put the plan together, help find the holes, you know." He was a shooter too, having been raised around guns. "I've been shooting my whole life," he said, although not so much in recent years. "I'd have to get back in practice," he admitted. Most important, perhaps, he noted that he was good at rounding up information. "I can gather intel," he said.

Curtis saw the intel as critical. "That's the biggest thing," he said. "Yeah."

It was like a talent show, at once serious but also lightened with wisecracks. Gavin joked, "I can run pretty fast when I'm chased. I can run tracks over your back if there was a bear after us."

When Dan laughed, Curtis poked fun at his gut. "You hang out with Dan, you don't even have to be very fast and you can still get away—no offense, Dan."

Later, Patrick playfully bragged about his driving. "I'm a driving motherfucker," he said, especially on back roads, which prompted Gavin to chime in, "I'm an awesome dirt driver."

Then, back to basics. It was Curtis's turn. "Commander?" Patrick said.

Curtis was thoughtful. "I think the planning side of it will be big," he said, and it went without saying that his army training would be useful tactically. And of course Curtis knew all kinds of weapons. In Iraq, he'd also faced incoming fire and watched comrades freeze up. "I've fucking yelled at guys right in the face to pull the trigger and they won't do it." It was an experience that had taught him to remain cool and calm under stress. Then there were explosives. He announced he'd already begun researching bomb-making online. He had no particular bomb expertise but exuded confidence. "We'll make our own."

That was Curtis's sum and substance. "I don't know what else you want me to say."

Dan thought Curtis was being too self-effacing. He quickly added to Curtis's skill set "leadership," just as Gavin spoke up to emphasize the importance of Curtis's "military experience, for sure."

Patrick's turn came, and he was not to be outdone. "I'm a good shot," he began. "I've got some medical background, was an EMT, a firefighter." Then there was "planning, coordinating, you know," and of course, growing up as a farmer, he'd learned to make pretty much anything from the stuff lying about the farm. Like the Renaissance man of white nationalism, he ticked off his many skills. He was most proud, however, of his knack for interrogation. "I mean, gentleman, I can go fucking primal." Dan had certainly seen firsthand Patrick as Jekyll and Hyde, what Dan called "going Stein." Patrick launched into a speech describing his talent for torturing "motherfuckers I hate and I want to get information out of." He noted that the occasion might arise when they'd need to kidnap and grill a Somali. "That's where, you know, I would love to shine." He said, "I don't know why that is, but I just, I can flip a switch and go to that place real fucking easy."

THEY ALSO devoted a fair amount of time to addressing the very purpose of what was now the third secret gathering—the first being in Brody's pasture in mid-June, followed by the two July sessions at Trish's. The subject was the makeup of the cabals: who was in, who was not.

Curtis had never wavered in thinking that the plot had to be closely held. "We can't get too many people involved in this because if one us fucking falls behind, gets fucking caught, we're all fucking done." His slogan was "Fucking small numbers," a stance that likely explained the aggressive approach he took toward the couple who arrived at the house soon after the four Crusaders had. The man, Nathan, had attended the July 8 meeting at Trish's for a brief spell and this time brought along his wife, Janina. Until now Curtis had been indulging Patrick's bid for new recruits, and they all had certainly given it their best shot with Trish. But Curtis now seemed impatient with the whole recruiting idea.

"You told her what we're going to talk about?" he said, referring to Nathan's wife.

Nathan laughed uncomfortably.

Curtis bluntly answered his own question: "Killing people and going to prison for life."

"Oh" was all Janina said.

The others joined in with the reality check, led by Patrick, who again rode his anti-Muslim high horse as he outlined a doomsday scenario: "Their objective is to breed you out of existence, to get into the school boards, every city council, the police force."

Curtis added, "This fucking goes on and on. It's fucking scary."

Patrick predicted that if Muslims were not stopped, "the planet is fucking done."

Given all that, Curtis demanded that the couple address the group's fundamental concern: "You gonna kill somebody if we tell you to?"

The meeting became strained. Patrick, maybe looking to ease up, complimented Janina, saying rumor had it that she was a really good shot. She smiled when her husband said it was true. But the couple hadn't yet answered the question, and when Janina vacillated, using the words *probably* and *maybe,* Curtis interrupted.

"I'll tell you what," he said. "I've seen a lot of guys that should've, could've—and never did."

Janina then mentioned her kids. "My babies," she said. "That's all I care about." It was the exact concern Trish had cited. Patrick mentioned the earlier meeting with the absentee host. "Things got a little heated there," Patrick said, which drew a chuckle from Dan, remembering the fireworks between Patrick and Trish.

"We understand the kid situation," Patrick conceded, and Dan acknowledged that deciding whether or not to join the Crusaders was hardly easy. "It took me a year to come around to this way of thinking," he said, drawing again on his putative awakening. "A year ago, you would've asked me, I would've said, 'Naw, I think I'll step back.'"

But, as Patrick had made clear, now was not the time to mince words. When it came to their duty of eradicating Muslims, every single one had to go. "We go on operations," Patrick told the couple. "There ain't no fucking leaving one behind." No matter the gender or age, he repeated, every Muslim had to be eradicated, even the women and children.

"If I'm on a mission?" he said. "The little fuckers are going bye-bye." He got no protest from his group.

Gavin said a young Muslim was a "TIT—terrorist in training." Curtis said that sparing the children risked detection. "I don't want nobody that can talk and point and say, 'Yeah, I can draw a picture of 'em.'" Dan indicated he was no different. He turned to Patrick. "Remember that time we went and drove around," he said, "and there's little fucking Muslims in their dress, and there's a mother." He was dredging up the winter day he'd ridden around Garden City, showing Patrick where Somalis lived.

Patrick nodded—of course he remembered.

"They're out there all decked out, you know, a little three-year-old or something," Dan said. He replayed Patrick's next move—making a finger-gun, aiming it at the small girl, and pretending to shoot her, a mime performance underscoring that eradication of Muslims meant killing every one of them. Dan then told the couple how in that moment he understood he had to decide if he had the stomach for killing children.

"Up to that point I didn't know if I could," he said. The outcome was nothing short of a revelation. "I realized it has to be done, you know?" Dan said.

Dan saw that Patrick was looking at him approvingly, and he knew he'd succeeded in exploiting the moment to further burnish the story of his evolution into a Crusader. He'd turned the incident—which in real time had left him horrified—into fodder to strengthen his persona as Dangerous Dan, a move that actually said more about his evolution as an FBI informant.

The cockroaches gotta go, as Patrick always liked to say. "To save the country, to save the future for my kids, my grandkids, your kids and grandkids," summarized Patrick a little while later. "That's what this is all about."

WHEN ALL was said and done, Nathan and his wife bowed out—just like Trish and the handful of others they'd met with. Sympathetic to the Crusaders' cause and passionately anti-Muslim, the potential recruits nonetheless would not go on the attack. Later Dan asked Patrick and Curtis what had happened to Nathan, and the two were evasive, as they'd been concerning Brody, saying only that Nathan wasn't part of things but not to worry, he wouldn't turn them in. He was still with the KSF, they said, although he rarely joined the nightly Zello calls anymore.

In a way, Curtis had won out; he'd wanted the group to stay small, and so it would—a foursome consisting of him, Patrick, Gavin, and Dan. In their view, the nation's fate rested in their hands, and by their actions they would inspire a patriotic uprising to cleanse America of the Muslim stain. That July 18 the group finally wrapped up their meeting at Trish's house deep into the night. Dan brought up the importance of secrecy, saying they had to assume they were being watched. "I don't know if we are," he said, "but you take all those things into consideration."

Curtis said, "Dan just brought up a good point." Security had to be uppermost in their minds. "Every time we have a meeting, every time we talk or anything like that, we've just got to fucking plan that they are listening." Cell phones were to be deposited in their cars prior to every meeting, he said. On calls, use codes, say little.

Curtis stressed that their bond of secrecy was their greatest protection against law enforcement, especially the FBI, from catching wind of their intentions. "They will make you talk," he warned of the FBI. "I don't know if you guys agree with that."

"They will," Gavin nodded.

"Oh, yeah," Dan concurred.

The FBI had ways, Curtis said. "They will make you talk. I don't care how fucking bad you are."

Gavin was the one who finally noticed the late hour; he rose and said he needed to split, which prompted Patrick to seek a bottom line for their sprawling discussion before everyone left. "Where do we start?" he said to the commander. "What do we do?"

"We need to fucking pick something out in Garden City," Curtis said, "and start fucking planning it."

The one caveat, Curtis said, was if suddenly Dan got intel that busloads of new refugees were arriving. They might want to kick into action on short notice if that were to happen. But otherwise they should take the necessary time to select a location.

Patrick seemed satisfied. "If we can pick where we want to start, we can start recon fucking right away."

Curtis then suggested they meet weekly. The question was where. Was there a location that was both secure and equidistant from their hometowns — Dan from Garden City, Patrick from outside Dodge

City, Curtis and Gavin from the Liberal area? When one of them mentioned the truck stop in the tiny town of Sublette as basically halfway, Curtis shook it off as too public, not a place where they'd be able to talk openly.

Gavin offered a solution: "My office." He meant the office of G&G Home Center, his family's business in Liberal. "We can meet in there any fucking time." It wasn't a perfect solution; Dan and Patrick faced an hour-long drive. But it was certainly secure, and with security of paramount importance, the matter was settled. G&G Home Center in Liberal would basically serve as the Crusaders' home office.

By the time they walked out of Trish's house it was nearing midnight, and everyone was pretty much spent. "I'll be in touch," Gavin sighed to Dan as each was climbing into his vehicle.

"All right, bro," Dan said. "Take care."

Dan headed down the dirt road under a full moon, the headlight beams of his Chevy Impala cutting across the flat fields. He called FBI agent Amy Kuhn to report he'd left Trish's and would be back in Garden City in about twenty minutes. She said she'd meet him at the FBI office—unless, that is, he worried they might be following him.

Dan didn't think so. "They're taking different ways back," he said. "I'll be okay."

He next called Brandon. "Hey, punk," he said, "I'm on my way back." He told his son that he first had to swing by the FBI office and wouldn't be home for another hour or so. He also told Brandon he was starving, was going to make a pit stop at McDonald's.

"What do you want?" he asked his son. "McChicken?"

That sounded good to Brandon. They ended their call.

"Whew, man, I'm tired," Dan said to himself—and to the recording device.

With the take-out order in hand a few minutes later, Dan parked his car in a lot adjacent to the FBI office. He walked in the dark through a row of barrier bushes to the rear of the office, where he gently knocked on the door. Within seconds it squeaked open. Kuhn and Robin Smith let him in, and Kuhn took possession of the device. "It's approximately 11:55 p.m.," she stated, "and this will conclude the recording of Minuteman."

By early summer, Dan's double life as Crusader and FBI informant had settled into something of a routine. It wasn't a dull, monotonous routine, however. It was marked instead by festering anxiety. Dan had never been much of a solid sleeper, suffering from periodic bouts of insomnia, so that on most days he'd get up before 7 a.m. already feeling tired. He'd then work with Brandon for a few hours on his son's landscaping and lawn jobs before it got really hot. He'd return home and nap for an hour or so—that is, if he could fall asleep. He'd spend the afternoon juggling online buying and selling as well as making sure his family's ongoing commitments were met—the kids' schooling and after-school jobs, his wife's medical appointments, and the household's everyday errands. Throughout, he'd take calls from Patrick, who phoned frequently, at random times. Patrick would just be looking to pass the time, blow off steam, talk about his dark hopes and dreams for a Muslim-free nation. What worked for Patrick, shouting into the phone and killing time while working in the field, was intrusive for Dan.

Dan usually managed to have dinner with his family unless he had to run off to a meeting—such as the secret recruiting sessions held at Trish's house—or attend a training exercise. Then, afterward, came the militia's Zello calls. They were held practically every night, usually lasting upward of two hours. In all, his undercover work had evolved over nine months from a casual calling into a full-time occupation. Dan, and his family, knew it had overtaken his life; the commitment deepened and dominated.

The Zello calls in particular became a centerpiece of the family's evenings. While Dan, and especially his FBI handlers, would have preferred to keep actual details of his involvement with the Crusaders from Cherlyn, Brandon, and Alyssa, it wasn't possible. The reason wasn't simply that the Day family was close, with few secrets kept and everyone sharing their daily lives. It was mainly that their shoebox-shaped house was small. Even if Dan had been determined to keep the militia calls off-limits to his wife and kids, the close quarters made that a physical impossibility.

The nighttime ritual started shortly after 9 p.m., when Dan stepped into the master bedroom and got set up on the bed, with the FBI's recording device positioned next to his cell phone. As Dan's compatriots checked in—Orkinman for Patrick, Sparky for Gavin, and so on—their voices were audible beyond the bedroom. The rest of the family was forced to get used to the often loud proceedings; they found a way to get on with their own business in other parts of the tiny house. Until the school year ended, Brandon and Alyssa were juggling schoolwork and socializing on their smartphones. In the living room, Cherlyn, substituting entertainment for reality, followed several television series featuring police and FBI procedurals. It was the equivalent of getting lost in a page-turner written by the likes of a crime novelist: Michael Connelly, Laura Lippman, or Ann Rule. When the shows ended and as Dan's meetings ran late, she'd head to bed. There was simply no way to avoid the activity on Dan's side of the room, so she would either listen in on the militia meeting or try reading a book. Eventually she'd manage to fall asleep.

During the initial phase of Dan's work, when the Zello calls were still a novelty and Dan seemed more a Peeping Tom for the FBI than someone playing the role of an active co-conspirator, he sometimes felt that the meetings sounded like a broken record of repeated rants: against Muslims and in support of gun rights, the Constitution, and readiness for when the SHTF. They dragged on, and because of Dan's general state of exhaustion, he actually fell asleep during an especially long one. After, as FBI technicians listened and transcribed the recording, they were puzzled by the sound of heavy breathing—and Dan had to explain that it was him, snoring.

Early on, Brandon considered the meetings oddly entertaining. He'd sit on his parents' bed and eavesdrop. When the participants reviewed that day's news, he was amused by how everyone thought his father was practically a genius, the way he talked so knowledgeably about what was going on around the world. Brandon knew his father had simply checked CNN online minutes earlier. Brandon was also fascinated and horrified by the group's obsession with the radical right-wing talk-show host Alex Jones and other similar conspiracy theorists who saw bogeymen everywhere. He'd listen, incredulous, as Patrick and the others heatedly cited the proliferation of wind turbines on the Great Plains as proof that President Obama had built underground tunnels to hide the UN troops he intended to deploy in order to stay in office a third term. Patrick insisted that the sleek turbines occupying thousands of acres—hundreds upon hundreds of them, right outside his hometown, Wright—were used to pump air into the tunnels so that the troops stationed underground could breathe. Brandon's jaw dropped as he listened to such malarkey, which sounded almost comical. But in fact Patrick and his cohorts were dead serious.

Brandon's sister, Alyssa, meanwhile found nothing entertaining about the calls. To her they were a horror show. She'd have homework to finish or was just trying to relax and fall asleep, and she wanted the chorus of darkness to stop. But no way. Her bedroom closet aligned with her parents' closet, and the shared wall made it seem as if they were all in the same room. The Zello call was on a speaker, so that the FBI recorder could pick up the dialogue, which meant Alyssa heard everything loud and clear—and what she heard distressed her: the hate, the endless expletives, and the blood-curdling descriptions of what a caller would like to do to a Somali, the president, Hillary Clinton—take your pick. That her dad joined in and was all rah-rah, acting as a cheerleader, was further upsetting. She imagined the men as hulking, three-hundred-pound rednecks. *Monsters*, she thought.

Once, when curiosity got the better of her, she left her bed and went into her parents' room. She studied her father; his face looked normal

—it was her dad. But the words coming out of his mouth made it seem as if he were possessed. To reach an accommodation of sorts, she found herself tapping into lessons learned at school. After the debate season had ended, she'd joined a competitive acting group in the winter, which was run by the debate teacher. Unexpectedly, the acting exercises—a first for her—proved helpful as she processed the "weirdness" at night at home. Instead of despairing that her father had actually uttered certain unspeakable things, she drew a parallel to her acting class. Her father was not a monster, she'd tell herself; he was just pretending to be one, playing a role. By repeating that to herself, she put the awful talk on the other side of the paper-thin wall into perspective; it became background noise.

THE CALLS turned more menacing after the meeting on June 14, when Patrick had let loose his war whoop. There was a detectable shift in tone, and the talk became more urgent, more action-oriented. The number of calls increased too. The usual general Zello meetings with KSF members continued, but added on afterward were more private ones in the Zello chat room Patrick had created for the Crusaders. It allowed the four key members to plan, though they did not make specific plans for carrying out whatever plot they'd eventually agree on. Rather, they used this Zello call mainly to arrange a later, in-person meeting, where they'd be able to speak freely—Curtis consistently pushed this stepped-up caution. He was always after them to speak vaguely or employ their homemade code words. In addition to all that, Patrick began calling Dan afterward on his cell, a one-on-one that Patrick increasingly came to depend on, to sound off.

Dan's work for the FBI was eating up more and more of his time as summer progressed. No surprise, then, that between the time commitment, his cumulative tiredness, and the mission's ever-increasing stakes, there came a night when he faltered. It happened on a Zello call following the June 14 turning point, when Patrick was seeing if he could interest others in the militia to join the plot-in-progress. Ordinarily, after arranging the FBI device and his cell phone on his bed, Dan turned on the recorder to announce the date, the time, and the fact he was recording the KSF on a Zello call, identifying Curtis and Patrick per their rank. Once the recorder was up and running, Dan next pushed the Zello button on his phone to enter the meeting. This time, however, he carelessly reversed the order. He was already connected into a live Zello call when he began speaking into the FBI recorder, robotically reciting from memory his standard introduction: the date, the time, and, using his KSF moniker as well as Curtis's, continuing: "This is Minuteman here at a KSF meeting with Ichiban . . ."

Dan stopped in midsentence. He'd glanced down at his cell phone and realized he was already on the Zello call, and that others were on it too. He froze. If he'd been half asleep moments before, he was wide awake now. There followed a hard quiet, as eerie as a cold winter stillness across the prairie. He didn't dare say another word as his mind reeled, as he asked himself, *Do they know? Is it over? Should I go get my gun?* He didn't know what to think, and he waited.

Curtis spoke first. "I'd like to know what the hell that was."

Dan said nothing. Of all the people to mess up with—Curtis.

Someone else asked, "What the hell was Dan saying?"

Dan couldn't tell who that was.

"Saying something about me," Curtis replied, his tone suspicious.

Dan felt as if he'd stopped breathing. Then he heard a voice that was all too familiar.

"You're fuckin' paranoid," Patrick called out. "Damn it, Commander, you're gettin' old—old and paranoid. You're seeing little helicopters and shit above you."

Laughter started and, following Patrick's lead, others teased Curtis too. Dan had an opening and he took it, summoning as best he could a good ol' boy guffaw. "I was just joking, man," he said. "What the hell. I was just screwin' around with ya. Sorry 'bout that."

The meeting got underway, but Dan stayed on edge. Brandon and Cherlyn joined him in the bedroom, having heard the commotion and noticing something was not right. They saw that Dan was agitated, perspiring. When the meeting ended, Dan anxiously explained to them the misstep; still uncertain, he called his FBI handlers in a semi-panic to report the possible security breach. The next day, the agents forwarded the recording to analysts who, after listening, thought Dan was okay, that the razzing had worked to distract everyone from the blunder. Dan was relieved but emotionally spent—a near miss, he thought. And he'd been rescued from a potentially bad outcome by none other than Patrick himself.

THE STRESS was a slow burn, like smoldering coals. It wasn't as if Dan was in a perpetual state of fright. In his view, "there's a difference between being scared and being concerned." And he was now, as he put it, always concerned when he was in the company of Patrick, Curtis, and Gavin. "I was going out there by myself," he said of the situation. "I never knew if they'd learned that I was working with the FBI. I didn't know if I was going to go sixty miles—drive sixty miles from my hometown, from my home—and be set up when they found out." That's what became constant—the worry that his life was in danger at each and every meeting.

The stress flared into other aspects of family life. Near the end of her freshman year, Alyssa had started dating a boy—her first boyfriend ever. She was fully aware she'd become enthralled in the new relationship, part of being a "crazy in love teenager," as she later called it. The young couple were together a lot, and Dan began acting more protective. When Alyssa asked about going out at night, Dan initially refused to let her. He cited his undercover work, how it had now taken a turn and become more dangerous and uncertain. Something could happen at any time, he warned her. They had to be cautious and stay safe. Bottom line: he didn't want her out at night.

But Alyssa fought back, arguing with her father: "This is SOOO stupid. Nothing's going to happen." She and her boyfriend were just going to a movie theater. How could that be dangerous? In the end, she usually managed to wear Dan down, convince him to let her go out on a date.

Even so, as his concern ramped up, Dan introduced his version of an emergency-response plan. By then, it had become his practice to assemble his wife and kids in his bedroom to update them on his undercover work, provide a periodic risk assessment of sorts. Just as the Zello calls were taking an ominous turn, so too did the family meetings. Dan was increasingly anxious for everyone's safety. He had always been careful to never tell Patrick where they lived in Garden City. He'd led Patrick to think they had an apartment. But, as he told his family, Patrick would be able to figure out the address quickly if he really wanted too—and Dan feared that if his FBI cover got blown, Patrick would "go Stein," meaning that he and the others would immediately want to hunt him down. There was a chance, he said, that they'd show up in the middle of the night.

Dan instituted certain defense measures. He got a dog, a pit bull he named "Sarge" after his late father, a World War II army sergeant. He figured both dog and man shared similar physical traits—short and stocky, always ready for a good fight. Then he placed an AR-15 semi-automatic rifle at his bedside, within arm's reach. He hid a handgun in a kitchen cabinet, informing Cherlyn and Brandon about its exact location. And he put a shotgun in the basement. If Patrick and his allies busted into the house to get at him, he imagined that the pit bull would sound the alarm while going for the intruders. Meanwhile, he'd rush to the front while Cherlyn and Alyssa stayed in the back bedroom and

A replica of the Statue of Liberty, a beacon of freedom and liberty, stands in front of the courthouse in Garden City. *William E. Fischer Jr.*

Dan Day (center), a junior, pictured in the Garden City High School yearbook, 1984.
Finney County Historical Society

All photos are courtesy of the US Department of Justice unless otherwise noted.

Patrick Stein.

Curtis Allen.

Gavin Wright.

ABOVE: Patrick Stein hung these posters in his trailer home.

LEFT: KSF commander Curtis Allen's militia card.

Meeting 1

Mc
Brody
Shelby
DAN
Curtis

1) Small Incidents – 1–3 @ time
2) Recon – Recon – Recon
3) Surveillance of mosques
4) Housing Locations – Mapped
5) Shiite vs Sunni War
6) Mexicans vs Cockroaches

EXH 97-a
Page 9

Patrick Stein's to-do list for the initial meeting he called to discuss attacking Muslims in southwest Kansas, in retaliation for the ISIS-inspired terrorist killings at the Pulse nightclub in Orlando, Florida, on June 12, 2016.

FILE NUMBER:	266T-KC-7542690-1D7
DATE:	06/14/2016
TIME:	6:00 p.m. (1800 hours)
RECORDING NUMBER:	1D7
LENGTH OF RECORDING:	03:23:58
LOCATION:	GARDEN CITY, KANSAS / LIBERAL, KANSAS
PARTICIPANTS:	S-73282 (Confidential Human Source)
	PATRICK STEIN
	BRODY BENSON
	SHELBY LEWIS
	SA AMY KUHN (FBI)
	SA ROBIN SMITH (FBI)

This is SA (Special Agent), this is SA Amy Kuhn. It is June 14th, 2016. It's approximately six (6) o'clock p.m., and I am turning on a recording device to give to Minute Man to go to a meeting with Patrick Stein up by Hutchinson, Kansas.

SA KUHN:	(on phone) Hello, okay. Yeah, we're pulling in and you're being recorded just so you know. Bye.
CHS:	(Walking) (music in background) OK, I'm here, they dropped me off (unintelligible). I'm walking through the mall right now. I'll be out there in a second. Uh, I'm walking towards that side. Okay. Hello, Hello, Hey. It's going to be, I might not be able to call you. The phone's going dead okay. Tell mom that okay. I love you, bye.
CHS:	Mm, fuck. Oh, sheez. Talk about a bad fucking day. ← 13 A
STEIN:	Well, I guess so.
CHS:	Sorry about that, man. Oh, shit. Gonna make it in time for the?

The meeting that Patrick Stein organized on June 14, 2016, was the first one recorded by the FBI informant Dan Day. This is the first page of the transcript of that meeting, with Dan Day referred to by his code name, "Minute Man," and identified as CHS, or confidential human source.

Halima Farah (far left), Ifrah Ahmed (second from right), and friends at the community dinner to celebrate Somali culture at a Garden City public school, June 2016.
Benjamin Anderson

A group of attendees at the community dinner, June 2016. *Benjamin Anderson*

Adan Keynan's popular African Shop on West Mary Street in Garden City.

The Garden Spot Apartments on West Mary Street, the home of many Somalis and a target in the Crusaders' bomb plot.

An aerial view of the Garden Spot Apartments. The Crusaders met at Gavin Wright's G&G Home Center to decide where to place explosive devices at this site in order to kill as many Somalis as possible.

Gavin Wright's business in Liberal, Kansas, where the Crusaders met to plot their attack against Muslims in Garden City.

Not enforsing our Borders. Illegally
Bringing in Muslims by the thousands.
Top US Officials Being above the
Law. Top officials in our Govt
Taking Donations & Bribes From
Foreign Nations. The U.S. Govt
passing Laws & executive orders that
go directly against the Constitution
Allowing U.S. Companies to "pack up"
& move totally overseas destroying
our manufactoring & JOB BASE. The
Current Administration is even giving
Jobs to overseas Companies & importing the
LABOR. We have to take A stand.
TAKE A stand Before its too Late too!
IT Might Already Be! We are
trying to do just that with this
manifest. We know whats going
on! This is A wake up Call to
everyone else. All the people who
Care about this country, Everyone
who know's somethings wrong but
have been afraid to Admit it. Any
Groups that Believe in the
Constitution. It's Time. The Govt,

Media and all the different
Social Media [illegible] have brainwashed
This Country into A lull-ness, A Lackadasical

Making foreign treaties that the people,
including our Representatives Cannot
even see. Signing agreements & laws
with the U.N. completely stripping
us of our Constitutional Freedoms.
Current Congressmen being above the
law ~~& [illegible]~~

Euphoria that could care less what
the Govt. Does. Well the time
has come for us that do Care to
Take A stand. It's Time to do
what the Govt hopes we will never
do!! that's Come together as A
nation, as A people. We must
begin to make our voices heard
while we still Can. Remember—
A Divided people have no voice.
And that's exactly where we are
now: Divided. This is a [illegible]

America I want to share
some information with you.
~~The Govt~~ Over the Last Few
years the main stream Media
+ Govt. has Been telling you,
Veterans, Christians, & Assorted
Groups are Domestic terrorists.
I Am basically all the above.
and I am A threat to no person.
What all these groups have
in Common is this. They Believe
in the Constitution. They Believe
in Reinstating the Constitution.
The Constitution the very Govt.
keeps Ignoring. In the near
Future you will see Certain
Actions to Reinstate our Constitution
And you will also see the Govt
& Media telling you we are
Domestic terrorists. Please Do not Fall
For this. We the people have to take
Back Control of our Govt.

Excerpts from the manifesto that Curtis Allen was drafting for release to the national media after the Crusaders' bombing attack on Somalis in Garden City.

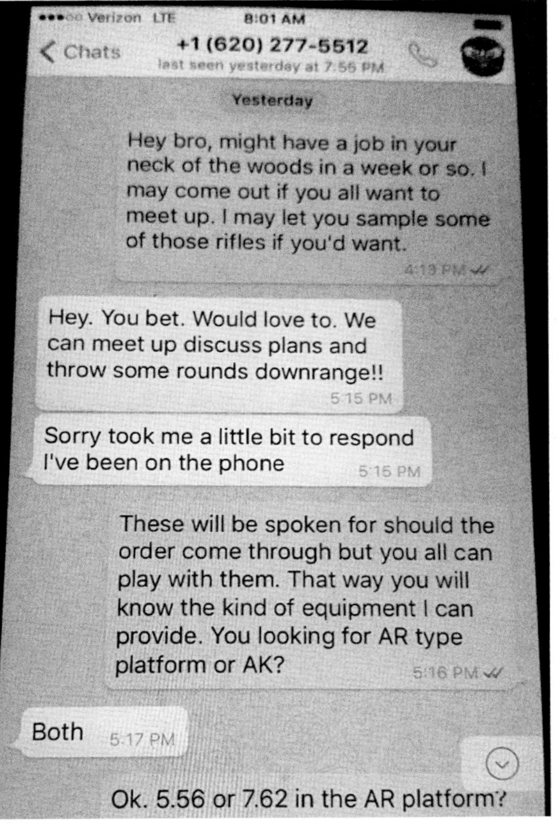

ABOVE: The trailer home (center) that Curtis Allen shared with his girlfriend.

LEFT: Texts between Patrick Stein and the FBI undercover operative "Brian" about meeting in Kalvesta in October 2016 to shoot automatic weapons and continue discussing the attack on Somalis.

The prosecution team in the 2018 federal trial of *The United States of America v. Curtis Wayne Allen, Patrick Eugene Stein, and Gavin Wayne Wright.* From left to right: Assistant US Attorney Anthony M. Mattivi, Assistant US Attorney Risa Berkower, Assistant US Attorney Mary J. Hahn, and the FBI agents Amy Kuhn and Robin Smith. *Anthony Mattivi, with permission of the trial team*

Adan Keynan, Benjamin Anderson, and Dan Day in the African Shop, August 2019. *Courtesy of the author*

Dan Day (left) receiving a community service award from Michael Utz, the Garden City police chief, November 2020. *Cherlyn Day*

alerted 911. Brandon's job was to race to the basement, grab the shotgun, and surprise the home invaders from there.

During these discussions Dan also mentioned that at some point in the investigation they all might have to suddenly flee Garden City and enter witness protection, a possibility that did not go over well at first with Brandon. Like his younger sister, he was in the throes of a new relationship with a girl, who happened to be his sister's best friend. He didn't like the idea that the entire family might simply have to disappear. He wanted to explain the circumstances to his girlfriend, so that if they did have to leave, she would know why. Dan balked at first, but Brandon persuaded him that she could be trusted. He then followed his father's instructions to disclose only the basics, and his girlfriend, although taken aback by the news that Dan had infiltrated a militia for the FBI, promised to keep the secret.

THE PREPARATIONS helped ease Dan's mind a bit, but they didn't stop the worry demons from haunting him, especially in moments when he was by himself and had plenty of time to think—like during rides, which could take up to an hour or more, to Crusader meetings. He'd have ample time to take stock of his undercover work—and to consider the price paid beyond the physical tiredness. For example, the risk, which he'd once viewed as principally involving him only, now extended to the rest of his family; this fact left him feeling guilty for ever having agreed to do the FBI's bidding. The way the Crusaders discussed what they'd like to do to landlords and their families for renting to Somali refugees—the threats of robbery, rape, and murder—chilled him to the bone and contributed to his mounting anxiety about the family. What might happen to them if his role as an informer was exposed?

Then there was the persona he'd cultivated. Maintaining his facade—convincing Patrick Stein, Curtis Allen, and Gavin Wright—that he was right with them, arm in arm in their anti-Muslim crusade, exacted a toll. It wasn't just that he had to be careful about how he talked when he was with them, ever mindful of the FBI dictum that he could get along and go along with the cabal but not plant ideas or introduce specific actions. Rather, it was the content, the words they shared, oozing with bigotry and bloodthirsty determination to go after Somalis. Like when he announced he had been transformed, ready to murder Muslim children as necessary to the extermination plan. Making these statements left him feeling soiled and anti-Christian. It ate away at him. Though he was not a regular churchgoer, he considered himself a religious person.

The rabbit hole of soul searching deepened. Dan started questioning the use of deception, the very foundation of his work. He wrestled with the idea that, put simply, lying was immoral. The Crusaders' goals were certainly abhorrent, but the massive deceit he'd constructed in order to infiltrate the group went against biblical teachings about mendacity. This thinking tied him up in knots.

Beset by an apparent FBI-informant midlife crisis, Dan talked to his son, a natural outlet because of their closeness and Brandon's deeply religious outlook. It was not unusual for them to discuss God and spirituality; they'd actually had testy talks over the past year, when Brandon disclosed that he was seriously considering converting to Catholicism. Dan first shared his angst with Brandon in late June, just as Patrick was pushing for additional recruits. Initially Brandon just listened as his father described his inner struggle to justify the undercover work. He saw that his father was looking for reassurance that he was doing the right thing morally, despite the risks and lies. Brandon didn't know what to say exactly, except to be generally supportive, tell his father that he was doing the right thing, and that God understood. They prayed too.

A few weeks later, in early July, Dan again confided in his son. This time, however, Brandon was ready. He had prepared just as he would for a debate competition at school; he had done his homework, found evidence that supported his position. He told his father the story of the unlikely biblical heroine named Rahab. In the book of Joshua, Rahab, a "harlot" from Jericho, protected two Israelite spies from capture by lying to her fellow Canaanites regarding their whereabouts. The lie gave critical aid to the Israelites in their eventual defeat of the Canaanites and takeover of Jericho, their promised land. Rahab's deception served the greater good—it was an act of bravery and faith illustrating the power of God.

Moreover, Brandon argued that his father's false front did not even trigger considerations as to whether lying was ever ethically justifiable. In his research he'd discovered that the "prevailing theological opinion" on lying was that, by definition, it meant withholding information from people who were entitled to it. Patrick and his supporters were *not* entitled to information about Dan's undercover role. Why? Because if they knew the truth, it could result in injury, or worse, to the Somalis, to Dan, and to his family. Without Dan's monitoring, the Crusaders might more easily carry out their deadly plot and elude detection. Ipso facto, Brandon's father had good reason—an obligation, even—to maintain his mask.

As the summer progressed, Brandon's reassurances helped Dan work through moments of self-doubt. "I prayed about it," Dan said of his FBI persona and the moral dilemma it imposed. "I felt a peace come over me, like that's what I was supposed to do. So I continued."

By July 2016, the FBI case agents Amy Kuhn and Robin Smith had acquired a fuller sense of Patrick Stein's volatility and dangerousness, mainly from Dan's interactions and his secret recordings but also from other sources. One was Patrick himself. He could not contain himself, despite Curtis's warnings to the group to keep their heads down on social media. On July 4 Patrick posted on Facebook an Independence Day screed that, while falling short of outing the Crusaders' secret intent, sounded off on every one of his hot-button obsessions. "I'm a RACIST for criticizing our COCKROACH loving potus and his MUSLIM BROTHERHOOD CABINET!!" he sneered. "I'm a TERRORIST because I'm not afraid to stand up for what's right . . . I'm a TROUBLEMAKER for supporting the 2nd Amendment."

Confirmation came from another source four days later, on July 8. That day, Patrick paid a visit to a cousin, a sergeant on the Dodge City police force. Still in recruiting mode, Patrick said he and a few select associates were aiming to confront the Muslim problem in the area. His cousin's reaction was not supportive in the way Patrick was hoping for, however. Afterward the sergeant wrote an email to his chief, laying out his concerns about Patrick's heated rhetoric. The chief considered the email and decided to forward it to the resident FBI agents, Kuhn and Smith, in Garden City. The agents quickly followed up. They made no mention of the open investigation of Patrick and the Crusaders. Instead the agents told the chief they appreciated the heads-up, asked that the sergeant get in touch if he heard anything else from Patrick, and said that they'd take it from there.

Patrick might be the unpredictable live wire, but Curtis, in his own way, proved to be another one to watch. Calm in tone by comparison, he was capable of flaring up unexpectedly—a lesson Dan would learn when the Kearny County Fair came to an end. Most KSF members returned for the last day: Patrick, Dan, but not Gavin, who needed to staff his home center in Liberal. Others included Trish and her husband.

Their daughter by this time had won the turtle race. Curtis came with Lula, whom he was living with.

On the ride to the fairgrounds, Curtis mentioned to Lula that at some point he'd be meeting privately with Patrick and Dan. Lula wasn't surprised; she already knew Curtis and the others were up to something. It was hard not to, having moved back in with him. Curtis, whose hearing following his military service wasn't 100 percent, had been putting the nightly Zello calls on speakerphone. He did the same for his separate calls with Patrick. Like members of Dan's family, Lula therefore heard plenty of their talk about Muslims, President Obama, and the end of the world. Curtis had also begun to plunk himself down in the living room recliner after dinner to watch YouTube videos on how to make homemade explosives.

Lula decided she had little use for Patrick. She'd not taken a shine to him when Curtis first introduced them at an IHOP in Dodge City. And it had only gotten worse. There was the night Curtis and Patrick were talking on the phone when someone knocked on their trailer's front door. Curtis handed Lula the phone, saying she should talk to Patrick while he went to see who it was. Lula and Patrick chatted awkwardly for a moment; then Patrick started asking how she was feeling after her cancer treatments. Without really waiting for an answer, he then asked a question that gobsmacked her: if her next cancer scan did not come back good, would she be willing to do something for the sake of the country?

"What might that be?" she wondered aloud.

Would she become a suicide bomber for them?

Patrick continued his pitch, saying he'd asked another friend, a woman named Jennifer who had breast cancer, if she'd consider doing the right and patriotic thing. But Lula, recovering from the shock of his proposal, interrupted him. She told Patrick, no friggin' way. Suicide bomber? Good for the country? She didn't think so. Besides, her scans were going to come back good. She was a warrior, she said, and had no doubt she was going to beat the cancer that had worn her down but not broken her. End of conversation.

EVERYONE MET up at the recruitment table that the KSF militia had staffed all week at the fair. On display were photographs of the damage caused by tornadoes on July 7. They had ripped through Eureka, Kansas, about 270 miles east of Garden City, and some KSF members had driven there to assist locals in the days after the tornadoes had touched down. Though about ninety homes and a mill had been damaged, no serious injuries or deaths had occurred. The recruitment table was also stocked with informational materials promoting aspects of the militia favored by Trish, Daniel, and other "preppers." They saw the KSF as a community-focused group that ensured members' safety, provided survival training, and safeguarded constitutional rights in the event of a natural disaster, civil unrest, or a government breakdown. The goals of its spin-off, the Crusaders, were of course not included in the public display; its operation was a closely held secret—more or less. Because of Patrick's failed bid to recruit additional conspirators, other members of the militia were aware of those goals.

The group spent the afternoon enjoying the last of the fair. A large barbecue had been set up at one end of the grounds, but by the time they headed over and got in line, all the picnic tables were filled, so they carried their food back to their booth. Members of militias from Missouri and Colorado attending the fair wandered over. With Patrick around, the conversation inevitably turned to Muslims. He and Curtis jokingly proposed a dark and terrorizing stunt. In coordination, they said, their militia groups should pick a day when each group would take a pig (an animal that Muslims considered unclean), slit its throat, and then release it into a local mosque, creating a squealing bloody mess. The idea got a round of laughs, with everyone agreeing that it would surely send a clear signal to Muslims: they were unwelcome, no matter where they sought to settle.

Lula also overhead Patrick and Curtis talking with Dan about his volunteer work at Catholic Charities, where supposedly Dan was working to obtain inside information from the resettlement agency about the next arrival of Somalis to Garden City. The fair was actually the first time she'd met Dan Day in person, though she'd heard his voice plenty of times on the Zello meetings. For a while late that afternoon, the two had found themselves at the booth by themselves, so they sat around making small talk. She thought him harmless, a big marshmallow.

For his part, Dan was naked that day. Not naked in a gun owner's sense of the word, meaning weaponless. He had his pocket carry, as always. He was naked in that as an FBI informant, he lacked his usual recording device. The unit had malfunctioned prior to his leaving the FBI office in Garden City. The agents had tried to get it to record properly, but it kept shutting down. Even so, they had wanted Dan to bring the device along to capture dialogue at any point that it happened to be functioning. They'd said the decision was Dan's, of course. But he told them he didn't like the idea. What if, while malfunctioning, it began emitting a strange sound? The device might give him away. He wasn't comfortable taking that chance and had rejected the idea of carrying it, a rare instance of refusing to do as the agents asked.

The fair ended officially at dusk, and as the organizers began closing down the grounds, Patrick reminded Curtis that he wanted to have a quick meeting. Dan wasn't sure if Patrick was talking to him or only to Curtis. He asked, "You talking about me too?"

Patrick gave him a look. "Yeah," he said, as if Dan was being thick-headed. "You're in it." Patrick wanted to set a date to meet at Gavin's workplace so they could start drawing up an actual plan.

Their vehicles were parked in different parts of an overflow lot, so they decided to move them together, next to the fair's horse arena. Dan retrieved his Chevy Impala and pulled in close to Patrick's vehicle. Curtis drove up with Lula; she left to use the restroom and stayed in the car after she returned. Patrick cranked up the music in his truck, and Curtis tossed his cell phone into his car. He ordered Patrick and Dan to do the same. Curtis then walked over and, like some homeland security officer at an airport checkpoint, gave them each a quick pat down. Curtis had never done anything like that before to verify that they'd left their phones behind. The move drew a chuckle from Patrick, but it gave Dan the willies. Had he agreed to bring the tiny recording device, it would have been in his pants pocket, and Curtis likely would have felt it. Not that Curtis would recognize it as a recorder, but he would certainly have wondered what the strange object was. He'd probably have asked Dan some uncomfortable questions, which hopefully he would have been able to deflect. Privately, Dan was relieved he'd refused the entreaties of his FBI handlers.

Patrick and Curtis got going again about the fate awaiting landlords and anyone else, including the mayor of Garden City, who was supportive of Somali refugees. That got Patrick talking animatedly about the need to pick a date to meet at Gavin's workplace and get going on a plan of attack. Then Patrick's phone rang. The three were standing outside Patrick's truck: Patrick at the driver's side, Curtis at the front on the same side, and Dan also at the front. Patrick took a few steps away to take the call. Curtis and Dan were left waiting for him to finish.

Dan was propped against the front hood as Curtis slowly turned away from Patrick and toward him. Dan noticed that Curtis was pulling a handgun from the small of his back as he pivoted in his direction. Legally speaking, Curtis was not supposed to possess, never mind carry, a firearm, due to a domestic battery conviction. He had always ignored the ban, however, and in recent years he had accumulated a small arsenal of weapons, nearly twenty in all.

For that reason, Dan was accustomed to seeing Curtis carry—they all carried, all of the time. But he was *not* accustomed to seeing a Glock 9mm semiautomatic pistol pulled on him. Especially when from day one, the first lesson his dad had taught him was to never point a gun at someone unless you intended to shoot. Plus, Dan knew full well that the Glock, for all its positive attributes, was not equipped with an external safety, which was why he'd stopped carrying one and had gone with the safer Ruger SR9c. The Glock could more easily go off by mistake.

Dan was in semi-shock as Curtis leaned forward and positioned the weapon about two inches from his forehead. Curtis said, "Dan, if any of this gets out, I'm going to put a bullet in your fucking head." The security-obsessed Curtis was at his most paranoid, yet cold and calm in demeanor. Dan felt tied up in knots, at once scared to death and pissed off, and over the next few seconds the anger won out; he reacted instinctively to confront the threat.

He warned Curtis, "If I ever find out it comes from *you,* I'll be the one to put a bullet in *your* fucking head." He shook with rage. "And your girlfriend's head."

Dan then heard Patrick whooping it up. He'd ended his call and was entertained by the sudden standoff at the front of his truck. "Yeah, all right!" he yelled.

Curtis put his pistol away and chuckled. "I just wanted to make sure we're clear," he said coolly. Trying to calm Dan, he said he'd been basically joking around.

Joking around? Hadn't that been Dan's spin—saying he was just messing around—when he'd screwed up with the FBI recorder at the start of a Zello meeting and Curtis got all suspicious? Was this a case of what comes around, goes around? Some kind of payback on Curtis's part? Whatever the reason, the sudden armed challenge left Dan both rattled and furious. He reported the threat to his FBI handlers later, at their debriefing. The moment had truly spooked him, even though Patrick and Curtis laughed it off. Picturing Curtis pointing a pistol at him,

Dan now figured Patrick wasn't the only one to worry about. It seemed Curtis was just as likely to go gunning for him at home if all hell ever broke loose about his undercover work.

THE CRUSADERS finally held their first meeting at Gavin's G&G Home Center ten days later, on July 31. The Sunday morning drive for Dan, from Garden City to Liberal, was quiet and quick. He'd never been to Gavin's business before and found it was located on the outskirts of town, set on a corner lot of scrub grass along Highway 83, a simple prefab trailer serving as both a showroom and Gavin's office. Gavin made a fresh pot of coffee. Curtis had them put their phones in an empty office and then shut its door.

The inaugural meeting proved to be a dud, however. Patrick ended up a no-show; he later explained that an unexpected emergency required his attention. Curtis, Gavin, and Dan then contended with a KSF member who appeared out of blue. The member was the same guy Dan had dealt with in the winter, who'd claimed to have Claymore mines. It had led to the mini-FBI operation to seize the items, which turned out not to be mines at all. Now the guy came into the trailer, talking a mile a minute, saying he'd heard rumors they were planning something. He wanted in. The threesome played dumb, acted as if they knew nothing. They didn't like the guy, didn't trust him, and suspected he was high, either on speed or some other drug, the way he talked gibberish and clearly hadn't slept in a while.

"I just don't understand anything about what you're saying," Curtis said at one point. Then, a few minutes later, Curtis became impatient and cut the guy off. "You gotta go," he said. They ushered him out.

Once he was gone, Dan said dismissively, "He talks, fuckin' big talk, and then later he won't even fuckin' remember, remember half the shit you tell him."

They hung out a bit longer, even after it was clear Patrick wasn't going to make it. Curtis asked Dan how it was going at Catholic Charities, whether he'd been able to get inside yet. Dan said not yet, but he was trying—even though he wasn't. They gossiped about different people they knew, and Dan entertained Gavin with the story of his passing out in the field at the June 14 meeting. "That was fuckin' weird, man," Dan said. "I remember a little bit, but then I get up, and they said I passed out again, and then the ambulance."

"That's fuckin' hilarious," Gavin said. It was a classic militia story now.

They called it quits late morning. "I don't think we can talk about anything without the XO here," Curtis concluded. The session, in the end, had been much ado about nothing. They'd have to reconvene another time, hopefully in the next week or so.

But in the interim, they did get to enjoy another bonding experience. The KSF, including Patrick, went camping at state-owned Jetmore Lake, about an hour east of Garden City. Not limited to the hardcore Crusaders, this was a broader KSF gathering, with some militia members bringing along their spouses. The small lake, popular for swimming and fishing, was partially surrounded by trees but mostly the area was open and flat. There was a shooting range too. Everyone seemed to have fun, save for fighting off chiggers, the nasty little bugs that were hard to spot and left bites that itched like crazy. The group set up tents, got a big bonfire going, ate homemade chili, and drank lots of beer. They blared music and lit up cigars. Dan pulled out a bottle of Crown Royal apple whiskey he'd purchased on the way out. He passed it around, faking a slug when it was his turn. No way did he want to get hammered when he was on an overnight assignment, especially in the company of Curtis.

For his part, Curtis was in full party mode, kicking back. But even as he tied one on, there arose from the boozy haze yet another moment of truth between him and D-Day.

Dan had just handed Curtis the Crown Royal when Curtis locked eyes on him. "Dan Day," Curtis said, nodding his head slightly, then repeating the name. "I can't figure you out."

Dan met his look. "What's there to figure out, man?"

"I don't know," Curtis said. He had a faraway look. Was it the whiskey or the look of someone turning a thought over in his mind? "I guess nothing," he finally said.

Dan replied, "I am what you see, you know."

Nothing further was said. Dan hoped to keep it that way.

And Curtis passed along the Crown Royal to the others at the bonfire.

5

"GO BIG OR GO HOME"

Later that same week, on August 4, 2016, the Republican presidential candidate Donald J. Trump strode onto the stage of the historic Merrill Auditorium in downtown Portland, Maine, to deliver another of his hate-filled, blistering attacks against Muslim immigrants. To a near-capacity crowd of about eighteen hundred, and to the dozens of reporters on hand, he targeted Somali refugees in particular, fully aware that Maine had emerged over the years as a primary destination in the Somali diaspora. Nearly ten thousand Somalis had been resettled in Maine—the whitest state in America—primarily in two cities, Portland and Lewiston.

"Somali refugees," shouted Trump. "We admit hundreds of thousands into Maine and to other places in the United States, hundreds of thousands of refugees. And they're coming from among the most dangerous territories and countries anywhere in the world." It was insane and disastrous policy, he claimed, ensuring high crimes, lawlessness, and infiltration of Islamist terrorists into the United States as refugees. "This could be the great Trojan Horse of all time," he roared to thunderous applause, adding that his opponent, Hillary Clinton, "wants to have them come in by the hundreds of thousands."

The remarks came at a moment when his repeated call for a Muslim ban had again taken center stage in the campaign for the White House. The prior Thursday, at the Democratic National Convention in Philadelphia, a Muslim American who was the father of a US army officer killed in Iraq had denounced Trump's relentless smears against Muslims. Invoking his son's military service, Khizr Khan said of the GOP nominee, "You have sacrificed nothing and no one." Waving a pocket-sized version of the Constitution, he continued, "Let me ask you: Have you even read the United States Constitution? I will gladly lend you my copy."

The speech by Khan, a Harvard-educated lawyer who became a US citizen in 1980, after emigrating from Pakistan, proved riveting, seen by millions of television viewers and described by pundits as one of the convention's most unforgettable highlights. In its wake, Trump could not sit idly by; instead of displaying a modicum of deference to parents of a Muslim American soldier killed by a car bomb, he mocked Khan and his wife, Ghazala. When he was roundly criticized for callousness, he tweeted defensively, "I was viciously attacked by Mr. Khan at the Democratic Convention. Am I not allowed to respond?" And by the time he'd taken the stage in Maine, he'd chosen to further ramp up his anti-Muslim campaign messaging, first by warning of the dangers of Somali immigrants and then by taking direct aim at his Democratic rival, as well as President Obama. "He's a founder of ISIS. He founded ISIS!" Trump told a crowd of cheering supporters in Florida several days later, stressing the president's full name when referring to the "administration of Barack Hussein Obama." Trump added, "I would say the co-founder would be crooked Hillary Clinton."

The candidate's remarks in Maine and Florida—outrageous in their disrespect and mendacity—were applauded by far-right extremists, white supremacists, neo-Nazis, and militia supporters who'd come to expect such histrionic performances in the fourteen months since Trump had first announced his run by promising to build a massive border wall to block Mexican "criminals" and "rapists" from illegally entering the United States. During the past year Trump had won endorsements from a bevy of high-profile white nationalists, as well as leaders of the Ku Klux Klan and the growing militia movement. The latter included several of the "Patriot" occupiers of Malheur National Wildlife Refuge the prior winter, one of whom had launched a profitable online business selling FUCK ISLAM T-shirts. Meanwhile, the chairman of the American Nazi Party was ecstatic. "We have a wonderful OPPORTUNITY here folks, that may never come again," said Rocky J. Suhayda. "Donald Trump's campaign statements, if nothing else, have SHOWN that 'our views' are NOT so 'unpopular' as the Political Correctness crowd have told everyone they are."

In their corner of the country, the self-anointed Crusaders of southwest Kansas were enthralled by the breakout support for Trump. Patrick, Curtis, and Gavin all viewed the 2016 election as critical to the nation's future, and their August meetings, secretly recorded by their fourth co-conspirator, Dan Day, featured a surge in intense hate for their candidate's frequent targets, Hillary Clinton and President Obama. To them, Trump was "the Man," and his staying power had seemed to give them and any like-minded fan permission to let rip a boundless torrent of bigotry and barbarism.

In one exchange, Patrick called Obama's mother—a native Kansan—a "fucking dumb cunt." He said, "To think, a five-cent fuckin' rubber could have prevented that motherfucker from ever being on the planet."

"He's a dirtbag," Gavin said.

"Worse than that."

"Yeah," agreed Gavin, "'cause I've even known dirtbags I could hang with."

"Yeah," Patrick said.

Gavin continued: "I wouldn't even hang with that motherfucker if you paid me a million dollars, I wouldn't fuckin' care."

Patrick said, "I can promise you one thing, if I ever got within a hundred yards of that motherfucker."

"He'd be dead?"

"Yep."

"Yeah," said Gavin. "I could sacrifice my life for that one, I think."

In another session, the group worked itself into a lather fantasizing about an armed road trip across state lines to assassinate "the bitch" Hillary Clinton and her family. Curtis got things rolling: "What if we go to fucking Arkansas and kill everyone involved?"

"Oh, I'd love to, dude," Patrick said. "I'd kill every goddamn one of them."

"Start with fucking Chelsea," Gavin suggested.

The resulting funeral, they realized, would draw targets galore. "You know Obama would be there," Gavin said. "They'd all be there—all of them would be there because they'd be paying their respects to Clinton."

It would be a shooting gallery. Or they could set off a bomb that would take out Obama, along with other officials such as the vice president, Joe Biden, whom they called "Fuckin' stupid Uncle Joe."

"That's, like, the wet dream right there," Gavin gushed.

"We go to Arkansas and kill everybody with that last name," Curtis repeated.

"I would have to go home and jack off after I was done," laughed Gavin.

Patrick one-upped him. "I'd do it while I was there, dude. I couldn't wait."

"Push the button. Push the button," Gavin said.

IN HIS own small way, Curtis began campaigning for Donald Trump. He and his girlfriend, Lula, planted a TRUMP/PENCE sign on the tiny lawn outside their home in Liberal, despite the fact that residents of the trailer park, mostly Hispanic, were upset at Trump's call for a border wall. Situated on a corner lot, the sign got plenty of exposure. When the couple walked around at dusk, taking in the evening air, Curtis engaged neighbors in talk about the election, wanting to know whom they were voting for. He strongly urged them to back Trump, attacked "crooked Hillary," and didn't mince words denouncing Muslims, especially Somalis, saying they were stealing their jobs at the local meatpacking plants.

Midsummer was also a time when relations between Curtis and Lula began to sour—again. They'd initially gotten along fine after Lula had moved back in, in June. Curtis was attentive to the fact her cancer treatments had left her tired and weak. Normally weighing about 120 pounds, she had faded to about 92. Curtis took her out to eat so that she wouldn't have to cook. Plus, they'd get the pleasure of the restaurant's air conditioning. Sometimes Gavin joined them for a beer.

Then the arguments started. By August, Curtis seemed moodier and preoccupied. He was spending less and less time at home. Lula suspected that he was cheating on her, what she called a "conflict of interest." Indeed, over the prior year Curtis had become a semi-regular at the local VFW post and the Branding Iron Restaurant and Club, where he'd been known to hook up occasionally with an available female patron.

Lula also didn't like the fact that he spent more and more time at G&G Home Center with Gavin, Patrick, and Dan. And when he was at home, he was either taking part in a nighttime Zello call, talking on the phone with Patrick, or ensconced in his recliner, watching YouTube videos and studying books on making explosives. Curtis was hard of hearing but refused to wear any kind of hearing aid, so he kept the TV and speakerphone blasting at a high volume. There was no escaping the noise. He loudly played the CD recording of one favorite book—*The Anarchist Cookbook*—so often that Lula came to know its bomb-making recipes by heart. She began thinking about breaking up and contacted a friend about the possibility of moving in with her, in the event that she did decide to bolt.

THE CRUSADERS were not the only ones noticing a cultural change induced by a Trump's corrosive campaign rhetoric. Ifrah Ahmed, comfortably settled into life in Garden City after her arrival three years earlier, detected the shift—sometimes subtle, sometimes not—both at work and around town. She liked her job at the Tyson meatpacking plant, where her responsibilities had continued to increase; she'd gone from being an interpreter to a supervisor of workers in the "harvest," or slaughterhouse. She began realizing that many of her white colleagues were cheering for Trump. She had expected them to be put off by his comments, as she was. This was America, after all, a country, she thought, that "prides itself in diversity and acceptance." It was why, as a refugee in Nairobi, she'd prayed to be allowed to resettle in the United States rather than other free countries, such as Canada or Australia, where her sisters had been sent. But her co-workers apparently were not put off. One, a veterinarian, someone she liked and whose company she enjoyed, had returned from a rally, excited to have had his picture taken with the candidate. The vet tried to soften her impression of Trump, telling her that he wasn't against all immigrants, just illegal ones. Ifrah, who counted Mexicans among her circle of friends, countered that immigrants, whether legal or not, were simply looking for a better life for their families. "Just because they are illegal doesn't mean they are going to harm you," she said. The two had come to a stalemate, and they agreed to disagree.

One day Ifrah was with a friend, browsing the clothing racks at a Target store, when she noticed a man eyeing them. It turned out he was a security guard, and when Ifrah and her friend stepped into a fitting room, the guard was fast on their heels. He ordered them to put down the clothes; a testy exchange ensued. Ifrah wanted an explanation for the intrusion. What had they done wrong? The guard said he was following his gut; he had a feeling they might be shoplifters. He said flat out that he didn't trust them. In all the times she'd shopped at the store, Ifrah had never before experienced profiling. Then, on a weekend night at a dance club she frequented, the disc jockey at one point trained the spotlight on her, her cousin, and a transgender Tyson co-worker. Over the club's sound system, the DJ declared he sure hoped that Trump would *make America great again.* The women tried to laugh it off, but Ifrah found the moment unnerving.

She received yet another jolt when she toyed with the idea of finding a new apartment. Spotting a promising listing, she called the landlord. The man was pleasant on the phone, inviting her to come by for an application. When she did, the landlord's demeanor took a turn. Seeing Ifrah, he said he didn't rent to Somalis.

Ifrah said, "Excuse me?"

He repeated his statement: no Somalis need apply. Ifrah left, stunned by the sheer bluntness.

These shunnings became the kind of thing Somalis shared while gathered socially in the back of Adan Keynan's African Shop. Meanwhile, Adan was having his own troubles. He'd received additional warnings from the city's zoning office that his store was operating illegally—the latest one on July 29. The letter recapped previous warnings: he needed to move. It wasn't as if Adan had not tried to do so. Next to his store on West Mary Street there was a vacant space in a little shopping center, for example. The asking rent was $900 a month—a figure he could afford. But when he went in person to the leasing office, the rent suddenly doubled. It was now $1,900 a month, an amount blatantly overpriced for the area and one he could not afford. Adan brought up the lower figure that had been posted publicly, but the landlord shrugged, saying only that the original listing had been a mistake.

Adan tried submitting an application for another space, this one next to the gas station across the street from his store, but it was rejected. He was told the store was being taken off the market. To test that claim, he had a friend—a white person—apply. The friend was quickly approved, but when both men appeared at the rental office, the landlord started saying they were too late—he'd just rented to another party. Still, the space sat unoccupied. Adan was upset. The most recent warning had extended the deadline another thirty days, to August 29, but what was he supposed to do when landlords were snubbing him, not wanting to rent to a Muslim?

Even so, Adan, Ifrah, and their fellow Somalis, while alert to an uptick in profiling, still considered most Garden City locals welcoming and "warmed-hearted," as Ifrah put it. Relationships they'd established over the prior year with the county hospital executive Benjamin Anderson and Dr. John Birky were a stark contrast to the cold shoulder they sometimes got elsewhere. Inviting each other into their respective homes had been a first for everyone involved, and their friendships continued to solidify, most recently through a medical emergency.

It was after supper one night when Benjamin got a call from Halima Farah, phoning from the apartment at the Garden Spot complex on West Mary Street where her mother, Sara, and Adan Keynan lived. Benjamin detected an urgency in Halima's voice as she explained that her mother was in excruciating pain. But Sara was afraid to go to the doctor, Halima said. Could he do something? In response, Benjamin called Dr. Birky, and together they drove immediately to Adan's apartment—not for dinner this time, but to do a house call. The doctor had Sara lie down on the rug on the living room floor. Then he conducted a musculoskeletal evaluation, carefully examining her joints, muscles, and bones and testing their range of motion and their symmetry. He also looked for any tenderness and areas of unusual warmth. The exam involved plenty of touching, and both Benjamin and Dr. Birky understood the significance of the moment—the trust that had developed between them and the Somalis made it possible for Dr. Birky to touch Sara in his professional capacity. A Muslim woman was permitted physical contact only with her husband or a family member. Even a hug or a handshake was seen as strictly off-limits. Yet Sara let Dr. Birky conduct the exam in front of her husband and daughter, and he did so in a gentle, calming manner.

The doctor suspected that Sara's hip was affected by severe arthritis and suggested that she follow up with an orthopedic specialist to determine exactly the cause of her pain. The information alone was comforting and seemed to reassure not only Sara but also Adan and Halima. Right away Benjamin began mulling over how to make that next step happen. Through his work as a rural hospital administrator he'd had dealings with Angel Flight, the nonprofit network of volunteer pilots who for free fly people needing medical attention, using their own planes and covering expenses out of their own pockets. Benjamin reached out to the group, put in a request for transportation, and followed up. So, near the end of August, Sara boarded a plane at Garden City Regional Airport. She flew first to Lincoln, Nebraska, where she switched to a second plane, which flew to Rochester, Minnesota. Sara was accompanied by a medical student that Benjamin knew, and Benjamin was in Rochester to take her to the appointment Dr. Birky had arranged with a specialist at the world-renowned Mayo Clinic. Further testing verified Dr. Birky's hunch: Sara's hip was the problem, and the orthopedist recommended that she eventually undergo surgery for a hip replacement.

For Sara there was the relief of knowing what was wrong and why —knowledge gained from a whirlwind late-summer trip out of her insular Somali community in Garden City and into what was for her a great unknown. She'd never flown on such a small plane and felt as if she was being treated like royalty by the volunteer pilots and hospital personnel. Benjamin could tell that she seemed overwhelmed by it all, yet also appreciative—as were Adan, Halima, and their friends. He and

Dr. Birky could also tell the trip had been a big deal to the Somalis—a matriarch from their community had gone off and returned two days later, unscathed. Many of the refugees harbored horror stories of past mistreatment and botched procedures from putative medical personnel in their homeland. Here, the intervention had been a success, and Benjamin, Dr. Birky, Adan, Sara, Halima, Ifrah, and the rest sensed that cross-cultural ties had been strengthened. They not only could coexist but also at times be one another's keepers.

"THIS RIGHT HERE," PATRICK said, using Google Earth to point out the West Mary Street location in Garden City. "This entire fucking complex chuck plump full."

Patrick, Curtis, Gavin, and Dan were gathered around the computer in Gavin's G&G Home Center, staring at the sixty-inch monitor tacked to the wall. Patrick zoomed in on one unit in particular. "This is their goddamn mosque right here," he said.

They deposited a pin to mark the Garden Spot Apartments at 312 West Mary Street.

"What is this big complex here?" Curtis asked, noticing a similar-looking set of low-slung brick apartments across the street, at 304 West Mary Street.

"More cockroaches," Patrick said.

"Fucking all of them?" Curtis said.

"Yeah, buddy."

Dan added, "There's another mosque, uh, Burmese mosque over here."

"They're all Muslims?" Curtis seemed incredulous that so many Muslims were squeezed into two sprawling apartment complexes right across the street from each other. How convenient. It was the Muslim equivalent of a cattle feed, where livestock were kept densely corralled and fattened for the slaughterhouse.

"Yeah, yeah, yeah, yeah," Dan said.

It was Monday afternoon, August 8, their second attempt to begin actual planning after the initial effort, on July 31, had been aborted when Patrick was a last-minute no-show. This time everyone was present. Dan, after driving down from Garden City under cloudy skies, had arrived at about 1:20 p.m. He found Patrick already there with Gavin. While waiting for Curtis, the three killed time talking about guns they owned and tornadoes they'd either experienced or known people who had. Looking around the spiffy trailer office that served as a sales showroom, Dan asked Gavin about the business; Gavin talked at length about how his entrepreneurial father had started a mobile home company in Garden City in the late 1960s, which he and his brother had recently taken over, creating G&G.

Dan was attending without backup of any kind—which was now routine. Because of this he had purposely chosen a chair on the far side of the table where they sat, rather than the inside bench. In Dan's mind, if something went awry, he didn't want to find himself stuck behind the table. To have any chance at all, he needed to be free to jump up and flee as directly and quickly as possible. For their part, his FBI handlers, Amy Kuhn and Robin Smith, had scouted the modular office trailer's location to see if they might establish surveillance for Dan when he was inside. But they realized immediately that it wasn't feasible. The office was located on a street corner, a stand-alone structure in an isolated and wide-open part of town. An unmarked vehicle planted down the street would stick out after a while on the blank canvas that was the surrounding area. If agents were discovered outside, monitoring the meetings, Dan's safety would be at risk.

Gavin's suggestion that they use his modular office trailer for their meetings was therefore a good one. It was a safe haven of sorts, where Gavin had full control. It was private and available basically whenever the group wanted to get together. When Curtis arrived soon after Dan did, they followed the precautions Curtis had been adamant about: they locked the door to prevent an unexpected visitor—say, a customer—from walking in on them; they turned up the background music—the Australian heavy metal band AC/DC was a favorite—to guard against what Curtis believed was the NSA's omniscience, its ability to monitor everything from its massive data center in Utah; and, out of an abundance of similar concern, they tossed their smartphones into a separate room.

"Put them back there, yeah," Gavin said, indicating a corner room.

With that they got down to business. "Can you bring it up?" Curtis had said to Gavin at the computer, meaning a 3D map of Garden City on Google Earth. For the next four hours the men debated potential targets, a discussion that was hardly linear and often digressed into related topics: best methods and targets for the attacks and actions to publicize their crusade. Should they target landlords who rented to Somalis? Landlords' families? Garden City officials supportive of immigrants? What about the refugee center in town and the several church organizations providing assistance to Muslim refugees? Or instead of striking in Garden City—which Gavin called "fucking nowhere"—what about a larger, more attention-getting urban area? Wichita? Chicago? Washington, DC? As the group bandied about these various people and locations, both nearby and far afield, they kept coming back to Garden City's Muslim-occupied apartments, mosques, and businesses. While studying the Google Earth map, they spent considerable time dropping "cockroach pins." Patrick and Dan were the best informed because of the drive-around they did when they were aligned with the Three Percenters. The two served as Garden City guides.

"Basically this whole fucking complex," Patrick said, pointing out the stretch along West Mary Street.

Dan nodded, adding, "Yeah, it's kind of a cluster."

Patrick continued: "This whole complex, and then this whole motherfucker right here." Down the street a bit Patrick and Dan then identified the two main Somali businesses—Adan Keynan's African Shop on West Mary itself and, on a back street a block away, the Somalia Wany Mall. Referring to their previous surveillance, Patrick reminded Dan how they'd staked out the African Shop. "Sat right here that one day in front of that building," he said. "Remember them guys come out of the building."

Dan did remember, and he also recalled the owner's vehicle parked out front. "That's where the—that white van was."

Curtis and Gavin took it all in. "Sand niggers," Gavin said.

When it came to killing Muslims, automatic weapons equipped with silencers and rocket-propelled grenades (RPGs) were methods that at various times were proposed and debated, but the group was drawn mainly to deploying big-time explosives.

"What would do some significant damage?" Patrick asked Curtis, the emerging go-to guy on bombs, given his military background and interest in them.

"Fifty pounds of fucking ANFO," Curtis said authoritatively, using the abbreviation for ammonium nitrate/fuel oil, the bulk industrial material favored in bomb making.

IEDs, or improvised explosive devices, had the sweet smell of payback because they were the radical Islamist weapon of choice, as demonstrated in a number of failed bomb plots involving homegrown warriors for the Islamic State. In Portland, Oregon, for example, the Somali-born immigrant Mohamed Mohamud was thwarted in 2010 while trying to detonate a car bomb at a Christmas tree–lighting ceremony teeming with holiday celebrants of all ages. In 2011, in Lubbock, Texas, a Saudi immigrant named Khalid Ali-M Aldawsari, a chemical engineering major at a local college, was busted while rounding up chemicals and equipment to manufacture a bomb in furtherance of ISIS's violent holy war; targets he'd considered included the Dallas home of former president George W. Bush. The prior year in Florida, the ISIS devotee Harlem Suarez was arrested in Key West while preparing a "timer bomb"—a backpack loaded with explosives and galvanized nails. He had planned to leave it unattended at a public beach and detonate it by using a cell phone. There was also the ongoing case, right there in Kansas, involving an ISIS-inspired Wichita man who'd been arrested outside the Fort Riley military base while readying a thousand-pound car bomb. John T. Booker, who'd pled guilty in federal court, was awaiting sentencing.

Explosives would give the Somalis a taste of their own, but more was at stake for the Crusaders—a historical legacy. Patrick and the others viewed their actions in grander terms, as a new chapter in the centuries-old religious conflict between Christians and Muslims. Patrick said their plan was "like the beginning of the fucking Crusades."

"That's it," said Gavin, likewise embracing the historical significance.

"Knights Templar," Patrick asserted. They would be the modern equivalent of the order of devout Christian soldiers who had protected Christians traveling to the Holy Land in the decades after Jerusalem had been freed of Muslim control in 1099.

"Crusades 2.0," Patrick continued.

Dan repeated the phrase, thinking, *How clever: Crusades, the second edition.* "I like that."

"Motherfuckers," Patrick said.

TALKING ABOUT bombs was one thing; getting their hands on them was an altogether different affair. Expertise in explosives was a big hurdle. Dan might know a lot about guns, but bombs? Next to nothing. He'd had no idea what Curtis meant when he'd said "ANFO" and only later learned what it stood for. Patrick often postured as the know-it-all but didn't know much more than Dan. So it fell to Curtis and Gavin, the latter drawing on his skill as an electrician, to take the lead in the Crusaders' self-education in Explosives 101. And the two were adamant that the only sensible approach was to keep their heads down, avoid trafficking in the black market, and manufacture their own devices.

"We could make the shit," Gavin said matter-of-factly at one of the group meetings at Gavin's office.

Curtis felt the same way: do it yourself. Attempting to purchase bombs would be risky and foolish.

"You're going to get set up," Gavin said. "You buy TNT or something, or C-4, somebody is gonna turn your ass in."

In fact, the two were already making headway. Curtis had gotten ahold of books about bomb making and was going through them at home as if studying for an exam, and at G&G's office he and Gavin had spent parts of their workdays scouring the Internet for more information. "We printed off, what, fucking one thousand pages the other day," Gavin bragged. "Every fucking manual you would think of. How to build guns, how to fucking, whatever, make explosives, triggers." The two were building an archive.

The news caught Dan off guard. His eyes followed Gavin's pointing finger, and he spotted the stack of documents—about a foot tall—sitting on Gavin's desk. He had no idea Curtis and Gavin had been getting out in front on their own in terms of research. Curtis also said something else during the long meeting that afternoon that made Dan realize his commander had been putting plenty of thought into their plan. Curtis kept stressing the need for explosive words to accompany an actual explosion, as a kind of one-two punch. "Like fucking Bersinski," Curtis said, torturing the name Ted Kaczynski, the so-called Unabomber who had issued a manifesto in connection with his periodic bombings, which started in 1978 and continued for fifteen years. During that time he killed three people and injured twenty-three others. The Unabomber's manifesto had made it into "fucking papers all across the country," including, Curtis said, the *New York Times*.

"That's what we got to do," Curtis said. Their manifesto, he emphasized, would not only make crystal clear the reason for their actions, but it would also "trigger the other like-minded people across the nation to fucking stand up and start doing the same thing we're doing." Which was going after "Muslims and Government," he said in summary.

Though surprised, Dan needed to show that he was on the bandwagon. He endorsed the persuasive power of a manifesto to inspire the like-minded. "Can you imagine if they rose up," he gushed. It would be an awesome uprising. "Everybody's ready," he said.

"That's what I'm saying," Curtis said.

As they did with most issues, they went around and around as to what the statement should say, the timing of its release, and the way to distribute it in order to maximize national attention; most of these questions were left unresolved for the time being. Except for one critical piece: the author of the opus. "We need a fucking wordsmith for that kind of shit," Gavin had noted. He added, "I'm not a wordsmith."

Dan certainly couldn't volunteer—imagine an FBI informant penning the group's radically violent white-supremacist treatise. He kept his mouth shut.

Curtis said that he was like Gavin and didn't see himself as deft with the written word. But as the meeting wore on, he was the one who finally stepped up. "I'll write something, guys," he announced. "I can do that." Reiterating his strong belief in the crucial value of the document, he said, "It'll trigger everybody in the fuckin' country."

Minutes later, as the meeting dragged on and the others had digressed into complaining about President Obama and government inaction, Curtis blurted out, "Who's got a notepad?" It was as if he wanted to get started putting to paper the ideas whirling around inside his head.

Gavin laughed at his friend's eagerness. "I got a legal notepad," he said. "I bet you want a fucking pencil too."

In the days that followed, Curtis did indeed buckle down and get to work. Lula would be finishing up in the kitchen as Curtis settled into his recliner. He began mixing writing with viewing YouTube videos on the manufacture of explosives. In longhand, he composed blocks of text he'd then share with the others for discussion and approval.

"The KSF is watching," began one draft. "We are taking down names.

Names of people in Congress, the house of representatives, both state and federal. We are going to one day hold every single elected official responsible for their action. Mark our words, Mr. President. Everyone will be held accountable for their oath to the Constitution."

By late afternoon, they'd had enough. "Dude, it's 5:30 already," Dan observed. Their session had been a meandering one—it hardly adhered to a tight agenda the way a corporate board meeting might—but they felt that the contours of their plan were taking shape. Curtis would start writing something up, and the others would continue researching explosives.

Critical, though, was finalizing the attack's focus—and soon. "We need to figure out a target," Curtis said. For homework they were each to pick one. Then at the next meeting they'd exchange their top locations and decide on a prime target once and for all. "Pick the targets, starting working on the manifesto, put all ideas together next time," Dan said in summary.

To shorten the commute for Dan and Patrick, the group briefly discussed meeting halfway, in Sublette, Kansas, but then agreed that Gavin's office was best. As Gavin said, "It's a lot more secure here, definitely.

"There ain't no fucking bugs in this place unless Curtis put them in here," he joked.

They all laughed. Dan too.

Minutes later, Dan and Patrick left the office and walked together toward their respective vehicles. They shared some grievances, ranging from their impatience about drawing up a plan to griping about their drive to Gavin's office—about an hour for Dan from Garden City and even longer for Patrick from outside Dodge City. "Freakin' damn near two hours," Patrick said. They both seemed tired and not all that excited about their return trips home.

Dan, however, wanted to leave Patrick with the right impression. He didn't want Patrick thinking that Dan's complaints indicated that his commitment had wavered. To the contrary. Not one iota. "I still fucking want to do something with fucking cockroaches in Garden," he told Patrick.

"Oh, I know," Patrick said. "I do too."

Of course Dan didn't mean it. In fact, he was troubled by the decision that they each go home, mull over options they'd discussed with the visual aid of Google Earth, and then pick a favorite target for attack. There was always the issue of entrapment—that fine line between reacting to the others' scheming and proactively leading the way. But that legality was something he'd basically gotten accustomed to managing. His discomfort was caused by something else. What if they agreed on the target he pushed for and it happened—something bad, where Somalis were hurt, or worse? That's what gave him a long pause: the horrible outcome would be on him—on his conscience. With operational planning actually underway, he didn't like the thought. The last thing he wanted was blood on his hands.

He told his handlers as much, and the FBI agents went to work reassuring him. For Dan to push for Somali targets in Garden City was hardly a case of first impression, they said. Heck, Patrick and the rest had discussed the various apartment complexes ever since February, when Jason Crick and the Three Percenters held a field exercise conducting surveillance in Garden City. Coming into the next meeting and lobbying for those targets would simply mark the umpteenth time—not the first—they'd considered them. Legally speaking, he was covered. He wasn't introducing the idea; rather, he was pressing for sites the others already clearly favored. It would simply look like he was all in.

But the conflicted feeling concerned acting gung-ho about a particular target to bomb, even if this advocacy was legal. The potential nightmare of spilling Muslim blood was haunting Dan. In response, the agents tried flipping this worry on its head. It was actually in the interest of public safety that he step up for a local target rather than stay quiet as others weighed targets in Dodge City, Wichita, or even farther away. The reason? The FBI field office was less than a half mile away from the apartments, and Dan, a lifelong resident, knew the lay of the land intimately. Garden afforded the best opportunity for them to maintain an up-close and inside handle on the Crusaders' actions.

Dan felt better.

THE NEXT meeting happened to fall on the day after a police shooting in Milwaukee, Wisconsin, which instantly grabbed national headlines. Police on Saturday afternoon, August 13, shot and killed a twenty-three-year-old Black man, following a traffic stop. The man, who was armed, had run from the car and tossed his firearm. An officer giving chase then shot Sylville K. Smith in the arm and chest. By nightfall, mourners and angry protesters were rallying in the city's Sherman Park neighborhood, confronting more than a hundred assembled officers. There was some smashing of windows, rocks were thrown at police, and businesses were set on fire.

On Sunday, Wisconsin's governor, Scott Walker, announced he was deploying the National Guard. Several protesters were arrested during the overnight riots, and one police officer suffered a head injury when a brick was thrown through his cruiser's window.

"You see where Milwaukee got burned to the ground?" Patrick said, practically the first words out of his mouth as he, Dan, Gavin, and Curtis convened at G&G Home Center.

"Too bad they don't try that shit around here," Gavin said. "Now you got that nigger with Black Lives Matter saying that, oh, if Trump wins, we're all gonna fucking protest. Well, y'all can go to jail with the rest of them motherfuckers as far as I'm concerned."

"Either that or get hung," Patrick said.

"That's right."

Patrick and Gavin went on a roll, relishing their racist riff. Speaking in an authoritative tone, Patrick issued a stark warning to Milwaukee's

Blacks. "We'll thin you motherfuckers out just like we'll thin the fucking cockroaches."

Gavin liked that. "It probably wouldn't hurt this country to do some population thinning."

"Absolutely," Patrick said.

"Fucking idiots," Gavin said.

The coarse commentary on the news was like verbal calisthenics in bigotry; it got the team warmed up for the business at hand, as the meeting of Sunday morning, August 14, was called to order. On the heels of the pep talk with his handlers, Dan was more assertive this time, a noticeable departure from his usual posture of mostly listening and offering supportive feedback. Putting himself into the thick of the target talk, seeming to be aching for action even if only rehashing locations already on the table, he demonstrated that he'd taken the homework assignment to heart—which also bolstered his persona.

"I was thinking," he interrupted early on to kick-start the meeting's agenda.

Patrick, as if surprised by his initiative, joked, "He had some thoughts."

Curtis was all ears, though. "Let's hear it."

Dan mumbled. "The, uh—"

"Nice and loud!" Curtis said.

"The Somali Mall," Dan suggested, referring to the Somalia Wany Mall.

They were hunched over a map of Garden City, which Patrick had asked Dan to print out in preparation for the session. "No cameras back there," Dan continued, as he pointed to the store on the map. "You can drive right up in the back."

"I know you can, 'cause I've done it," Patrick said.

In addition to the Somalia Wany Mall, Dan mentioned the larger store owned by Adan Keynan as a possible second option. That is, if they wanted to blow up a Muslim business. But, he said, the African Shop might be riskier, given its location on a busy thoroughfare, West Mary Street. "It's too public," he said, whereas "this one is set back."

With that the foursome began a lengthy discussion on finalizing a target. Patrick wondered again about an out-of-town mark, at one point mentioning he'd heard of an upcoming gathering of Muslims in Chicago.

The idea was roundly rejected. "That's a long ways," Dan said.

"You're talking about going up there and spending weeks?" Curtis asked.

"I don't see it's very realistic," Gavin added.

Eventually they circled back to the two apartment complexes across from each other on West Mary Street. "I can almost guarantee you every one of those fuckers are Somalians," Dan said of the tenants. "There ain't no white people."

"I like the mosque idea myself," Patrick said, as they all recognized the merits of timing an attack during prayer, when a large number of Muslims would be in the makeshift mosque created out of one of the apartments, specifically the unit just across the driveway from Adan Keynan's, at the entrance to 312 West Mary Street.

Curtis decided they should conduct additional surveillance, check for security cameras, and assess the area where Somalis prayed. "We need to look at the building and see what kind of fucking building it is."

"Take some pictures," Gavin said.

"How many people will be there during prayer?" Curtis asked. "Find out numbers."

Curtis thought Dan should enter the grounds and go inside the unit to inspect the space, see if it was wide open or had walls.

Patrick was incredulous. "White boy going into a cockroach mosque," he mocked. He didn't think so.

Curtis pushed back, saying Dan could pose as a city inspector and simply walk around.

Gavin agreed. Just act, he said, "like you own the place, take a clipboard."

Curtis conceded that any one of them would certainly be noticed by the Muslims socializing outside when not at work. "I mean, they sit down there like a street gang," he said. "You drive by there, they look at you, stare you down."

Trigger-happy Patrick saw that as an opportunity, however. "You know that's what makes it real fucking easy for a goddamn drive-by, pop about ten of the motherfuckers out."

But for all the back-and-forth—and sarcastic banter—they had clearly reached a consensus on a target: the Muslim housing complexes and mosque. From this point on, that would be their bull's-eye. Dan, as if to acknowledge this milestone, said, "I'll tell you what, if this could happen in Garden City, America, a little fucking town—and we take out a mosque. That's gonna put fucking fear into people everywhere," he said.

"Dude," Patrick added, "anything we do is going to put fear in their ass."

"I DON'T know anything about explosives," Dan said halfway through the meeting. The discussion had turned to possible ways to deliver the big bang. Dan had plenty of questions about the delivery system, the actual explosives, and the timetable. They explored the idea of obtaining a dumpster to fill with explosives, which they would then set near the mosque. To minimize suspicion, they could slap an official sticker on it, to make it look like a city-owned receptacle. But Dan didn't think Garden City maintained dumpsters in the apartment complexes, so the arrival of one without notice might arouse suspicion. In a digression, Curtis expressed envy for Timothy McVeigh's means. "If we had a fucking U-Haul truck, something cold like that, we can just back that motherfucker up . . . fill that motherfucker with a thousand-pounder."

Gavin was equally impressed by McVeigh's powerful explosives in Oklahoma City. "Yeah, he took down, what, twenty-five stories?"

They talked about using heavy metal trash cans packed with explosives, but the idea that got the most traction was car bombs. "We go find this fucking hundred-dollar car or steal a fucking junk car and pack a hundred pounds of fucking ammonium nitrate in the trunk of it," Curtis said. Pointing on the map to a spot across from Adan Keynan's apartment, he continued: "Back it up into that first stall here, do one there, do one here, park one on the building over here." Four cars in all. Referencing the frequency with which radical Islamist terrorists employed car bombs, Curtis mentioned rough justice. "Use the same shit they use against us," he said.

They all repeatedly stressed the importance of their newfound focus on the mosque—and prayer time. Patrick said, "I want those motherfuckers jam-packed."

Curtis laughed and said, "We want them to be praying and then meet that motherfucker [Allah] all at the same time."

Peppered into the talk about cars was talk about the actual explosives. Curtis in particular began mentioning components they had to round up—and much of this was over Dan's head, given his basic ignorance about bombs. To Dan's surprise, Curtis disclosed he'd already secured about twenty pounds of one key ingredient—ammonium nitrate powder.

"I don't know shit," Dan interrupted, puzzled about the size and look of the improvised explosive devices Curtis and Gavin were talking about making. "I'm trying to figure out how big it's going to be. I mean, what's it going to be in—like a five-gallon thing?"

"No, in the back of a trunk," Gavin said.

They had to purchase a bunch of supplies, and they needed to be smart about it. “I don’t want it shipped to my house because I already ordered a bunch of aluminum powder,” Curtis said. “Sooner or later it’s going to be flagged.”

The solution, Gavin offered, was to have supplies purchased online shipped to G&G Home Center rather than to anyone’s home. The business address probably wouldn’t draw as much attention. To get started, they divided up the to-do list that Curtis had drawn up. Dan would do more reconnaissance of the apartment complex, to take photographs and check for any security cameras. Gavin was tasked with buying a chemistry kit, a beaker, and other glassware; Patrick, fertilizer and a rock tumbler that could be used to crush cans into aluminum powder. Curtis mentioned that some components might be pricey, and it became clear during their wide-ranging discussions about targets and supplies that their plot involved financial costs. It went without saying: no one had deep pockets.

Patrick was undeterred, though. “You got credit cards?” he asked rhetorically early on. “It’s time to start maxing those motherfuckers and fuck out the payments. ’Cause it ain’t gonna matter in a few months, boys.”

Curtis, meanwhile, promised to continue working on their manifesto, saying he’d already made substantial headway. He’d begun compiling a list of grievances against the federal government, which included “illegally bringing in Muslims by the thousands” and failing to enforce the country’s borders. For an opening, he addressed the manifesto to “the U.S. Govt. and for the American People.” He wrote, “With this document, we are going to attempt a ‘forced wake up call.’ American people, you have to wake up while there still might be time to stop our Govt from totally selling this country out.”

With that, they questioned again when they should release the document. Gavin thought suspense would build if they distributed it to the media prior to the bombing. They'd demand that its contents be aired. "Send it to Fox News," he said at one point.

"That's just a start," Curtis said.

"Make it a national thing, not just a local thing," Gavin said.

Ignoring it would be at the public's peril, noted Dan. "If they don't put it out—*boom*."

"Yeah," Curtis agreed.

Patrick had thought the manifesto should go out immediately *after* the bomb attack. "First crack out of the box," he'd said.

Dan agreed, saying that this course of action seemed customary. "If you look around most bombers, they take credit for it a day or so later after it's done."

Patrick chided him for his choice of words. "I don't want no goddamn credit," he snarled. "I just want the motherfuckers to know why it's happening,"

Besides the timing of release of the manifesto, Dan wondered about the timetable for the bomb attack. Earlier in the summer there'd been talk about planning it for the anniversary of 9/11, but that no longer seemed feasible. They'd made progress, to be sure, but he couldn't see them being good to go by then. "So you think we should set a date, a goal?" he asked.

"I don't know if we need to set a date," Curtis replied. "We just need to get it done." Curtis talked up their individual tasks, and he also indicated that he was eager to start conducting tests.

Dan was surprised. Tests of explosive materials? He didn't know whether Curtis was exaggerating or was in fact ready to do that. Either way, it gave him pause. *They're making 'em,* he realized, keeping the thought to himself, and that was a reminder: *This is 100 percent real.*

Curtis stressed how they had to be certain the IEDs that he and Gavin were planning would actually work. He didn't want to set them all up and then discover the bombs wouldn't detonate. "We don't want them to go out there and tow a truck off or a car off and then find five hundred pounds of explosives in the trunk," he said. That would be a big-time bust.

But Patrick had faith. "I know it'll work," he said. Indeed, he'd exuded full confidence since the start of the Sunday gathering, distilling into a few words the group's hopes for the work at hand. In fact, he'd stumbled onto a slogan of sorts to capture the awesomeness of exterminating Muslims. The goal, he'd said, was "go big or go home."

BASED ON THE INTELLIGENCE that Dan provided to the FBI following the back-to-back meetings in August, the agents calculated that the Crusaders' plot to commit mass murder was progressing. Out of the usual hot rhetoric, the steady stream of verbal venom, and the digressions into all manner of topics, a clear bottom line had been reached: they had chosen their target—the Somali apartment complex—and their means—improvised explosive devices (IEDs). In fact, bomb making increasingly preoccupied the foursome, especially Curtis and Gavin, who were often together, now that Curtis had begun working part-time in sales at G&G Home Center.

FBI agents Amy Kuhn and Robin Smith had plenty to consider: Should they warn Muslim refugees of the developing danger? Should they notify state and local law enforcement that a cell of a local militia was intent on carrying out an act of domestic terrorism that, if successful, would kill hundreds of people? The agents, consulting with their supervisors, decided against alerting the Somalis. The point of the investigation was to prevent the Crusaders from executing their plan. To disclose that the militia offshoot was targeting the 312 West Mary Street apartments, the agents concluded, would terrify refugees and likely cause panic. Word of the threat could easily spread beyond their community and make its way to Patrick Stein and the others. They couldn't risk it.

They also resisted the inclination to brief local law enforcement. The issue was one of trust—a genuine concern about leaks. The agents had been informed that some officers in local police departments were members of the Kansas Security Force, including a patrol officer in the Garden City Police Department. They also knew that a dispatcher for the Kansas Highway Patrol was involved in militia activity. If these militia-minded officers got word of the FBI investigation, they might tip off the Crusaders. "Southwest Kansas is a very rural and small-town area, and a lot of people know a lot of people," said Amy Kuhn as she sized up the situation. A native of southwest Kansas, she knew firsthand this fact of rural life. She and Smith "didn't want to have somebody find out and perhaps provide information." They couldn't take that chance. Too much was at stake. Not just the FBI's investigation, but Dan's life as well.

The overall strategy was to keep as tight as lid as possible on their work. Besides, and most important, the FBI had Dan — its eyes and ears inside the cabal, providing the best possible intel through his recordings of the Crusaders' conversations. Between the in-person meetings, the Zello calls, the separate calls with Patrick, and regular contact with the FBI handlers, Dan's work as an informant had become basically full-time.

It didn't mean there weren't exceptions to the FBI vow of secrecy, though. For example, Kuhn and Smith had worked on previous cases with an agent for the Kansas Bureau of Investigation, or KBI, who happened to live in Liberal. The agents let her in on what was percolating in the office of G&G Home Center, knowing she'd keep a low-key eye on things and be close by to lend assistance if, unexpectedly, the Crusaders kick-started some kind of impulsive action and quick intervention was needed to snuff out the danger.

The agents also began ramping up the probe to match their "risk assessment": that the Crusaders' evolving activities portended trouble. Within days of Dan's debriefing of the August 14 meeting, agent Smith prepared paperwork to expand the investigation beyond its early focus on Patrick Stein to officially include Curtis Allen and Gavin Wright. Curtis was a "radicalizer/recruiter" involved in "militia extremism," as Smith described him in the internal documents that he submitted for approval to the bureau's special agent in charge (SAC) in Kansas City on August 17. Smith did the same for Gavin Wright the next week, on August 22, with the SAC's say-so to investigate both men for "militia extremism" coming just days after Gavin had used PayPal to buy online laboratory equipment on Curtis's wish list. The items—a five-piece set of beakers; a hot-plate magnetic stirrer with dual controls; a slender, ten-milliliter graduated cylinder; and a set of three-milliliter disposable eyedroppers—were all basic, must-have equipment recommended in bomb-making manuals.

The FBI obtained authorization from a federal magistrate to use surveillance devices—known as a pen register and a trap and trace device—to capture incoming and outgoing call numbers on Patrick's and Curtis's smartphones. They also got approval to set up a so-called geofence around G&G Home Center—a virtual boundary surrounding the business—so that whenever Gavin and Curtis entered or left Gavin's workplace, their cell phones would trigger an alert to the FBI.

Because Patrick used a smaller cell-phone carrier, which wasn't capable of being tied into the newer geofence technology, the agents had to turn to an older tech trick to monitor his whereabouts. They got court approval to hide a GPS tracking device on Patrick's red Chevy pickup truck. And to help install it, they enlisted Dan to figure out a ruse to distract Patrick while Smith and an FBI technical agent surreptitiously went to work. Dan did come up with a plan, although its execution didn't go as smoothly as hoped. Dan started by calling Patrick with a story that he'd been vetting a potential new member and was eager to have Patrick, as the militia's executive officer, meet the prospect in person. Patrick hemmed and hawed, complaining he was in harvest, busy all day in the fields, but Dan pushed. The prospect, a trucker, was coming through Dodge City, and Dan said he'd arranged for them to meet at the IHOP on Wyatt Earp Boulevard. Dan promised to buy Patrick lunch, and that clinched it.

Dan deliberately parked in the space farthest from the restaurant. Patrick followed suit, parking his truck next to Dan's car. The plan called for the FBI techie and Smith to install the tracking device while Dan and Patrick ate lunch and awaited the arrival of the militia prospect. Smith was to notify Dan with a text message when the device was set. It was a good plan, simple and straightforward. The problem became Dan's phone—a new one at that. Earlier in the day Amy Kuhn had taken Dan to the AT&T store in Garden City to buy a replacement for Dan's old Samsung smartphone, which was breaking down. The agents didn't want the unreliable phone messing up the operation. But the new phone that she bought for Dan—an inexpensive prepaid model—turned out to be a lemon. As he sat across from Patrick at the IHOP, he couldn't get the phone to work. Smith had said it would take only fifteen minutes to attach the tracking device to the truck, but as time passed, Dan grew worried. He had no way of knowing whether the task had been completed. Patrick saw Dan fiddling with the phone and wanted to take it from him, to see if he could make it work properly. Dan didn't want Patrick anywhere near the device—what if a text from Smith suddenly popped onto the screen? Then Patrick, in keeping with his personality, erupted in righteous indignation when Dan said the phone was brand-new. Patrick insisted on taking Dan down to the AT&T store in Dodge City and demanding that they either fix the phone or swap it for another one.

Dan did everything he could to keep Patrick seated in the booth, buying time to be sure the agents weren't interrupted. They even got to talking about Dan's cousins in Oklahoma, the ones who were part of a criminal enterprise trafficking in guns and drugs—the canard Dan had concocted earlier in the year to burnish his credentials when first cozying up to Patrick and the Kansas Security Force. Patrick had been fascinated ever since and on occasion would ask Dan about this connection. Over lunch Dan shared he had an upcoming "mule run"—a drop for which he'd make some easy money. Patrick was at once intrigued and concerned, admonishing Dan that he had better be careful. Dan agreed. He knew doing drops was risky; he needed the money, though.

But eventually Dan couldn't corral Patrick at the table any longer. Patrick was impatient, wondering where the hell the guy was that Dan wanted him to meet.

Dan groused that the militia prospect was apparently a no-show. He apologized profusely to Patrick for screwing up his day—although Patrick did get a free lunch.

As the two walked out of the IHOP, Dan was holding his breath—and as they crossed the parking lot, he was instantly relieved to see that no one was still monkeying around Patrick's truck. Patrick left annoyed, and Dan left angry. When he arrived at the FBI office in Garden City, he nearly lost it with his handlers, complaining that a stupid, cheap phone had nearly compromised him. Couldn't the Federal Bureau of Investigation see to it that he at least had a decent phone? He'd never snapped at the agents like that, and the outburst made him realize how stressed he'd been while stalling Patrick at the IHOP.

The agents worked to calm and reassure him. Plans, however carefully crafted, do go awry at times. But this one had worked out: the tracking device was installed successfully. They explained to Dan that it and the other new measures taken in late August were designed to beef up the bureau's ability to monitor the group more closely. In that same vein they informed Dan that another, and even more significant, turn in the case was in the offing—one that would further enhance oversight of the Crusaders. They told Dan they had someone they wanted him to meet, someone the FBI had decided to bring on board in order to slow the group's bomb-making activity and then—if all went well—to assist in steering the investigation into domestic terrorism in America's Heartland to a final and orderly climax.

DONALD J. TRUMP, campaigning nonstop throughout the summer, happened to arrive in Wisconsin to woo much-needed Black voters on Tuesday, August 16, just three days after the fatal police shooting of a young Black man in Milwaukee. It was an ill-timed, awkward visit, to say the least, but one that had been on the Republican nominee's schedule well before the shooting that had sparked what was being called the Milwaukee Uprising, with its angry protests and occasional rioting. During his daytime visit to Milwaukee, Trump held no press conferences but attended a closed fundraiser, met privately with local law-enforcement officials, and sat with Fox News to tape a town hall meeting. Then, when he did deliver prepared remarks—intended to court Black voters—he did so in a nearly all-white suburb, West Bend, about forty miles northwest of Milwaukee.

"I am asking for the vote for every African American citizen struggling in our society who wants a different and much better future," he told the largely white audience that had turned out at the Trump for President rally. Finally addressing the police shooting, he reiterated pro-police, law-and-order talking points that hardly seemed likely to draw Blacks into his camp. The past two days of violence, he said, were "an assault on the right of citizens to live in security and to live in peace." Those who criticized police seeking to maintain law and order "share in the responsibility for the unrest in Milwaukee."

In typical Trump fashion, the candidate did not let facts get in his way. He argued on Fox News that the police shooting of Sylville Smith was likely justified, falsely asserting that "the gun was pointed at his [a police officer's] head, supposedly ready to be fired.

"Who can have a problem with that?" he charged. Then, perhaps suspecting he was on thin ice factually, he added offhandedly, "Maybe it's not true. If it is true, people shouldn't be rioting." In truth, the victim, while armed, was tossing the handgun over a chain-link fence as the officer chasing him fired his weapon, striking him the right arm. Moments later the officer, standing over Smith, fired a second shot, this time into Smith's chest, killing him. The officer later said he thought Smith's hands were moving toward his waist.

Trump's appearance in West Bend unleashed a Twitter storm. Many pounced on the disconnect between the message—an appeal for Black votes—and the venue—a suburban convention center filled with whites. One Black activist issued a warning that Trump might well surprise pollsters and win the White House. "This isn't a game, y'all," tweeted DeRay McKesson @deray. "This 'African-American' outreach speech was meant to polarize."

Indeed, Trump's spreading of falsehoods had long become business as usual for the presidential hopeful, a key campaign tactic to garner headlines, notoriety, and ultimately, political power. It was the kind of stuff that Patrick, Curtis, and Gavin consumed constantly on social media—and were often entertained by it—no matter the veracity of Trump's statements. The threesome delighted, for example, in the year-long feud between Trump and Megyn Kelly, the popular Fox News host. The clash between candidate and media celebrity had started the previous August, when Megyn Kelly questioned Trump during a GOP debate about calling women he disliked "fat pigs, dogs, slobs, and disgusting animals." Trump responded on Twitter like an attack dog, denouncing Kelly as a "loser" and a "lightweight," and later, on CNN, he accused Kelly of not just taking a cheap shot but relishing it, saying, "There was blood coming out of her eyes, blood coming out of her wherever." Now, a year later, in August 2016, a story about Kelly suddenly began trending on Facebook. The headline was "Breaking: Fox News Exposes Traitor Megyn Kelly, Kicks Her Out for Backing Hillary."

Patrick and the others high-fived the apparent fall of Trump's media foe.

"Good," Gavin said when Patrick mentioned the apparent firing. "Fuck her."

No argument from Patrick. "Fucking bitch," he said.

"I haven't watched her since she fucking pulled that shit with Trump," Gavin said.

In fact, the story was not true but rather a hoax that had gotten past Facebook's supposedly functional content screeners. It was an Internet mess for the social media giant to sort out, and hardly a concern for the Crusaders, who enjoyed the trending report as if it were based on fact.

"She's so in the bag for fucking [Hillary] Clinton it's ridiculous," Patrick said. He began fantasizing a final smackdown on Fox News between the outgoing Kelly and Trump. "I would love to see Donald Trump on her," he said. "He would rip her to fucking shreds."

MEANWHILE, AS Donald Trump was making his way through Wisconsin and elsewhere, fueling discord, and as the Crusaders followed fake news about a perceived foe of Trump, a local Garden City group, the Noon Lions Club, held its monthly noon luncheon. The polar opposite of the Crusaders, this collection of civic-minded locals, young and old, men and women, routinely invited guest speakers to discuss their work, the point being to promote understanding and community spirit. This month's meeting featured two speakers. One was Dr. John Birky, who'd been working with the hospital administrator Benjamin Anderson to find ways to mingle Kansans with the Muslim refugee community. Dr. Birky introduced the keynote speaker—Mursal Nayele, the extroverted multilingual Somali who had been working with city officials in community outreach. In promoting the talk, the Noon Lions Club had asked Mursal to "share his story" of immigrating to a new land. After the meeting, a photograph of Dr. Birky and Mursal was posted on the club's Facebook page.

6

GUYS, MEET BRIAN

WHEN THE FBI AGENTS Amy Kuhn and Robin Smith first told Dan, at the end of August, that they wanted to bring an undercover agent on board, the news came as a surprise. But it wasn't as if Dan thought, *What the heck? Why bring in someone else? Don't they trust my work?* It was not like that at all. Instead, Dan regarded an undercover joining the terrorism case as an affirmation of his work—that based on his infiltration and secret recordings, the FBI was now kicking its investigation into higher gear. It made everything seem real. Participating in the evolving conspiracy to kill hundreds of Somali refugees had of course been bone-chillingly real. But this development somehow made it seem even more so. Yet Dan felt some relief too. Having an undercover around meant he wasn't going to have to go it alone anymore. He'd been on his own as the FBI's informant for most of the year, at times fearing for his safety, and now maybe he'd have some help.

But though Dan was surprised, this move was standard for the FBI, part of its playbook in counterterrorism investigations. In the case out of Portland, Oregon, for example, where the Somali-born immigrant Mohamed Mohamud had planned to detonate a car bomb at a holiday tree-lighting ceremony, two FBI undercover operatives posing as radical Islamists had befriended Mohamud in time to stop him. In another FBI sting, undercover operatives had posed as foreign terrorists to intervene before Harlem Suarez could carry out his plan to set off an explosive-loaded backpack at a crowded Florida beach. In the 2015 Kansas case of John T. Booker, undercover informants played a key role in Booker's arrest for plotting to detonate a car bomb outside the Fort Riley military base.

The practice of bringing in "undercovers" was par for the course. The bureau even had a formal undercover program; an assistant director of the FBI counterterrorism division once described the undercovers as a small group of experienced law-enforcement personnel, often drawn from state and local police agencies, who were "trained and certified as UCEs (undercover employees)." They were viewed as "highly valuable, non-fungible assets" in the post-9/11 age of terrorism. The FBI division chief said the bureau went "to great lengths to effectively train them and protect their true identities" so that they could participate in high-risk undercover operations throughout the country.

This change in the case did not at all reflect personally on Dan, his handlers explained. And the benefits were several: the undercover would give the FBI a second source of information, meaning once they found a way to involve him in the cabal, the undercover would be positioned to monitor the men either alongside Dan or possibly at times when Dan was not present. The FBI was increasingly concerned that Patrick would go rogue, the way he talked up the idea of riding through town and gunning down Somalis. They were also concerned about Curtis and Gavin, who were pushing ahead on explosives and often worked apart from Dan and Patrick at G&G Home Center. Dan could not be everywhere at once, and a second set of eyes could potentially expand the FBI's oversight.

Then there was the added value of involving an undercover who'd been trained for this kind of work and possessed expertise that Dan did not, especially when it came to explosives. In late August, as discussions about bombs advanced and became more specific, Dan sometimes felt confused and fearful. He knew next to nothing about the chemicals and components that Curtis, Patrick, and Gavin were talking about. The undercover, explained Kuhn, was knowledgeable about explosives. He could talk the talk of IEDs and was better able to assess risk.

Dan had no beef with any of it. The FBI was turning things up a notch in the belief that Patrick and the others were a determined bunch. Bringing in the undercover was seen as a way to slow the men down. He'd attempt to present other, albeit phony, alternatives to their bomb-making scheme, and by doing so create a misdirection that would allow investigators to take control, gut the plan, and end the threat.

In short order, the agents began compiling justification for the move, working their way up the chain of command to win approval from FBI headquarters, a time-consuming process they knew would take weeks.

DAN HAPPENED to be with his handlers at the FBI office on the morning of September 1 when, unexpectedly, his cell phone rang. It was Patrick. He was calling Dan about setting up a meeting for the next day, Friday, in Liberal, at Gavin's G&G Home Center. Patrick had already confirmed with Curtis and Gavin. He realized the meeting was on short notice, but he was feeling antsy. They couldn't be dawdling and allowing days, even weeks, to go by.

"I was thinking about 10:30," Patrick said.

"Yeah, uhh," Dan said, seemingly caught off guard. "Lemme think." Then, regaining his footing, he said, "Yeah, I can make it."

When the call ended, Dan looked at his handlers. Kuhn was the first to say it, but they all knew that the next day's meeting was Dan's opening. They began hashing out how Dan could steer the conversation to the undercover. Dan had already set the stage—albeit unwittingly. His bid early on to buff his militia persona with a tall tale about having Oklahoma cousins involved in a criminal enterprise now provided a fortuitous opportunity. He could exploit that fake story and spin something around the idea that Dan's connection to black-market traffickers could be a boon to the Crusaders. What was originally résumé-building bluster could now serve as a natural segue to introduce the undercover-*cum*–arms dealer as someone able get his hands on materials and weapons they so fervently desired. It was as if Dan had planted a seed months before just for this very moment. He had even recently sweetened his story by disclosing to Patrick at the IHOP that he was doing "mule runs," a new morsel further stirring Patrick's curiosity.

Thinking Patrick was already primed, Kuhn said, "It's probably likely that Stein is going to bring up your explosives connection." If that happened, she suggested that Dan try to act vague and noncommittal. "You tell them," Kuhn said, "I don't know a lot about explosives, but usually they're able to get what people need." She also suggested this alternative wording: "If you guys know specifically what you need, I can ask them. I can't promise that they're going to be able to come up with it. I can tell you they're usually pretty good at it."

Dan nodded, taking it all in. They tackled the impact of Dan's recent embellishment of the story about his mule runs during his meeting with Patrick at the IHOP. It was the kind of thing that would excite Patrick, and his calling around to arrange a meeting for the next day might indicate that he had said something to the others. "It is very possible," Smith said, "that Patrick has told Curtis or Gavin or both that you are far more into somebody."

That would be fine, Smith said, except for one thing: Dan must be careful not to "push things timeline-wise." The undercover wasn't on location yet. Nor had final approval, although expected, come through. "We have to be careful how quickly we build this," Smith said. "If they want to talk direct, that then steps up the timetable significantly." What if, Smith said, "Curtis tells Dan, 'I want to talk to these guys myself.'"

Dan would have to finesse the situation—at once dangling the undercover while slow-walking any sort of immediate contact. The two

FBI agents considered possible approaches, with Kuhn saying that if his cohorts wanted an immediate face-to-face, Dan could take, in effect, baby steps: he could promise to reach out to the contacts to test their willingness to meet, then get back and report that the contacts had said, "No, not yet," that they were extremely cautious and first wanted to learn more about Patrick, Curtis, and Gavin and their specific needs. This stalling tactic would allow time to get the undercover operation set up and in play for later in September.

Mulling over everything, Smith said, "Okay, we can do that. We can do that." Conceding that he sounded like "a broken record," the veteran agent reiterated that he wanted to be certain they got everything in place to bring the case to its "endgame."

He said, "We just got to be careful how—I don't know how else to say it—how fast we get this snowball rolling."

WHEN DAN arrived on time for the meeting the next morning, September 2, it turned out he did not have to worry that his proposition would take off on a fast track, before the FBI was ready. The subject of the weapons trafficker came up, to be sure, but there was also plenty else on the agenda. The meeting would be the group's longest to date—about six hours—and Dan was privy to (and recording secretly) the kind of specific planning that verified the FBI's concern that the advancing plot needed to be corralled, and soon. The nature of the gatherings had clearly evolved. Those in the early summer had revolved around Islamophobic rhetoric, often led by Patrick, coupled with a conviction to do something to exterminate the "cockroaches." The hate-filled talk continued, but in the late summer the meetings focused on translating those words into action by devising the nuts and bolts of an actual plan.

"Let's get to figuring out what we want to do," Curtis ordered as they got started.

"What we need to buy," Gavin said.

"Did you bring the manifesto?" Patrick asked.

"Yeah," Curtis said.

They spent several hours honing the plot. They considered the possible delivery systems for the fertilizer bombs Curtis had assigned himself to make. They revisited using industrial-sized trash cans altered to explode toward the apartments at 312 West Mary Street. Inside these containers they could stuff nails, ball bearings, and Sheetrock knives or, as Gavin said, "anything that can kill and maim." Dan was assigned to see whether Home Depot or Menards carried them, and at what cost.

They continued exploring the idea of using car bombs, with Curtis pointing out on a map of the apartment complex the places where they'd park the vehicles to create a "circle of explosives." He sounded at times like a teacher giving a lesson in IEDs, sharing the knowledge he'd gained from studying books and videos on creating bombs. He mentioned various chemicals and materials—things like ammonium nitrate and aluminum powder—and said he'd already purchased some of them. He said his focus was making blasting caps as the critical first step, because without a detonator, no fertilizer bomb would ever be complete. "We can make a blasting cap up," he said confidently.

"That's what you need a hot plate and shit for?" Patrick asked.

"Yeah," Curtis said.

Gavin added, "It got here the other day."

Curtis also made clear they'd want to run a test on anything he put together.

"Oh, yeah," Gavin laughed. "'Cause we don't want it being a dud!"

From explosives they turned to the manifesto, and like would-be authors enrolled in a writing workshop, each one offered feedback on Curtis's latest draft. Patrick asked, "Do you want it to say, you know, illegal immigrants, or do we want it more focused directly at the fucking Muslims?"

Curtis thought for a moment and agreed, saying he'd already mentioned Muslims plenty and should add denouncing illegal immigrants, "'cause they're all over."

They talked about precautions they should take to prevent the manifesto from being traced back to them once it was distributed. Everything used in its production should be brand-new—paper, word processor, printer—and then destroyed. "No fingerprints on anything," Gavin said.

"Motherfucking gloves the whole time," Patrick said. "No hair."

Dan chimed in. "They can get DNA off it."

"Dude," Patrick chuckled, "we should have full fucking CDC suits on!"

They certainly didn't want to mail manifestos from Garden City, so other locations were considered. Gavin suggested Colorado Springs. Or Amarillo, Texas. Curtis thought they could send a bunch to state militia commanders they trusted and "have them drop it in the fucking mailbox in Louisiana."

The goal, of course, was press coverage: to get the manifesto into the hands of what Gavin called "every fucking swinging dick" in the media.

"The AP," Patrick said.

"NBC, CNN, fucking Fox," Gavin said.

"*New York Times,*" Patrick said.

"Everybody," Gavin said.

"KSN," Dan added, referring to the NBC-TV affiliate in Kansas.

"That's it," Gavin said. "The little ones too."

Curtis, a huge fan of Alex Jones, wanted to call Jones's radio show live. "I got fucking Alex Jones's phone number."

Patrick said they could call Sean Hannity and "that stupid fuck Glenn Beck too."

Curtis was fixated on Alex Jones, though, saying the right-wing conspiracy theorist reached "like twenty million people, thirty million people a week."

Gavin loved the idea, noting, "Everybody that listens to him is a patriot."

Most important, Curtis continued, was that Alex Jones would champion their cause. He could picture Jones reading the manifesto out loud and declaring, "Listen to this call to arms" and "We need to do something."

Talk of massive news coverage triggered a group chant of sorts, as the Crusaders reminded themselves of the purpose for exterminating Muslims and the existential stakes involved. "It's about a fucking country," Curtis said. "You need to take a stand."

"Or we ain't gonna have one," Gavin said.

"It's fucking history, man, in the making," Dan said.

THE NEW item on the agenda, though, was Dan's black-market contacts. Within minutes of arriving, he made his move, raising the subject with Curtis and Gavin. "I have some fucking connections," he said. Underworld ties through "family, back east, Oklahoma."

Curtis said, "I already know all that."

Just as expected, Curtis already knew something. Dan forged on, proffering the idea that they could tap the family connection in previously unforeseen ways. "I put out there," he said, "if there was any way to get, uh, any kinds of, you know, anything. Explosives, anything. I put it out there.

"I got an answer," he said. "Yes, maybe. You know?"

"From a family member?" Curtis asked.

"Yes," Dan said.

"All right," Curtis said.

"Okay," Dan said.

Curtis asked, "So what's the deal?"

Dan launched into a rambling pitch aimed at enticing the others while keeping the contacts shrouded in mystery. He said, "These people were the fuckers in charge," and not actually his cousins. They were people his cousins worked for. "They fucking intimidate me," he said. "They're the real deal." And as he'd told Patrick, he'd been making mule runs. "I made some extra money here in the past couple of months." He said he didn't even know what exactly was secreted in the trunks of vehicles he'd taken to drop-off locations—whether they contained weapons or drugs. "I don't ask," he said. "I don't tell.

"Is it worth the risk?" he asked rhetorically, now on a roll. "Fuck no," he said, answering his own question. "But I need the money."

Curtis said, "Depends on what they're paying you."

Dan gave them a number: "Two thousand bucks."

Gavin was wide-eyed. The loads, he said, must be "something special, I'm sure."

"Is it worth prison time?" Dan wondered, and again didn't wait for anyone to reply. "Nothing's gonna be worth prison time." Even after answering himself yet again, he kept going, a chatterbox for once. "I mean, I go on a—"

But Curtis interrupted him. "Okay, okay," he said. "So get on with the deal."

"Okay, all right." Dan buckled down. He said the contacts told him that getting weapons, explosives—whatever—was a definite possibility. But he said they wanted him to be more specific about what the group needed. And he said the contacts wanted a better sense of where he was coming from—"a one-man show" or what?

"I ain't gonna lie to these fuckers," Dan said, an unsubtle way of saying that the arms dealers were heavy-duty dangerous. "I told them it's a group thing."

The bottom line: Dan had opened up a channel that was a potential game-changer in terms of the Crusaders' capability and timetable. "From here on out, it's, you know, it's up to you guys. It's, you know, what exactly you want, and if they can provide it, okay?" He could set up a meeting—if that's what they wanted. "They did this shit for a long time, and that's what I know," he said, emphasizing the traffickers' bona fides.

He'd completed the pitch. He'd mumbled some, stumbled on his wording at times, but thought he'd done a good job introducing the idea that connections through his law-breaking cousins could be useful to their bomb plot—*but,* and this was crucial, he'd made clear that it was up to the others whether or not to go down that path. Dan figured he'd managed to walk a fine line, setting up a sting but not entrapment.

Patrick offered full-throttle support. To Dan's disappointment, though, Curtis and Gavin seemed less sure—not rejecting the idea outright, but hesitant.

"I don't want to know who they are," Curtis said.

Gavin added, "I don't want them to know *who I am.*"

The four debated the issue throughout a meeting that had begun at midmorning and was lasting into late afternoon, as they refined their bombing plot and their manifesto. They kept asking Dan lots of questions, grilling him about the kinds of weapons and materials the traffickers could obtain, and, an important consideration, at what price, given the fact they did not have deep pockets. Time and again, whether the inquiry was about the various explosives, weaponry, or price points, Dan said he didn't know. His strategy was to convey little more than the fact that he'd made initial contact—his lack of answers offered a way to slow down the process and, equally important, to encourage an in-person meeting.

"I was hoping that you might have, you know, an idea of prices," Patrick complained after Dan kept saying, "I don't know."

BUT THE price question ended up inspiring Patrick and Gavin to riff on how they might cover costs. Patrick observed that he'd gotten the sense from Dan that the arms dealers might be willing to "trade out," or barter.

Gavin caught the drift. "Cooking stuff for them," he said.

The two then excitedly described how they could set up a lab to provide methamphetamine in exchange for weapons. Having once had a crystal meth lab, where he'd manufactured "good shit," Patrick felt fully competent to do this. Gavin said he'd once done the same—making, buying and selling product. "When I was buying, they were like $16,000 a pound, but that was back in the fucking eighties." Making meth, both claimed, was in their wheelhouse. It wouldn't be hard to do.

And Dan was encouraging, saying he thought the traffickers would be "very fucking interested" in that kind of arrangement.

What did Dan think the traffickers would pay for meth? Curtis wondered aloud.

Dan didn't have the answer—once again. "Depend on the purity," he guessed.

Patrick suggested they produce a sample, test the market.

Curtis mulled the idea, then agreed it was a decent first step. "I say we do it."

From there they speculated animatedly about the benefits of Dan's connections. It was as if Dan's lack of particulars had further stirred their interest. Could Dan's contacts get them dynamite? Mortar rounds? Rocket-propelled grenades?

"Fucking land mines would be great," Patrick said, sounding almost giddy.

"Try C-4," said Curtis, the chief bomb-maker, referring to a plastic explosive. "Tell them what we mostly need is blasting caps." Dan busily took notes, drawing up a weapons wish list. Curtis laughed, saying that when Dan showed the list to his contact, "he's going to look at you like you're fucking insane."

Curtis was clearly interested—teaming up with Dan's traffickers would quicken the pace of their activities. "We need to get this going," he reminded everyone. "We ain't got enough time, guys—this is gonna happen in less than a hundred days." But he also resisted Dan's repeated suggestion of direct facetime with the strangers. Meeting with them was an unnecessary risk, he said; he was fine with Dan serving as the group's lone trade representative.

"You do it," he told Dan at one point.

DRIVING BACK to Garden City, Dan called home immediately. "Is Mom doing okay?" he asked Brandon. His son reported that she was fine. Dan then called the local Walmart pharmacy to confirm that prescription refills for his wife were ready; they were. Then he swung by McDonald's to buy a medium-sized extra-value meal with a Dr. Pepper.

He had plenty to think about. He'd left the meeting a bit disappointed by the mixed response. He knew the FBI wanted all of the Crusaders to embrace the plan involving the undercover. In truth, though, he knew he shouldn't have been surprised at the fact that Curtis and Gavin ran hot then cold, at once intrigued but hardly an easy sell. Curtis, especially, had always been the most security-conscious of them all, to the point of obsession. He was the one who regularly nagged at everyone to toss their smartphones into an empty office at G&G Home Center before they talked; the one who wanted background noise going at all times, preferably hard rock on either a radio or CD player; the one who insisted on face-to-face planning, eschewing the Zello calls; heck, he'd put a gun to Dan's head at the county fair in Lakin as a loyalty test. He warned them, to the point of nagging, about maintaining high alert. "Once we blow the mosque up, we're terrorists," he'd said matter-of-factly.

Curtis had even wondered aloud, at one point during the meeting, whether Dan was getting played. "You might be talking to the fucking CIA guy," he'd said. Even so, there was no denying the temptation. Curtis and Gavin both recognized the operation would go faster if they were to tap Dan's resources. And so they did encourage Dan to learn more — to take the list back to his contacts, see what they could get for them, and whether they'd barter for drugs. Curtis, as always, had his eye on blasting caps. "We need blasting caps," he emphatically said to Dan.

Gavin, the bomb-making sidekick, concurred totally. "Blasting caps would be the biggest deal," he said. "Making them," he told Dan, "is the hardest part.

"You can do it, but it's the hardest part. Because it's the most unstable."

IN THE days that followed, Dan kept after Curtis and Gavin about his black-market contacts. Not a whole lot changed, though. Curtis and Gavin enthusiastically urged Dan to forge on, but neither warmed to the idea of accompanying him to a confab — although Gavin eventually budged, saying he would go if a deal depended upon it.

Dan did have an ally in Patrick, however. And the two commiserated for hours on the phone about their collaborators' stubbornness. Curtis was far too uptight, they complained. There was a huge difference between caution — a good thing — and obsession. Curtis's insistence that they stay off Zello for fear of being monitored, for example, risked slowing the plot to an exasperating crawl, and Dan indignantly derided the claim. "Commander was saying he guarantees that the feds have been listening to every single thing we've said on Zello," he said, drawing on his role-playing best to sound deeply offended. "I disagree with that."

Patrick agreed completely, insisting they needed more, not less, communication — "a shitload of communication," he ranted, "for this thing to come off anytime in the near future." He ridiculed Curtis for behaving as if the four of them were on the FBI's Ten Most Wanted List. "We are nothing to the federal government, the NSA, the CIA," he said. "I mean, in order for them to catch everything we talk about literally? They would have to have somebody on all four of us twenty-four hours a day." And Patrick took umbrage at Curtis's criticism that they were being lax. "I'm not going to, you know, sit there and be basically accused of being the one that's going to cause us to fucking get caught." Curtis, he said, needed to chill out. "He needs to get on some fucking paranoid medication," Patrick wisecracked.

DAN WENT into the next meeting—on September 11, of all days, the anniversary of the terrorist attacks—all set to resume talking about his contacts. He informed the others he'd had no luck finding trash cans but did come bearing other gifts—the mortar and pestle he'd bought at Target, a chore Curtis had assigned to him. Gavin certainly was pleased. He took the items, placed them in a closet, and then he and Curtis together announced they'd reached a milestone: they now had everything on hand to start manufacturing the components of a bomb.

But just as Dan got ready to kick-start the pitch, there was a hard knocking at the door—which Gavin had locked, as he did for all their meetings. Standing outside was Lula Harris. She was looking for Curtis. She apparently had tried calling but got no answer—the phones were in another room for the meeting—and so she'd decided to drive down to the office to find him.

The tension between the two was palpable. The couple had not been getting along, as Lula continued to suspect that Curtis was seeing other women. She also resented running his errands; he'd recently told her to go to Walmart and buy several Tracfones, the low-cost cell phones that were difficult to trace. To make matters more annoying, he'd acted mysterious about it, refusing to say exactly why he would want disposable burner phones when he already had a smartphone. In any event, her sudden presence cast a pall over the proceedings. They couldn't discuss anything of substance in front of her, and so the meeting was cut short.

Dan left for home; further discussion about his contacts would have to wait for another day. But however frustrated he might have felt, he could take comfort in Patrick. The XO was all in about the potential arms dealers. He'd told Dan exactly that, in no uncertain terms, during one of their many private phone calls. "We really need to try to get together with them," he'd said. "We need to talk face to face so we can get down to some, you know, serious chat."

A FEW DAYS later, Dan drove to the FBI office to meet, at last, the undercover. He followed his usual routine, with one modification. For months he'd parked at a bank behind the office on Campus Drive. He'd walk across a tree-lined grassy strip to the FBI's back door. The idea was to be as inconspicuous as possible. But then the branch manager at the Garden City State Bank had noticed, and he did not like Dan using the lot. Dan began finding notes stuck under his windshield wiper that read DO NOT PARK HERE! Dan showed them to Amy Kuhn and Robin Smith. They rolled their eyes; the bank's spacious parking lot was never full. But rather than argue, they had Dan find a new spot. According to the altered routine, Dan would turn off Campus Drive onto a side street and into the parking area for a cluster of two-story wood-framed apartments. He could leave his car there unbothered for hours.

So he pulled into a space at the weathered fence separating the apartments from the plaza housing the FBI office and cut the engine. He missed his Chevy Blazer, which had crapped out on that long, crazy, and terrifying day in June when he'd recorded the Crusaders for the first time. He looked forward to the day he could afford to buy another SUV or, even better, a truck. Not that he was complaining. He appreciated having the maroon Chevy Impala that the FBI had paid for; he was just dreaming.

Dan went through an opening in the fence and walked behind the plaza, past the rear entrance to a dentist's office, and toward the FBI's gray back door — the only one equipped with an overhead camera. His mind whirled as he knocked to let the agents know he was there. Blending the undercover into the plot was proving to be a challenge. His proposal had caused friction among the Crusaders, no question about it. And now? He didn't know what to expect from the undercover. Even if he did manage to arrange an audience, would the guy the FBI had drafted be able to pull it off? He worried too that no matter how effective the undercover's performance as a like-minded white nationalist hungry to rid the country of Muslims, the others would reject him: no, we don't need any help, we're doing just fine on our own. What would be the FBI's next move then? Worse, what if Curtis and Gavin somehow caught on, and the entire investigation unraveled?

But his worry began to ease the moment the newcomer stood up from the conference table to shake Dan's hand. It wasn't that the undercover was especially imposing; he was of average height, maybe in his midthirties, and muscular, like he worked out. It was his presence. During his introduction he managed to at once convey friendliness and a warning: *don't fuck with me.*

Dan right away wondered if the undercover might be ex-military, possibly from the US Navy SEALs or some other special force. In fact, during the conversation that followed Dan learned the operative was on loan from an urban police department; he'd been part of the FBI's undercover program for a decade, since 2006. He had participated in a slew of investigations. Some involved drugs and weapons trafficking; others, terrorism and explosives. In all of the cases he had created what he called a "legend," a backstory to fit the particular circumstances. He'd also adapted his appearance to fit a particular locale. He might grow a heavy beard or a mustache, or shave his head — like a master of disguise. The one thing he didn't alter, though, was his voice. The undercover had never been to Garden City before, and to assume the role of a big-time weapons supplier, he wasn't about to try mimicking some kind of redneck twang; he spoke to Dan in a generic tone that came naturally, as if he were originally from somewhere north. It came across as no-nonsense, though. He sounded like someone taking charge.

Dan, Kuhn, Smith, and the undercover sat down and went over the case. Dan learned that more undercovers were on their way to Garden City to pose as members of the gang, and they would devise a plan to infiltrate the plot once they arrived. The undercover was already aware that Curtis and Gavin were resistant to outsiders while Patrick was welcoming—and so they would start by working on Patrick.

The undercover exuded confidence, which was a relief. Dan felt the investigation was in good hands. After the meeting they chatted for a while, but it wasn't like they got chummy. Dan left not having learned a whole lot about the new arrival. In fact, for security reasons, Dan would never learn very much about the undercover's career or his personal life. In official FBI records, he was known simply as UC-5276. To Dan and the Crusaders, he was Brian.

WHILE DAN WAS BEING introduced to the undercover operative, Curtis and Gavin were busily at work at G&G Home Center. They'd converted the kitchen into the equivalent of a high school chemistry lab. Glass beakers, cylinders, and a hot plate with a mechanical stirrer—which Gavin had purchased using PayPal—were arrayed on the counter, along with a digital scale, safety goggles, and the chemicals Curtis had rounded up. The mortar and pestle Dan had bought at Target were also on hand. Curtis's notes and the recipes downloaded from the Internet were spread out on a table. He and Gavin weren't looking to role-play as two teenage kids turning water into wine, however. Hardly. Instead, they were set to make a dangerous compound that even to a chemist was likely a mouthful to pronounce: hexamethylene triperoxide diamine. To scientist and nonscientist alike, calling the compound by its acronym was much simpler: HMTD.

Producing HMTD was painstaking, time-consuming, and dangerous. The chemical compound was the volatile key ingredient in a blasting cap—and that cap was the critical component of an improvised explosive device, or IED. Whether set off by a spark, a flame (such as from a match), or any other bit of heat, the blasting cap was used to ignite a bomb's main explosive charges. As the triggering device, a blasting cap was called a "primary explosive" in bomb-making circles, and during Curtis's self-education as a budding bomb maker he had long ago learned that making a detonator was not easy—a lesson he'd been informing the others about for weeks now.

HMTD was not available commercially, but its three ingredients were. Hydrogen peroxide and a citric acid powder, such as vitamin C ascorbic acid, could be found in many households. The third ingredient—hexamine—was used in fuel tabs, the small cubes of white powder that burned slowly and for a long time. Campers and backpackers loved them for their size and utility in heating up a cup of soup or coffee.

Using the mortar and pestle, Curtis and Gavin ground the fuel tabs into a fine powder. To combine everything, they used the hot plate and automatic stirrer — although it was solely the mechanical stirring function they intended to use. Heating the concoction was to be avoided entirely, given the instability of the ingredients as they reacted chemically. In fact, it was best to pack ice around the container to monitor its temperature; if the materials, heating naturally, got too hot, they could explode. Chemists called that unwanted outcome a "runaway reaction."

Curtis poured the hydrogen peroxide solution into the container. Then he mixed in the citric acid and hexamine. The solution was stirred — slowly and continuously, and it became a waiting game for the chemistry to do its magic. The solution was clear initially, as the solid powders — the citric acid and hexamine — dissolved. Then, as the chemicals reacted, the mixture began to turn white and cloudy, and then, as more time passed, it thickened and turned even cloudier. Curtis had to be hoping that Lula would not make one of her unexpected drop-ins, as she seemed inclined to do of late. Earlier in the summer she'd begun bringing him lunch, which he'd appreciated. She'd usually called ahead then. Now her unannounced visits felt like spying.

Nearly six hours later the solution was transformed into a solid white powder. The process had gone smoothly, just as Curtis had seen it done on a YouTube video. Curtis and Gavin were ready to conduct a test, to see what they had. Curtis took a pinch of HMTD from the batch — about one gram — and put it inside a tiny paper tube. It was like rolling a joint. He reinforced the tube with masking tape. Into one end he stuck a short fuse, resembling a fireworks fuse, which is often called a hobby fuse. The men considered going outside, but decided it was too windy. Instead they stood at the stove, over which they spread a piece of plastic.

Curtis asked Gavin for his Bic lighter; he flicked it to get a flame.

The explosion was instant — a hot fireball.

Both men jumped back. The hair on Curtis's finger was burnt off.

The two traded wide-eyed looks.

"That was fuckin' awesome," Gavin said.

It was their eureka moment. They'd made a blasting cap.

NEARING SUNSET a few days later, Sunday, September 18, the Crusaders pulled in one by one at the truck stop along US Highway 83 in Sublette, Kansas. Dan had called for the meeting—the first time he'd ever done so. It would be quick, he'd told the others, so that he could share the latest news from his black-market contacts. He hadn't wanted to talk on the phone or in a Zello meeting—which Curtis, for one, certainly appreciated. For everyone's convenience they'd picked the tiny town of Sublette to meet; it was located about halfway between Garden City and Gavin's G&G Home Center in Liberal.

Dan had left Garden City from the FBI office, where at 6:06 p.m. his handlers had turned on the secret recording device: "This is Special Agent Robin Smith with the FBI," Smith had said. "I am here with Minuteman. He is about to travel down to Sublette, Kansas, for a meeting with some or all of the Crusaders." The drive took Dan south out of town, past rows of grain silos and acres of corn and alfalfa fields stretching across the Great Plains. During its descent the bright-yellow sun gradually turned the western horizon an amber color. The trip took Dan only about a half hour, and when he pulled into the U Pump It truck stop he saw that Patrick, Curtis, and Gavin had arrived just ahead of him.

They gathered in the unpaved lot adjacent to a low-slung building that housed a Subway sandwich shop and, next to it, the U Pump It convenience store, which featured Champs Chicken and Baskin-Robbins ice cream. Noisy eighteen-wheel haulers of cattle and grain occupied the large dirt lot, and trailers rumbled up to the Conoco gas pumps to refill their tanks. Now that an undercover was part of the case, and with several others to arrive in Garden City, the FBI wanted to move ahead to get Brian blended into the bomb plot. Dan was to deceive his cohorts, stating that his connections had gone over the wish list and were good with the next step: a meeting.

Dan got out of his car and approached the others. "What's up?" Patrick said.

Right away Dan noticed that Curtis and Gavin were unusually buoyant—laughing and kidding each other—and he wondered why. Then, after they'd left their smartphones behind and were walking across the gravelly lot toward the Subway shop, he found out. Curtis and Gavin were bursting with real news that easily trumped Dan's fake news.

The two had "tested that shit"—HMTD—and Gavin called the occasion "badass." He and Curtis then launched into a reenactment of the high-five moment, while Dan, stunned by the surprising development, went mute.

Gavin was the one to set the stage for the kitchen-*cum*-lab. Curtis, he said, had matter-of-factly stated, "Let's try this."

"I was gonna do it outside," Curtis chimed in, "but the wind was fuckin' blowin' so bad."

Dan managed to ask, "You did it inside?"

"Yeah, over the stove," Gavin said.

"On the fuckin' stove!" Curtis said, as if in hindsight that had been a crazy choice, given what happened next. Then he cut to the chase: "I just lit it with a Bic lighter."

"It was like *woosh, woosh,*" Gavin said. "Probably a fire this big around." He made a shape with his hands, about the size of a soccer ball.

"Burnt all the hair off my finger," Curtis said.

The wannabe chemists laughed hard. "I was like, whoa, fuck," Gavin said.

And they marveled at how little HMTD they'd used.

"You only need a gram," Curtis said.

Gavin was still in rapture. "I felt the percussion off of it," he said, almost breathless, "and I was standin' probably from me to him, and he did it right in front of me."

Dan tried to act as enthused as the rest, and he teased Curtis: "Man, you're lucky your clothes didn't catch on fire." The remark got a new round of guffaws.

Gavin continued to point out how little had been necessary, about the same amount as a crushed aspirin.

"That's all?" Dan said.

Patrick, impressed, simply said, "Oh fuck."

"I mean, it was nothin', man," Gavin said.

Curtis disclosed that he'd made more since, including a batch the day before, which Gavin guessed amounted to about sixty grams. Curtis wasn't so sure it was sixty, just that it was a "coffee filter full." Both Patrick and Dan looked enthralled.

But Dan was reeling—scared even, confronted with the fact that Curtis and Gavin had successfully made a detonator. He'd learned enough about bomb making at this point to know that the blasting cap was the hardest part. In relatively short order, they'd be ready to blow up Somalis.

IT WAS Curtis who interrupted the victory lap, turned to Dan, and reminded him that it was his meeting. "Tell us what you're talkin' about," Curtis said.

Dan fumbled at first, as if still in shock, then found his footing and gave an update on "my people, my guys." He said he'd shared the weapons list, "you know, the wish list," and his guys had replied they'd be able to help out. Better still, things could happen really fast. They wanted to see him the next week, business related to a mule run. They'd be in the area and would give Dan twenty-four hours' notice on time and place. They could all meet.

"Meet with us?" Curtis asked.

"They said bring you guys," Dan said.

"I don't see why we need to even meet 'em," Curtis said.

"I'm just goin' by what they told me," Dan replied.

It was déjà vu: on the one hand everyone saw a huge upside in working with the arms dealers, but Curtis and Gavin questioned the need to meet face-to-face. Curtis reiterated his view they'd all be better off "if nobody knew anybody." Not surprised by Curtis's typical conflicted views, Dan was ready to debate the issue.

"Here's the deal," he said. "They got their way of doin' shit, they've been in business for a long time. I mean, these are some bad motherfuckers."

If his contacts wanted a group huddle, he wasn't about to argue with them.

"I understand," Curtis said.

"I don't have no leeway," Dan said. The black marketeers were not be taken lightly, he added, and required utmost respect. "They scare the shit outta me," he said. "You see these fuckers, you'll know."

Even so, Curtis and Gavin wondered why they should trust the arms dealers. "I don't know 'em, you know what I mean?" Curtis said. For the next several minutes he and Gavin peppered Dan with questions, just as they had the previous week. Did Dan always deal with the same guy? Different guys?

Patrick wanted to know if Dan's cousin would be there, saying that would be reassuring.

Ultimately, Curtis asked, what if Dan were to just tell his contacts they had to go through him because his partners didn't want to meet.

Dan didn't mince words. "They're gonna say, 'Fuck no,' forever." He feigned frustration, insisted he was caught in the middle. To the weapons traffickers he'd gone out on a limb and vouched for the Crusaders. To the Crusaders he was now vouching for the traffickers.

"You're vouchin' both ways," Gavin said.

"Damn straight," Dan said. "My ass is on the line."

Patrick considered the predicament funny. He needled Dan. If something went "haywire on their end? Or our end?" He smiled, told Dan, "You're fucked."

"No shit," Dan said.

"I'm just makin' that clear," Patrick said, laughing.

Patrick's grim humor seemed to take the edge off. Everyone agreed they wanted things to work out, despite reservations—even Curtis, who'd noted that their position was stronger, now that he and Gavin had made a detonator. "If this other thing works out," he said at one point, "we won't need 'em anyway."

But Dan laid it on thick—how the arms dealers had made it clear they'd be willing to help. How much help? He didn't know yet. And they'd also indicated a willingness to barter, or to even help out if they were short on cash to pay for the explosives. That's why they should all meet—to sort everything out. "I'm vouchin' for ya—that's getting us in the door!" Dan reiterated.

Patrick, putting the shoe on the other foot, said he could see why the arms dealers might be so adamant. "I might even be the same way," he said. He explained that if he were one of them and was going into a business transaction with new people he'd never met, "I might wanna, like, look people in their fuckin' eyes. 'Cause I can tell a lot by that.

"Look you straight in the eye, talk to you, you know?"

They continued talking in circles, with Curtis at one point directly addressing his overriding concern. "Even the best, lowest fuckin' down and dirty groups have fuckin' narcs in 'em," he said. He challenged Dan: any chance his contacts were in fact police?

"Oh, no, no," Dan said, pretending astonishment at the question.

"That's my only fear," Curtis continued. "We're being set up."

Dan said, "I guarantee you. I guarantee you they're not—"

Patrick interrupted. "I ain't even worried about that."

Eventually, Curtis advised Dan to simply be straight with the weapons traffickers—say they'd just rather not meet as a group "unless it's required." It was their preference, but not one cast in concrete.

Gavin added, "We'll do what we got to do."

With that, Gavin checked the time and announced he had to go. Nearly thirty minutes had gone by and Dan had billed the meeting beforehand as a quickie. "We done?"

Dan recapped: once he heard the time and place, he'd call everyone.

"We'll figure it out," Gavin said.

"This'll be the first meeting, you know," Dan said. "Then things can happen fast."

Patrick said, "We ain't gonna pass up the opportunity."

SIX DAYS later, Dan stood at the end of a gravel road, looking out at a small lake. Run by Finney County for public use, it was drying up. While at other times during the year you could get around in a small boat, maybe fish a little, it was now only a large pool. Several hundred yards beyond was a cluster of trees. The greenery stood out because practically everything else in sight was the muted brown color of dry grass. Dan thought his son, Brandon, would like this spot; they both shared a love for the Great Plains. Outsiders might see boring sameness; Dan and Brandon Day saw a prairie paradise of soft, rolling hills, with occasional farms and a quiet seclusion that was ideal for deer hunting.

No one was else was around—except, that is, Dan, the two FBI agents, Brian, and the handful of undercover operatives who'd joined the investigation. It was Saturday, September 24, one day ahead of the Sunday meeting Dan had arranged between Brian and the Crusaders—depending, of course, on who could make it.

When Dan had told his FBI handlers about Curtis's blasting cap, Kuhn and Smith were as alarmed as he'd been. It was an "oh shit" moment, as one said later, and had rocked the agents' ongoing "threat assessment," the process by which they evaluated whether the Crusaders' actions posed a clear and present danger. Concerns about Dan's news were several. For one thing, a detonator signaled a breakthrough in the group's bomb-making prowess. Just as important, Dan had been unaware of this development, raising the specter that he was getting sidelined when more than ever they needed him to be in the mix. The last thing they wanted, as Kuhn said, was for "him to get cut out and then we find out that something bad had happened." The FBI needed to get Brian involved as soon as possible for the sake of everyone's safety—the Somali refugees, their informant, Dan, and even the targets, Patrick, Curtis, and Gavin. It would be Brian's task to slow the Crusaders down in the manufacture of their improvised homemade explosives.

They'd spent the week hashing out a plan. It was standing room only in the windowless conference room in the FBI field office in Garden City—another half dozen or so undercover operatives and support staff had arrived. It looked at times like a Hollywood casting call. The operatives mainly wore jeans, boots, and work shirts. Some had long hair; some had a shaved head. Some had facial hair, some not. Physically, they were rock solid, and all were veterans of special operations. Sizing them up, Dan had thought none of them looked like they worked at desk jobs, and he saw in the motley crew the same kind of no-nonsense confidence he'd detected right away in Brian.

Deliberations were disrupted at one point by a knock at the rear door. Everyone in the conference room saw, on the surveillance camera, that a man in a conservative suit was outside, his face contorted in anger as he pounded on the door. It was the bank manager, and the two FBI agents right away realized he was there to complain about the bunch of vehicles, belonging to the undercover operatives, parked in the bank's lot. Smith excused himself and went outside to deal with the problem. When he returned, he told everyone to move the vehicles. Smith, fed up, soon after closed his personal account at the bank.

Brian had floated the idea of staging their meeting in a local bar, if Dan or the agents could think of a place that would be suitable. He'd used bars, preferably dive bars, in other investigations—their rundown, dark ambience was conducive to criminal and conspiratorial conversations. To Dan, the idea revealed Brian's background in city policing, and right off he thought the idea wouldn't work in small-town Garden City. He told the group as much, that he didn't think Patrick and the others would feel comfortable in such a public place, where they might run into someone they knew.

It was agent Robin Smith who was aware of the lake preserve and had suggested they use it. The location was indeed out of the way—about forty-five miles northeast of Garden City and then another ten miles along dirt roads north of Highway 156 in Kalvesta, Kansas. The back roads took them past the ghost town of Ravanna, one of many small towns dotting the Great Plains that had shriveled up and died after Big Ag gobbled up the family-owned farms. In its heyday, around 1900, the town center boasted a bank, a general store, a newspaper, and a cheese plant. But today the crumbled stone foundations of the courthouse and schoolhouse, and a nearby cemetery, were Ravanna's only remains. Driving almost another mile north, they reached the county's remote lake area. Other than logs positioned to designate the parking area and a concrete structure housing a public bathroom, there was little sign of human activity. Few were interested in visiting the tiny lake that wasn't.

Now on location, Dan took it all in as Brian and the others got the lay of the land. The investigators began a walk-through of the next day's plan—a dress rehearsal of sorts, as they decided where to park the vehicles and where people should stand during the encounter. Dan had already contacted the Crusaders to say he'd gotten word from the arms dealers that they would be in the area on Sunday. He'd explained again that the traffickers were coming through to settle up with Dan regarding a mule run, and it would be a good time for everyone to get together. It was a meet and greet, and would go fast. Gavin had replied that he was going to Colorado for the weekend; Dan encouraged him to return in time. Curtis had been noncommittal. Patrick, in the midst of harvest and long workdays, had said that a rainy day would be best for him, as he'd be able to break away from the fields. There actually had been scattered showers the past few days, so Patrick told Dan he was on.

For the next hour or so, the investigators blocked out how they hoped the introductions would unfold. Brian involved Dan, but it got to the point where Brian was feeding him lines he should say to Patrick and whomever else might show up. The direction felt a little heavy-handed, as if Dan wouldn't be able to think on his feet and needed to memorize words Brian was composing for him.

Dan spoke up, said he'd mostly been doing fine over the past ten months. "Man, let me do it my way," he said. Brian backed off. It seemed Brian even appreciated it that Dan had asserted himself—at least that was the feeling Dan got afterward, when they'd finished rehearsing and the undercovers asked Dan where in Garden City they could get a fine steak. They were in Kansas, after all. Dan didn't hesitate: Samy's Spirits & Steakhouse, no doubt about it—and the undercovers invited Dan to join them. That Saturday night they all sat on the restaurant's rooftop deck under a starry sky. They ate fancy steaks, drank whiskey shots, and got ready for the real deal the next day.

THE VERY same week, so much was ramping up—Curtis's lab work on the one hand, the FBI's bid to get Brian up and running on the other

—and to top it off, Lula Harris did happen by G&G Home Center at what could only be considered an inopportune moment. She arrived at lunchtime, carrying a bag full of Kentucky Fried Chicken, and walked right in. She spread the food out on the dining table adjacent to the kitchen, the same table where Dan and the others usually sat when they were meeting. She even brought along enough for Gavin, who was holed up in his office, talking on the phone. He barely gave her a nod.

Thirsty, she walked around the kitchen island to get a drink of cold water from the refrigerator. It was after she'd closed the refrigerator door and turned that she saw the hot plate on the island's lower shelf. On the hot plate she saw a beaker with a stirrer, and in the beaker she saw what could best be described as a white substance. Her mind flashed to their trailer's living room, where for weeks Curtis had plopped himself down in the recliner to watch YouTube videos. It had become a flashpoint in the escalating tension, the way he'd watch videos over and over again, taking notes, paying her little attention or none at all. It had gotten to where she had no choice but to watch the videos too—and now her mind's eye cut between the videos and the countertop, and she took inventory of materials common to both—hot plate, stirrer, mortar and pestle, beaker, and so on. She recalled the part in one video where fuel tabs were being explained, at which point Curtis had ordered her to go into the spare bedroom—his so-called man cave, where he kept guns, ammo, and all manner of supplies—to rummage around, see if they had any fuel tabs. She'd found only a few packs, so Curtis had gone online to order a new supply. Just the way he'd ordered a glass stirrer online, which he'd taken with him one day to G&G Home Center.

When Curtis came over, she asked him, What the hell were he and Gavin doing?

He didn't answer her directly, just began describing some items on the counter, explaining who had bought what—the stirrer, the mortar and pestle, which was upside-down and apparently drying. But Lula knew the answer, and it rattled her: they were making explosives. And with that she also realized Curtis had been dead serious all along and was actually following through on threats to do something to the refugee Muslim population.

ON SUNDAY, THE DAY after their rehearsal, Dan arrived in Kalvesta just after the noon hour. It was quiet, but every day was quiet in Kalvesta. He drove his Chevy Impala past grain silos, a radio tower, and the main enterprise in town, Kalvesta Implement, a family-owned dealership selling a broad array of new and used farm machinery, from tractors and mowers to balers and axial rotary combines. Continuing a few minutes east of town on Highway 156, he pulled off into the empty lot that he and the FBI agents had picked for its isolation as a good spot for him to meet up with Patrick. Dan turned off the car, sat, and waited. Patrick, driving from Dodge City, would be arriving from the opposite direction.

Dan had left home in plenty of time to reach Kalvesta first. Once they'd met, he would lead Patrick to the lake preserve, where Brian and his crew waited. It seemed to him he was spending all his waking hours working on the case. Cherlyn had recently commented he'd grown more anxious of late and tossed in bed at night more than usual. He half-jokingly figured the fitful nights must mean he was working on the case around the clock. His wife was at once frightened and worried for him —scared that the Crusaders would catch on that he wasn't loyal to their cause and track him down. She could be reassuring too, giving Dan pep talks about doing the right thing and how well-suited he was to perform the role he played for the FBI. She'd cite his work at the detention center and his proven ability to manage criminals, talk their language, really be alert to danger, and be a step ahead of them. Then there was their Christian faith. They prayed, and Cherlyn believed that Dan's infiltration of the Crusaders was something that God had planned, something that Dan was specifically designed to do. Her words helped bolster his spirits. Even so, Dan looked forward to the day when this would all be over.

Within minutes Patrick appeared in his dirt-encrusted pickup truck. Dan rolled down his window. They shouted greetings without getting out of the vehicles. Dan signaled for Patrick to follow, and Dan backtracked about a mile into town. Directly across from the machinery dealership he turned right off the main street. The gravel road stretched flat for miles, straight into the horizon. The road was rutted, the ride bumpy, and the Impala kicked up so much dust that Dan could barely see Patrick in the rearview mirror. He could tell, though, that Patrick had dropped back a bit, to stay clear of his car's dust storm. Within a couple of miles they reached a broken-down, boarded-up structure that long ago was a one-room schoolhouse. It was painted red, and in its time it could have served as an illustration in one of Laura Ingalls Wilder's Little House on the Prairie books.

Dan turned left at the schoolhouse onto a dirt road that didn't look much different from the one they'd been on—rutted, flat, and straight. This one headed in the direction of Ravanna, the ghost town, and after a few more miles he took a right onto yet another barren road. He thought he'd taken the turn to the lake preserve, but after a few minutes he realized he'd turned too soon. Dan didn't know if the mistake was due to nervousness or the fact that he'd ridden in one of the FBI's vehicles for the rehearsal. To get back on track, he had to call agent Kuhn. He stopped and turned around, making sure Patrick couldn't see him making the call. Kuhn was able to direct him to drive farther toward Ravanna, and soon Dan recognized the correct turn. The mix-up caused a ten-minute delay, and it was another few minutes before he spotted the access road to the lake preserve. Dan headed down that final stretch.

Brian and several undercover agents posing as members of Brian's criminal outfit were already set up and waiting. Brian stood with one crew member some thirty yards below the parking area, near barbed-wire fencing. Two others were posted at the entrance to the parking area itself. Brian was in contact with other agents shadowing Dan's progress, while another two, armed with long-range rifles, were hiding out of sight in the cluster of trees beyond the lake. In all, a dozen law-enforcement personnel were involved in an undercover capacity, as a sniper or as part of the broader tracking team. Brian had a hidden recording device much like the one Dan used, which he'd already turned on.

"They gotta be lost," Brian said when Dan's expected arrival time came and went. Then his phone rang; it was an agent on the outer rim of surveillance. The agent confirmed Brian's hunch—Dan had indeed taken a wrong turn. "Okay, okay," Brian said. "I figured that's what happened." Probably Dan's nerves, Brian told his caller. "It is what it is."

Then two vehicles emerged in the distance. "Subject in his truck way behind our guy," Brian said, observing Patrick's pickup trailing behind Dan's Chevy Impala as both vehicles kicked up clouds of dirt. Brian interpreted the gap between the two vehicles as something working in their favor. He said, "The good thing about them coming down this way is he is sizing us up the entire time, and if he still shows up, then he has at least bought into it so far." In other words, Patrick had plenty of room to bolt, but he hadn't.

Brian watched the arrival unfold according to plan. Two of this men walked over to Dan and Patrick as they got out of their vehicles. The idea was to create an aura of power by having subordinates initially check Patrick out, give him the once-over as a security measure. They didn't want Patrick thinking he could have immediate access to the top man. "They're greeting each other," Brian narrated into his recorder. He eyed the action as Dan and Patrick were next instructed to leave their phones behind in their vehicles. "This guy's being friendly so far," Brian said. The lead agent was then quick to spot that Patrick was open-carrying a SIG-Sauer P250 9mm semiautomatic handgun. Brian said, "Subject Stein has a gun on his right hip." Notification that Patrick was armed was transmitted to the snipers hiding in the trees and to agents participating in the surrounding coverage.

Dan had a small gym bag, which he handed to one of the escorts. It contained the money he'd purportedly gotten as payment for the gun run he'd just completed for the outfit—the handoff being the reason for this meeting. In front of Patrick, the crew member took a moment to tally the cash. When he was done, he counted out $2,000 and gave it to Dan. Dan took the money and made a show of counting it himself. "Wanna make sure you guys aren't rippin' me off," he joked. He and the crew members began razzing one another.

Dan was acting as if he already knew the two escorts from previous mule runs, and as they walked to where Brian was standing, they made small talk about Dan's cousin and about football's Kansas City Chiefs and the start of their season. But Dan was to act as if he'd never met the boss before, making Brian's presence something special. The explanation for it was that Brian was en route to attend to other undisclosed matters and thus able to make a quick stop.

Brian looked at Patrick and said, "Uh, who's this guy?"

"Double D's buddy," one of his men answered. Double D was Dan Day.

"Okay," Brian said. But instead of greeting Patrick, which would have been expected, Brian turned his attention to Dan. "Hey, what's up, man?" he asked. "Haven't met you but it's nice to meet you. Looks like it worked out again?"

Dan said, "Yeah, everything went good, man."

The idea was for Brian to seem aloof, play hard to get, so when he acknowledged Patrick's presence, his tone was noncommittal. "What's goin' on, bro?"

"Nice to meet ya, brother," Patrick said.

Some others introduced themselves—one was named Mark, another Ryan. Patrick made the rounds, shaking hands vigorously as they were offered.

Brian asked of no one in particular, "So why is he here?"

It was as if Brian needed reminding.

Dan said, "This is the guy." Brian's face remained blank. You know, Dan said, the guys with "the list." He continued: "The other two weren't able to show up."

"Oh, okay, all right," Brian said, acting as if now he remembered. But even then he remained standoffish, turning again to Dan with queries about the delivery. Brian was making it clear that his own business concerns would come before Patrick's.

"Everything work out, though?"

"Everything was good, man," Dan replied.

Brian appeared glad to hear it, and he told Dan business generally was going well, that demand was up, which would mean more opportunity going forward. "More business, and more often," he said. He asked Dan, "You game for that?"

"Oh hell yeah, man, as much as you can feed me, man."

"Okay," Brian said.

Brian then paused and looked out toward the shrunken lake. "Do they stock this? Do you know if they stock this?" He was still not ready to address Patrick.

Dan said, "Man, you know what? I really don't know."

"What's that?" Brian said.

"I really don't know," Dan said. "They used to."

"They used to?" Brian said.

Breaking his silence, Patrick interjected, "We got good pheasant hunting out here."

The non sequitur prompted comments from everyone about favorite hunting spots, nearby and beyond. Meanwhile, Brian huddled within earshot with a key subordinate. He asked about the accounting of monies Dan had delivered.

"It's good," the underling told Brian. "We're good."

And with that Brian was finally ready.

"All right," he told Patrick. "Let's talk."

Brian signaled to Patrick to follow him to his truck.

"Glad to finally meet you," Patrick said as he climbed into the red Ford pickup.

Brian had reason for wanting them to be alone. The pretext was to allow for a private one-on-one between the Crusader and the high-level arms dealer. For investigatory purposes, however, Brian maneuvered alone time to conduct his own assessment of the terrorist threat, independent of any possible influence Dan might have by his own words or actions. Brian was, in effect, the case's "fresh set of eyes," tasked to evaluate the seriousness of the bomb plot against Garden City Somalis, as described by Dan and his FBI handlers in their reports. Moreover, he'd be looking to establish a rapport with Patrick, the first step in insinuating himself into the plot in hopes of controlling it.

He began by saying he knew from Dan that Patrick's group wasn't flush with money. But before they got into particulars, including how Brian might be able to assist Patrick's group, he needed to make certain Patrick was on the right side—not aligned "with all those jihadis blowing people up and shit." It was why meeting in person was important. The last thing Brian wanted was to see his armaments going to "fucking jihadis to go blow up people that I care about." That would be the worst, he said, and if Patrick were somehow looking to aid and abet radical Islamists, "you better get out of my fuckin' truck."

Patrick laughed out loud; it seemed he could barely process the idea that Brian might be thinking he was on the Muslims' side. The idea was absurd, and he assured Brian that the opposite was true—he wasn't looking to assist Muslims, far from it. He was looking "to take them out."

"I'm cool with that," Brian said.

"Every one of them motherfuckers need to be fucking eradicated."

No argument there, Brian said. "Just wanted to make sure you guys aren't fucking with any of those guys." Now they could talk, and over the next few minutes Patrick worked to impress Brian and establish his bona fides as a Somali slayer. "You'll probably be seeing some news coming out of western Kansas in the near future," he predicted.

Brian took out the handwritten list Dan had provided as the basis for discussion. He said he needed clarification about some of the items —blasting caps, for example.

"You want mechanical or electronic?"

Patrick said that, as far as he knew, "electronic—something that we can wire up and, you know, like detonate with a cell phone type deal."

Brian acted alarmed. You want to get that idea out of your head, he warned Patrick. "You ever get telemarketer calls?" he asked. "Ever get phone calls from people you don't know?" Brian had seized on blasting caps as a teaching moment. He said, What if you guys were *not* ready to go but had already tied the cell phone into the bomb so that when the phone rang, its electrical current would detonate the bomb. "What if someone accidentally calls your number?" Brian pressed, "What's gonna happen?"

Brian didn't wait for Patrick's reply. "You're going *boom*."

"I follow what you're saying," Patrick said, sounding both humbled and impressed by the arms dealer's acumen. It was clear that, more than ever, he wanted Brian to participate, and to advocate for that outcome, he declared the need to come clean. "I'm gonna be straight with ya," he said. "We're no fucking bomb experts here—just fucking country boys that, you know, are sick of seeing these motherfuckers coming into this country." Left unsaid was the fact that Curtis and Gavin had already achieved a breakthrough—a homemade blasting cap.

Brian pretended to let Patrick's words sink in. Then he spoke: "You and I are on the same page." It was an affirmation—the meeting of two anti-Muslim minds.

Brian reviewed some pricing. Blasting caps, he said, were "fifty bucks a pop." It appeared they were building an IED using fertilizer. "It's going to take a lot of that," he said.

But Patrick said, no worries. "I'm a farmer," he said, "and I can get that shit by the fucking truck load."

Okay, good, Brian said. Then there was a tube-fed grenade—that would be $150. Pineapple grenades were also on the list. "Those are like eighty bucks a piece." Patrick wanted to ask about a couple of items not listed—fully automatic weapons and an RPG, or rocket-propelled grenade. Brian replied, "I can get you automatic weapons." But, he added, "Those are expensive." For example, for an AR-15 rifle "you're looking at about two thousand, twenty-five hundred. For an AK-47 you're looking at about two thousand."

Patrick floated the idea of bartering. "Just to put it out there," he said. "Is there any possibility, instead of dealing all strictly in cash, of like doing some trade out?"

"What would you trade me?"

Crystal meth. "I did some manufacturing back in the day," Patrick said.

Brian fell silent as he mulled the proposal. Then he said that before agreeing to a drug trade, he'd want to talk to some people at his level, see if they'd take it. But another very real possibility, he said, was a price break. He was open to reducing prices, given the fact they were like-minded about the "infestation." Brian said, "If I can keep my hands clean, I might do something for you guys, hand it off, and you guys go do your thing."

Patrick liked the sound of that a lot.

Brian pushed Patrick for clarity about his crew, who exactly he'd be dealing with and whether they were trustworthy. Was it just him and Dan?

"Me and him," Patrick said, "and then there's two others."

"And can you trust those two others?"

"Yes, absolutely." Patrick wanted to erase any doubts. "Yep, no question."

"Okay," Brian said.

They'd covered a lot of ground in only about ten minutes. Brian acted as if he needed to keep moving. This was, after all, an initial meeting, a first impression to ensure there was both common ground and trust. Security and trust were paramount. "There's a reason we meet out here," he said about the preserve off the beaten path. "There's a reason we talk to people only if other people vouch." The implication was clear: Patrick was fortunate to have Dan Day vouching for him and the other two Crusaders who were not present.

Brian concluded he needed a few days to make up his mind. But he gave Patrick every reason to feel encouraged. "Sounds like you guys are doing good things out here, man," Brian said. "Give me a couple of days and I'll get back to you."

Patrick's only apparent misstep was asking for contact information. Brian refused. "I'm not gonna tell you that now." He used different phones for each transaction, he said, a business practice to better protect himself. It was his protocol. When he was ready he'd reach out to Patrick. "I'll just say it's me—the guy you met out in the field."

Nonetheless, Patrick seemed to have passed the audition hands down. "I can't wait to get it started, bro, to be honest with ya," he told his new best friend, the lead black-market arms trafficker. Then, as if eager to deliver a punch line he knew would win him a racist rave, Patrick revealed his moniker.

"My call sign is Orkinman," he blurted.

Brian let go a hearty laugh. "Exterminator, huh?"

"I hate fucking cockroaches, and that's exactly what them motherfuckers are."

Brian opened his truck's door, signaling the session was over. Patrick opened his side. Dan and everyone else were waiting for a report, and Brian announced, "We're good." Everyone acted pleased, telling Patrick how great it had been to meet up and make a connection.

Patrick didn't seem to want to go, the way he worked the small group, saying, "Nice to meet ya" and "See ya guys" and "Look forward to talking to you guys some more." He said to Brian, "You done with me. I'll go on ahead and get out of here."

Brian nodded. Good idea. He was going to speak briefly to Dan, but Patrick had permission to leave. Patrick and Dan gave each other a look: be in touch soon.

Then Brian, Dan, and Brian's crew watched as Patrick drove off. Brian said, "He's clearing on out, so what we are gonna do now is we're going keep our talking minimal about stuff because we are recording things, okay? Don't say your name. Don't say my name. Don't talk about any specifics. Let's just shoot the breeze about the pond, or the hunting."

Even so, they couldn't help but comment on the close encounter with Patrick Stein. Brian had wondered beforehand if Patrick would be angry and volcanic, given his terrorist aims, but instead he'd been "personable."

Someone else recalled Patrick's arrival: "He's got a big ole pair of farmer mitts, doesn't he?"

Brian agreed, for sure. "He's sturdy. His handshake. He's a sturdy boy—a farm boy." Everyone agreed the meeting had gone well.

Brian asked Dan, "You feeling all right?"

"Yeah," Dan said.

"Good job, man."

DAN AND Brian rendezvoused back at the FBI office that Sunday night. "We need to accelerate this" was Brian's message to the case agents

Kuhn and Smith. Patrick had come across a bit wobbly in his personal knowledge about the actual manufacturing of explosives, but there was no question that he and his cohorts had devised a plan to kill Somalis, one that was gaining momentum. Patrick's commitment was unwavering, his hatred for Muslims ran deep, and the danger index was high; the Crusaders were going to do something, and the investigative team needed to act quickly. Brian needed to fast become part of their plan so he could assert influence and steer them away from building their own bombs.

In fact, Dan and Patrick were on the phone before the day was out. Patrick could barely contain his excitement, all gung-ho about his talk with Brian in the truck and yakking like he was jacked up on speed or something like it. Patrick marveled at Brian's resources, gushing that he could get the Crusaders just about anything they wanted. You name it, he had access. Patrick continued his drumroll about his monster hookup with the high-ranking arms dealer on Zello calls with Dan, Curtis, and Gavin. Dan began trying to cut Patrick off, saying he was busy and had other things to attend to. Dan was looking to lower his profile and allow for a budding bromance between Patrick and Brian.

Then two days later, on September 27, Brian did reach out to Patrick. He sent an encrypted message at 3:41 p.m., using WhatsApp: "It's the guy from the field."

Three minutes later Patrick replied, "Hey man. How's it goin'?"

"I'm on this side of the dirt," Brian wisecracked. "So, good."

"LOL."

Brian delivered his decision: he would assist the Crusaders. He stressed, however, that he was taking a big risk by putting a partnership on such a fast track. "I'm only working with you because I like what you stand for and you are a straight shooter," he explained.

Patrick meanwhile expressed holy gratitude at having met Brian at such a pivotal moment in the group's planning—someone as fed up as he was and willing "to put some wheels in motion to address the infestation of these fucking cockroaches!" It was not by chance or coincidence, as he saw it, but by divine intervention, the work of "the man upstairs."

He assured Brian he was making the right decision, describing in a number of ways his own long-standing devotion to their cause—even a willingness to die for it. Patrick didn't expect to make it to January 2017, he told Brian. "I might come home in a pine box," he typed. It was something he'd already reviewed with his parents and two sons. "Brother, I have never been more serious, more prepared, more ready and willing to defend this country, the Constitution, and the citizens at all cost," he said. "I do all of this in the name of Jesus my God and for my kids and grandkids and future generations."

And he addressed lingering doubts Brian might harbor about his comrades. "The other people I work with feel exactly the same way I do," he said.

"And we are all ready to take action."

7

"WILL, DETERMINATION, AND DEDICATION SECOND TO NONE"

TWO DAYS AFTER THE inaugural meeting on September 25 between Dan, Patrick, and the faux weapons dealer "Brian" at the isolated lake preserve in southwest Kansas, the director of the FBI, James B. Comey, settled into a leather chair in a wood-paneled Senate hearing room fourteen hundred miles away, in Washington, DC. The FBI director was making a scheduled appearance before the Senate Committee on Homeland Security and Governmental Affairs. Still fresh on everyone's mind was the June massacre at the Pulse nightclub in Orlando, Florida, where the ISIS supporter Omar Mateen slaughtered forty-nine people in the deadliest act of terrorism since 9/11. More recently—just ten days earlier, in fact—there'd been bombings in New York City's Chelsea neighborhood and in Seaside Park, New Jersey. Three pipe bombs, wounding thirty-one people, had been detonated by an ISIS-inspired Afghan Muslim and US citizen named Ahmad Khan Rahimi. Rahimi was arrested after a shoot-out with police.

The title of Comey's address on September 27 was "Fifteen Years After 9/11: Threats to the Homeland." "Preventing terrorist attacks remains the FBI's top priority," he told the senators in the crowded room in the Dirksen Senate Office Building. Throughout his talk Comey focused exclusively on threats posed by radical Islamist terrorists and "homegrown violent extremists," or HVEs, recruited by the Islamic State of Iraq and Syria, known for short as either ISIS or ISIL. "These threats remain the *highest* priority and create the most serious challenges for the FBI, the U.S. Intelligence Community, and our foreign, state and local partners," he said. "ISIL is relentless and ruthless." Comey described in detail some of the methods the organization used to recruit and "propagate its extremist ideology," citing in particular its "widespread reach through the Internet and social media." The terrorist group, he said, "has proven dangerously competent" in using online videos, private messaging platforms, and other social media networking sites to "spot, assess, recruit and radicalize" vulnerable sympathizers in the United States to carry out attacks. He likened the law enforcement challenge to not just looking for "needles in a nationwide haystack" but also trying to figure out "which pieces of hay might someday become needles."

The FBI director's remarks echoed those he'd given the prior year, in July 2015, at an appearance before the same committee—and, to be sure, attacks by HVEs had proved a durable threat. The Orlando and New York City attacks were bloody reminders of that fact. But Comey's narrow focus on radical Islamist militancy as America's singular terrorist threat failed to account for an evolution in terrorism at home—namely, the ever-more-frightening spike in far-right violence, especially against Muslims. In 2015 white supremacists and bigots had accounted for an estimated 260 assaults and other hate crimes against Muslim citizens and refugees—a 78 percent increase from the previous year. And in many instances perpetrators used the very same tools Comey had cited as ISIS's go-to methods for organizing an attack—Facebook and other social media platforms, along with encrypted text-messaging services. In fact, the dangers posed by domestic terrorism would go largely unacknowledged by counterterrorism officials for several more years—not until late in 2020 did the US Department of Homeland Security, in its

"Homeland Threat Assessment," candidly call violent white supremacists the "most persistent and lethal threat" in America, overtaking ISIS, al-Qaeda, Hezbollah, and other foreign terrorist groups.

There was one major difference, however, between Comey's remarks from 2015 and those of September 2016. FBI agents on the ground had begun responding to the shifting landscape—the dangerous uptick in white nationalism and Islamophobia. In keeping with Comey's analogy, his agents had detected a new kind of needle in the nationwide haystack, and in Kansas, the FBI agents Amy Kuhn and Robin Smith had homed in on the Crusaders as one needle in particular. The Garden City case was part of the investigatory pivot—counterterrorism resources were now being devoted to domestic violent extremism.

COMEY AND national counterterrorism officials may have been slow to recognize this burgeoning brand of terrorism, but independent researchers were not. It was the Center for the Study of Hate and Extremism at California State University, San Bernardino, that had documented the 2015 spike in assaults, ranging from shootings and arson at mosques to verbal threats—findings it had released just weeks prior to Comey's appearance in Congress. Scholars tended to cite two key factors driving the escalation—backlash from the latest round of ISIS-inspired attacks, such as the one in Orlando, along with persistent, unprecedented anti-Muslim messaging in national political discourse—most notably from Donald J. Trump. On the campaign trail Trump's call for a Muslim ban and a national registry of Muslims living in the United States were centerpieces of his presidential platform. "There is a lot of negative rhetoric," Brian Levin, the center's director, noted after the release of the new data. "The negative rhetoric is causing the hate, and in turn the hate is causing the violent acts."

Studies and statistics were making headlines, but to Muslims feeling under siege, the increase in attacks was all too familiar—in short, old news. In April 2016, for example, a surveillance camera outside a coffee shop in Washington, DC, captured footage of a woman dumping a cup of hot liquid onto a Muslim woman's head while calling her a "terrorist" and a "worthless piece of Muslim trash." The assailant claimed to be a supporter of Donald Trump. In June an elderly Muslim riding his bike home after attending prayer at his mosque in Queens was viciously beaten by two men who jumped him. Later that same month, in Minneapolis's Dinkytown neighborhood, two Somali men suffered gunshot wounds when a local man opened fire on their car. In July a Muslim couple returning to their Staten Island home found a note waiting for them, which said, "I'm going to kill you Muslim bitches. You're ISIS. I'm coming for your baby." In August a Somali woman, new to the town of Little Falls, Minnesota, was told by two men who came to her front door that unless she moved out, they would burn her house down. Then early in September two Muslim women with their babies in strollers were accosted on a Brooklyn street by a woman who knocked one stroller over, tried to rip one mother's headscarf off, and screamed, "This is the United States of America, you're not supposed to be different from us!" Most recently, on the fifteenth anniversary of 9/11, a mosque in Florida had been set on fire by a man who'd posted on his Facebook page, "All Islam is radical . . . and should be considered TERRORIST." Flames leaped from the Islamic Center of Fort Pierce after a motorcycle-riding arsonist tossed at it a bottle filled with flammable liquid. Victimized Muslims in nearly every instance were quoted in the media, reciting a mantra of fear: "I'm scared. I'm scared."

These and similar incidents had become the talk of Muslim communities around the country, including the one in Garden City, where Somali refugees living in the West Mary Street apartments, working at the Tyson meatpacking plant, and frequenting Adan Keynan's popular African Store shared their concerns about the worsening treatment of Muslims in America. Adan; his wife, Sara; Sara's daughter, Halima

Farah; and their friends Ifrah Ahmed and Mursal Naleye—they'd all sensed the big chill in one way or another. Adan remained preoccupied with the zoning officials' insistence that his store was noncompliant. The deadline for him to cease operations had come and gone at the end of August, and he worried he'd lose his business any day, maybe have to leave Garden City altogether. Told he might be able to appeal the city's judgment, he was trying to decide on his next move as summer turned into fall. Of course neither he nor any of the others had a clue about a terrorist conspiracy—or that targets had been placed on their backs.

MEANWHILE, IN the days following his introduction to Brian and his cohorts, Patrick worked to get the Crusaders together for a debriefing. But given their respective work responsibilities—with Patrick in the middle of harvest and likely the most hard-pressed—another week went by before they could. For the early evening session on Wednesday, October 5, they again chose the truck stop in Sublette. Patrick quit early to head down; Dan came after spending a day with his family and prepping with his FBI handlers; Curtis was back and forth between his trailer home in Liberal and G&G Home Center, where he felt relieved to escape the nearly constant tension at home with Lula; Gavin mainly manned the shop at G&G. In the early afternoon he spent some time on Facebook, checking on some of his favorite pages, including Being Patriotic. He'd become a regular follower, liking the way the group regularly trashed Hillary Clinton and championed gun rights. Today the page featured a catchy anti-immigrant meme: a photo of a bearded man wearing a Vietnam War veteran's cap with this accompanying text: "Veterans Deserve the Best. Illegals Deserve Nothing." Gavin shared the meme with his Facebook friends, including Dan, Patrick, and Curtis. Little did he know that Being Patriotic was one of a number of fake accounts Russian operatives had created as part of a covert effort to fan hate and chaos in the US presidential race.

Once inside the Subway shop the Crusaders pulled chairs around a table in a corner and were barely seated when Gavin announced that he and Curtis had "set off one."

"You made one?" Patrick asked, totally surprised. He'd been ready to talk about Brian but was stopped in his tracks by Gavin's report of a second test.

"Yeah," Curtis said, without a trace of braggadocio. "With blasting caps."

"Out in the parking lot," Gavin said.

Patrick asked, "What'd you make the blasting cap with?"

"That HMTD powder that we made," Curtis said.

Dan was also stunned—a second successful test had been conducted, yet he'd been unaware of it. His mind grappled with the news; he pictured Curtis and Gavin stepping outside into the parking lot with one of Curtis's homemade detonators; the pinch of HMTD powder tucked inside a paper wrapping with a fuse sticking out; Curtis putting a match to it; the explosion.

Gavin provided a voice-over: "It blew pretty good," he said. "*Boom,* and it was done." Disintegrated everything except for a tiny bit of fuse, he said. Created a hole in the ground "that was, uh, an inch deep." Gavin said they hadn't tried fertilizer this time, just tested the blasting cap. Next step was to use a cap to ignite fertilizer-based explosive material.

Dan seemed bewildered. "I'm in the dark about everything," he said, as the others kept talking about the test. Then later on, and with some urgency, he asked Curtis point-blank how close he was to an actual bomb with "the stuff you got right now?"

"I can do it tomorrow," Curtis said. "Make up a two-pounder, something like that."

No one seemed to notice amid the patter, but Dan was unable to suppress mumbling his dismay. The hidden recording device, however, caught it. "Oh, fuck," he said.

Curtis was apparently riding a wave of confidence. He matter-of-factly laid out his ideas for the final phase of bomb making. In his research, he'd mainly investigated two types of fertilizer bombs. Both involved repurposing fertilizer as the bomb's key ingredient. One involved ammonium nitrate fertilizer. By itself ammonium nitrate was not explosive, but it became highly volatile when mixed correctly with aluminum powder. The mixing was simple—for equipment, a Ziploc plastic bag sufficed. Bomb experts called it the "shake and bake method." Weaker versions of the mixture were used commercially to make explosive targets for firearms practice, with Tannerite being the most popular brand. In bomb-making circles, the ammonium nitrate fertilizer bomb was known as a secondary explosive, meaning it was set off directly by a detonator—such as a blasting cap.

The second type involved urea fertilizer. A urea nitrate bomb was made by dissolving the fertilizer in a solution consisting of water and nitric acid—a process called nitration. Once chemistry did its thing, urea nitrate—a white powder and the key explosive material—was formed. International terrorists favored making homemade explosives out of urea nitrate, given the low cost and easy availability of urea fertilizer. This type of bomb was used in the February 1993 truck bombing at the World Trade Center's north tower, which killed six people and injured more than a thousand.

The urea nitrate fertilizer bomb was considered a tertiary explosive, meaning its explosive material—the urea nitrate—was too insensitive to be ignited directly by a blasting cap. It required an intermediary charge, or booster. The process had three steps—the blasting cap was ignited, which ignited the booster, which then ignited the urea nitrate. For the booster, a compact malleable explosive known as C-4 was often preferred. C-4 came in blocks or sticks and was affixed to the bomb package. Given its stable makeup, C-4 also required energy to kick off. This was the sequence of events: a blasting cap triggered the C-4, the C-4 exploded, and the urea nitrate bomb was then triggered. A fifty-pound bag of urea fertilizer cost about twenty dollars. A bomb built with about 350 pounds of urea fertilizer was powerful enough to flatten a sprawling one-story building—such as the apartment complex on West Mary Street in Garden City, where Somali refugees lived.

Dan grew increasingly uncomfortable as he listened to Curtis talk about how they were practically ready to go, now that the hard part—the blasting cap—was out of the way. Curtis had done homework on both types of fertilizer bombs while he'd worked on making HMTD for the caps, and now in the Subway shop he seemed to be leaning toward a urea fertilizer bomb, the one requiring a booster. As he explained the second test in the parking lot to Dan and Patrick, he referred to the cap as "a pre-charge," meaning it would detonate a booster, such as C-4. The blasting cap, he explained, would ignite the C-4, and the C-4 would trigger the bomb. "If we can get like a quarter stick of C-4, or half a stick of C-4, that would set off the charges."

Here Curtis showed some interest in Brian, though previously he'd remained stubbornly wary of him. He turned to Dan and asked, "Can you get C-4 from him?"

MEETING BRIAN, the high-level arms dealer, was of course the other major topic of the pivotal meeting of October 5. "That brings me to that very subject," Patrick said by way of transition, after they'd digested Gavin's news of the second blasting-cap test. "This guy knows his shit when it comes to explosives," he said. "That's his exclusive fucking business. That's all he does. Guns, explosives—pretty much of any kind."

Like a couple of texting pals, Patrick and Brian had continued exchanging messages right up to the previous night. For his part, Brian was looking to arrange a second meeting, hopefully with everyone there, to persuade the Crusaders to drop their own efforts and leave the manufacturing of bombs to him. That way the FBI would be in charge. Patrick, meanwhile, was looking to solidify his connection to the big-time trafficker and bring Brian's expertise and resources to bear on finalizing the Crusaders' plot. They traded messages about all manner of weapons and explosives—long guns, handguns, grenades, dynamite, blasting caps, C-4, electronic detonation devices. "I can make you something that will take care of that address," Brian bragged, referring to the Somalis' apartment complex.

Patrick did not hold back, revealing in dozens of texts the full monty of the bomb plot. The target date was after the presidential election. "We should have everything ready by the ninth of next month," he said. "We are going to blow up a mosque when they are at their prayer time and they are packed in there like sardines. This is in a location where a select few pieces of shit property owners in this town are housing these bastards."

He was upbeat about the prospect of partnering up, seeing it as way to ensure that the Crusaders got "it right the first time with as few complications as possible, so that people from miles and miles away will take note at the beautiful job we did!!" It would only be the beginning, he said. "Hell, if things go like we want them to it will inspire others in a HUGE way to build the same kind of projects all across the country." Muslims would be on the run.

The two traded thoughts about the best delivery system for IEDs at the West Mary Street apartments. Brian advised that cars would work better than the trash bins the Crusaders had considered. "Which do you think will get more attention? Your getting a ton of garbage cans delivered or some random nobody's buying used cars for cash?" He said they'd need only two cars to hold the explosives needed to level the apartments. "I can build what is needed in one car per building," he said.

Patrick replied, "Nice. That will simplify things so much."

More than once Brian made a point of telling Patrick that he needed to view the target apartment complex himself, to see what the buildings were made of. "Once I have all that, I can make something that will work." The real reason for this requirement, though, was to slow down the Crusaders in order to gain control over them. Brian also kept working on the question of trust and continued pushing to meet Patrick's partners.

"Look them in the eye. You understand?"

"Understand completely, bro," Patrick said. He promised to try.

Brian pressed for further reassurance. He typed another text: "Your other people on board? I haven't met them/know them. I've looked you in the eye."

"Yes, they are," Patrick insisted.

DOMINATING THE messages was a feel-good vibe. To move matters along, Brian told Patrick he'd be returning to the Garden City area—"a job in your neck of the woods in a week or so." He proposed hooking up again, even offered to bring along some of the automatic weapons Patrick had shown interest in at their first meeting. "I may let you sample some of those rifles if you'd want."

Patrick was over the moon. "Would love to," he typed. "We can meet up, discuss plans, and throw some rounds downrange!!" Then, trading texts the night before the Crusaders were to meet at the truck stop, Patrick brimmed with excitement at the possibility of combining forces to go after Muslims. "Orkinman enjoys his work and really gets into it. Making canoes out of their fucking heads is my specialty."

"We could always use more canoes," Brian replied.

"OMG. LMFAO."

Brian explained he was willing to put in "money, time, and effort" and go out on a limb to help because he shared in Patrick's belief that Muslims must be eradicated. He pledged to keep costs down as well. "I support/share your ideologies. I want you to be successful and to do so without getting hurt."

Patrick thanked him again for "any and all advice, thoughts, concerns, expertise etc. that you can provide." Like he'd said when they first met, he and his group were first-timers in the explosives game.

"But the will, determination, and dedication are second to none."

WHEN HIS turn came at the Subway shop meeting, Patrick was eager to talk up Brian; he reenacted their interactions, from the first introduction at the lake preserve through the texting that followed, leaving little doubt how he felt about the high-level arms dealer.

"This guy is very Christian," he told the group, ticking off Brian's positives the way a membership director of an exclusive club would outline an applicant's qualifications—the difference being, this exclusive club was a killing cabal. "He's a stand-up individual," Patrick continued. "He only does this shit for causes, if you will. The right causes."

Dan seconded Patrick's assessment, emphasizing as well that Brian was "the top dog at what he does. He don't have to ask permission about whether he can do shit."

Patrick began by replaying their awkward arrival, saying the first thing to happen was Dan doing "his little transaction deal"—delivering cash to settle up for a mule run. Patrick said Brian acknowledged Dan but seemed stumped about Patrick's presence. "He fucking looked at me and he said, 'Who the fuck is this guy and why is he here?'" Patrick paused to chuckle, as if for dramatic emphasis. "I was like, Oh, fuck, oh, shit, here we go." But Dan had bailed him out, mentioning the weapons list and "who I was and why I was there."

Patrick was unable to satisfy the others' baseline curiosity, however—specific questions about where Brian was from, where his men were from, or the trucks' license plates. Oklahoma? Another state? Gavin at one point teased, "What kind of fucking GI are you, man? You gotta get information."

Patrick confessed to feeling a bit freaked out by the circumstances—surrounded, in the middle of nowhere, ten miles from the nearest main road. "When you're walking into a group of five motherfuckers, and you know they're all packing, and you know none of them, I guarantee you I ain't lookin' at no fuckin' tags. I'm keeping my eyes on everybody."

Gavin was entertained, but Curtis not so much. "So what's the news?" the group's commander said, seeming impatient. "I'm sorry, but there's some new stuff, right?"

Patrick wasn't going to be rushed. He narrated how, after the introductions were finished, he and Brian had gone off to talk privately in Brian's pickup. Once inside, Brian first insisted on clarifying their terms of engagement. "The reason he wanted to meet with us personally," Patrick said, "is because he wanted basically to look everybody in the eye, to get a feel for them, and to make sure that what he was going to provide wasn't going to the hands of the jihadis." Patrick, chuckling, said he'd made it crystal clear that Muslims were the target, "and he really got interested then, you know. He is all about that."

Patrick's gut reaction? Totally impressed with Brian's competence and expertise in explosives. He cited, for example, how Brian had strongly advised against relying on a cell phone to activate a bomb's blasting cap. "He said, 'You want to get that idea out of your head.' And I asked him why and he said, 'Well, think about how many people there are in the United States and how many phones are out there.'" Brian, he said, warned him, "Who's to say while you're wiring everything up, you get one of the bombs ready to go, and you make the last connection. It's all good to go, and somebody dials that fucking phone? You go bye-bye."

"Yeah, and that ain't good," Gavin said, an understatement.

The one-on-one could not have gone better, Patrick said. "We hit if off really very well." Brian had acted all gung-ho, supporting their patriotism and their plans. "He's chomping at the bit to be part of it; however, he's also very fricking cautious."

Gavin, in Colorado that weekend to visit his ninety-four-year-old grandfather, expressed regret that he'd missed out. "I sure would have been there if I could have."

The bottom line: Patrick had explained the group's goals to Brian, and with that, Brian had committed to do anything he could to make things happen. Patrick's recommendation? To view Brian as a golden opportunity. "This way might be the way to go," he said. No matter how much progress they were making with Curtis's blasting caps, anything they did was going to be "a first-time deal." The stakes were too important to mess up due to inexperience, especially when they had the chance to team up with a pro. Patrick exclaimed, "By God, when that motherfucker goes off, I want the whole fucking building to come down. I want the mission accomplished, okay?"

Even with Patrick's rave review, however—which was on his own firsthand meeting with Brian—Curtis continued to voice skepticism, sounding almost resentful at times at Patrick's embrace of Brian and his apparent bomb-making prowess. Curtis was the one who'd put in the time and hard work to become a bomb-making autodidact. He'd gotten past the difficult hurdle of making HMTD for a functional blasting cap. The rest would fall into place once they rounded up the fertilizer and converted it into explosive material. Curtis again questioned the need to go outside their bubble.

The debate that ensued followed a pattern that had remained consistent since Dan had introduced his connection to a weapons dealer. Dan and Patrick pushed for the partnership, with Patrick becoming an even more vociferous ally of Dan's as his own relationship with Brian got underway. Curtis and to a lesser extent Gavin both voiced reluctance, and the discussion grew heated at times.

"What's he going to build?" Curtis asked. He wanted specifics.

"He didn't say," Patrick replied, "and I didn't ask."

Curtis pressed him about the drug bartering. "He willing to trade still?"

Patrick said he wasn't certain. They hadn't yet discussed bartering in detail.

"Hmm" was all Curtis said. Then, after a pause, he asked, "You haven't discussed trading? Trading *something*? I thought you did." He seemed annoyed at the dearth of substantial information. Patrick hadn't been able to tell them where Brian or any of his crew were from. Not a big a deal, really. But this? This was getting to the heart of any so-called alliance.

"Nope," Patrick answered.

"That's the only way we're going to be able to do it," Curtis said.

"Yeah, no shit," Gavin concurred. "Unless we hit the fucking lottery."

Then there was Curtis's unwillingness to meet Brian, though Dan had been calling him about it, separate from the group, and urging him to reconsider. "We're leery of meetin' his ass," Curtis said, referring to himself and Gavin. Curtis added later, "I don't want to meet him."

Patrick was ready to throw up his hands at Curtis's pigheadedness.

"These ain't just fuckin', you know, curbside fuckin' drug dealers, or arms dealers," he said. "The guy that I'm dealing with, he works all over the country. There ain't a state in the union he don't fucking work in, or have customers in."

Lastly there was Curtis's concern about a trap. He questioned yet again Brian's emergence the previous month, at such a key moment in the group's planning. Was the timing too good to be true? "And it's like, now he's going to build us something." Curtis was suspicious. "It's starting to sound like a CIA setup, or FBI setup." He laughed half-heartedly at his words, knowing they had become a refrain for him, even now, in the face of Patrick's endorsement of Brian. Maybe it made him sound paranoid—although he was, albeit unknowingly, actually close to the truth, and too close for comfort, for Dan.

Patrick had heard it all before. "Dude," he said, "don't think I haven't thought about the same thing." But wasn't that getting a bit tired at this point? He'd vetted Brian, in person and through encrypted text messaging. Then there was Dan. Patrick reminded everyone that their trusted cohort had deep ties to Brian's outfit and had vouched for him. "The only reason I've went as far as I have with this guy is because of this guy right here." Patrick seemed frustrated by the recurring complaints about money and deceptions. He pushed back. "Here's the deal on this guy," Patrick said. "He is willing to put his own money into it. It's not just us putting money into it. And he will put the time into it.

"He will build it and what he builds, he said it'll take out the whole fucking building."

It was point, counterpoint.

Then Curtis softened. He'd squawked and complained—just as he'd done previously. But previously he'd never slammed the door shut, and he didn't do so this time either. Instead, by meeting's end he was acknowledging the benefits of being with Brian.

"I'm cool," he said, as Patrick and Dan kept trying to talk sense into him.

Curtis's take was this: Patrick and Dan should continue playing out the string with Brian, see if money was not going to be a problem and if Brian could deliver on his promises. Curtis even reiterated his specific interest in C-4. He ordered Dan to get a price from Brian for "a stick of C-4" and, while he was at it, the price for "a couple of blasting caps." Meanwhile, he and Gavin would continue working on their own homemade IEDs. Why cease production? "We've already got everything for it," Curtis said.

So a two-track strategy emerged, one with a built-in insurance plan. If Brian went dark on them for whatever reason, they'd still be ready to act. Gavin thought Curtis's plan made sense. "We can't get the shit," he said, meaning if Brian fell through on the bombs, "we're going to have to make it."

"Right," Curtis said, and with that, the commander had spoken.

UNDER FAIR SKIES, DAN, the informant; his FBI handlers, Amy Kuhn and Robin Smith; the undercover arms dealer, Brian; and a slew of other agents and supervisors pulled into the parking area at the lake preserve outside Kalvesta, Kansas. They'd made the forty-minute drive from Garden City to rehearse Brian's second meeting with Patrick the next day, October 12. Dan would be there, of course. Less clear was whether Curtis or Gavin, or both, would surprise everyone and show up.

The early afternoon weather was warm but not hot, given the cloud cover, and a breeze blew across the barren terrain. Dan had gotten a ride this time with agent Kuhn. Not because he'd taken a wrong turn en route to the first meeting, just that there was no reason to add another vehicle by having him drive alone. There were already more vehicles on the premises than at the first rehearsal—a caravan of pickup trucks and SUVs kicking up dust across the miles of dirt road leading to the preserve. There was also nearly double the personnel; a dozen or so had participated in the first meeting, either in an undercover capacity or working surveillance from a distance.

The reason for the added manpower was the added firepower. Brian, to further ensnare Patrick while cementing his bona fides as a weapons trafficker, had promised Patrick he could sample the guns that were the staple of his black-market deals. Kuhn and Smith had already jumped through bureaucratic hoops to get approval from headquarters in Washington, DC, for the use of automatic assault weapons that were otherwise illegal—guns capable of emptying a thirty-round magazine in a split second. The cache had arrived from the FBI laboratory in Quantico, Virginia, and included the M16 assault rifle, first used by American troops in the Vietnam War in the early 1960s, and the extremely popular AK-47, which dated back to World War II. The AK used a 7.62-millimeter high-velocity round, which could rip through a body, shattering bones and destroying organs, and was considered one of the deadliest weapons ever.

With guns in play, the risk of something going dangerously awry increased. The agents were not expecting trouble from Patrick, or his cohorts if they came, but they had to plan for that possibility, for the safety of their undercover operatives, their informant, Dan Day, and even their target, Patrick Stein. Beefed-up measures meant extra bodies and assets, and they'd held several plenary sessions at the FBI office in Garden City prior to heading out for the afternoon rehearsal. The quickness with which the FBI mobilized its resources left Dan a bit wide-eyed. Having learned that cell phone coverage was poor at the lake preserve, the FBI had technicians set up a portable cell-phone booster, which was kept out of sight, as were all of the surrounding support services. Once again snipers would be hidden in the trees a few hundred yards away; in the event of gunfire, agents would drop to the ground, and the snipers would aim only at anyone who was standing. In addition, a SWAT team would be on call nearby. More agents were posted in the broader perimeter, and arrangements had even been made for aerial surveillance. Dan didn't know whether they'd be using a drone or a high-flying aircraft; he simply understood that no matter how hard he stared upward, he would never spot it in the sky. Nearby too was a helicopter, on standby in case gunfire caused injuries, or worse. The protocol for its use: if an FBI agent was hit, both an ambulance and the helicopter to airlift the wounded would be summoned instantly. If one of the targets was hit, just the ambulance would be called. In other words, the helicopter was for FBI only. Dan had sat silently as supervisors reviewed the operational plans, but upon hearing about the helicopter rescue protocol, he wondered where he fit in—he was neither FBI nor a target. He cleared his throat noisily, as if to say, Hello? His handler, agent Kuhn, the one who probably knew him best, caught on. She interrupted the presentation to note that Dan was to be "treated as FBI." The clarification was accompanied by lighthearted apologies—of course he was included. They had not meant to imply that he'd been overlooked.

Then, at the meeting, they'd diagrammed the shooting exercise. And now at the lake preserve Dan watched as Brian and the others performed a walk-through, reviewing where they wanted the trucks to park and where, down below the parking area, a makeshift shooting range had been set up. It's where Brian would park his pickup loaded with weapons, and Dan saw that pumpkins purchased from Walmart—dozens and dozens of them, in all shapes and sizes—had already been scattered beyond the fencing. It seemed like a Hollywood set for on-location filming. And just as in a movie, this scene was fake, constructed to support an illusion: that a clandestine encounter with a weapons dealer was taking place. But any similarities ended right there.

Having Patrick use the assault rifles wasn't just for show. It was part of a strategic ploy intended to advance the legal case. The moment Patrick pulled the trigger, the government had a chargeable offense—it being a felony to discharge a weapon that continued firing until the shooter either released the trigger or the magazine was emptied, and an AK-47 could fire six hundred rounds in a minute. If on short notice the agents needed to act quickly, Patrick's illegal action gave them the power to take him into custody. "We want to put automatic weapons into their hands in case they become an immediate danger to the public," Kuhn had written in the FBI paperwork seeking authorization for their use.

When Kuhn sought approval, they were hoping to have all three Crusaders on hand, but those hopes were diminished by the time the rehearsal was underway. In the days following their meeting in Sublette the prior week, on October 5, both Dan and Patrick kept up their efforts to convince Curtis and Gavin to attend. Gavin had seemed to thaw but then came up with reasons why he couldn't make it. Curtis was fine with the idea of doing business with Brian but wouldn't budge on meeting him. "I don't know what would make them come on board," Dan had griped to Patrick. It was one thing for Curtis to be cautious, he said, but "paranoia will overtake everything." Both complained that Curtis was way too mistrustful — although Patrick was quick to remind Dan that if not for him vouching for Brian and going way back with Brian's outfit, he'd harbor suspicions. He'd read plenty online describing how the FBI takes down terrorist bomb plots. "You know the FBI always catches their fucking ass like right before they get ready to set it off," he said. "If it wasn't for you, and the fact that you know these people — fuck, I wouldn't even consider it."

Dan just nodded and said, "Right."

Even without their presence, though, the FBI figured it had ample evidence against all of the Crusaders at this point — from Patrick's direct involvement with Brian and especially from the many hours of Dan's secret recordings, chronicling the terrorist conspiracy from its inception in June until this moment. In fact, the FBI's endgame was coming into focus as agents readied for the second meeting at the lake preserve, and it was strikingly similar to Patrick's description of the FBI's terrorist busts. Tactically, Brian was to finalize the plan that he would be the one to manufacture the bombs. That would put the FBI in the driver's seat. Then they'd set up another meeting for Brian to hand off bogus IEDs to Patrick and the others. Finally, as the Crusaders executed their plot — setting up the cars loaded with phony bombs outside the mosque on West Mary Street and getting ready to detonate them — agents and a SWAT team would descend in force. In the ideal scenario, everyone would be there: Patrick, Curtis, and Gavin. Dan would be taken into custody as well. In anticipation, prosecutors had begun amassing the necessary legal paperwork — affidavits and probable cause for search warrants and the criminal complaint. There were of course no guarantees, but agents and federal prosecutors at this point felt they were on what one prosecutor called a "nice, steady path to a takedown." The plan was to do it within forty-eight to seventy-two hours of the November 8 presidential election.

On the overcast day when Dan and the agents were rehearsing their parts, Brian took to his smartphone to make arrangements for the next day's meeting. "Tomorrow," he texted Patrick early in the afternoon, "I'll start heading your way."

"Sounds good, man," Patrick replied. "Look forward to meeting up again."

THAT SAME afternoon in Liberal, about a hundred miles south of the rehearsal in Kalvesta, Lula Harris fumed inside the trailer home she shared with Curtis. She was fed up. Fed up with Curtis and his sleeping around—his "conflicts of interests," as she called them. Fed up with feeling used—she'd fronted Curtis $2,100 when she'd moved back in so that he could pay his lot rent, and he'd basically stopped repaying her. Fed up with caring for the little puppy he'd brought home one day when she was still feeling worn out from cancer treatments earlier in the year. Come the afternoon, all she wanted was a short nap, but the frisky, yapping puppy demanded her attention, like a new baby. Fed up that Curtis was barely around anymore, either to care for his puppy or, more important, her. He used to go off to work with Gavin at G&G Home Center three days a week at most. Now it was like he was there every day, all day. The list of grievances had reached the tipping point.

She headed for G&G, which was less than three miles away, and after she parked her car, she walked directly into the office trailer. Curtis was indeed present, at once surprised and annoyed to see her. Lula said they needed to talk—about the money, about the women, about the damn puppy outside in her car. The couple went outdoors where Curtis got mad, saying he and Gavin were busy. She repeated her demand—that they go home and talk about the problems in their relationship—the money, the women, and the puppy.

Curtis turned toward her car; he had a solution for the puppy problem—kill it.

"You kill that puppy," she yelled, "I'll call 911."

Curtis glared at her. He smashed his phone in anger, jumped into his truck, and roared off. When Lula reached their trailer a few minutes later, she saw that his maroon GMC Yukon Denali was already there. When she entered the trailer, she saw Curtis had begun piling her things on the loveseat in the living room. He came out the bedroom with another armful. They argued. Lula demanded, "Where's my money? Where's my money?"

Curtis swore and shouted he'd call the bank, make some kind of arrangement. He continued to throw her clothes onto the loveseat and then across the floor, his way of saying he was done.

Lula followed him toward the back bedroom, ordering him to pick her things up off the floor. If he didn't, she threatened again to call the Liberal police. Curtis was not impressed: "You're gonna need more than 911 today," he yelled at her. They stood in the narrow hallway, confronting each other. Curtis grabbed Lula's purse, then went after the smartphone in her left hand. She wouldn't let go. They struggled. He twisted her hand. It hurt. She squirmed and broke free. She stepped over her things on the floor and hurried outside, as he screamed from behind her. She noticed that several of their neighbors were in their tiny yards, watching, as if rubbernecking a traffic accident.

Curtis stood in the doorway: "You call 911, I'll kill you and your family," he said. Then he went inside and came back out, carrying weapons. He loaded them into his truck. He repeated the process a couple of times. He went to her car and removed a gun he kept in the console. While he did this, Lula dialed Gavin, thinking he was probably ready to close the office for the day. She thought maybe he'd come and get Curtis, take him out for a beer, calm him down. This would give her time to remove her belongings in an orderly way.

Gavin was unsympathetic. Curtis, he told her, was also frustrated with the situation. Lula tried explaining she had good reason to be upset, but Gavin cut her off. He repeated the line that Curtis had gotten extremely frustrated. Then Gavin hung up on her.

Curtis climbed into cab of his truck, slammed the door shut, and drove off.

No goodbye. Nothing. Lula stood alone in the tiny yard decorated with rocks that they had painted red, white, and blue during happier days. She dialed 911.

CURTIS AND Gavin, each driving his own vehicle, left work together a little after five o'clock. A few hundred yards down the road from G&G Home Center they spotted the flashing blue lights of several Liberal police cruisers. Both men slowed down and pulled off to the side of the street called Country Estates. Seconds later the cruisers arrived, lights afire. The police vehicles stopped in a way that boxed in Curtis and Gavin, so that neither could, on impulse, try to take off. The officers exited their vehicles and drew their service weapons. The two Crusaders looked puzzled: what the fuck?

The stop was made within forty-five minutes of Lula's 911 call. She'd reported an assault, given a description of Curtis's truck and its license plate, and said he'd probably be found at G&G Home Center. While one patrol officer staked out Gavin's office and had indeed spotted the truck, another went to the mobile home to interview Lula. The officer saw evidence of the couple's dispute—the living room was littered with her clothes and other things. Looking around, he also saw plenty of weapons, ammunition, and military manuals. Lula got emotional as she recapped the fighting: Curtis grabbing at her, his storming off, his yelling and threats. Then she went further. She told them about what she'd seen a few weeks earlier at the home center—the lab equipment and strange chemicals. Then she dropped a bombshell: she said Curtis and Gavin were making explosives to kill Muslims.

Explosives? The officer updated the 911 call, triggering what one supervisor later called an "elevated response." The seemingly standard domestic call had taken a sharp turn into a far more serious matter. It meant that when Curtis and Gavin had left the office and climbed into their vehicles, the police who pulled them over shortly after were not making a routine traffic stop. For those—a speeding or a red light violation—the officer would approach the driver's window and politely ask for license and registration. This was different, something known in police parlance as a felony traffic stop.

With guns drawn, the officers shouted at Curtis and Gavin to get out of their trucks: "On the ground! Hands on your head!" Soon a couple more officers hustled across the field, rifles in hand; a police captain named Jason Ott pulled in behind his colleagues; there were now multiple police vehicles on the scene, lights flashing. Ott ran along the side of Curtis's truck to confirm no one was hiding inside. Curtis and Gavin obeyed the officers' command and lay down as they were cuffed with their hands behind their backs. Curtis fell silent but Gavin got mouthy; he protested the harsh treatment and demanded to know why the hell they were being detained. Ott and the arresting officers were initially skimpy with information, disclosing only that Curtis had threatened someone's life. With that, officers pulled Curtis to his feet and ushered him into the back of a police cruiser. In a cursory search of his truck that was part of the arrest, police found piles of ammunition, AR-15 magazines, an AK-47 magazine, and a Glock handgun magazine—all loaded. They found a tool used for making silencers for firearms or suppressors.

Gavin watched in disbelief. He complained, "What the hell does any of this have to do with me? Why am I on the ground cuffed, you guys pointing guns at me?"

By this time, with both men handcuffed, the officers had holstered their own weapons. One officer then told Gavin that the complainant had also said Curtis was making bombs.

Gavin thought, *Oh shit,* but managed to say, "I don't know nothin' about that."

Captain Ott said, "She says he's making them in your shop."

"There ain't nothing in my fuckin' office but work stuff."

Ott said, "How about you let us take a look?"

Gavin said, "No, no way. Can't do that." Gavin then said something about being only a co-owner of the business, so he couldn't be letting police on the premises unilaterally.

Ott said, "Okay, if you won't allow a search, then we'll get a warrant."

"I'm not hiding anything from you guys." Gavin was trying to sound conciliatory.

"Right," Ott said.

The police had no reason to hold Gavin, however. They removed the handcuffs and let him go. In a panic, Gavin headed to his home, just across the state line in Oklahoma. His mind reeled as he tried to think of what to do—clean house, so to speak. One of the first steps he took was to make the short drive to Space Station Secure Storage in Liberal. Hoping no one was watching—and hoping police would never know about unit F2, rented in his brother's name—he punched the access code at the electronic gate. Once inside the fenced-in complex, he went to the unit and unloaded some files and printed materials he'd scooped up from his office. He tried to figure out what to do next.

Curtis was taken to the Liberal Police Department, where he was processed and held. Meanwhile, Captain Ott drove out to Curtis's trailer. It was about 6:30 p.m. He had Lula Harris repeat what had happened during the quarrel with Curtis. She recapped events and then continued talking about how Curtis, Patrick, and Gavin were plotting something "big" against Muslims. She said Curtis was making explosives at Gavin's workplace because the mobile home was not air conditioned and the substances Curtis used were extremely volatile. In the living room Ott and a patrol officer saw how-to manuals for making bombs and weapons such as an AR-15 rifle. On a side table they spotted a CD with the label ANARCHIST COOKBOOK. Lula handed Curtis's silver spiral composition notebook to one officer, who flipped it open and read aloud: "America, I want to share information with you," from Curtis's opening passage. The officer continued reading. A few sentences later, Curtis had written: "In the near future you will see certain actions to reinstate our Constitution and you also see the Govt. & Media telling you we are domestic terrorists. Please do not fall for this. We the people have to take back control of our Govt." The officer closed the notebook and handed it to Ott. "This is a manifesto," the officer said. Ott read a few more paragraphs to himself, then put it down. He'd wait for a search warrant to be secured before delving further.

Lula then showed the police captain Curtis's "man cave," a bedroom set aside for his collection of weapons and ammunition. The small room was piled high, wall to wall, with weapons and reloading supplies. One bullet-loaded belt caught Ott's eye immediately—it contained .50-caliber cartridges. The .50-caliber bullet was big and powerful, nearly 5.5 inches in length and known for its armor-piercing force. The US military used the heavy-hitting bullet in sniper rifles and M2 Browning machine guns. Ott held up one of the bullets and asked Lula, "Does Curtis have a gun that will shoot this .50 cal?"

Lula said yes, but the weapon was not in the trailer at that moment. She said it might be at Gavin's house. Or Daniel's. She wasn't sure. Curtis stored things at Daniel's place, outside Liberal. Daniel was a member of the militia that Curtis commanded, the Kansas Security Force. She told Ott what she knew about Curtis's militia activities with KSF.

The bomb-making CDs and manuals, the draft manifesto, the .50-caliber cartridges and the weapons: Ott took it all in. A domestic call had morphed into domestic terrorism.

He said, "This is above my pay grade."

NEAR THE end of the rehearsal at the preserve, Dan's smartphone rang. He looked and saw that Patrick was calling. He, Robin Smith, Amy Kuhn, Brian, and others were down below, where the shooting gallery would be staged the next day. Dan yelled over to Smith, who was standing near a gate. "Stein's trying to call me," he said. The FBI agent was dismissive, told Dan to call him back later. They needed to finish up first.

Dan had no problem with that. Patrick frequently called, just wanting to vent. But then he got a text message from Patrick—"911," it said. Dan told the agent that Patrick was now texting him. "I need to get this, man," he said. "Patrick's saying it's an emergency."

Smith said, "Okay, go ahead."

Dan stepped away from the group. Brian, his curiosity piqued, accompanied him. They climbed into a Jeep parked nearby. Dan put his cell on speakerphone and returned Patrick's call—and that's when the FBI first learned about Curtis Allen's unexpected arrest by local police in Liberal.

Patrick talked excitedly but didn't have much information beyond the news that Lula Harris had called the cops on Curtis, who had been taken into custody. Brian texted Smith that Dan was on a call with Patrick. The FBI agent ran over in time to hear the tail end of Patrick's urgent report—that Liberal police had stopped Curtis and Gavin at gunpoint, handcuffed them on the ground, taken Curtis in, and let Gavin go. Patrick said he was going to try to get more information. Dan said to keep him informed. They hung up.

Brian and Smith immediately told everyone—and the scramble was on. Smith and Kuhn knew they needed to get to Liberal as fast as possible. Their worries were twofold. First, the local police, in the dark about the federal investigation, could inadvertently mess everything up in their contacts with Curtis or Lula or whomever. Early on the agents had made the strategic decision not to notify their state and local counterparts about the terrorism case—which went against their usual practice of working collaboratively. They'd done so out of extreme concern for the security of the investigation and for Dan's safety—the possibility of leaks at the state and local levels. Dan was especially at risk—always on his own when meeting with Patrick, Curtis, and Gavin. Not only did the open, flat terrain make close surveillance impossible, but the small-town nature of Garden City meant Smith and Kuhn were well known as federal agents; they always had to assume word would get around if they were spotted here, there, or anywhere in the area. The agents and federal prosecutors had operated on the belief that if Dan's role was discovered, the others would not hesitate to kill him, and for that reason the probe was a closely held secret. Now, in the wake of Patrick's news, they worried they might end up paying a price for that decision, since local police had no idea what was up.

The second concern was that Curtis's arrest would set off Patrick and possibly Gavin. Would they start destroying evidence and go on the run? Or worse, decide to hurry up and conduct some kind of violent attack on their own against Somali refugees in Garden City? Suddenly, so many unknowns. Of course, the team abruptly ended the rehearsal—and for that matter, perhaps the next day's planned meeting with Patrick would never happen.

Everything was in flux, the impact of Curtis's arrest unknown. Given that Lula had mentioned explosives, the FBI agents knew that within minutes they'd be getting a call from Liberal police to alert them about a matter within their jurisdiction. The agents quickly decided that they needed to act as if the report was news to them, rather than attempt to disclose everything over the phone—including why they'd kept the case so secret for so long. The agents wanted to get the Liberal police to freeze in place until they got there and could take stock.

Kuhn jumped into an FBI vehicle with a supervisor and left for Liberal. Smith did not have his FBI vehicle, so he needed to stop in Garden City to retrieve it while en route to Liberal. He and Dan climbed into a Suburban driven by an FBI technician. They rumbled along the dirt road to get to Highway 156. The drive to Liberal from Kalvesta usually took at least ninety minutes. But Smith had no intention of obeying the speed limit. "*Faster,*" he yelled at the driver. "*Faster.*" On the way, Smith did get a call from the Liberal police officer he knew, Captain Jason Ott. Smith listened as Ott summarized the situation, then, playing dumb, said, "Okay, sounds like you got a problem." He also learned that Ott had contacted Adam Piland, an agent for the Kansas Bureau of Investigation, who lived in Liberal and was unaware of the operation related to the Crusaders. Smith knew Piland too. Smith promised that he and his partner, Amy Kuhn, would be in Liberal as soon as possible—everyone there should sit tight and await their arrival.

So much for feeling they were on a steady path toward a takedown.

JASON OTT, THE POLICE captain, had his officers secure Lula and Curtis's trailer home while he drove Lula down to the Liberal Police Department. FBI agent Amy Kuhn arrived first from Kalvesta, at about 8 p.m., and agent Robin Smith, after dropping Dan off at home in Garden City and switching to his FBI vehicle, arrived soon after. Selectively, and over the course of the next day, the agents revealed the full contours of the terrorism case, first to the KBI's Adam Piland, who was in the KBI's Special Operations Division, and then to Captain Ott of the Liberal police. The agents also immediately got in touch with their FBI supervisors in Kansas City and with Tony Mattivi, the lead federal prosecutor. Evidence and explosives teams at both the federal and state levels were notified. The Liberal police of course remained involved, as did the sheriff of Seward County, whose deputies were in charge of booking and holding Curtis at the county jail. Each was notified on a need-to-know basis that they had a far more serious matter on their hands than a local couple gone bad.

Curtis had been taken to an interview room equipped with a video camera. Kuhn, observing him on a monitor, noticed that Curtis appeared calm, just sitting there silently without showing any outward signs of worry. No surprise, really; he had always been the most wary and disciplined Crusader, perhaps because of his military background. She and the KBI's Piland entered the interview room, hoping to engage with Curtis. But he had little to say except that he was hungry. Kuhn had someone get fast food from the McDonald's a few minutes from the station. But once he got his food, Curtis "lawyered up," meaning that he would not respond to questions from Kuhn and Piland without his lawyer present.

Then, in a different room, Kuhn and Piland settled in with Lula and asked her to start again from the beginning. Beyond information about the couple's troubled relationship, Lula added more details about Curtis's intense hatred for Muslims and his supply of bomb-making materials—beakers, scales, and stirrers. She described how she one day saw a white powdery substance cooling in an ice bath on the counter at G&G. She mentioned again Curtis's friend Daniel and the fact that Curtis kept weaponry at Daniel's because their trailer was so cramped. It was well after midnight before they finished up the interview, at which time Lula was taken to a domestic violence shelter nearby. The agents talked about having her show them exactly where Gavin lived the next day. Lula said she would cooperate with police and testify if need be, but she made it clear that she had no intention of staying in Liberal. She did not feel safe anymore, she said. In fact, within the week she would uproot herself from the mobile home and leave town for good, along with the $15,000 the FBI had given her, to assist in her relocation.

While Kuhn and Piland met with Lula, Ott worked on search warrants for the mobile home, Curtis's truck, G&G Home Center, and Daniel's property, about twelve miles northwest of town. Police contacted Daniel about Curtis's arrest; Daniel and his wife voluntarily came to the station, where FBI agent Smith explained the case as an instance of domestic violence. He asked about Curtis's cache—and stayed clear of mentioning anything about bombs and terrorism. Daniel was not happy that he had caught the attention of law enforcement, and he made the point that in Kansas there was no law against owning firearms of all kinds and ammo in unlimited amounts.

Meanwhile, Ott worked through the night on the warrants, and the next morning he, the KBI's Piland, and a police team headed out to Daniel's property, handed the warrant to Daniel, and conducted a search. They found little in the two small houses on the rural property but located firearms and ammunition stockpiled in a tornado shelter under a garage. The cache included a .50-caliber BMG single-shot rifle—a weapon able to fire the powerful, armor-piercing 5.5-inch bullets that had caught Ott's eye when he'd initially surveyed Curtis's "man cave" in the trailer. Then the police returned to the mobile home and took a detailed inventory of Curtis's weaponry there; on closer inspection they found a can containing a bag of aluminum powder—the key ingredient for making an improvised explosive device when mixed with ammonium nitrate fertilizer. In Curtis's truck police found more ammunition but no firearms. They did find additional bomb manuals; Curtis's business cards as commander of the Kansas Security Force militia; and his iPad, with a sticker attached to one side that read ISIS HUNTING PERMIT. The search team kept busy itemizing and documenting everything it seized, including an estimated metric ton of ammunition in boxes and cans or lying about loose. The size of Curtis's arsenal, both at the trailer and at Daniel's place, was eye-opening even to the Liberal police veteran Jason Ott, who considered himself a collector and a "gun person."

THE FBI case agents and prosecutors were adjusting on the fly as they worked through Tuesday night to assess the possible fallout from Curtis's arrest. Meanwhile, Brian, his fellow undercover agents, and Dan had to stay on track, act as if they knew next to nothing about the tumult. Brian reached out to Patrick following the arrest, the pretense being to continue updating the next day's meeting. He was also looking to detect if Patrick had grown suspicious. "5 tomorrow," he texted Patrick, giving him a time.

Patrick replied with an emoji: two thumbs up. He asked, "Same place as last time?"

Brian said, "Tell Dan and the boys. I'll let you know tomorrow."

So far everything seemed to be holding fast.

For his part, after Dan got home at dusk on Tuesday he briefed Cherlyn and the kids. The takedown plan was unraveling, he said, and the next forty-eight hours would be touch and go. And news of Curtis's arrest wasn't just rippling through law enforcement; it was making the rounds in militia circles as well, most notably the Kansas Security Force. Dan monitored the chatter to see if it strayed beyond the domestic-violence-related arrest. He said little and mostly listened during a quick KSF meeting on Zello. No one seemed to know much. Lots of questions with few answers.

Patrick jumped in, shared what he knew so far, and promised to find out more. Because he was dealing with the authorities at the Liberal police station, Daniel was not in attendance, which was fortunate. Daniel knew something the rest did not—the FBI was in town, which was strange. The bureau did not ordinarily get involved in a domestic violence case. Something else had to be going on.

This meant Patrick was unaware of FBI involvement. Had he known, the agents' rush to get a handle on the startling turn of events would be further complicated. Patrick might suspect he was being set up and pursue any of several possible courses of action, none of them good. One official considered the possibilities: Maybe he attends the meeting with Brian as scheduled, but when he gets his hands on an automatic AK-47, he "goes postal" and starts killing everyone—Brian, other agents, and Dan Day. Maybe he bails from the meeting, destroys evidence so that the case falls apart, and remains free to try to kill Somalis, more determined than ever. Maybe he goes rogue and right away goes after Somalis in Garden City or tracks down Dan Day to assassinate him. After all, similar things had happened. The previous year, in Overland Park in eastern Kansas, the former Ku Klux Klan leader who had been convicted of killing three people at a Jewish community center thought he was terminally ill with emphysema when he'd carried out the fatal assault—it was sort of a swan song, a final gesture. Maybe Patrick would view the collapse of his history-making plot to exterminate Muslims in Garden City as his equivalent of a terminal illness; after all, he'd told Brian when they first met that he did not expect to live past January.

The federal prosecutor, Mattivi, now in regular contact with the FBI agents and their bosses, was convinced that, at a minimum, Patrick would be a no-show at the meeting with Brian in Kalvesta.

Besides Daniel, noticeably absent from the Zello meeting was Gavin. Kuhn and Smith assumed he was hunkering down in his mobile home but didn't know for sure. They asked Dan to check on him, take his pulse in the wake of the police stop. When Gavin failed to join the Zello meeting, Dan decided to give him a call. It was 9:35 p.m. when he did.

"Hey, Gavin," he said.

"Sir," Gavin answered.

"Hey, this is Dan."

"Hey."

"I know you probably don't want to talk very much, but, uh, you doing okay?"

"Oh, yeah. I'm fine."

The two Crusaders talked for nearly a half hour, during which they continually looped back to certain topics. Lula Harris was one; she was referred to as "a bitch," "whacked," and "a fuckin' liar" for igniting so much trouble. "She's lost her mind," Gavin said. "They should throw *her* in jail." Gavin several times replayed his handcuffing by the police. "I'm like, 'What the fuck, this is a bit excessive, isn't it?'" he said. "Why am I on the ground cuffed and people walkin' across pointin' guns at me?" He claimed to be aghast when police brought up bomb making. "Making fuckin' IEDs is what the cop said. 'You know what an IED is?' I go, 'I watch the fuckin' news, yeah. I'm not stupid. I mean, they do 'em over in Iraq and Iran and Afghanistan all the time. I hear about it all the fuckin' time. Yeah, I know what it is. Do I know how to make one? No! Have I seen anyone make one? No!'"

He said police asked him how Curtis spent his time outside his work at G&G Home Center. "I go, 'Fuck, I don't know. I'm not his mommy.

Or his daddy.' I said, 'I don't get into my employees after hours. It's none of my fuckin' business what he does.'"

Gavin said he'd told Patrick he was quitting the group, that he'd deleted everything from his computer. "I'm done," he told Dan. Besides, he said, he knew nothing about manufacturing bombs. "I can't tell 'em anything," Gavin said, his voice going flat. He repeated—stressed, in fact—that he'd seen no evil, heard no evil, and spoken no evil. "I don't know anything, Dan," he said. "I want to keep it that way."

Dan found the remarks confounding at first: Gavin wasn't talking to the police anymore; he was talking to him, a fellow Crusader—so-called Dangerous Dan.

Gavin continued: "Like I told them, I don't know anything."

Dan thought, *Don't know anything? What about the meetings at G&G, where we spent hours finalizing a plan and rounding up bomb-making supplies using his PayPal account? What about the breakthrough moment when he and Curtis had made a blasting cap?* Gavin had been the one so eager to share the news at the Subway shop in Sublette—news that had shocked Dan. Gavin said they'd "tested that shit," meaning HMTD, and it had been "badass." Then Dan realized Gavin must be thinking their call was being intercepted by the police. Gavin was playing to them, professing innocence. But even as Dan concluded he'd figured out the game, listening to Gavin describe himself as simply a "business owner" was hard to take.

"All right, man," Dan finally said.

"All right, see you, bud," Gavin said.

"Be in touch," Dan said, but he was thinking, *What a bunch of crap.*

GAVIN WRIGHT continued his know-nothing talk first thing the next morning, Wednesday, October 12. He showed up unannounced at the Liberal Police Department shortly after 8 a.m., complaining he'd been barred by an officer from entering G&G Home Center. The FBI's Smith and Kuhn, both of whom had been up all night, were at a nearby restaurant, having breakfast with some Liberal officers, when they got the call about Gavin. Returning to the station, Smith and the KBI's Piland led Gavin into a windowless interview room. Coffee was set up all around, like shots of whiskey at a bar. Smith was dressed in blue jeans, an overcoat, work boots, and a camo cap, which he took off and flopped onto the table. The weather had been clear and comfortable during the rehearsal in Kalvesta the prior afternoon but had turned cold overnight, as a front moved across the plains. Smith's state counterpart, Piland, wore jeans and a flannel shirt, his sleeves rolled up. Gavin wore a blue windbreaker and blue jeans. When Gavin took a seat on one side of the tiny table in the cramped room, Smith sat directly across from him, with Piland off to the side.

Gavin didn't wait for a cue. He had a business to run, he said. Not being able to open up his shop added insult to the injury of the police stop the previous afternoon. "To put it mildly, I'm not very happy," he said, leaning toward Smith and rubbing his chin.

Smith said, "I understand that, uh, you had some dialogue with an officer—"

Gavin interrupted. "You don't understand it at all. They pointed guns at me, bud. Threw me on the ground and handcuffed me—and I didn't do anything."

Smith nodded. He opened his thick notebook and feigned a folksy patience. He suggested that Gavin start at the beginning, and so Gavin gave a rambling account of the prior afternoon's events involving Lula and Curtis. Smith interrupted to ask for clarification about the couple's relationship, acting as if he needed help following Gavin's story when he knew full well all about Curtis, Lula, and life at G&G. He zeroed in on Curtis Allen, asking Gavin how well he knew Curtis. Gavin minimized the extent of their relationship, saying Curtis had just begun working in sales at G&G and that he rarely saw him outside work. He and Curtis might grab a beer on occasion at the local VFW, he said.

Smith took a shot across Gavin's bow ten minutes into the interview. He asked, "How important is respect when you want to close a deal with a customer?"

"Huge," Gavin said.

To let the point sink in, Robin Smith put down his pen, then his coffee, and then he extended his hands across the table toward Gavin, open faced, as if reaching across a great divide and saying, C'mon, man, now's your chance. If you want to come clean, now's the time. Smith then shifted in his chair, pulled out his FBI business card, and handed it to Gavin. He pointed out one telephone number in particular, the one he could call at any time, twenty-four hours a day.

"I want to be able to take you at face value," Smith said. "But I have some issues."

"I understand, I guess," Gavin said. "I don't know what issues you'd have with me."

"I have some things I need to understand and clarify."

"Okay," Gavin said. "That's why I'm here."

But Gavin persisted in advancing a narrative about Curtis and their relationship that did not match the one the FBI agent knew to be true.

Smith grew restless. He interrupted Gavin's bid to distance himself from Curtis. "So, what is it you wanted to come talk to us about?" he asked.

"Why I can't open my business this morning?" Gavin said his brother was angry that he wasn't able to open up; and he had a meeting with a city official about a new project he needed to prepare for, and yet a police officer was saying he couldn't enter G&G.

Smith said the officer was simply following instructions, awaiting a search warrant.

"I understand that."

"Why do I need a search for your office?" Smith asked. The agent had had enough; the dancing around was over. "And not for legal reasons —what am I looking for?"

"I don't have a clue."

Smith took a sip of coffee. "Not even the slightest?"

"No," Gavin said. "Not even the slightest."

Smith said, "Back to that respect issue."

Seconds later Smith's tone changed, much of the folksiness gone. "You don't have any idea why we need a search warrant for your business office?"

"No," Gavin repeated. "Other than what the cop said last night."

"Which was?"

"That his wife [Lula] told them that he was making bombs, is what the cop told me," Gavin said, becoming agitated. "I go, 'Not in my office, he's not.'"

"What do you know about that?"

"What do I know about what?" Gavin said.

Smith leaned in. "Do you know anything additional about Curtis and the bombs?"

"No," Gavin replied emphatically. "I don't have a clue."

Smith delivered a rapid-fire series of questions. The interrogation was full on.

"You don't know anything else about Curtis Allen?"

"No."

"Nothing at all?"

"Not personally."

"You ever go shooting with Curtis Allen?"

"No."

"You ever attend a group meeting with Curtis Allen?"

"No."

"He never invited you to a meeting with a group called Kansas Security Force?"

"No."

"You're not a member of a militia?"

"No!"

Six questions, all answered in the negative. Smith warned Gavin about the "hole of untruthfulness" he was digging for himself.

Gavin said he was sorry if Smith felt that way.

"You don't have to apologize," Smith said, adding that it wasn't just a feeling. "I know," he continued cryptically, stopping short of revealing that the FBI had the tapes.

The session was effectively over. When Gavin showed up, Smith had not expected much more than "a bullshit waste of time." But of course he'd had to go along, see if his hunch was wrong — maybe Gavin would be cooperative. But no way; he'd experienced what Dan had during their call the prior night: Gavin insisted that he knew nothing.

"Gavin, don't lie to me," Smith finally said.

"I'm not lying to you," Gavin replied.

Seconds later Smith closed his notebook and stood up. He turned toward the door, saying he and Piland needed to check on some things. Gavin sat alone for a bit, then got up and left the police station on his own. He kept to his word, doing what Patrick called "laying low," and did not have further contact that day with either Patrick or Dan. At night, however, he returned in the dark to Space Station Secure Storage to hide another milk crate filled with notebooks, bomb manuals, and chemical supplies, including some aluminum powder.

LATER THAT same afternoon Dan sat in his Impala, waiting for Patrick. He'd pulled off Highway 156 in Kalvesta at the same spot where they'd rendezvoused for the first meeting. The sky was mainly clear, the temperature around fifty degrees—pleasant conditions, overall. It was about 4:30 p.m. and darkness wouldn't come for another three hours.

The twenty-four hours since Curtis's arrest seemed to have passed in an instant and, just like his FBI handlers working furiously in Liberal, Dan had not slept much. He took stock of his awkward conversation with Gavin; the fact that Gavin and Patrick had also talked following the police stop had sunk in. It meant that in addition to learning about Curtis's arrest on a domestic charge, Patrick had surely learned that Lula Harris was blabbing to Liberal police about bomb making. Yet Patrick never mentioned anything about that during the Zello meeting afterward. He'd only ranted against Lula for siccing police on Curtis for a bogus domestic complaint. And Dan figured Patrick had good reason to keep that to himself—none of the KSF members on the Zello call were part of the bomb plot. Some might *suspect* something was up; after all, in July the Crusaders had tried recruiting a select few to the cause, to no avail. But none had specific knowledge, and for Patrick to have gone there on Zello would have been completely reckless. Plus, Patrick was unaware of the FBI's presence down in Liberal. Knowing Patrick, he'd assume the local police were in way over their heads, trying to sort through Lula's mad ravings, and he'd figure they wouldn't be able to connect her to either him or Dan, each located more than sixty miles north, in Garden City and Dodge City, respectively. It was a reminder of the beauty of social media, how the Crusaders had been able to find one another despite living many miles apart in their militia version of the meatpacking Golden Triangle: Dodge City, Garden City, and Liberal.

Wishful thinking on Patrick's part, all of it, but Dan, more than anyone, knew how eager Patrick was to fulfill their destiny and how ecstatic he'd been to have met a big-time weapons dealer like Brian. Even so, during the morning meeting at the FBI office, which was becoming even more crowded as more agents and supervisors arrived at the Garden City field office from Kansas City, there'd been palpable anxiety that the investigation might be coming undone. They had to act like everything was still on, however. By early afternoon Brian had reached out to Patrick to confirm the location. "Same place," he'd texted Patrick at 12:25 p.m. "Let Dan and your boys know."

Patrick had replied, "Okay, will do."

Then Dan and Patrick talked briefly by phone to finalize meeting up along the highway in Kalvesta. Both interactions were matter-of-fact, without any sign of apprehension. To Dan, it meant Patrick, while worked up like everyone else, wasn't about to bolt, or worse; he was staying the course. Others on the case might be thinking he'd flee, but Dan thought he'd show.

He was right. Within minutes Patrick pulled in next to Dan, right on time. Patrick was unshaven and wore a camo cap and dark sunglasses. He looked tired, coping with the demands of the bomb plot and his day job—farming. The corn was picked; he'd finished planting wheat earlier in the week; he was trying now to get the milo cut, although the morning dew had gotten in the way, since milo needed to be dry. But despite looking haggard, he was pumped up to get going, and Dan wondered if he'd done some meth.

Ten or so miles north, Brian and his crew of undercover operatives were set up at the preserve. "This is UCE 5276," he said, after turning on a secret recording device. The sound of gunfire could be heard in the background, as other agents took warm-up shots at the pumpkins. "Today's date, October 12, 2016. The approximate time is 5:01 p.m." Brian wasn't sure what to expect from Patrick, but one thing he and all the agents knew for certain: the original takedown plan was history. There was no longer any time for the FBI to make a fake bomb by month's end, orchestrate a handoff to Patrick, Curtis, and Gavin, and then arrest everyone the moment they tried to detonate it. The case had to be resolved sooner—as soon as possible, in fact—in a manner short of the ideal. The question now was how to engineer a new finish. Brian would be watching Patrick for signs of suspicion over the course of their meeting, starting with their target shooting at the pumpkins and then a ride-around in Garden City to see the real targets: the Somalis.

Dan pulled into the parking area, followed by Patrick. Just as before, they were escorted down the dirt slope to the barbed-wire fence, where Brian waited. Brian's truck was parked there too, its bed open to reveal weapons and ammunition.

"Looks like they're havin' some fun down there," Dan said.

"Hell yeah," Brian said. "That's what it's all about, isn't it?"

"How you doin', man?" Patrick said. "Nice to see you again."

"Good, how are you, brother?"

Gunfire drew everyone's interest.

"Havin' a little fun, are ya?" Patrick said.

Brian said, "Hell, yeah, come on down and join the fun, man."

Patrick was ready and eager. "Didn't know they had a shootin' range up here."

"The range is where the guns are, my friend," Brian said.

"There you go," Patrick said.

"Grab a couple of mags and come on."

Patrick moved toward the shooting spot, and as he did, several of the undercover agents casually surrounded him, but not so they would be in a better position to watch Patrick shoot. It was a security precaution. The agents were staying tight on Patrick in case they needed to pounce and disarm him.

"That's a piece of artwork right there," Patrick said about the AK-47.

Brian made small talk while they set up, asking Patrick about his harvest.

"Weather's kinda shut us down for a little bit," Patrick said. "Little too wet, yeah, for milo. We had a shower that went through last night."

Then Brian asked, "Where's your other boys at?"

"Just me and Dan," Patrick said.

"Your other boys aren't comin'?"

"No, huh, uh" was all Patrick said—for now.

Brian had to act as if he knew nothing. "Okay," he said.

Patrick's gun was loaded and ready. "Wanna give 'er a try?" Brian asked.

"Sure," Patrick said.

Patrick took aim and fired at the pumpkins.

"Little high," Brian said.

Patrick fired again.

"There you go. There you go!"

"Dead punkin." Patrick smiled. He emptied the magazine and got a new one.

"Have fun, bro," Brian said.

"Can we go auto?" Patrick asked.

"Just tear it up," Brian said.

Patrick fired away. Then Dan took a turn. Then Patrick shot again, both the M16 assault rifle and the AK-47. Pumpkins made for good targets, thick and tough and holding up until a relentless barrage of bullets splattered chunks of orange flesh every which way.

"Oh yeah," Dan said after a series of pops, "I love that sound."

"That is sweet, man," Patrick said in awe, adding seconds later, "That is fuckin' badass," and then, after firing another round, he simply said, "Wow." He blasted away at the targets, the bullets making a thumping sound. "Good sound," he said. "I'd love for that to be a fuckin' raghead."

Brian's men provided a steady supply of thirty-round magazines. Brian offered shooting tips and, as they finished up, noted that the target practice had proved his point—the guns he sold might be used and somewhat beat up, but they were of high quality. "You asked me if we get good stuff," he told Patrick in a tone of I-told-you-so.

Patrick was completely convinced. "Those are sweet," he said. "Very sweet."

Brian's men began putting away the weapons, as everyone talked excitedly about how clean they emptied out and were relatively quiet when firing. Patrick joked, "Shit, these fuckers look so good, I'd date one of them." Brian, Dan, and the others laughed.

Concern about Patrick's state of mind had subsided; he was fully engaged.

It was time too for Brian to zero in on pending business. "Hey, Dan," he said. "Why don't you go on, grab your car, man." Dan thanked everyone for the chance to shoot the automatic weapons. He retrieved his Impala and drove the short distance down to where they'd been shooting, so that Brian's men could load the weapons into his trunk. He was pretending that he'd be making a delivery after leaving. But instead, he'd head to the Garden City Regional Airport, where agents would take possession of the weapons. Meanwhile, Brian signaled to Patrick to head over to his truck for a private conversation. The singular attention from the top man was supposed to make Patrick feel important and to further seal their connection. But the one-on-one had an important investigatory purpose—to once again gather direct evidence from Patrick, without Dan being present, so that no one at some later date could claim that Dan had stage-managed Patrick's involvement.

"Had fun with those, did you, man?" Brian asked as they climbed into his truck.

Patrick said he'd liked the automatic AK-47 the most.

"Those are gonna be $3,500 a piece," Brian said.

"Really? Complete, just like it is?"

"Just like it is, come with its mags and all."

Brian segued into the bomb plot in progress. He asked Patrick whether he and his partners had talked about money to pay for explosives and weapons he'd be willing to provide at reduced prices. Patrick hesitated, then said he needed to share something.

"We've had a little situation develop," he said.

"Okay," Brian said slowly. He was acting cautious. "Good or bad?"

"Bad."

"Okay."

Patrick told Brian the story of Curtis's arrest the prior afternoon on a domestic charge, how Curtis's girlfriend, Lula Harris, had called the police on him. "He fucked up and, according to her, attacked her and threatened to fuckin' kill her."

Brian acted taken aback. "Do we need to be worried about that?" he asked.

"Um," Patrick said, "at this point, no, uh, that's all clear down in southwest Kansas."

Brian peppered Patrick with questions about a possible breach in security. Did Lula know Patrick? Did Lula know about their new business dealings? Did she know about the plan? "Is he stupid?" he said, referring to Curtis. "Did he talk to her?"

Patrick sought to be reassuring. He minimized his own contact with Lula, saying he'd only met her once or twice and that she was "a freakin' witch from hell." He insisted that Lula was ignorant of "any of the particulars" of the plan.

But when Brian questioned him further, Patrick conceded that Lula had seen Curtis watching videos and studying manuals about making bombs. "She knows enough to be dangerous, I guess, if you want to put it that way." Even so, Patrick didn't see her as getting in their way. "I'm actually thinkin' that, you know, she's probably already done the damage that she's wantin' to do."

But what about in the aftermath of the attack? Brian asked, "Is she gonna put a lot of heat on you after this thing?"

The question gave Patrick pause. "Yeah, uh, I don't, well, honestly,

I can't answer that question, I don't know." Patrick seemed to turn the matter over in his mind. "She doesn't know enough to make sense of anything," he said, as if considering one alternative. "But I guess if somethin' like this was to happen, like real soon, um, that is a concern."

"Okay." It was as if Brian were asking, What are you going to do about that?

Patrick finished his train of thought: "She's somebody that, really just to be fuckin' real blunt, just needs to disappear."

Not a bad idea, Brian acknowledged, knowing full well that the FBI now had to consider Lula Harris a potential target.

The crisis Lula had created—as well as her possible fate for causing it—became a recurring note as Brian pushed for clarity on the impact of Curtis's arrest on the Crusaders' intentions. Brian acted as if he needed help keeping straight the identities of his two partners, since he had never met Curtis or Gavin. Patrick explained that the one sitting in jail—Curtis—was their point man on manufacturing explosives—or, as Patrick put it, "intimately involved."

"Oh man," Brian said. "So he's out of the picture then?"

"Well, yeah," Patrick replied.

"And he ain't gonna talk?" Brian pressed.

"No," Patrick said emphatically. Time and again during their discussion, he guaranteed that Curtis and Gavin were totally trustworthy. "Both of 'em," Patrick told the seemingly worried arms dealer. "They ain't gonna say a word."

8

PLOT INTERRUPTED

Brian ended what had turned into a quasi-inquisition of Patrick regarding Curtis's arrest, so that they could finish packing up and reconvene in Garden City, where Patrick was going to show Brian exactly where the Somalis lived and prayed. They departed separately from the shooting range but drove in line toward Garden City. "The shooting seemed to go well," Brian said hopefully to two undercover agents riding along with him. Even so, as they had already seen, things could change in an instant. Keeping a close eye on Patrick in the truck's rearview mirror, he said, "The trick is to make sure he stays with us the whole time." Then, as Patrick drifted farther back, Brian pleaded, "Come on, bud, stay with us." Nearing Garden City, the agents suddenly spotted a Finney County sheriff's cruiser pulled off to the side of the road; the officer was apparently conducting a speed trap. "We would really not want to have a stop happen right now," Brian fretted. After all, a police stop in Liberal had turned what had been a carefully planned endgame into improvisational policing. "It's almost humorous at this point," he said darkly.

Brian pulled into the parking lot of Buffalo Wild Wings. He and the others looked back for Patrick. "Here he is," Brian said. "That's him, right? In that red truck?" It was Patrick; he'd stayed with them. Patrick parked his Chevy pickup and climbed into the passenger seat of Brian's.

The plan was for some of Brian's men to go inside the restaurant and get a table while Brian, two of his men, and Patrick drove around before it got too dark. In his role as an arms dealer doing his due diligence, Brian right away resumed questioning the Crusader about Curtis's arrest. "Why don't you keep tellin' me about what happened with your guys," he said. "'Cause, uh, I'm gonna be honest with you, it's got me a little concerned."

Patrick recapped the situation — Curtis was the one in jail and Gavin, "free as a bird," had notified him that he'd be checking out for the time being. Both men, he said yet again, could be trusted unequivocally.

Brian listened intently, taking stock. "Sounds like Curtis is gonna be out for a bit?"

Patrick concurred.

Brian continued: "Gavin is not wantin' to do anything 'cause he's scared."

Patrick chose to put it differently: "He's just layin' low."

Brian spoke. "I shoulda asked you this before I even started drivin' anywhere," he said, as if wondering aloud whether they had any reason to be in business at this point, given the circumstances. "What do you guys want me for?" he asked. Wasn't it game over?

"Leaves me and Dan to pick up the slack," Patrick said. He was undeterred.

"You guys are still wantin' to do what you were plannin'?"

"We're still wantin' to take care of some business."

"Sure." Brian went along with him.

"It's getting' bad over here, man," Patrick said.

The conversation turned to the business of bombs. They talked about the timing of the attack, whether it had changed. Patrick said no; they were still aiming for November 9, the day after the vote for the next president: Clinton or Trump. They talked about logistics. Patrick conceded that with their chief bomb maker now sidelined, he and Dan were going to need Brian to put everything together. "We're plannin' on, you know, deliverin' it." Patrick mentioned having $300 in cash and bartering in crystal meth to help subsidize the effort—and he mentioned he'd "spent a nice little chunk on the, uh, the fertilizer."

"So you have the fertilizer?" Brian asked.

"We was gonna build everything," Patrick said. "Do everything ourselves."

"Do you still have that fertilizer?"

"Yeah," Patrick said.

"How much do you have?"

"Probably close to three hundred pounds. Maybe a little over."

"We could use that."

Brian became fixated on Patrick's offer to provide an IED's key ingredient, as if realizing fertilizer could be the basis for a next meeting in the FBI's now unscripted effort to bring the case to a climax. There was no time to orchestrate a takedown as originally planned—for the FBI to produce a fake bomb, stage a transfer, and then arrest Patrick as he and Dan tried to set it off. But at least Brian had a way to keep things going while the FBI and the Department of Justice prosecutors sorted everything out. He and Patrick then discussed other logistical matters—the use of vehicles to hold the explosives as opposed to trash bins, for example, as well as other materials Patrick said he had, such as aluminum powder, another component he said Curtis had acquired. But Brian focused on the fertilizer, leaned into it as the next move. He reviewed the new plan, saying that once Patrick delivered it to them, "we'll mix it up, and we'll hand it off to you and Dan."

"Okay," Patrick said, concurring.

"You guys go do your thing," Brian said. "That sound reasonable?"

"Sounds wonderful."

Minutes later, Brian revisited fertilizer, just to be certain about it.

"So, you still have the fertilizer that we could use?" he asked.

"Yup."

"We might take you up on that."

"It's about sixty miles east of here."

Patrick was referring to his home in Wright, Kansas, just outside Dodge City.

"We can figure that out, man," Brian said.

The two men talked as they made their way in Brian's truck across Garden City to West Mary Street, with interruptions in the bomb confab for Brian to ask for directions or for Patrick to give them. When they drove past Adan Keynan's store, Patrick, as terrorist tour guide, interrupted to say, "Here's the little fuckin' haji's store."

"This?" Brian asked, looking to his right.

"The African Shop," Patrick said.

They next drove past the Garden Spot Apartments at 312 West Mary Street. "What we have here are Somalians," Patrick said. Residents mingled about, dressed in robes and scarves. "This is their fuckin' mosque on this end right here," he continued. "That's where they pray to fuckin' haji."

Studying the scene, Brian said, "Oh, man." They talked about where to position bomb-filled cars. Patrick also pointed out a second apartment complex, also occupied by Muslims, across the street. They talked about attacking both at the same time.

"It's easier to do 'em both," Brian said.

"Then you ain't gotta worry about heat," Patrick noted.

One of Brian's men agreed. "Once you do one, the heat's on."

"Yep." Patrick laughed. "Especially with these freakin' bastards we got around," he said, meaning FBI agents in the local field office. The FBI went out of its way to protect Muslims, he complained. "Those son-of-a-bitches do everything they can to help 'em."

"I don't think anybody likes the FBI," Brian said, with a straight face.

Despite feeling bone-tired from farm work and "dealin' with this shit all night," a reference to Curtis's arrest, Patrick seemed energized by the ride-around, so much so that as they were finishing up, he resurrected an idea he'd long nurtured. "Let me throw somethin' else at ya," he said, then described his fantasy of kicking in doors of Somali-occupied apartments, armed with a gun and a silencer, to "cap every motherfucker in the place." That Patrick still entertained the idea of going rogue and shooting Muslims was concerning.

Brian would have none of it. "You're gonna get caught fast doin' that," he said. "Let's focus on this one."

Patrick's volatility got Brian worrying again about Lula Harris—the latest cause for alarm. "You've said that one gal needs to go away," he said returning to their discussion of her fate. "Do you think that needs to happen?" He wanted to be sure Patrick wasn't going to go after her.

Patrick replied that he hadn't decided; he needed more information about the harm she'd done. "But I will let you know if that is, you know, a definite issue."

Brian insisted that Patrick keep him posted and that if he decided to do something about her, "Let's talk about it."

Most of all, Brian urged that they buckle down and stay on track: Patrick delivers the money and three hundred pounds of fertilizer; Brian assembles the bombs; Patrick and his cohorts detonate them. "Then we can move from there and do stuff later, after it clears," he said.

Music to Patrick's ears. "You have no idea how much I'm lookin' forward to this."

Before returning to the restaurant Brian asked about the fertilizer one last time.

"How long do you need to get that fertilizer for us?" he asked. "If I call ya and say, 'Hey, we're gonna be there in a day or two days, will you be able to bring it up to us?"

Patrick said yes, for sure, "providing I'm not in the milo field." He said late at night was best. "When we're cutting milo, we can only cut 'til about sundown, then it gets too wet."

Brian would keep that in mind. He invited Patrick to join him for wings and beer, but Patrick begged off, saying he needed to crash, get some sleep. Patrick was thankful, though. "I appreciate you comin' down, man," he said. "Fuckin' rock on with those sweet-ass rifles."

Brian smiled. "Yeah, they're nice, right?"

Patrick left. Brian went inside to grab some food with the other undercover agents before heading back to their hotel. By concentrating on Patrick's fertilizer, he'd put in play a reason for their next encounter. When exactly that would be was up to the FBI brass. Maybe in a few days? Or even the next week?

Little did he know it was going to be way sooner than that.

NEAR MIDNIGHT, the FBI agent Robin Smith strode with purpose down the hotel's hallway to the room where the undercover agent Brian was staying. He knocked hard on the door. For his part, Smith had already pulled one all-nighter, having hurried to Liberal following word of Curtis's arrest on Tuesday afternoon, where he and his partner, Amy Kuhn, then worked through the night. Immediately following his interview with Gavin Wright at the Liberal PD first thing Wednesday, he'd hurried back to Garden City to join the team monitoring Dan and Brian's late-afternoon target practice with Patrick in Kalvesta. Afterward he drove to Garden City Regional Airport, met up with Dan, and babysat the weapons until they were loaded onto a plane bound for Washington, DC. He'd touched base several times with Kuhn, who'd remained in Liberal for the search of G&G Home Center, and then headed home, hoping to finally steal some rest. Except that after he fell onto his bed, within minutes his phone began ringing. The call meant he'd be pulling another all-nighter.

Smith knocked again at Brian's door. This time Brian answered. Smith could tell he'd woken him up. Smith said the decision had been made: it was time to take them down. Not in a few days. Not next week. But the very next day, Friday. The denouement was at hand.

Top officials in the FBI and the Department of Justice, in Kansas and Washington, DC, had just completed a video teleconference on a secure system. With the unanticipated turn in the case, sessions involving high-level officials had picked up, and this one was convened to assess the latest encounter with Patrick Stein. It didn't take long to recognize that Patrick's fertilizer could be used to orchestrate his arrest, an opportunity one prosecutor called a "no-brainer." The more difficult question was the timing: how long should they let things play out? Prosecutors, with an eye toward a future trial and the strongest possible case, favored stringing out the charade right up to the moment the conspirators thought they were detonating a bomb. But in this instance, that plan no longer seemed viable. The situation was too combustible on several fronts. Patrick seemed bonded to Brian, even enamored of him, but would that hold? Then there was Lula Harris—would Patrick decide she needed to go? The FBI urged immediate action, and so, with the prosecutors on board, the ruling came down from the top to Smith, his partner Kuhn, and other agents in the field—do it now.

"Here's what's gonna happen," Smith said, as he brought Brian up to speed. The other undercover agents were then notified. Everyone involved, including several high-ranking FBI supervisors from the Kansas office, conferred through the night with counterparts at headquarters in Washington, to draw up a plan and organize additional tactical resources, such as a SWAT team and a hostage rescue team, or HRT. Not long after daybreak, on Thursday, October 13, Brian took the next step: he texted Patrick.

"Hey, brother," he said. "Can I get that stuff from you tomorrow?"

It was 8:06 a.m. No response. Thirty minutes passed.

Patrick finally replied: "Yes."

The investigators were relieved.

Patrick continued: "Can you make it either early morning or late evening?" He explained why: "Will be in the field otherwise." Then, apparently wanting to oblige, he said, "If not, that is okay too. I can just leave the shop unlocked for you. Give you directions to pick it up."

Brian said, "Does around 7 in the morning work?"

The dialogue was underway to plan a handoff.

DAN SPENT that Wednesday night at home. He felt a bit in limbo, an unfamiliar feeling after so many months of focused work. He'd succeeded in hooking Brian up with Patrick, and as their bromance blossomed, Brian, along with the other undercover agents, had essentially taken over moving the investigation forward. Dan had been sidelined to a degree, which in terms of timing wasn't so bad. He was due to head out of town on Friday morning for Pratt, Kansas, more than 120 miles away, for a reunion of "first cousins" from Kansas and beyond—Oklahoma, Arizona, and Oregon. He, Cherlyn, Brandon, and Alyssa were counting on seeing all those cousins on his side of the family, and Dan didn't want to disappoint.

He did learn that Brian's ride-around in Garden City had gone well. Patrick had called afterward to report that the alliance was intact. He'd also raised a new and sensitive topic: Lula Harris. Patrick said he and Brian had talked about her at length, how she posed a serious risk to their plans. Patrick wanted to know what Dan thought—whether they should kill her.

Dan was caught off guard but instinctively went into his default mode—hemming and hawing, urging that they slow down. They had a lot of stuff going down at the moment and didn't want to go off on some tangent that would distract them from their main objective. It was reminiscent of the moment the previous winter, outside the Dollar General store, when Patrick spotted a couple of Somali women, raised his gun, and began screaming how he wanted to shoot them right then and there. He'd talked Patrick down back then, and he tried to do so again. Dan told Patrick they needed to think carefully about Lula Harris, and before he could give Patrick a straight answer, he first wanted to get with his cousin—the one who was part of Brian's organization. He'd ask for his cousin's take on the situation, since this was something more in his cousin's world than his. Patrick said that made sense. He'd just wanted to put the idea in play; she was a real concern for them.

Patrick's cold-bloodedness was once again on full display—something Dan had experienced many times over, nearly a daily diet of it, in his guise as a die-hard Crusader and white supremacist. But he'd never accepted the bigotry as normal and was indeed repulsed by it. In fact, while they were shooting at the lake preserve in Kalvesta a few hours earlier, a strange and discomfiting thought had crossed his mind. Patrick was firing the automatic AK-47 at the time, whooping it up and wishing the targets were Muslims—"cockroaches," as Patrick always said. The joy on Patrick's face seemed boundless as he blasted pumpkins, imagining they were Somalis, surrounded by men he believed were newfound soul mates, united in their white-hot hate. Dan then thought how the joke, if it could even be called that, was on Patrick—how Patrick actually had *no friggin' idea* how much FBI firepower had been trained on him, not just in the immediate vicinity from the undercover agents who encircled him but in the trees beyond, where several FBI snipers were hiding. Dan imagined how all that firepower could instantly blow Patrick apart like the pumpkins in the patch, and he realized suddenly that he did not feel sorry for Patrick Stein at all. The thought was hardly a Christian way of thinking, but things had come to this. It was how he felt.

Dan made sure that night to review the defense measures he'd instituted at home early in the summer: an AR-15 semiautomatic rifle positioned at his bedside, a handgun kept in the upper shelf of a kitchen cabinet, the shotgun in the basement for Brandon to go and get if need be. The pit bull, Sarge, that he'd acquired had proved both a welcome pet and a convenient alarm system, barking whenever someone approached the house. In a late-night call with Robin Smith, Dan described what Patrick had said about Lula Harris. He could picture his handler shaking his head in dismay and disgust. Smith then updated Dan—a takedown was imminent. The finish line was in sight. Smith said he'd come by the next day, Thursday, to discuss it further. Dan replied that it sounded good to him, and he'd be around.

BEFORE DAWN on Thursday, October 13, Robin Smith drove back down to Liberal to meet up with his partner. He'd not slept, whereas Amy Kuhn had managed to grab a couple of hours of sleep—that was it. Kuhn was keeping a secret from everyone, including her longtime FBI partner; she was newly pregnant. Her husband, a Dodge City police officer, was adamant that she pace herself, but that hardly seemed possible after putting nearly a year into the case. Kuhn had accompanied investigators during the search of Gavin's G&G Home Center, where instruments and substances used in bomb making were recovered, including goggles, a thermometer, hydrogen peroxide, and urea fertilizer, one of the two types of fertilizer that can be converted into explosives. In a kitchen drawer they found a blasting cap that Curtis had made, along with traces of HMTD, or hexamethylene triperoxide diamine, a detonator's key ingredient. In the desk in Curtis's office they found bomb recipes, *The Anarchist Cookbook,* revisions in the "wake-up" manifesto he was drafting for release after the bombs had been detonated, and random notes on how to make crystal meth. Later searches of Curtis's truck and Gavin's storage unit yielded the mortar and pestle Dan had provided, the magnetic stirrer, and the hot plate—all of which were used in making blasting caps.

Smith and Kuhn, together with an FBI official from Kansas City, huddled with the Liberal police chief and the county sheriff to fully disclose the terrorism case. Then the agents drove back to Garden City. For the rest of the day, and into the night, Kuhn hunkered down in the office to work on the documents that prosecutors needed for the criminal complaints they were completing. For his part, Smith began making the rounds, notifying local and state officials, especially Garden City's police chief, Michael Utz, given the fact that his town's several hundred Somalis were the Crusaders' targets—people like the store owner Adan Keynan, his wife, Sara, her daughter, Halima Farah, and Halima's friends Ifrah Ahmed and Mursal Nayele, all of whom were active in the community.

Dozens of federal agents continued arriving in Garden City. Meanwhile, Brian stayed in touch with Patrick by cell phone. Patrick had agreed right away to Brian's suggestion that they meet first thing Friday, at around seven o'clock, but he wanted to hold off pinning down a location as he continued coping with the crisis caused by Curtis's arrest.

"I will send you the address later today if that's okay," he texted Brian. "Still dealing with the BS I told you about. Things are dying down but still a fucking mess." He took off on Lula Harris, calling her a "no good lying conniving worthless cunt that is in the same category of the fucking cockroaches." He said her potential to create further trouble was "weighing heavy on me right now and may need to be taken care of at some point."

"Sounds like it," Brian replied. He wanted to make it seem he was supportive. But he also didn't want Patrick doing anything in haste. He said, "If it needs to be done, grab what info you can on her and bring it with you when we meet tomorrow a.m."

By late afternoon Thursday, Brian still had not pinned down the time, place, and manner of the handoff. He texted Patrick not long after 5 p.m. to kick-start the final round of planning. "I'm gonna need all 300 lbs," he said, to get things going.

Patrick assured him that all was good. "Not a problem," he said. "There is probably a little over 300 pounds if it was weighed up but I know there's at least 300."

"Perfect."

Brian poked around some more about Lula Harris. "Got the info on the bitch?"

"Working on that as we speak," Patrick said. "Just getting in from the field." It was all Patrick had to say, likely a reference to the conversation he was having with Dan.

By nightfall on Thursday they still hadn't decided on where to meet. Brian needed to know, as federal tactical resources were mobilizing. "Can we meet in Dodge?" he texted Patrick, knowing Patrick lived outside Dodge City, in Wright, Kansas.

He added, "We should be near there around 7."

Patrick said, "Yes, that would be fine."

"Thanks, bro," Brian wrote.

Patrick typed an emoji in reply: two thumbs up.

IT WASN'T until late that Thursday night that FBI agent Smith was finally free to swing by Dan's house—he'd been tied up for hours, notifying other local officials and keeping up on logistics for the takedown, now that Brian and Patrick had settled on Dodge City as their meeting spot. Smith and one of his supervisors pulled up in front of Dan's house, something the agent had never done before, for security reasons. Dan was waiting, and he jumped in. Robin parked on a darkened street nearby, so that they could talk and get caught up. Dan mentioned the uproar on the Kansas Security Force's private Facebook chat room, with militia members sharing the latest rumors regarding Curtis

Allen and the police investigation in Liberal. This time Daniel was in attendance, all riled up. He posted a copy of the search warrant for everyone to see, and he yelled about police going through his house and storage areas, looking for Curtis's guns and ammo. Fortunately Patrick was not on Facebook to hear Daniel's harangue—meaning that Patrick remained unaware that the FBI had a role in the fast-breaking events. KSF members seemed scared during the chat, Dan told the agents; some announced they were dropping out, deleting their KSF account on Facebook and any other evidence of militia membership.

The agents then had Dan follow up on the status of Lula Harris—a matter of peripheral but continuing concern—and both were seated quietly in the car as Dan put his call on speakerphone. The conversation didn't last long; Patrick said he had a lot going on, and so Dan was quick in summarizing that he'd run everything by his cousin, and his cousin had advised that a decision for something this big had to be Patrick's, that Patrick was in charge, with Curtis now in jail. Dan said he'd back Patrick up, but the decision was his to make. Patrick listened, then said he'd figured Dan would say something along those lines. He was still thinking through what to do, he said, and that was that. They finished their call.

Smith updated Dan about the next morning's takedown—just hours away, really—and reminded Dan that both he and Brian would be taken into custody to maintain the fiction that they were both involved in the plot. He said Dan was unfortunately going to have to cancel his family trip to Pratt. Dan then made a request: given his occasional back troubles, he did not want to be handcuffed from behind. Okay, Smith said, and they came up with a plan: when agents moved to cuff him, Dan should balk, cite his bad back, and ask to be cuffed in front. Smith would make sure ahead of time that the SWAT team would abide by the request, even wrote a note to himself so that he wouldn't forget to remind the team.

Dan then had a realization: the plan made no sense.

Smith asked what he meant.

"Patrick didn't ask me," Dan said.

"What?"

Dan said he'd talked to Patrick at least twice since Patrick had met with Brian, and never once had Patrick mentioned he wanted Dan to help with the fertilizer delivery. Even when they'd talked just minutes ago, it wasn't as if Patrick had ended the call saying, "Okay, bud, see you in the morning." In other words, if Dan showed up at the crack of dawn when Patrick had never even invited him to come along—well, need he say more?

No, he didn't. Smith and his supervisor had an oh-my-god moment, catching on immediately to the mistake in the making, the likely result of little to no sleep and nonstop work. Smith regained his bearings, announced it was settled then: Dan should indeed get himself to Pratt for the cousins' reunion. Just as well that he'd be out of town during the takedown.

The FBI agents were in a hurry and had to keep moving. They dropped Dan off and headed back to the local field office a couple of miles away, where Kuhn was at work. Dan went inside and told his wife the latest. Cherlyn thought her husband looked different. Never in their marriage had they gone through such a long stretch when they had not shared everything. Dan of course couldn't keep the fact of his informant work from her—not with the regular meetings on Zello projecting loudly through their small house. But Dan had refused, plenty of times, to discuss specifics; he'd kept secrets. Her constant worry was that he'd fall under the influence of Patrick and the others, that their views would win over his mind and soul, and so she'd prayed often for his safety and for God's protection, so that he would not turn into one of them. Looking at him now, she knew that it had not happened. Instead she detected her husband's characteristic calm, which for a time had been absent.

Dan did feel relief. He'd juggled twin fears for so long. One had to do with his own safety—the fear that the others in the militia would discover the truth, and he'd be a dead man walking. The other had to do with the safety of others—the fear that Somalis in Garden City would be slaughtered if he and the FBI failed them. He'd been scared plenty: the time he'd passed out in the middle of nowhere and the time Curtis had put a gun to his head at the county fair. He'd lived a dangerous lie and felt worn down by it, but now, as he made small talk with his wife about when to leave for Pratt the next morning, he realized too that in the morning the big lie would come to an end. They talked a bit more about the trip, then headed off to bed. For the first time in a long time Dan slept soundly through the night.

THE FBI AGENTS AMY KUHN and Robin Smith met up before dawn in the parking lot of the Boot Hill Casino and Resort in Dodge City. It wasn't difficult to spot each other; though the western-themed casino was always open, the parking lot was largely empty. After meeting up with Dan late Thursday night, Smith had gone back to the office, where he found Kuhn buried in paperwork. He was wondering what he should do next and offered to help her write up the search warrant affidavits. But she insisted he go home, get some rest. Something about too many cooks in the kitchen. Kuhn was thinking that for the next day's operation, which would hopefully include questioning Patrick Stein once he was custody, one of the two FBI case agents needed to be somewhat coherent. Smith obeyed his partner, went home, and slept for a couple of hours. Over the course of their partnership they'd developed a custom: on "important mornings" Kuhn would stir Smith with a wake-up call. It wasn't necessary this time; he awoke on his own a few hours later. Kuhn had managed a short nap too, after leaving the field office at around 2:30 a.m.

She joined Smith in his car and together they drove the short distance to the Village Square Mall. Smith found an out-of-the-way spot at one end of the mall's sprawling parking lot, across from where Brian and Patrick were scheduled to meet—at the McDonald's. The tactical team, Brian and the undercover agents, had chosen the fast-food restaurant for its convenience—located an easy ten-minute drive for Patrick down Highway 50 from his trailer home in Wright, Kansas—and for its open parking area, suitable for a tactical operation. In a way, the case had come full circle. McDonald's was where Kuhn had dropped Dan off to meet Patrick on June 14, for what would become the start of the Crusaders' criminal conspiracy to develop weapons of mass destruction. The same location was now the spot where, if all went according to plan, the conspiracy would be crushed. Smith parked his car so that he and Kuhn had eyes on the restaurant across the way. The SWAT team was in charge of the takedown; Smith and Kuhn would approach afterward. They sat in the dark and waited.

PATRICK GOT things going with Brian at about 6:30 a.m. "How far out of town are you?" he texted.

Within minutes Brian replied that he was already in Dodge City. "Grabbing food at mcd's," he said.

Patrick voiced concern about the weather, its effect on the fertilizer. The temperature had fallen during the night and there was a light mist. "Not sure it's a good idea to load and haul this stuff as wet as it is this morning," Patrick said.

Brian assumed the fertilizer was in bags.

"We'll just throw it in the bed of the truck," he said. "And we'll cover it after."

"It's in paper sacks, yes—like feed sacks," Patrick said. "Okay, I'll load it up and head that way." He asked Brian which McDonald's to go to; there were two in Dodge.

"I'm at a mall," Brian said. "Let me find the name of it."

"I know where u r at."

"Okay," Brian said. "See you soon."

Two thumbs up from Patrick.

Less than thirty minutes later, at 7:12 a.m., Patrick announced he'd arrived, texting, "I'm going through the drive-through at McDonald's and I will meet you after."

Brian didn't wait; he and a couple of his men went outside. Meanwhile, other undercovers, posing as early-morning patrons, remained stationed inside. Brian directed Patrick to park his truck next to his. "What's goin' on, brother?"

"It's wetter than hell this morning," Patrick said.

First things first: they transferred six fifty-pound bags of fertilizer into Brian's truck. "We'll cover it up," Brian said, to hide it and keep it dry.

Patrick noted that one bag, "this sack here, has a little bit of a tear in the bottom of it."

Then Brian pivoted. "Wanna go in and talk?" he said.

The two found a spot with privacy, although Brian was secretly recording everything on a hidden device and agents had them surrounded. For the next fifteen minutes it was as if Brian was walking Patrick through a checklist—a final accounting of evidentiary threads developed over the previous weeks. There was the fate of Lula Harris. "What's your decision on that fuckin' bitch?" Brian asked, once they were seated.

Patrick said he was "leanin' towards it's gonna have to be taken care of." If she could cause so much harm to somebody she supposedly cared about, meaning Curtis, "she'll do that to fuckin' anybody." He didn't think she was of immediate concern, however. "My main concern is like, uh, after it happens," that once they blew up the Somalis' apartments, she'd "think, 'Hmmm, well,' and then, you know, she'll call the fuckin' cops." He indicated that after the bombing was when he'd be forced to decide what to do about her.

Then, Curtis and Gavin. Brian asked, "None of those two are talkin'?"

Patrick was emphatic. "No. No. No."

"Okay."

"They're golden," Patrick said. "If they talk, they're in just as deep as I am."

Then there were the explosives: using Patrick's fertilizer, Brian said, he'd have the bombs ready within a week—bombs he promised would pack enough power to level the Muslim-occupied apartment buildings on both sides of West Mary Street. "Those two buildings and more," he said.

"Sweet," Patrick said. He expressed gratitude that Brian had come along when he did. Curtis may have gotten them over the hump, mastering the making of blasting caps, which was the hardest part of building homemade explosives, but there was no way around the fact that they were neophytes. Brian was the real deal. "You know what the fuck you're doin'!"

Brian soaked up the compliment. He summarized how to discharge the bombs he'd be providing—place them near the mosque, flip a switch, pull the trigger. "That simple, bro." Brian said the bombs were "gonna make a big mess. Both those areas are gone."

"Good," Patrick said.

"I know that's what you wanted."

"It's nothin' but fuckin' cockroaches, man," Patrick declared. "There is no place in this fuck' country for them sons-of-bitches." He repeated it: "No place."

Brian mentioned that the victims would most likely include Somali children. "I mean," he said, "I'll be honest with you, are there a bunch of kids there?"

Patrick said that kids surely lived in the apartments, although he didn't recall seeing many during his drive-arounds. It was as if by bringing up the children, Brian was giving Patrick a chance to have second thoughts. But that factor gave Patrick no pause. He didn't respond with something like "Heck, I'd never considered that possibility." Instead, he didn't seem to care. He simply said, "I been after them motherfuckers for a long time, dude." He was "stoked."

"I hear ya," Brian said.

Sensing how that might have sounded, Patrick added, "I'm not a morbid sick motherfucker, you know, most of the time. Except against these motherfuckers."

Brian laughed. "It'll be good, man, I'm tellin' ya." Finishing up, Brian said he'd be available to instruct Patrick and Dan. "If you have a question, let me know, but when we bring 'em up here, we'll sit down and go through 'em with ya, show you how to use 'em."

"Cool," Patrick said.

"It should be pretty, pretty easy, man,"

Patrick took the moment to step back, look at the big picture. "This could be a fuckin' fruitful relationship, you know, if all goes off without a hitch." He said "the motherfuckers"—Muslims—were everywhere. "This is only the beginning," he said.

More patrons arrived, including a gaggle of kids, and so Brian and Patrick stood, chatting like two guys who'd met for a breakfast Happy Meal before getting on with their day. Patrick complained that the sudden drop in temperature had cut short his harvesting the prior night. "The shit went clear to sixteen on us, so we had to shut down."

OUTSIDE, PATRICK admired Brian's late-model Ford pickup. He started to ask about its gas mileage when members of the SWAT team suddenly converged from every which way, weapons trained on the pair.

"GET THE FUCK DOWN!" one yelled.

Brian acted ambushed, shouting, "Fuck, fuck, what the fuck is this? Who are these motherfuckers?"

The agents moved in forcibly to handcuff both of them behind the back. Patrick resisted, suffering scratches on his forehead during the struggle. "Fuckin' arm," he yelled. "Goddamnit."

The agent would have none of it. "Bring your fuckin' arm back. Bring your arm back." They seized the SIG-Sauer P250 9mm semiautomatic handgun he'd come armed with.

"Let's go, let's go," another agent shouted at Brian, pushing him toward a nearby van. As he was led away, Brian yelled, "Who the fuck did this?"

Once inside the vehicle, Brian and the agents dropped the charade. The agent apologized for the rough stuff. Brian laughed it off, said no worries, and made ready to turn off the hidden recording device.

"Beautiful," he said, to close out his role as an illegal weapons trafficker.

Kuhn and Smith pulled up to take Stein into custody. The agents put Patrick in the back seat. Smith drove, while Kuhn sat in the back next to Patrick, whose hands were in cuffs. Patrick fumed but said little during the seven-minute ride to the Ford County Sheriff's Office. Later he would be transported to the Sedgwick County Sheriff's Office in Wichita, where he'd be reunited with Curtis and Gavin. Curtis would arrive from Liberal; he'd been held there since his arrest on Tuesday. Gavin had been taken into custody in Liberal about the same time Patrick was arrested; he was stopped on the road and surrounded by a hostage rescue team.

It was in Wichita that Patrick was able to conduct a head count: him, Curtis Allen, and Gavin Wright. But no Dan. Where was Dangerous Dan Day? That evening, in a frantic call from jail to his mother, with a hardness to his voice, he said he needed her to do something.

"You got something to write with?" he said.

"Yep," his mother said. "Go ahead."

Patrick instructed her to contact one of the Kansas Security Force members on Facebook and send that member the following message: "Dan Day—*D-A-Y*—is a goddamn Fed." He said it was urgent, and to tell that member, "Get the message out. Dan Day—*D-A-Y.*"

Then he said, "We were fuckin' infiltrated, Mom."

MURSAL NALEYE was about to leave his apartment later that Friday morning to attend noon prayer at the mosque when he noticed texts and voice messages on his smartphone. They were from Michael Utz, Garden City's police chief. The chief wanted Mursal to call him back as soon as possible; the matter was serious. That was all he said.

The police chief had maintained the relationship he'd forged with Mursal the previous year, and the Somali had proved an effective liaison between police and the city's Muslim population. Utz now needed Mursal more than ever; the chief had been briefed by FBI agent Robin Smith about the terrorism case, and he'd just now gotten word that two co-conspirators had just been arrested. The Department of Justice and the FBI were planning a press conference for late in the afternoon, in Wichita. Utz wanted to get out in front of the news, so that the Somali community would hear about the plot from him first.

Mursal had no idea why the chief was calling, however. He returned the call immediately. The chief's voice was calm but urgent: he wanted Mursal to meet him at headquarters at 1 p.m. and to bring as many Somali elders as he could round up. The chief did not say much more, just that he would be sharing information of vital importance.

It was a big ask, and not only because of the short amount of time. In Somalia, police were feared, often because of corruption and harassment. But Mursal trusted the chief, and his fellow Muslims trusted him, so he began making calls, telling those he reached about the chief's request but unable to explain it. The worst he could imagine was that a Somali had gotten into serious trouble, or had died, or had done something crazy. Rather than speculate, he just kept saying the chief "needed us." He knew better than to tell them to meet at the police department; few if any of them had ever been to the station. Instead he instructed everyone to gather at their unofficial community center: Adan Keynan's store.

When he arrived, Mursal was met with a steady stream of questions: What do the police want? Why do we have to go to the station? He still had no specifics, just told everyone that they did not need to be afraid, that the chief had assured him nothing bad was going to happen. They headed downtown, with Adan driving a handful of Muslims in his white van while others took their own cars. Some Somalis were scared to enter the station; back home a scenario like this might be a run-up to extortion, a beating, a kidnapping, or some other harmful event. Mursal was coaxing them inside when Utz came out. The chief said they'd done nothing wrong, but that he had something very important to share with them.

He led them upstairs to a second-floor conference room, where chairs had been set up. Utz was accompanied by the officer in the department who was Somali. Utz explained the foiled terrorist plot to bomb the two apartment complexes on West Mary Street, and Mursal translated his words. The audience was stunned. The chief urged calm and asked that the elders spread the word through the Muslim community, and to workers at the Tyson meatpacking plant, where a shift change was due at four o'clock. He asked too for their help in organizing a community meeting for the next day, where he and other officials would be on hand to offer reassurance and to answer any questions. Three suspects were now in custody, he emphasized, and the message to take away was that everyone was safe.

The chief's hope in alerting the elders in advance of any media reports was to avert panic. The Somali contingent clearly appreciated the respect he'd shown them, but they were shaken nonetheless. They began speaking anxiously in Somali among themselves. Mursal, for one, began to cry. He thought, *You worship, go to work, you sleep and eat, and you do your basic life. You don't do anything wrong—and somebody is trying to kill you?* It seemed unimaginable. *Why?* he asked himself. *What did I do? Why do they hate me so much?* The meeting ended after twenty minutes, and when Mursal left, he was still feeling unnerved.

IFRAH AHMED was finishing her shift at Tyson when news of the plot began circulating by word of mouth at the sprawling plant on the outskirts of Garden City. She'd left her phone in her car, meaning she'd missed many calls, from Mursal and others. She was focused on her job as a production supervisor, overseeing seventy workers dressed in white frocks, who were "harvesting"—or slaughtering—cows on the floor. She was making sure her team was following protocols and staying safe.

Then her boss reached her, told her that some bad guys had been planning some bad stuff aimed at the Somali community. Ifrah phoned

Mursal, who filled her in about the meeting at the police station, and she then headed to West Mary Street and the Garden Spot Apartments. That's where her friends were, people who were family to her, and in her mind the safety of her fellow refugees, whom terrorists had planned to slaughter, had replaced her thoughts of workplace safety at Tyson. She found that Somalis and the other Muslim tenants were in a collective fog. She saw fear in their faces, and she knew that the disclosure of the bomb plot had triggered frightening memories of the violence they'd escaped by leaving Somalia—the car bombs, civilian warfare, and deadly attacks by the terrorist groups al-Shabab and ISIS. She was feeling the same way.

To Ifrah, the scene was surreal, as if she were in a movie, and the rest of that day and into the next she heard others saying what she was thinking, as if reading her mind: they'd come to the United States seeking safety, found refuge in Garden City, only to wake up one day to learn that a terrorist group—not al-Shabab, not ISIS, but a domestic terrorist group called the Crusaders—was preparing to bomb them. Emotions ran high. Some Muslims retreated into their apartments, afraid to go out. To protect themselves, especially their children, many were thinking they would have to move, flee Garden City, just as they'd once fled Somalia, and Ifrah found herself leaning in that direction. She called a cousin in Minneapolis and told her to prepare a bed because she'd decided to head north. It was as if the bombs had gone off—not literally, of course, but in terms of the impact the bombshell news was having. As word of the plot raced through the community, causing fear, it seemed that an exodus of Muslims from Garden City might be in the offing. If that happened, the Crusaders would be able to pat themselves on the back. They would have achieved at least part of their goal—to rid the area of Muslims.

By late afternoon, televisions all over town were tuned in to news of the government's press conference in Wichita. Mursal, for one, had made his way to the Tyson plant for the B shift and was watching on one of a number of TVs located in offices and lunchrooms. He'd continued his outreach on behalf of the police chief, briefing plant managers and huddling with workers to reassure them. Even so, as Kansas's acting US attorney, Tom Beall, described an investigation "deep into a hidden culture of hatred and violence," Mursal became emotional again; he saw several of his co-workers crying quietly.

Meanwhile, in the African Shop, Adan Keynan was busier than ever, as he and Sara provided hot tea, food, and comfort to Muslims viewing the large-screen TV in his back room. For Adan, news of the plot was gut-wrenching; he and Sara's corner apartment was within feet of the mosque targeted by the terrorists. Police and city officials might say everything was going to be okay, that the plotters had been arrested. But how could they be sure? *In life,* he thought, *there is no guarantee.* And he was still facing a personal crisis—the city's order to cease and desist, as he was, in their view, operating his store illegally. That time bomb was ticking as well. It felt like a one-two punch. Maybe he should pack up and leave too.

Then things turned—the efforts of Police Chief Utz, other city and law enforcement officials, Mursal, and a cohort of Somali elders paid off. Several hundred people showed up for a meeting early Saturday afternoon in the parking lot of the apartment complex at 305 West Mary Street. FBI agent Robin Smith was there, and he helped break the ice by approaching some Somali kids to kick a soccer ball around. Utz, the county sheriff, and two FBI officials spoke briefly about the investigation and then took questions—and soon enough they were surrounded by appreciative Somalis.

"Thank you, FBI," one Somali man told a reporter from the *Garden City Telegram,* who was covering the event live on his smartphone. The rally was then followed by a candlelight vigil, where residents turned out in a show of support for the refugees, holding posters that read WE LOVE OUR SOMALI NEIGHBORS. Dr. John Birky and Benjamin Anderson, the county hospital CEO, showed up, hoping to build on their year-long effort to bring locals and Somalis together. Dr. Birky in particular was sought out by reporters, and in interviews with the Associated Press and Mary Louise Kelly on NPR's *All Things Considered,* the young doctor said more work was needed to overcome cultural barriers. "There is a level of distrust sometimes and even fear of immigrant communities," he told Kelly, adding he'd gotten past feeling that way once he'd befriended Somalis in town. He told the AP that the refugees arriving in Kansas simply wanted to assimilate. "They're trying to make a better life for their families here," he asserted. "They want to pursue the American Dream." Benjamin, meanwhile, jump-started a project with the help of college students, whereby Somalis and locals went into each other's homes for meals. He called it "Guess Who's Coming to Dinner?" In the ensuing coverage of the bomb plot and its fallout—in local, national, and international media—one resident even cited the replica Statute of Liberty that stood in front of the Finney County Courthouse in Garden City, and said, "I see Garden City as the Ellis Island of the Plains."

The message, conveyed at the Saturday rally by Chief Utz and reinforced time and again after, was clear: "You are safe," Utz told the crowd. The plotters may have been driven by bigotry, he said, but the city's Muslim immigrants needed to know this: "You are all Garden Citians." The gatherings and outpouring of support proved cathartic. Some refugees left, but most, including Ifrah, did not. She called her cousin and said to forget what she'd said; she was staying. Likewise, Adan Keynan was not going anywhere. In a brief, one-paragraph typewritten letter "To Whom It May Concern" at city hall, he said he'd decided to appeal the adverse zoning ruling against his African Shop. The letter was dated November 9, 2016—by coincidence, the very day the Crusaders had planned to carry out their attack to exterminate Muslim "cockroaches" and "wake up" America.

DAN DAY watched the news coverage of the government's Friday afternoon press conference surrounded by Cherlyn, Brandon, and Alyssa in their hotel room in Pratt, Kansas. His FBI handlers had called at about 6 p.m., told him Patrick and Gavin were in custody. They asked if he'd seen the press conference. "What press conference?" Dan said. They explained that Kansas's acting US attorney, Tom Beall, and their boss, FBI special agent in charge Eric Jackson, had announced the arrests at a press conference in Wichita. Dan could hear in their voices both excitement and relief. It's what he felt too. He'd been wondering all day long about the planned takedown, and now he knew it was done. Flipping open his laptop, Dan right away found the coverage—video, audio, and text from media all around the world. He clicked to CNN, then Fox, then local Kansas stations, and he and his family listened to Beall say the Crusaders had been charged with conspiring to use a weapon of mass destruction against Somali immigrants in Garden City, Kansas. Beall and Jackson provided some details about the militia group's plot, drawing on specifics that FBI case agents Smith and Kuhn had provided in their reports. Beall mentioned bomb-making materials, recipes for improvised explosive devices, the manifesto—all part of the group's plot to kill Muslims and destroy the Somalis' mosque and apartments. He mentioned too that a "confidential source" and an undercover agent had infiltrated the group, providing the FBI with inside information that enabled agents to thwart the attack. Beall of course did not identify the informant by name, although Patrick was doing so in militia circles.

Dan took it all in, his family at his side. Cherlyn felt excited that his secret life was over and that Dan was out of danger. They left the hotel for the Friday night reunion cookout, where news about the case was a hot topic among the forty cousins and their families. Except for sharing his role as an informant with a sister, Dan kept quiet. The next morning he cut the trip short. He was restless and felt wiped out, even though he'd slept better the previous night. He didn't really want to be around people; he simply wanted to rest, and so after the family returned to Garden City that afternoon, and while a rally and candlelight vigil supporting Somalis unfolded less than a mile away, that's what he did. He slept.

For their part, Dan's FBI handlers, Smith and Kuhn, did not attend the press conference. Having handed off Patrick in Dodge City to agents from the Kansas City main office, they'd headed back to Garden City, making a short detour to drop off some of Patrick's personal belongings at his mother's. They listened to the press conference in the car, and as they did so, they also continued to process the long, strange interview they'd had earlier with Patrick, back at the sheriff's in Dodge City. It was rather haunting.

Going into the interview, the agents knew it wasn't going to be one in which they'd be trying to coax a suspect to confess or at least cooperate. They had the goods on the Crusader—hours and hours of incriminating recordings, nearly all of them Dan's work, along with Brian's recordings toward the end of the case. They weren't going to adopt good-cop, bad-cop roles or use any other interviewing technique to get Patrick to fold his hand and give it up. They didn't need a confession. What they were interested was an explanation for the group's actions: in short, the why.

Kuhn had gotten a sample of what was to come during the interview at the end of the short car ride from McDonald's to the sheriff's department. Patrick had noticed the crucifix necklace she was wearing, and when they were getting out of the car, he muttered something under his breath. Kuhn wasn't able to catch all of it but heard him basically call her faith into question, saying that if she were a true Christian, she'd be on his side, since he and his fellow Crusaders were trying to do good. Kuhn just shook her head.

In the interview room, Smith got things started.

"Why are we here?" he asked Patrick.

"Because I'm a patriot, bro. I love my country. I love the people in it."

"I'm listening."

"I'm a fucking Christian. And I don't like it when people want to kill my people."

"I'm listening."

"That's all they want to do."

"They being?"

"Cockroaches."

Patrick let that word hang in the air, then asked for some more coffee.

Kuhn took a turn. "You said you're a patriot," she said.

"Yeah," Patrick said.

"You're not a criminal?"

"No."

"Explain that to me."

"We have enemies within our borders that are sworn to kill every fucking one of us."

"Who are these enemies?" Kuhn asked.

Patrick grew annoyed. "You know who they are," he said. "Don't—"

Kuhn interrupted. "I'm not patronizing you."

The interview had morphed into a quasi debate, the contestants arguing about the meaning of patriotism across a table that was as wide as the Grand Canyon in terms of irreconcilable differences. The agents and the terrorist shared the same physical space—an interview room in the county sheriff's department—but not the same concept of America.

"I'm a patriot," Patrick kept insisting, "ready to do everything I can to save this nation from going over the cliff." He continually challenged the agents. He asked mockingly, "Do you know anything about Muslims? Have you done any kind of research on them? Do you know? I mean, c'mon, dude, I would think you of all people, you and anybody else in the FBI, would be more knowledgeable, and have more information, and know way more than me, just Joe Blow stupid fuckin' farmer, about Muslims or Islam."

Muslims despised and killed Christians, he declared, and "we invite them to the country?" Patrick looked disgusted. "They're not productive fucking people."

Kuhn said, "You don't believe there's any productive Muslims in this country?"

"Tell me what are they doing that's productive."

"There's some that are in the military, fighting for the United States."

Patrick dismissed that fact, calling any Muslim in the US military a spy feeding intel to the enemy. He then taunted her and Smith for arresting him, Curtis, and Gavin. "You're taking down the very fucking people who are willing to give their life to save yours. Do you not get that?" The FBI agents were traitors, he said. "You don't give a fuck about your country."

Enough was enough—and Smith pushed back hard. His words weren't the final ones in the meandering session, as the parties talked in circles and past one another, never coming close to common ground. But the rebuttal might as well have been the last word, because Smith seemed to be speaking not only for himself but for most Americans.

You know, the veteran agent said, "the amazing thing about the United States of America and the Constitution that we live under is you're entitled to that opinion." He let that sink in before repeating it: no matter how appalling Patrick's views, he would not try to deprive him of the right to that opinion. And, he added, he would not deprive him of the right to participate in the country's political process. But more important, Smith said, he would not interfere with Patrick's right to life—which is exactly what Patrick and his partners had plotted to do against the Muslims living in Garden City, Kansas.

Smith said, "I won't kill you because you believe differently than me."

Debate done, and on Monday, October 17, the three Crusaders accused of domestic terrorism were arraigned in federal court in the case officially called *The United States of America v. Curtis Wayne Allen, Patrick Eugene Stein, and Gavin Wayne Wright.*

EPILOGUE: TRIALS

THREE MONTHS AFTER THEIR ARREST, as the Crusaders sat in their cells, the Somali Adan Keynan arrived at Garden City's administrative center on the morning of January 10, 2017, to fight for the survival of his business, the African Shop. He made his way to the center's Commission Chambers, where the Board of Zoning Appeals was awaiting the start of his hearing. Four of the five-member board were seated in tall black-leather chairs behind a half-moon-shaped desk. (One member was absent.) The hearing room was carpeted in a neutral, institutional beige, its walls partly wood-paneled. The BZA looked out on a room filled to capacity with interested listeners.

In the decade Adan had lived in Garden City, he'd never been to the chambers before. He was not there alone, however. In addition to Somalis and immigrants from other African countries who'd come to show support, people like Dr. John Birky and the hospital CEO Benjamin Anderson had come to testify on Adan's behalf. For months the two had worked with Adan to better understand the zoning officials' ruling that the shop was being operated illegally—classified as a "Department Store," which was not a "permitted use" in the "1–2 Medium Industrial District" where the store was located. The two had lobbied local legislators, and over the summer they had even spent time with Adan, looking for a new location—a frustrating and failed effort during which they saw firsthand what Dr. Birky called a "white price and East African price for rent." Moreover, on the heels of the thwarted terrorist bomb plot targeting Adan and his Somali neighbors, they saw the hearing in a new light—no longer a mundane matter involving the arcana of zoning but a trial whose subtext was tolerance. The key question, as Benjamin saw it, was this: were Somalis welcome?

Adan, dressed in a suit and assisted by an interpreter, spoke first. "I am worried that I will have to move out of the store," he began. In brief comments, he stressed the store's role in the Muslim community—and the impact its closure would have. "People might not be able to stay here if they can't get the food and things they need from their culture," he said. "I ask you to give me the right to stay where I am for the people of our community."

Then one by one a number of others spoke. Some supported the ruling as it stood, saying the issue wasn't whether Somalis were welcome but rather the integrity of zoning regulations. "They need to follow the rules," one property owner said. "They opened [the store] up with total disregard." Most, however, advocated for Adan, and they knew they couldn't build their case around culture—the fact that the store was central to Somali life, where Somalis could buy their tea, rice, foodstuffs, and clothing items found nowhere else. Or that it was a community center for Somalis, a place to gather, as they had on the day the news broke about a bomb plot to kill them. They had to talk the talk of zoning, and to do that, they argued that the shop had been incorrectly defined as a Department Store and should instead be considered a "convenience store"—which, according to zoning rules, was allowed in an industrial zone. The store was comparable to the gas station across the street that had a "food mart" as part of its operation—and which was deemed legal as a convenience store. Adan's shop was no Walmart or Target or big-box store; it was a family-run small business.

Dr. Birky noted that items sold in Adan's store were foreign to most residents in town, and "it does take a minute to translate what we see there." But however unfamiliar the brands might be, they were actually the foreign equivalent of American products—the clothing, personal items, and frozen food found in any roadside convenience store.

Meanwhile, Benjamin blended the arguments related to culture and zoning. "It's a small store, the size of a convenience store," he said, and also "an invaluable resource for the African people of Garden City who are an invaluable human resource for the workforce here; the two are inextricably bound." To him, based on how the city defined a convenience store, "this is pretty black and white." The board, he concluded, should rule in Adan Keynan's favor.

It did. By a 3–1 margin, the Board of Zoning Appeals voted to reclassify the African Shop as a convenience store. Adan, his friends, Dr. Birky, and Benjamin left the hearing room ecstatic; later they celebrated at the shop, over a meal of African food. Everyone, especially Adan and Sara, felt relieved that the zoning crisis at long last had been resolved. The victory ended his "many sleepless nights" worrying about the business's fate, as he told a local reporter later. It meant he'd be staying put in Garden City.

NEARLY TWO and a half years after the Crusaders' arrest, on March 28, 2018, Dan Day stood ready to enter Ceremonial Courtroom 238 in US District Court in Wichita. Ordinarily the presiding judge, Eric F. Melgren, occupied Courtroom 408 on the fourth floor, but because there were three defendants as well as teams of lawyers for both the government and the defense, the trial was moved to the expansive refurbished courtroom. And Courtroom 238 had a gallery large enough for spectators and the journalists covering the case. The trial had been underway for four days when Dan's time came. Already Lula Harris had testified for the prosecution, as had Brody Benson, who'd hosted the June 16 meeting where Dan passed out and where Patrick and Curtis truly got their terrorist goals underway. Several FBI agents had testified, and the Liberal police captain, Jason Ott, who'd responded to Lula's domestic assault complaint and was involved in Curtis's arrest, had just finished up.

During previous testimony Dan had waited on standby; he hung out in the prosecutors' offices at the courthouse, always in the company of FBI agent Robin Smith. He'd spent months in preparation, going over the secret recordings and evidence with the lead prosecutors, Anthony Mattivi from the Department of Justice's Topeka office and Risa Berkower from the DOJ's Civil Rights Division in Washington, DC. When word finally came, Smith escorted Dan down the halls of the granite courthouse, which had been built in the mid-1930s. Its front lobby featured two imposing oil-on-canvas murals showcasing the state's pioneering past. One, *Kansas Farming,* depicted a romanticized display of agrarian life on the Great Plains—rolling hills, tall corn, sunflowers, a bountiful fall harvest, and farmers and their families.

Standing with his FBI handler at the doorway to Judge Melgren's courtroom, Dan realized he didn't feel as nervous as he'd thought he would. He'd been anxious, for sure, during the preceding days, but now that it was time to testify, he just wanted to get on with it. He hadn't seen Patrick, Curtis, or Gavin since the arrests. They'd been held without bail while awaiting trial. Early on, a crude map of the jail's layout was found in Patrick's cell, which suggested he was cooking up a plan to escape. Dan knew full well the trio would be seated at the defense table with their lawyers. He'd been advised by the prosecutors not to look over at them but straight ahead as he entered for the first time.

Dan did just that when a court officer pushed open the swinging door and he walked in. He saw that the room was filled with spectators, reporters, members of the Crusaders' families—and also the twelve jurors in the jury box, who'd be deciding the case. He thought the room's restored and historically accurate appearance was breathtaking—the high ceilings, the glowing chandeliers, the polished dark wooden tables, chairs, and benches. The judge instructed him to step to the front, to be sworn in by a court clerk. Dan didn't know it, but he, the judge, and, for that matter, all of the defendants were practically neighbors—not just native sons of Kansas, all of them, but from the same corner of the state. Eric Melgren had grown up in southwest Kansas on a cattle and wheat farm. He was a first-generation college student, served in the Department of Justice as Kansas's US attorney for six years, and had been a judge for a decade, ever since his appointment in 2008 by then president George W. Bush.

Dan could feel everyone's eyes on him, including those of the defendants, as he walked toward the witness box. But he resisted exchanging looks with the Crusaders and was sworn in by the clerk. Berkower, one of the prosecutors, greeted him. "Good afternoon," she said.

"Good afternoon," Dan said.

Berkower then asked, "Dan, in 2016, did you help the FBI break up a plot by these defendants to blow up a building in Garden City, Kansas?"

"Yes, I did."

It was the start of testimony that would continue for the next five days. Mattivi would later say that in nearly two decades of trial work, he'd never seen a government's key informant testify for so long. Indeed, on one of those days the judge quipped, "Mr. Day is resuming his oh-so-familiar seat in the witness box." And it was only a matter of time before Dan did trade looks with his former militia mates. They looked so different—clean-shaven and wearing pressed suits—that he almost didn't recognize them. Patrick had even dyed his hair, maybe to hide some of his premature gray, Dan thought. But beyond cleaning up their appearance, little else seemed to have changed. If looks could kill, Dan would have been dead. Curtis, the one Dan always figured hadn't liked him, was particularly transparent about his loathing. From his place at the defense table Curtis gave Dan the middle finger, and then another time he made a movement with his hand to suggest firing a gun. Curtis thought he was being sly, but a US marshal noticed the gesture and told Curtis to knock it off.

LAWYERS FOR the Crusaders framed their defense around a theme of entrapment and government abuse of power, saying if not for the FBI —with Dan Day as its errand boy—none of the defendants would be on trial. "The FBI created and directed all of this," said Rich Federico, Curtis's federal public defender. Plus, the lawyers asked, where was the bomb? The Crusaders may have talked a mean game, but, Federico said, "There was no bomb, there never was any weapon of mass destruction." Jurors should instead view the investigation as an instance of government overreach, an infringement of the rights of free speech and association protected by the First Amendment, no matter how repulsive that speech might be. Tapes of their clients contained harsh, foul language "full of hatred," Federico said, "but hatred is not a crime in this country." In short, the men were big talk, no action—except the actions they were seduced into taking by corrupt FBI agents and their informant.

Each lawyer sought to distinguish their client from the rest. Gavin was a "very lonely man" who'd recently moved to the Liberal area to open a branch of the family business. He'd had a hard time making friends and so when he met up with Curtis Allen, "having a friend was a welcome relief." In the end, argued his attorney, Kari S. Schmidt, "Gavin Wright chose friends who were bad for him." Curtis, meanwhile, was an Iraq war veteran who had returned home a changed man, deeply wary of the federal government and then lured into doing things he would never have done otherwise. Patrick's lawyer knew there was no way he could run from his client's bigotry, so he got out in front of it. To be sure, he said, Patrick was someone "who at times has allowed his prejudice and his hate to consume him." Patrick referred "to Muslims as cockroaches, talked about them as an infestation, and would refer to himself as Orkinman." The defense attorney, James R. Pratt, went so far as to predict that jurors would end up not liking his client at all. "You will despise the things you hear him say on these recordings," he said. But, Pratt argued, Patrick's likability was not on trial. "You will need more than a dislike of Patrick Stein to find him guilty." Patrick's legal jeopardy had also gotten much worse after the FBI searched his home following his arrest: 149 images of kids engaged in sexual activities were found on his laptop and two thumb drives, which had led to a separate criminal charge of possession of child pornography.

Throughout, the three were also depicted as victims of unceasing Islamophobic rants from both the far right and Donald J. Trump, who, to the shock of pollsters, pundits, and a majority of American voters, had won key swing states, and with that, enough Electoral College votes to defeat Hillary Clinton in the 2016 election. For starters, Pratt argued at one point that Patrick had learned to hate from the right-wing media. "For years Patrick immersed himself in right-wing news and ideals: Sean Hannity, Michael Savage, and Alex Jones." Patrick then became an "early and avid supporter" of Trump, a candidate who at the climax of his campaign repeatedly warned that Muslim and Somali immigrants settling in the United States provided ISIS with a rich pool of potential recruits. Prosecution of the Crusaders could therefore not be viewed in a vacuum, the lawyer argued, but had to be seen in the larger sociopolitical context "of one of the most rhetorically mold-breaking, violent, awful, hateful, and contentious presidential elections in modern history, driven in large measure by the rhetorical China shop bull who is now our president."

Most of all, though, the defense targeted Dan Day as an unreliable narrator—the enabler of the government's sinister entrapment of their clients. Patrick's attorney asserted that without Dan's manipulations, "none of this alleged plot would have been possible."

Dan, the lawyers said, was a wannabe cop in "financial straits" who hit the lottery as a "paid FBI informant." Over fourteen months he'd been given a used Chevy Impala by the FBI and paid about $12,810 to cover gas and other expenses, including his emergency room bill after he passed out at the June 16 meeting; he received an additional and unexpected $15,000 cash payment after the arrests—for a total of nearly $33,000. "He was paid a lot," Federico said. To keep his gravy train running, Dan needed to deliver chargeable offenses. "He planted ideas," Federico exclaimed to jurors, his voice rising.

"Dan Day is not a truthful guy," Federico said.

FOR THE prosecution, fifteen civilian and law enforcement witnesses, along with more than five hundred exhibits, were presented over the course of a trial lasting six weeks. The militia member Brody Benson talked about the June meeting on his property following the massacre at the Pulse nightclub in Florida, and he described how he'd resigned, once he'd realized Patrick Stein was moving beyond words toward taking action. Lula Harris walked jurors through her troubled relationship with Curtis, focusing on his growing preoccupation with making homemade bombs and authoring the group's manifesto. FBI agent Amy Kuhn and other police witnesses testified about bomb-making evidence they'd seized, with Kuhn also describing at length Dan's work as a civilian informant, which began in the summer of July 2015, after the militia cookout held at Terrence Taylor's. While Kuhn was on the witness stand, an aunt cared for her ten-month-old baby girl back at their hotel.

FBI bomb experts gave jurors a primer on improvised explosive devices. They explained that the urea fertilizer Patrick had provided the undercover agent Brian was popular with terrorists making homemade bombs and that it was considered a "tertiary explosive," meaning once the fertilizer was converted into urea nitrate, the resulting bomb still required a booster and could not be denotated directly by a blasting cap. Bombs made from Patrick's three hundred pounds of urea fertilizer would have "completely destroyed" the Somalis' apartment complex, they said. Of course the undercover agent Brian testified; Judge Melgren allowed him to appear in disguise and to be identified by his pseudonym; the press and the public were sent to a courtroom on the first floor to view his testimony on a video feed. "Those measures are being taken solely to protect his undercover status with regard to other investigations unrelated to this case that he may be working on," the judge explained to jurors. Brian told of his role as a weapons trafficker, his bonding with Patrick as part of the FBI's strategy to take control of the bomb plot, so that the Crusaders would not blow up the apartments on their own, and to help steer the effort to a harmless conclusion. Jurors appeared riveted by the FBI video showing Brian and Patrick riding around Garden City after they'd been shooting at pumpkins, as they discussed the Somali targets.

But all eyes were indeed on Dan Day. He was the centerpiece of the government's case, the one to provide running commentary on the hours of secretly recorded Zello and in-person meetings. He detailed his infiltration of the Crusaders starting in late winter of 2016 and lasting through October, walking jurors through what prosecutor Mattivi would call the plot's three acts: the conspirators' initial coming together and the planning phase in the spring; the move from hateful speech to action throughout the summer, as they devised a plan; and the plot's end, with the arrests during that critical week of October 11, 2016.

For Dan, it wasn't as if life had returned to normal after his return from the cousins' picnic on the weekend of the Crusaders' arrests. The twin fears of working as an informant—fear for his personal safety and for the safety of the Somalis, should the investigation fail—had largely been dispelled, but embers still flickered. For one thing, he'd been outed online and was soon attacked on Facebook. Some said he deserved to be hanged; others said he should be shot. Several commented that although they were against the Crusaders' extremism, Dan was nonetheless a traitor to the militia movement for working with the FBI. Not surprisingly, worry flared about his family's safety. Returning home one night, they spotted a dent in the front door. Had someone tried to break in? Or had the dent always been there, unnoticed until now? No one could know for sure—an uncertainty that left them feeling vulnerable. Dan alerted the FBI agents, and the family was put up in a local hotel for a couple of days. To beef up home security, one of Dan's cousins installed a video camera on the exterior of the house.

Then came the nightmare. The first time he had it was about six months after the arrests, and it recurred. In it Dan wandered through the smoky remains of one of the Somali apartment complexes. The sky was dark; little fires smoldered; a burning smell filled the air. In the dream Dan was thinking, "I screwed up." Moving through the wreckage, he spotted a Somali woman, who faced away from him. As he approached she turned his way. In her arms she held the bomb-shredded corpse of a child.

Dan bolted up in bed, sweaty, his mind racing as it straddled sleep and wakefulness. He was asking himself if the bombs had actually gone off; had it really happened? "My worst fear coming true," he'd think, concerning the carnage in the dream.

In time, Dan found a way to relieve some of the stress—by talking with Dr. John Birky. He decided to reach out to him even though they'd never met. Dan didn't count the community dinner that Dr. Birky and Benjamin Anderson, dressed in traditional African robes, had cohosted, as an actual meeting, though Dan had attended in his role as a Crusader gathering intelligence about Somalis. Dan sent Dr. Birky a note on Facebook; the doctor responded, and the two started meeting at the library in Garden City to talk about the case and their experiences.

Over Dan's five days on the witness stand, prosecutors had him address the cumulative stress of maintaining his "persona"—portraying a

Muslim-hating white supremacist. "It wasn't fun and games," Dan told jurors. "It was hard on me, hard on my family." He admitted as well to having questioned, along the way, the amount of lying and deception required to sustain his fictional character—a moral dilemma he'd worked through with the help of his son, Brandon, who'd bolstered him by invoking the story of Rahab from the book of Joshua. In testimony at trial, though, Dan was forceful; no trace of that earlier self-doubt remained.

"You were asked a lot about the fact that you lied to these defendants to earn their trust," Berkower noted. "Do you remember being asked about that?"

"Yes, I do."

"And that's true, right, you did?" she said.

"That's true."

"In your mind, are all lies created equal?"

"No."

"Why not?"

"I lied to save a life," Dan said. "I would lie, anything, to save an innocent life." If this willingness to lie made him "sound like a bad person," he said, "I'll take that responsibility."

For his part, by the time of the trial, the veteran prosecutor Mattavi had abandoned the initial skepticism he'd expressed when FBI agent Amy Kuhn first suggested recruiting Dan as an informant. He'd held the opinion that Dan had too much baggage and would not be an effective witness. But Dan had held up fine, weathering attacks on his motives and credibility and never losing his cool. More than that, though, Mattivi had come to admire Dan's true grit in a role lasting far longer than he'd ever bargained for, which had put him and his family at risk.

In his closing argument, Mattivi recapped the evidence for jurors—emphasizing the Crusaders' own incriminating words contained in the tapes—and argued that, contrary to the defense lawyers' repeated assertions, the trial was not about government inference with the Crusaders' rights to free speech and assembly under the First Amendment. "You saw that the defendants didn't just express their views," Mattivi said. "They didn't just talk. They're not here because of their words." He cited their specific activities: choosing targets, devising a plan, revising it "to achieve maximum body count," researching explosives, making and testing a blasting cap, and, lastly, teaming up with a bomb maker, Brian. They were not engaged in protected political discourse; they were planning cold-blooded murder. "The defendants plotted to murder dozens of innocent men, women, and children.

"That's why this isn't a case about the First Amendment."

Mattivi wasn't quite done, though. "I want to say something about Dan Day," he said. It wasn't an afterthought; he'd saved his closing words for Dan, a tribute lasting nearly ten minutes. "Dan Day's not an FBI agent. He's not a trained operative. He's not a professional actor. Dan Day is an everyday guy who, when he found himself in the middle of a terrifying situation he never sought out, he dug deep into his soul, and he found a strength that he didn't know was there." In later interviews, Mattivi continued his praise, saying had it not been for Dan, "I really believe we would have been looking at a smoking hole at the West Mary Street apartment complex, with dozens and dozens of dead bodies everywhere."

MATTIVI HAD a formula for predicting how long a jury would deliberate—one day for each week of the trial. His formula failed this time. Instead of taking six days for the six-week trial, the jury returned its verdict in about six hours. Patrick, Curtis, and Gavin were convicted of conspiracy to use a weapon of mass destruction, as well as conspiracy to interfere with the civil rights of the Muslims living in Garden City.

Gavin was convicted of one count of obstruction of justice for lying to FBI agent Robin Smith when he went to the Liberal police department and insisted he knew nothing about the plot.

Before the Crusaders' sentencing, scheduled for the next year, some Somali refugees were videotaped, talking in personal terms about immigrating to the United States and the fear they felt when news of the plot broke on October 14, 2016. Adan Keynan, Ifrah Ahmed, and Mursal Naleye were among the Somalis whose videos were given to the judge as victim impact statements. In Ifrah's, she described seeking refuge in America in the pursuit of freedom and happiness, and she stated that Garden City was her home. She had voted in her first election as a citizen in 2017 and noted that she was an American, just like the defendants, and that she should not live in terror.

In their arguments for leniency, lawyers for the convicted men revisited the Donald J. Trump factor, arguing that Trump bore responsibility for their clients' criminal actions. This time, Gavin's lawyer went so far as to posit that the life sentences federal prosecutors were seeking would not have the desired deterrent effect against future violent attacks by white supremacists—not as long as the country had a president who persistently egged them on with inflammatory Islamophobic rhetoric. "Intellectual honesty requires this Court to confront a certain reality," Schmidt argued. "As long as the White House with impunity calls Islam 'a dangerous threat' and paints average Americans as 'victims of horrendous attacks by people that believe only in Jihad,' a mixed signal gets sent. The President warns Americans that radical Muslims are 'trying to take over our children.'" Meanwhile, that same president, Schmidt continued, praised as "good people" the white supremacists at a Unite the Right rally in Charlottesville in 2017; they had fought violently with police and civil rights groups, which resulted in a young woman's death when one of them intentionally rammed a car into counter-protesters. "As long as the Executive Branch condemns Islam and commends and encourages violence against would-be enemies, then a sentence imposed by the Judicial Branch does little to deter people generally from engaging in such conduct if they believe they are protecting their countries from enemies identified by their own Commander-in-Chief." To think stiff sentences in this case would deter future domestic terrorism, she concluded, "is simply a pipe dream."

For many, it was amen. For Judge Melgren, however, the argument was not legally relevant. Millions of people on both the right and the left consumed heated, partisan rhetoric from the media and public figures, the judge said, "but none of that explains or justifies anything remotely like what we're dealing with here." The men, he said, "made their choices." The judge rejected as well any assertion that the case involved the Crusaders' free speech rights, noting the "irony" in making such a claim—"the fact that an attack that was designed to interfere in the most horrific of ways with the First Amendment rights of individuals' freedom of worship is now being used as a defensive shield to say that this was just talk. That's what conspiracy is—a conspiracy is planning to carry out an event, and those plans are made, of course, largely verbally." Further, he brushed aside as irrelevant a fact repeated by the defense that the Crusaders never succeeded in manufacturing a bomb. "They were convicted of conspiracy," he said. "Whether they actually did it, whether they actually could have done it, they wanted to do it. They intended to do it. They planned to do it. The fact that they didn't do it and that, therefore, no one actually received physical injuries is of no credit to them." Indeed, had they succeeded, the judge said, the death and destruction resulting from their attack would have been worse than that unleashed by Timothy McVeigh in 1995, in Oklahoma City, when the fertilizer bombs he'd made leveled much of a federal building and killed 168 people. "In some ways," Melgren said, "I find this even more appalling, perhaps, than the Oklahoma City event. Of course people died there. Fortunately, no one died in Garden City. But this event was motivated by extraordinary animus on the basis of race, religion, and national origin." That animus, the judge continued, was antithetical to the nation's aspiration to tolerance and inclusion. He concluded, "I find that they were planning a significant horrific terrorist attack."

Finally, Melgren found that the defendants' statements to the court, their so-called apologies, were lame. Curtis, he said, seemed to express some remorse by writing, "To anyone who may have been put out or frightened by anything we did, I offer my sincere apologies and ask for their forgiveness." But he said he was "astonished" by Gavin's statement, which said the government had "painted me to be something that I'm not." Gavin must "still be in denial," the judge said. Lastly, Melgren said that Patrick—the "chief cheerleader for the hatred"—remained "starkly unrepentant" even after his arrest, apologizing only to his family for the "literal hell" the case has caused them.

Melgren in the end did not sentence the men to life in prison, which the prosecutors had asked for; instead he sentenced Curtis Wayne Allen to twenty-five years, which he called a "staggeringly long sentence, particularly for a man who's 50 years old"; he similarly sentenced Gavin Wayne Wright to twenty-five years, plus another year for lying to the FBI; and he reserved the harshest sentence for Patrick Eugene Stein—thirty years. Separately, another three and a half years were added to Patrick's term for his possession of child pornography.

SEVERAL WEEKS after the jury's verdict on April 18, 2018, a fifth-grade teacher in the tiny hill town of Shelburne Falls in western Massachusetts mentioned the case to her students during a morning meeting when current events were discussed. The teacher summarized the bomb plot against Somali refugees and the militia group's conviction. The kids—ages ten and eleven—were alarmed, especially upon hearing that after the incident many Somalis were afraid to even go outside. The class wanted to do something, and the kids decided to write to the immigrants living seventeen hundred miles away who had been the targets of the plot.

Ashleigh wrote that "when are [*sic*] teacher told us what had happened in Garden City I was so upset." Ruby said her "heart dropped," and asked, "Who would do such a thing?" Lydia admitted she felt "a bit scared" just hearing the news. "I don't understand why people think it is okay to harm people who have done nothing!" Natalie wrote that she felt "emotional, embarrassed, and in shock!" to hear that Americans would try to hurt other people because of their religious beliefs. Aiden, meanwhile, pulled no punches, exclaiming, "I was disgusted by what those people wanted to do to your town." Maybe, he asked, they could become pen pals? Fiona wrote that she hoped the class's letters would be shared among the immigrant families and their friends. Plus, she had an idea: "Visit Shelburne Falls!" Logan also urged a visit: "You will find that you will be treated with kindness."

The teacher, Patricia Perlman, filled an envelope with the students' letters—twenty-four in all—and mailed them to Garden City's manager, Matthew Allen. In a cover letter, she told Allen, "We often discuss current events; your story moved them very much. They wanted to reach out." City officials eagerly shared the letters with Somali elders and then came up with a way to showcase more broadly the fifth-graders' support for the refugee community. Fifth-graders from one of Garden City's elementary schools were videotaped reading excerpts from the letters. The footage mixed sweeping images of Garden City, news reports about the plot, and Muslims praying in the mosque, with those of the local boys and girls standing in the library, or at a playground, or in a classroom, reading aloud the words written by their counterparts in Massachusetts.

The uplifting video was posted on the city's website the next month, and in short order it had more than twenty thousand views, more than anything the city had ever produced. City manager Allen said, "It's a glimpse of what the world would look like if human beings treated each other the way fifth-graders treated each other."

THE VIDEO was titled "Infinite Hope"—which was certainly needed in a democracy increasingly torn asunder by violent militia members and far-right extremists. In October 2019 the director of the FBI finally acknowledged that threat in no uncertain terms when speaking to the House of Representatives' Homeland Security Committee. "More deaths were caused by domestic violent extremists than international terrorists in recent years," Christopher Wray told lawmakers. It was a message far different from that of his predecessor three years earlier, when James B. Comey appeared before a Senate committee to discuss homeland security and spoke exclusively about threats from radical Islamist terrorists, either homegrown or from abroad, and never once mentioned the upward trend in far-right violence. The Garden City bomb plot had become a harbinger of what was to come, a darkness that had deepened by 2020—the year of Donald Trump's failed bid for reelection—with intensifying alarm and amid a deadly coronavirus pandemic. On April 30, hundreds of protesters, many bearing arms and belonging to militias, occupied the state capitol in Lansing, Michigan, to demand an end to the governor's stay-at-home orders. Six months later thirteen men were arrested by the FBI in what was described as a domestic terrorist plot to kidnap Michigan's governor, Gretchen Whitmer. Then, after Trump's loss to Democrat Joe Biden, hundreds of Trump's supporters violently stormed the US Capitol on January 6, 2021, in a bid to halt the final electoral count and overturn Trump's defeat. The mob included neo-Nazis and supporters of the Proud Boys, the Three Percenters, and other militias. If not for their incarceration, Patrick, Curtis, and Gavin would likely have been there. Five people died as a result of the insurrection, and in its wake the one-term president Donald Trump was impeached a second time, a first in the country's history.

The Garden City bomb plot made international news in 2016—a foiled attack against Muslims that left a community shaken but physically unharmed. The case made headlines from time to time afterward too—mostly during the six-week trial in 2018, and then again during Judge Melgren's sentencing in January 2019. Then it faded, overtaken by the latest news, good and bad, breaking around the country and beyond. But it was a near miss that thankful local officials and residents of Garden City would never forget. By the fall of 2019, or nine months after the sentencing of the Crusaders, Dan had returned as best he could to a quiet family life. To help make ends meet, he'd resumed his buy-sell activity online. He coped too with worsening health—he suffered a heart attack and spent time in the hospital more than once.

Then, that fall he got a call from Michael Utz. The police chief asked if Dan was available to attend the Diversity Breakfast on November 8. Dan replied that he could; he was free on that day, as he was most every day, and so on that raw November day, he and his family arrived at a conference room in a local hotel. The room was packed with officials, residents, Somali elders, and other Muslims. In his remarks Utz talked about celebrating "the strengths of our diverse community" in the middle of America's Heartland, of all places, and he paid homage to Dan's work to protect that diversity and the civil rights of all people living in the Garden. When he was finished, and as those in the room stood and applauded, the chief called on Dan Day to step up to the podium—"the individual who came forward to make sure our community is safe." Whereupon he presented Danny Ray Day with the city's high honor, its Community Service Award.

ACKNOWLEDGMENTS

I want to acknowledge my friends and neighbors Scott Tromanhauser and Jennie Shaw. One Sunday afternoon in the spring of 2019, I answered my doorbell and found Scott standing there. "I have some people I think you should meet," he said. We went to his house, where he introduced several guests whom he and his wife Jennie were hosting for the afternoon. Three Kansans: Dan Day, Mursal Nayele, and Benjamin Anderson. (Scott and Benjamin knew each other from a health care leadership program at Dartmouth College.) The visitors were making a pit stop at Scott and Jennie's house en route from Dartmouth, where they'd been on a panel titled "Reconciliation," and back home to Kansas.

At that moment, only a few months had passed since the sentencing in Wichita of three white nationalists who had conspired to build bombs in order to kill Somalis in Garden City, Kansas. I was vaguely aware of the case, which had been in and out of the news since the October 2016 arrests of Patrick Stein, Curtis Allen, and Gavin Wright. Now, in my neighbor's living room sat the FBI informant who'd played a critical role in the FBI's domestic terrorism investigation, one of the Muslims who'd been targeted, and the hospital executive who'd been working with others in the Garden City community to bridge cultural gaps between longtime Kansans and Muslim refugees. It took a number of months to really get rolling, but those initial introductions proved to be the start of what is now *White Hot Hate.* Without Scott's knack for knowing a good story when he sees one, I would not be able to tell this one.

My friend and sometimes collaborator Mitch Zuckoff was once again on standby, always ready to talk narrative and discuss research challenges and any other bumps in the road. At Boston University, where I teach, I thank Bill McKeen, chair of the journalism department, for enthusiastically supporting this book. Likewise, Jenn Underhill, who helped me with my comings and goings in Kansas to do my research; and longtime colleague and friend Maggie Mulvihill for helping to arrange research funding for those trips. Two BU graduate students in journalism, Sofie Isenberg and Damian Burchardt, were a great help in researching a variety of topics and chasing down secondary sources. Jacob Boucher and his colleagues Joey Campos and Steve Theer are wizards in technology, and also, it turns out, great sounding boards for possible book titles.

In Kansas I met plenty of helpful people—and not just helpful regarding the book's reporting but also for getting around town and suggesting a good place to get a burrito or a beer. Most important was Dan Day; I'd like to thank him and his family for fielding any question I put to them. I want to thank Benjamin Anderson, who introduced me to Adan Keynan at his African Shop. It was because of the Somalis' trust in Benjamin that those whom I wanted to interview agreed to do so. I enjoyed the good company of Ifrah Ahmed, who hosted me for tea in her apartment with Halima Farah, and I thank Mursal for taking my periodic calls while he was on the road, driving eighteen-wheelers cross-country. I want to acknowledge Johnetta Hebrlee and Laurie Oshel at the Finney County Historical Society for their help in gathering newspaper clips about immigration trends in Garden City, Somali refugees, and the history of Garden City. They directed me to Holly Hope's memoir, *Garden City: Dreams in a Kansas Town.* It, along with

Sarah Smarsh's memoir, *Heartland: A Memoir of Working Hard and Being Broke in the Richest Country on Earth,* were must-reads.

I thank former assistant US attorney Anthony Mattivi, retired FBI agent Robin Smith, and agent Amy Kuhn for agreeing to be interviewed about the case; it wasn't until very late in the process that those interviews came about, but better late than never. I thank Bridget B. Patton, media representative, FBI Kansas City Division, for her help in making those conference calls happen. I thank Sean Moore, litigation support special in the US attorney's Topeka office, for sharing his knowledge of the trial exhibits, and also Scott Nace, for assistance in seeking access to public records. The clerks at the US District Court in Wichita were always helpful, and I especially thank Sarah Zepick for quickly getting back to me when I had a question about the docket or other procedural matters involving the federal district court.

For their ongoing support, I thank my editors and the team at Houghton Mifflin Harcourt. Bruce Nichols got me started and Rakia Clark expertly guided me to the finish line, while Ivy Givens and Lisa Glover oversaw the manuscript through production. They are all a joy to work with, as is Megan Wilson. I thank Susanna Brougham for her close, careful copyediting. My agent, Richard Abate, and Martha Stevens at 3arts Entertainment were there when I needed them; Richard is the best.

I have had a "family council" of readers whose comments along the way were always helpful: my brother John and my sons, Nick and Christian. Then there's my friend David Holahan; he was my first newspaper editor way back when, and it seems he has pretty much read every word I've ever written (not necessarily a good thing).

None of this would have been possible without my wife, Karin, and my daughters, Holly and Dana. They make sure I keep one foot planted in our daily lives while the other is planted (and sometimes stuck) in the book world. It's called balance, I'm told, and I'm grateful that they guarantee it. I could not do without it—or without them.

CHAPTER NOTES

PROLOGUE: A CALL TO ARMS

FBI RECORDINGS

Dan Day, Patrick Stein, and Brody Benson, June 14, 2016, Hutchinson, KS.

SWORN TRIAL TESTIMONY

Dan Day: March 29, 2018; April 3, 2018. FBI agent Amy Kuhn: April 10, 2018. Brody Benson: March 26, 2018; March 28, 2018.

COURT AND OTHER OFFICIAL RECORDS

Garden City Neighborhood & Development Services Department, zoning files regarding the African Shop, numbered GCBZA2014-09 and GCBZA2016-19.

OTHER SOURCES

For the description of the Pulse nightclub shooting, I relied on public records of the city of Orlando, available online at https://www.orlando.gov/Our-Government/Departments-Offices/Executive-Offices/City-Clerk/Pulse-Tragedy-Public-Records. I also consulted a study by Frank Straub, Jack Cambria, Jane Castor, Ben Gorban, Brett Meade, David Waltenmeyer, and Jennifer Zeunik, "Rescue, Response, and Resilience: A Critical Incident Review of the Orlando Public Safety Response to the Attack on the Pulse Nightclub," Critical Response Initiative, Washington, DC: Office of Community Oriented Policing Services, 2017, https://cops.usdoj.gov/RIC/Publications/cops-w0857-pub.pdf. For comments by Donald J. Trump I relied on *Politico* magazine, "The 155 Craziest Things Trump Said This

Election," November 5, 2016, https://www.politico.com/magazine/story/2016/11/the-155-craziest-things-trump-said-this-cycle-214420.

CHAPTER 1: THE ACCIDENTAL INFORMANT

SWORN TRIAL TESTIMONY

Dan Day: March 28, 2018; April 3, 2018; April 4, 2018. Jason Crick: April 11, 2018. Stephanie Burgess Blackburn: March 26, 2018. FBI agent Amy Kuhn: April 10, 2018; April 11, 2018.

COURT AND OTHER OFFICIAL RECORDS

United States v. Allen et al., Government's Motion *In Limine* to Preclude Improper Impeachment Evidence, March 12, 2018, p. 5. Defendant Curtis Wayne Allen's Sentencing Memorandum, October 29, 2019, pp. 32–35. Government Sentencing Memorandum, October 29, 2018. Letter from Steve Burgess, owner of Garden Spot Rentals. Garden City Neighborhood & Development Services Department, zoning files regarding the African Shop, numbered GCBZA2014-09 and GCBZA2016-19.

OTHER SOURCES

Dan Day's Facebook page, postings on August 25, 2015; August 31, 2015; September 8, 2015. Terrence Taylor's Facebook page. Garden City Noon Lions Facebook page, posting September 8, 2015. Mary Louise Kelly, National Public Radio, interview with Dr. John Birky, October 16, 2016, https://www.npr.org/2016/10/16/498135766/what-you-need-to-know-about-the-somali-refugee-community-in-kansas. James B. Comey, "Counterterrorism, Counterintelligence, and the Challenges of Going Dark," statement before the Senate Select Committee on Intelligence, July 8, 2015, https://www.fbi.gov/news/testimony/counterterrorism-counterintelligence-and-the-challenges-of-going-dark/layout_view. *The Wizard of Oz,* Metro-Goldwyn-Mayer, 1939, starring Judy Garland as Dorothy.

BOOKS, ARTICLES, AND REPORTS

Holly Hope, *Garden City: Dreams in a Kansas Town,* Norman, OK: University of Oklahoma Press, 1988. David Neiwert, "Far-Right Extremists Have Hatched

Far More Terror Plots Than Anyone Else in Recent Years," *Investigative Fund,* June 22, 2017. Janet Reitman, "U.S. Law Enforcement Failed to See the Threat of White Nationalism: Now They Don't Know How to Stop It," *New York Times Magazine,* November 3, 2018. Trevor Aronson, "Terrorism's Double Standard: Violent Far-Right Extremists Are Rarely Prosecuted as Terrorists," https://theintercept.com/2019/03/23/domestic-terrorism-fbi-prosecutions/. https://www.justice.gov/usao-ks/pr/kansas-man-sentenced-30-years-plot-explode-car-bomb-fort-riley. Donald D. Stull, "Harvest of Change: Meatpacking, Immigration, and Garden City, Kansas," a paper presented at the Kansas Economic Policy Conference, Lawrence, Kansas, October 13, 2011, http://www.ipsr.ku.edu/conferen/kepc11/HarvestofChange.pdf. Michael J. Broadway and Donald D. Stull, "Meat Processing and Garden City, KS: Boom and Bust," *Journal of Rural Studies* 22 (2006), 55–66, https://www.researchgate.net/publication/222596959_Meat_Processing_and_Garden_City_KS_Boom_and_Bust. Dr. Janet E. Benson, "Garden City: Meatpacking and Immigration to the High Plains," a paper delivered at a conference titled "Immigration and the Changing Face of Rural America," July 11–13, 1996, Ames, IA. Ted Genoways, "The Only Good Muslim Is a Dead Muslim," *New Republic,* May 15, 2001, https://newrepublic.com/article/142346/kansas-meatpacking-somali-muslim-refugee-murder-plot-trump-supporters. Diana Diaz, "Hungry and Desperate, Thousands of Somalis Trek to Ethiopia," March 25, 2017, https://www.unhcr.org/en-us/news/latest/2017/3/58d2585a4/hungry-desperate-thousands-somalis-trek-ethiopia.html. Al-Shabab, https://www.cfr.org/backgrounder/al-shabab.

NEWS ARTICLES

Clare Trapass, "The Untold Story Behind the Infamous 'In Cold Blood' Murder House—and Why It's for Sale," October 24, 2019, https://www.sfgate.com/realestate/article/In-Cold-Blood-Murder-House-Goes-on-the-Market-14558631.php. Associated Press, "Usually Dry Arkansas River Is Flowing Again in Southwest Kansas, June 17, 1985, https://apnews.com/35f6705b70f8dc719901f812ada8c9ad. Pam Zubeck, "One Rescuer Couldn't Even Swim," *Garden City Telegram,* May 29, 1985, p. 1. Photograph of Dan Day, 17, and Terry Johnson, 17, holding a salute cake, *Garden City Telegram,* June 15, 1985, p. 20. David Ramsey, "Walmart Issues Statement Denying Underground Tunnels Beneath Stores Used in Obama Plot to Take Over Texas: Really," *Arkansas Times,* May 5, 2015, https://arktimes.com/arkansas-blog/2015/05/05/walmart-issues-statement-denying-underground-tunnels-beneath-stores-used-in-obama-plot-to-take-over-texas-really. Tom Hamburger, "Hundreds Gather for 20th Anniversary of Deadly Oklahoma Bombing," *Washington Post,* April 19, 2015. *Huffington Post,* "John T. Booker, Jr., Kansas Man, Arrested in Plot to Suicide Bomb Fort Riley for ISIS," https://www.huffpost.com/entry/us-man-arrested-bomb-fort-riley_n_7041960. Author note: On May 23, 2016, Booker pleaded guilty to conspiracy to detonate a car bomb, and on July 24, 2017, he was sentenced to thirty years in prison, https://www.justice.gov/usao-ks/pr/kansas-man-sentenced-30-years-plot-explode-car-bomb-fort-riley. John Eligon, "White Supremacist Convicted of Killing 3 at Kansas Jewish Centers, *New York Times,* August 31, 2015, https://www.nytimes.com/2015/09/01/us/white-supremacist-convicted-of-killing-3-at-kansas-jewish-centers.html?auth=login-email&login=email. Author note: Miller was convicted at trial of one count of capital murder, three counts of attempted murder, and assault and weapons charges; he was sentenced to death on November 10, 2015. Kevin Murphy, "Kansas White Supremacist Sentenced to Death for Three Murders, Reuters, November 10, 2015, https://www.reuters.com/article/us-kansas-sentencing/kansas-white-supremacist-sentenced-to-death-for-three-murders-idUSKCN0SZ1HP20151111. John W. Fountain, "Needy Workers Wait for a Kansas Plant to Reopen," *New York Times,* July 10, 2001, p. 10. Barbara Vobejda, "The Heartland Pulses with New Blood," *Washington Post,* August 11, 1991, https://www.washingtonpost.com/archive/politics/1991/08/11/the-heartland-pulses-with-new-blood/3291f783-01f1-4565-956a-ecdbe6e6a7d2/. Rachel Seth, "Out of Africa," *Southwest Daily Times,* June 12, 1994, p. 1. Dolores Hope, "Somalis Find Refuge Here," *Garden City Telegram,* July 8, 1994, p. 1. Dolores Hope, "Somalis Help Each Other," *Garden City Telegram,* July 16, 1994. Joey Berlin, "Somalis Will Relocate," *Emporia Gazette,* January 30, 2008. Associated Press, "Somalis, Emporia Residents Struggle with Cultural Differences," January 15, 2008. David Klepper, "Garden City: America's Future?" *Wichita Eagle,* June 27, 2010, https://www.kansas.com/news/local/article1037443.html. Asifa Quraishi-Landes, "Five Myths About Sharia," *Washington Post,* June 24, 2016, https://www.washingtonpost.com/opinions/five-myths-about-sharia/2016/06/24/7e3efb7a-31ef-11e6-8758-d58e76e11b12_story.html. Angie Haflich, "Kearny County Hospital, Garden City to Host Benefit Concert," *Garden City Telegram,* September 25, 2015.

CHAPTER 2: MINUTEMAN

FBI RECORDINGS AND TEXTS

Dan Day, Patrick Stein, and Brody Benson: June 14, 2016, Hutchinson, KS. Dan Day, Patrick Stein, Curtis Allen, and Gavin Wright: August 14, 2016, and September 2, 2016, G&G Home Center, Liberal, KS. Texts between "Brian" and Patrick Stein, September 27, 2016.

SWORN TRIAL TESTIMONY

Dan Day: March 28, 2018; March 29, 2018; April 2, 2018; April 3, 2018. FBI agent Amy Kuhn: April 10, 2018; April 11, 2018. Jason Crick, April 11, 2018. Garrett Wright: April 12, 2018. Lula Harris: March 26, 2018. Brody Benson: March 26, 2018.

COURT AND OTHER OFFICIAL RECORDS

United States v. Allen et al., Patrick Stein Sentencing Memorandum, October 29, 2018. Opening Statement by Stein defense attorney James R. Pratt, March 22, 2018. Government's Sentencing Memorandum, October 29, 2018. Sentencing Hearing transcript, January 25, 2019. Memorandum and Order, Judge Eric F. Melgren, regarding Stein's pretrial detention, March 9, 2017. Opening Statement by Asst. US Attorney Risa Berkower, April 22, 2018. Curtis Allen Sentencing Memorandum, October 29, 2018. Opening Statement by Allen defense attorney Rich Federico, April 22, 2018. Opening Statement by Wright defense attorney Kari S. Schmidt, April 22, 2018. Government's Motion to Preclude Defendants' Witness Dr. Amy Cooter from Testifying and for *Daubert* Hearing, Exhibit 2, Cooter's notes of her interview with Gavin Wright, during which Wright describes a Zello call among KSF members in which Stein mentioned working on setting up a security detail for the Sharp family's return to Kansas, January 9, 2018. James Hearing: statements of Asst. US Atty. Anthony Mattivi, March 19, 2018. Pretrial detention hearing before Judge Melgren, February 24, 2017.

OTHER SOURCES

National Speech & Debate Association, https://www.speechanddebate.org/topics/. *The Oregonian,* "LaVoy Finicum, Neighboring Rancher of Cliven Bundy, Explains Refuge Takeover," January 4, 2016, https://www.youtube.com/watch?v=

yX6icu72bRg. Garden City High School yearbook, 1984. Maxine Bernstein, "FBI Authorized Some Informants to Engage in Unlawful Activity at Refuge," February 23, 2017, https://www.oregonlive.com/oregon-standoff/2017/02/defense_asks_retired_fbi_agent.html. Claymore mine explanatory video: https://www.youtube.com/watch?v=kDqaeMGMAWk. Proverbs 6:16–19, King James Bible. Kyung Lah and Brad Parks, "Woman Says She Was Feet Away When Shots Killed Oregon Occupier Finicum," CNN, February 3, 2016, https://www.cnn.com/2016/02/02/us/witness-lavoy-finicum-killed-oregon/index.html. Bryan Thompson, "Southwest Kansas Dinner Exchange Aims to Bridge Cultural Gaps," *High Plains Public Radio,* October 1, 2017, https://www.hppr.org/post/southwest-kansas-dinner-exchange-aims-bridge-cultural-gaps.

BOOKS, ARTICLES, AND REPORTS

Francesca Laguardia, "Terrorists, Informants, and Buffoons: The Case for Downward Departure as a Response to Entrapment," *Lewis & Clark Law Review,* 17:1, 2013.

NEWS ARTICLES

Justin Wingerter, "In the Case of John Booker Jr., Entrapment Is an Unlikely Defense," *Topeka Capital-Journal,* April 14, 2015, https://www.cjonline.com/article/20150414/NEWS/304149697. Jonathan Shorman, "U.S. Senate Candidate Prosecuted Domestic Terror: Key Cases Were Stings with Fake Bombs," *Wichita Eagle,* August 31, 2019, https://www.kansas.com/news/politics-government/article233543542.html. "The 155 Craziest Things Trump Said During This Election," *Politico,* November 5, 2016, https://www.politico.com/magazine/story/2016/11/the-155-craziest-things-trump-said-this-cycle-214420. Sam Levin, "Rebel Cowboys: How the Bundy Family Sparked a New Battle for the American West," *Guardian,* August 29, 2016, https://www.theguardian.com/us-news/2016/aug/29/oregon-militia-standoff-bundy-family. Judy L. Thomas, "Russian Facebook Posts May Have Inspired Militia in Kansas Bombing Plot, Expert Says," *Kansas City Star,* June 10, 2018, https://www.kansascity.com/news/politics-government/article212830274.html.

Julie Turkowitz and Jack Healy, "LaVoy Finicum: 'I Would Rather Die Than Be Caged,'" *New York Times,* January 27, 2018, https://www.nytimes.com/2016/01/28/us/lavoy-finicum-protester-killed-in-oregon.html.. Author note: Ammon

Bundy, his brother Ryan, and five others were acquitted by a federal jury of charges of conspiracy and firearms charges following a trial in US District Court in Portland, Oregon, in October 2016; in a separate trial in 2017, two other occupiers were convicted in federal court of conspiracy to impede federal officers. Rick Montgomery and Judy L. Thomas, "The New Face of the Patriot Movement Is a Kansas-Raised Teenager," *Kansas City Star,* February 27, 2016, https://www.kansascity.com/news/politics-government/article62911607.html.

Rick Montgomery, "'Patriot Princess' Victoria Sharp Still Traumatized a Year After Oregon Standoff Shooting," *Kansas City Star,* January 29, 2017, https://www.kansascity.com/news/state/kansas/article128921799.html. Hunter Woodall, "Kansas Mom Whose Kids Sang at Oregon Standoff Loses Custody," *Kansas City Star,* July 27, 2016, https://www.kansascity.com/news/local/crime/article92255522.html. Trevor Hughes, "White Domestic Terrorists Threatened This City of Refugees, Here's What Happened Next," *USA Today,* February 1, 2019.

CHAPTER 3: CRUSADERS 2.0

FBI RECORDINGS AND TEXTS

Dan Day, Patrick Stein, and Brody Benson, June 14, 2016, Hutchinson, KS. Dan Day, Patrick Stein, Curtis Allen, and Gavin Wright, July 31, 2016, G&G Home Center. Ibid., August 8, 2016. Ibid., August 14, 2016. Ibid., September 2, 2016.

SWORN TRIAL TESTIMONY

Dan Day: March 29, 2018; April 3, 2018; April 4, 2018. FBI agent Amy Kuhn: April 10, 2018; April 11, 2018. Brody Benson: March 26, 2018; March 28, 2018. Lula Harris: March 26, 2018. Garrett Wright: April 12, 2018.

COURT AND OTHER OFFICIAL RECORDS

United States v. Allen et al., transcript of Zello call, Exhibit D, in Government's Opposition to Defendants' Motion for Bond, September 27, 2017. Allen Sentencing Memorandum, October 29, 2018. Government's Response to Defendants' Motion to Suppress Facebook Warrant, January 22, 2018; see Affidavit in Support of an Application for a Search Warrant. FBI agent Amy Kuhn, January 17, 2018. Opening Statement by Allen defense attorney Rich Federico, April 22, 2018. Memorandum in Support of Motion to Suppress Evidence and Request for a *Franks* Hearing, January 11, 2018. Omnibus Affidavit for Search Warrants, January 11, 2018. Motion Hearing transcript, February 24, 2017, especially statements by Asst. US Atty. Anthony Mattivi. Government's Consolidated Response to Defendants' Motions *In Limine,* March 15, 2018. Judge Eric F. Melgren, Statement of Facts, January 15, 2019. Government's Opposition to Defense's Motion for Bond, Exhibit D, September 27, 2017.

OTHER SOURCES

Technical Sgt. Daniel Anderson, Arlington National Cemetery, Memorial Day 2013, https://www.youtube.com/watch?v=YmLT482wIm4. Bill Engvall, "Stupid People (Here's Your Sign)," https://www.youtube.com/watch?v=ZBjelRDKHUk.

NEWS ARTICLES

Oliver Morrison, "A Helpful Neighbor. A Proud Father. A Farmer's Kid. And, the FBI Says, Terrorists," *Wichita Eagle,* October 27, 2016, https://www.kansas.com/news/local/crime/article109081977.html.

Theodore Schleifer, "Donald Trump: 'I Think Islam Hates Us,'" CNN, March 10, 2016, https://www.cnn.com/2016/03/09/politics/donald-trump-islam-hates-us/index.html. Dave Boyer, "Donald Trump Doubles Down on 'Islam Hates America' Claim," *Washington Times,* March 10, 2016, https://www.washingtontimes.com/news/2016/mar/10/donald-trump-doubles-down-islam-hates-america-claim/. Jonathan Shorman, "Kansas to Withdraw from Federal Refugee Program, Gov. Sam Brownback Says," *Topeka Capital-Journal,* April 26, 2016. "African Center to Hold Event," *Garden City Telegram,* June 4, 2016. Nico Lang, "Donald Trump Backtracks on Orlando Gun Comments," *Advocate,* June 21, 2016, https://www.advocate.com/election/2016/6/21/donald-trump-backtracks-orlando-gun-comments.

CHAPTER 4: "THE COCKROACHES GOTTA GO"

FBI RECORDINGS AND TEXTS

Dan Day, Patrick Stein, Curtis Allen, Gavin Wright, and others, July 9, 2016, Lakin, KS. Ibid., July 18, 2016. Dan Day, Patrick Stein, Curtis Allen, and Gavin Wright, July 31, 2016, G&G Home Center. Ibid., September 2, 2016.

SWORN TRIAL TESTIMONY

FBI agent Amy Kuhn: April 10, 2018, during which she testified to the following about Shelby Lewis: "Shortly after the meeting, we believed she might be involved in the conspiracy. But as time played out, it didn't appear as though she was part of it." Brody Benson: March 28, 2018, during which he testified about his discussions the next day with Shelby Lewis by telephone: "I told her, you know, I didn't want to be any part of what was, you know, going on. And she kind of conferred the same idea . . . and I tendered my resignation with the KSF." Lula Harris: March 26, 2018; March 27, 2018. Dan Day: March 26, 2018; March 29, 2018; April 2, 2018; April 3, 2018; April 4, 2018.

Affidavit in Support of Application for the First Extension of a Mobile Tracker, Tracey M. Jenkins, a special agent with the FBI, October 6, 2016. Closing Statement by Stein defense attorney James R. Pratt, April 17, 2018. Government Sentencing Memorandum, October 29, 2018, which stated, in part: "Starting at age 24, defendant Allen has been arrested eight times for a variety of domestic violence, failure to appear, and driving offenses, including driving while intoxicated. For two of these early arrests, defendant Allen was placed on diversion. Yet despite completing diversion (twice), defendant Allen continued to re-offend, and two of his later arrests resulted in misdemeanor convictions, including a municipal domestic battery conviction. Under applicable law at the time, this domestic violence conviction prohibited him from possessing any firearms. Regardless, defendant Allen continued to obtain firearms, and at the time of his arrest in this case he possessed twenty-one firearms, fourteen of which he stored at a friend's house to avoid detection. Although the law has since changed since the time of defendant Allen's arrest on this point, defendant Allen's determination to circumvent applicable law to amass more than twenty firearms, despite knowing of his status as a prohibited person and having previously gone through two separate diversion programs, shows a consistent history of disrespect for the law."

NEWS ARTICLES

Josh Harbour, "Turtle Race a Staple for Kearny County Fair," *Garden City Telegram,* July 19, 2016. Judy L. Thomas, "Russian Facebook Posts May Have Inspired Militia in Kansas Bombing Plot, Expert Says," *Kansas City Star,* June 10, 2018.

CHAPTER 5: "GO BIG OR GO HOME"

FBI RECORDINGS AND TEXTS

Dan Day, Patrick Stein, Curtis Allen, and Gavin Wright, August 8, 2016, G&G Home Center, Liberal, KS. Ibid., August 14, 2018. Ibid., September 2, 2016. Dan Day and FBI agents Amy Kuhn and Robin Smith, September 1, 2016, Garden City, KS.

SWORN TRIAL TESTIMONY

Dan Day: March 29, 2018; April 2, 2018; April 3, 2018; April 4, 2018. Lula Harris: March 26, 2018. FBI agent Amy Kuhn, April 10, 2018; April 11, 2018. FBI agent Jonathan Tucker, Evidence Response Team, April 9, 2018.

COURT AND OTHER OFFICIAL RECORDS

United States v. Allen et al., Opening Statement of Allen's defense attorney Rich Federico, April 22, 2018. Government's Response to Defendant Wright's Motion to Suppress Evidence Obtained or Derived from Search of Oklahoma Residence, Attachment A: Affidavit in Support of Search Warrant, January 22, 2018. Government's Closing Argument, April 17, 2018. Government's Sentencing Memorandum, October 29, 2018. Government's Reply to Defendants' Response to Notice of Authorities, December 3, 2018. Government Affidavit in Support of Application for the First Extension of Mobile Tracker, October 6, 2016. Memorandum and Order by US District Judge Eric F. Melgren, January 15, 2019. Trial Exhibit 309, Gavin Wright's PayPal record dated August 19, 2016. Defendant Curtis Allen's Sentencing Memorandum, October 29, 2018. Consolidated Brief for the United States as Appellee, Appellate Case 19-3034, US Court of Appeals for the Tenth Circuit, May 8, 2020.

OTHER SOURCES

https://www.facebook.com/gardencitynoonlions/.

BOOKS, ARTICLES, AND REPORTS

Sarah Posner and David Neiwert, "How Trump Took Hate Groups Mainstream," *Mother Jones,* October 14, 2016, https://www.motherjones.com/politics/2016/10/donald-trump-hate-groups-neo-nazi-white-supremacist-racism/. Sarah Posner and

David Neiwert, "Meet the Horde of Neo-Nazis, Klansmen, and Other Extremist Leaders Endorsing Donald Trump," *Mother Jones,* September 21, 2016, https://www.motherjones.com/politics/2016/09/trump-supporters-neo-nazis-white-nationalists-kkk-militias-racism-hate/. Jessica Pressler, "The Plot to Bomb Garden City, Kansas," *New York,* December 11, 2017.

NEWS ARTICLES

Michael Shepherd, "In Maine, Trump Shares His View of US Threatened by Somalis, Other Immigrants," *Bangor Daily News,* August 4, 2016, https://bangordailynews.com/2016/08/04/news/in-maine-trump-shares-his-view-of-us-threatened-by-somalis-other-immigrants/. Stephanie Ebbert, "In Maine, Trump Takes Aim at Somali Refugees," *Boston Globe,* August 4, 2016, https://www.bostonglobe.com/metro/2016/08/04/donald-trump-speak-portland-maine/8V0I1INbzelYh3cgo7NPLN/story.html. Reporter's Notebook, "Gaffe Track: Trump Fires Back at Khizr Khan, Citing His 'Sacrifices,'" *Atlantic,* July 31, 2016, https://www.theatlantic.com/notes/2016/07/gaffe-track-trump-fires-back-at-khizr-khan-citing-his-sacrifices/493754/. Alexander Burns, "Ignoring Advice, Donald Trump Presses Attack on Khan Family and G.O.P. Leaders," *New York Times,* August 2, 2016, https://www.nytimes.com/2016/08/03/us/politics/donald-trump-gop.html. Peter Holley, "Top Nazi Leader: Trump Will Be a 'Real Opportunity' for White Nationalists," *Washington Post,* August 7, 2016, https://www.washingtonpost.com/news/post-nation/wp/2016/08/07/top-nazi-leader-trump-will-be-a-real-opportunity-for-white-nationalists/. Oliver Morrison, "A Helpful Neighbor. A Proud Father. A Farmer's Kid. And, the FBI Says, Terrorists," *Wichita Eagle,* October 27, 2016, https://www.kansas.com/news/local/crime/article109081977.html. Jaweed Kaleem and Matt Pearce, "Riots in Milwaukee After Police Shooting: 'The People Are Fed Up,'" *Los Angeles Times,* August 15, 2016, https://www.latimes.com/nation/la-na-milwaukee-unrest-20160814-snap-story.html. Author's note: The police officer, Dominque Heaggan-Brown, who fatally shot Sylville Smith, was later charged with first-degree reckless homicide. He was acquitted by a jury on June 21, 2017. Bill Glauber, Karen Herzog, and Hannah Schwarz, "Trump Courts Black Voters in West Bend Speech," *Milwaukee Journal Sentinel,* August 16, 2016, https://www.jsonline.com/story/news/politics/elections/2016/08/16/trump-addresses-milwaukee-unrest/88864016/.

CHAPTER 6: GUYS, MEET BRIAN

FBI RECORDINGS AND TEXTS

Dan Day, FBI agents Amy Kuhn and Robin Smith, September 1, 2016, Garden City, KS. Dan Day, Patrick Stein, Curtis Allen, and Gavin Wright, September 2, 2016, G&G Home Center, Liberal, KS. Ibid., October 5, 2016. Telephone call between Dan Day and Patrick Stein, September 4, 2016. Dan Day, Patrick Stein, Curtis Allen, and Gavin Wright, September 18, 2016, Sublette, KS. Dan Day, "Brian," and Patrick Stein, September 25, 2016. Text messages between Patrick Stein and "Brian," September 2016.

SWORN TRIAL TESTIMONY

Dan Day: March 29, 2018; April 2, 2018; April 4, 2018. FBI agent Amy Kuhn: April 10, 2018; April 11, 2018. FBI undercover "Brian": April 4, 2018; April 5, 2018. Dr. Jack Barrow, PhD, hazardous device examiner, FBI Explosives Unit: April 5, 2018. FBI agent John Tucker: March 27 2018. FBI agent Jason Miller, chemist forensic examiner: April 5, 2018. Lula Harris: March 26, 2018.

COURT AND OTHER OFFICIAL RECORDS

United States v. Allen et al., Declaration of Michael C. McGarrity, asst. director, Counterterrorism Division, FBI, in Government's Motion for Protective Order Pertaining to Testimony of FBI Undercover Employees at Trial, March 9, 2018.

NEWS ARTICLES

Amy Bickle, "Visitors Come to See What's Left of Short-Lived Southwest Kansas Town," *Hutchinson News,* March 27, 2015.

CHAPTER 7: "WILL, DETERMINATION, AND DEDICATION SECOND TO NONE"

FBI RECORDINGS AND TEXTS

Dan Day, Patrick Stein, Curtis Allen, and Gavin Wright, October 5, 2016, Sublette, KS. Texts between "Brian" and Patrick Stein on and after September 27, 2016, through October 14, 2106 (government trial exhibits 108, 110, and 111). Telephone call between Dan Day and Gavin Wright, October 11, 2016. "Brian" and Patrick Stein, October 12, 2016, in Kalvesta and then Garden City, KS. FBI agent Robin Smith and KBI agent Adam Piland, interview of Gavin Wright at the Liberal police station, October 12, 2016.

SWORN TRIAL TESTIMONY

Dr. Jack Barrow, PhD, hazardous device examiner, FBI Explosives Unit: April 5, 2018; April 6, 2018. FBI agent Jason Miller, Explosive Unit, FBI laboratory: April 11, 2018. FBI agent Amy Kuhn: April 10, 2018; April 11, 2018. Dan Day: April 2, 2108; April 4, 2018; April 8, 2018. "Brian": April 5, 2018. Lula Harris: March 26, 2016; March 27, 2018. Liberal police captain Jason Ott: March 28, 2018. KBI agent Adam Piland: April 9, 2018.

COURT AND OTHER OFFICIAL RECORDS

United States v. Allen et al., Defendant Allen's Sentencing Memorandum, October 29, 2018; see p. 35, where attorneys for Allen argue, "Many themes in the messaging, advertisements, and posts created and published by Russian operatives were central to the underlying motivations, speech, and state of mind of the defendants. Mr. Allen, Stein, and Wright unwittingly and unknowingly fell prey to the Russian's covert operation." Government's Response to Defendant Wright's Motion to Suppress Evidence Obtained or Derived from Search of Oklahoma Residence, January 22, 2018. Government's Response to Defendants' Motion to Suppress Facebook Warrant, affidavit by FBI agent Amy Kuhn, January 22, 2018.

OTHER SOURCES

Statement of James B. Comey, director, FBI, before the Senate Committee on Homeland Security and Governmental Affairs, September 27, 2016, https://www.fbi.gov/news/testimony/fifteen-years-after-911-threats-to-the-homeland. Statement of Michael C. McGarrity, assistant director, Counterterrorism Division, Federal Bureau of Investigation, before the House Homeland Security Committee, "Confronting the Rise of Domestic Terrorism in the Homeland," May 8, 2019, https://www.fbi.gov/news/testimony/confronting-the-rise-of-domestic-terrorism-in-the-homeland. Homeland Threat Assessment, US Department of Homeland Security, October 2020, https://www.dhs.gov/sites/default/files/publications/2020_10_06_homeland-threat-assessment.pdf.

NEWS ARTICLES

Matthew Daly and Eric Tucker, "Senators Press FBI Director on Response to Domestic Terrorism, Associated Press, September 27, 2016, https://www.denverpost.com/2016/09/27/senators-press-fbi-director-on-response-to-domestic-terrorism-threat/. Lindsey Bever, "Arrest Made in Arson at Orlando Gunman's Mosque, Authorities Say," *Washington Post,* September 14, 2016, https://www.washingtonpost.com/news/acts-of-faith/wp/2016/09/12/arson-suspected-in-fire-at-florida-mosque-attended-by-pulse-shooter-omar-mateen/. Lauren del Valle, "2 Muslim Women, Babies Attacked in Alleged Hate Crime in New York," CNN, September 10, 2016, https://www.cnn.com/2016/09/10/us/brooklyn-muslim-women-attacked/index.html. Matt McKinney, "Threat Against Somali Woman in Little Falls Investigated as Hate Crime," *Star Tribune,* August 19, 2016, https://www.startribune.com/threat-against-somali-woman-in-little-falls-scrutinized-as-hate-crime/390651081/. Rocco Parascandola and Mary McDonnell, "Cops Investigating Threatening 'ISIS' Note Left at Muslim Family's Staten Island Home," *New York Daily News,* July 20, 2016, https://www.nydailynews.com/new-york/nyc-crime/cops-investigate-isis-note-left-muslim-family-s-home-article-1.2718403.

CHAPTER 8: PLOT INTERRUPTED

FBI RECORDINGS AND TEXTS

"Brian" and Patrick Stein, October 12, 2016, in Kalvesta and then Garden City, KS. Texts between "Brian" and Patrick Stein on and after September 27, 2016, through October 14, 2106 (government trial exhibits 108, 110, and 111). "Brian" and Patrick Stein, October 14, 2016, Dodge City, KS. Telephone call between Patrick Stein and his mother, October 14, 2016. Transcript of Patrick Stein interview by FBI agents Robin Smith and Amy Kuhn, October 14, 2016, Dodge City, KS.

SWORN TRIAL TESTIMONY

"Brian": April 5, 2018. FBI agent Jonathan Tucker, Evidence Response Team: March 27, 2018; April 9, 2018. FBI agent Michael Miller, Evidence Response Team: March 27, 2018. FBI agent Amy Kuhn: April 11, 2018. Stein defense attorney Pratt reading October 13, 2016, text messages between his client and "Brian," April 4, 2018. Dan Day: April 2, 2018.

OTHER SOURCES

James Dobson, technical producer, *Garden City Telegram,* live videotaping of the Garden City Police Department discussion with the Somali community following the arrests of three bomb plotters, October 15, 2016. *Strangers in Town,* documentary by Steve Lerner and Reuben Aaronson, 2018. Mary Louise Kelly, "What You Need to Know About the Somali Community in Kansas," National Public Radio, October 16, 2016. Department of Justice, Office of Public Affairs, press release, October 14, 2016: "Three Kansas Men Charged with Plotting a Bombing Attack Targeting the Local Somali Immigrant Community."

BOOKS, ARTICLES, AND REPORTS

Ted Genoways, "The Only Good Muslim Is a Dead Muslim," *New Republic Digital Edition,* May 15, 2017. Jessica Pressler, "The Plot to Bomb Garden City, Kansas," *New York,* December 11, 2017.

NEWS ARTICLES

Eric Tucker and Roxana Hegeman, "3 Militia Members Arrested in Alleged Bomb Plot Targeting Somalis in Kansas," Associated Press, October 14, 2016, https://apnews.com/article/f73471c52d9941cfa8049cf093bcb3df.

EPILOGUE: TRIALS

SWORN TRIAL TESTIMONY

Dan Day: March 28, 2018; March 29, 2018; April 2, 2018.

COURT AND OTHER OFFICIAL RECORDS

Board of Zoning Appeals, Garden City, KS, minutes of public hearing, January 10, 2017, in appeal number GCBZA2016-19 regarding Adan Keynan's African Shop. *US v. Allen et al.,* excerpts from Opening Statements by defense attorneys Rich Federico, Kari Schmidt, and James Pratt, March 22, 2018. Closing Statements, April 17, 2018, and sentencing memorandums, October 2018. FBI agent Amy Kuhn, April 10, 2018. Author note: Defense attorneys, citing that Dan Day did not file federal tax returns in 2015 and 2016, called him a tax cheat; in response, Dan

Day testified that he did not file because he incorrectly thought he had not earned enough income to require a filing, especially with his wife being on permanent disability. He testified that in prior years, when he had worked full-time, he always filed tax returns and usually received a substantial tax refund. Closing Remarks by Asst. US Atty. Anthony Mattivi, April 17, 2018. Wright Sentencing Memorandum, October 30, 2108. Transcript of sentencing by Judge Eric F. Melgren, January 25, 2019. Author note: The defendants appealed their convictions to the Tenth Circuit Court of Appeals, which held oral arguments on December 14, 2020, and then issued a ruling upholding their convictions on January 25, 2021.

OTHER SOURCES

Copies of twenty-four letters by fifth-graders at the Buckland Shelburne Elementary School, Shelburne, Massachusetts, including their teacher's letter to Garden City's manager, Matthew Allen. Garden City's video "Infinite Hope," featuring local elementary school students reading the letters the city received from students in Shelburne, Massachusetts, https://youtube/mD5m1Vtuo1g. Statement of Christopher Wray, director, FBI, before the Committee on Homeland Security, US House of Representatives, October 30, 2019, https://homeland.house.gov/imo/media/doc/Testimony-Wray.pdf. Transcript of Garden City police chief Utz's remarks at the Diversity Breakfast, November 8, 2019.

NEWS ARTICLES

Scott Aust, "West Mary Businesses Allowed to Stay in Industrially Zoned Area," *Garden City Telegram,* February 11, 2017; Diane Broncaccio, "Local 5th-graders Reach Out to Kansas Students Following Bomb Threat," *Greenfield Recorder,* July 20, 2018.

SELECTED BIBLIOGRAPHY

COURT CASES

United States v. Curtis Wayne Allen, Patrick Eugene Stein, and Gavin Wayne Wright, US District Court, District of Kansas, criminal dockets 16-1-141-01, 02, 03.

United States v. Patrick Eugene Stein, US District Court, District of Kansas, criminal docket 17-10045.

United States v. John T. Booker Jr., US District Court, District of Kansas, criminal docket 15-40030-01-CM.

United States v. Khalid Ali-M Aldawsari, 749 F.3d. 1015 (5th Cir. 2014).

United States v. Mohamed Mohamud, US District Court, District of Oregon, criminal docket 3:10-cr-475-HZ.

United States v. Harlem Suarez, US District Court, Southern District of Florida, criminal docket 4:15-cr-10009-JEM.

Curtis Wayne Allen, appellant, v. United States of America, appellee, US Court of Appeals for the Tenth Circuit, Case No. 19-3034.

Patrick Eugene Stein, appellant, v. United States of America, appellee, US Court of Appeals for the Tenth Circuit, Case No. 19-3030.

Gavin Wayne Wright, appellant, v. United States of America, appellee, US Court of Appeals for the Tenth Circuit, Case No. 19-3035.

BOOKS AND ARTICLES

Aaronson, Trevor. "Terrorism's Double Standard: Violent Far-Right Extremists Are Rarely Prosecuted as Terrorists." theintercept.com (March 23, 2019).

Belew, Kathleen. *Bring the War Home.* Cambridge, MA: Harvard University Press, 2018.

Eichenwald, Kurt. *The Informant.* New York: Broadway Books, 2000.

Genoways, Ted. "The Only Good Muslim Is a Dead Muslim." newrepublic.com (May 15, 2017).

Hope, Holly. *Garden City: Dreams in a Kansas Town.* Norman, OK: University of Oklahoma Press, 1988.

Kakutani, Michiko. *The Death of Truth: Notes on Falsehood in the Age of Trump.* New York: Penguin Random House, 2018.

Laguardia, Francesca. "Terrorists, Informants, and Buffoons: The Case for Downward Departure as a Response to Entrapment." *Lewis & Clark Law Review* 17:1, 2013.

Marantz, Andrew. *Anti-Social: Online Extremists, Techno-Utopians, and the Hijacking of the American Conversation.* New York: Viking, 2019.

McCann, Anthony. *Shadowlands: Fear and Freedom at the Oregon Standoff.* New York: Bloomsbury Publishing, 2019.

Pachirat, Timothy. *Every Twelve Seconds: Industrialized Slaughter and the Politics of Sight.* New Haven, CT: Yale University Press, 2011.

Reitman, Janet. "U.S. Law Enforcement Failed to See the Threat of White Nationalism: Now They Don't Know How to Stop It." *New York Times Magazine* (Nov. 3, 2018).

Saslow, Eli. *Rising out of Hatred: The Awakening of a Former White Nationalist.* New York: Knopf Doubleday Publishing Group, 2018.

Smarsh, Sarah. *Heartland: A Memoir of Working Hard and Being Broke in the Richest Country on Earth.* New York: Scribner, 2018.

Tenold, Vegas. *Everything You Love Will Burn: Inside the Rebirth of White Nationalism in America.* New York: Bold Type Books, 2018.

Whitehead, Colson. *The Underground Railroad.* New York: Anchor Books, 2018.

INDEX

ABOUT THE AUTHOR

DICK LEHR is a professor of journalism at Boston University. He previously wrote for the *Boston Globe,* where he was a member of the paper's Spotlight Team, a special projects reporter, and a magazine writer. While on the Spotlight Team he was a Pulitzer Prize finalist in investigative reporting. Lehr is the author of eight previous works of nonfiction and fiction, including the *New York Times* bestseller and Edgar Award winner *Black Mass: Whitey Bulger, the FBI, and a Devil's Deal,* which became the basis of the Warner Bros. movie of the same title. *The Birth of a Movement: How* Birth of a Nation *Ignited the Battle for Civil Rights* became the basis for a PBS/Independent Lens documentary of the same title.